A Guide to Administering Distance Learning

Leadership and Best Practices in Educational Technology Management

VOLUME 2

The titles published in this series are listed at *brill.com/lbpe*

A Guide to Administering Distance Learning

Edited by

Lauren Cifuentes

BRILL

LEIDEN | BOSTON

All chapters in this book have undergone peer review.

The Library of Congress Cataloging-in-Publication Data is available online at http://catalog.loc.gov

Typeface for the Latin, Greek, and Cyrillic scripts: "Brill". See and download: brill.com/brill-typeface.

ISSN 2666-7010
ISBN 978-90-04-47136-8 (paperback)
ISBN 978-90-04-47137-5 (hardback)
ISBN 978-90-04-47138-2 (e-book)

Contents

Foreword

When I met Lauren Cifuentes several years ago at a Symposium for Quality Online Education at Texas A&M system, she quickly mentioned that the book George Saltsman and I wrote in 2005, *An Administrator's Guild to Online Education*, was her primary resource for starting and leading her online program. She thanked me for writing it and then gently reminded me it needed updating since the practice of online education has evolved and is more heavily used since 2005. Of course, she was right! A lot of things have changed in 15 years after our book was written that are important topics included in this new book such as the state authorization rule or the use of online learning for crisis situations such as the Covid-19 pandemic. In addition, this book gathers together essays from online learning experts such as Tony Picciano, Ray Schroeder, and Karen Swan, who have been involved in this field for almost three decades and have extensive experience in designing and leading online programs.

Yet, when you look at this book's collection of chapters, many of the same topics we found that administrators struggled with in 2005 are still within the scope of this book like strategic and transformational leadership, typical challenges and barriers that must be dealt with, policy development, a systematic process for course development, use of technologies, faculty support and professional development, student support and student success, and marketing. However, this book extends those topics with more anecdotes, more research, and draws from more experiences which makes this book an even more valuable resource for the higher education practitioner with additional topics such as program improvement, quality assurance, legal topics, ethics, and recruitment and retention.

When Lauren approached me with her idea for this book, I was thrilled to find she has the same passion and desire to help our colleagues in the field like George and I did in order to provide good sound resources for decision making, program guidance, and focusing on quality in online learning. As a dean of online programs myself for more than 10 years, there were so many times I needed a guide like this book to run to for possible recommendations or further research. This book is destined to become the next major resource for those leading, managing, or working in this exciting and increasingly important field as online education continues to impact higher education.

Kaye Shelton
Professor, Educational Leadership Lamar University

Series Editors' Foreword

The impetus behind our approaching Brill with the concept of *Leadership and Best Practices in Educational Technology Management* was to address the issue of the lack of comprehensive materials to guide educational technology leaders – including distance learning leaders – in their practice. For many years, Kaye Shelton and George Saltsman's 2005 influential book, *An Administrator's Guide to Online Education*, was one of the only books tailored specifically to the needs of online learning administrators. How fitting that Dr. Shelton provides the foreword to this book! The 2018 book *Leading and Managing e-Learning: What the e-Learning Leader Needs to Know*, is designed primarily for institutional leaders for whom online/distance learning fall under their jurisdiction, but who do not have a background in online learning, educational technology or instructional design. *A Guide to Administering Distance Learning* will become the leading reference for directors of distance learning and others who oversee the day-to-day operations of online/distance learning and whose responsibilities may be more extensive than their level of institutional authority. Lauren Cifuentes is uniquely qualified as an experienced faculty member and scholar who also served many years as a Director of Distance Learning at Texas A & M Corpus Christi. Dr. Cifuentes has experienced distance learning from all levels and has amassed the collective wisdom of many of the finest leaders in the field of online/distance education. This is a book written by those who have "walked the walk" and for those who are currently walking the walk. *A Guide to Administering Distance Learning* is a fitting addition to our book series.

Anthony A. Piña and Christopher T. Miller

References

Piña, A. A., Lowell, V. L., & Harris, B. R. (Eds.). (2018). *Leading and managing e-learning: What the e-learning leader needs to know.* Springer.

Shelton, K., & Saltsman, G. (2005). *An administrator's guide to online education.* Information Age Publishing.

Preface

In 2020, in a matter of weeks, hundreds of thousands of courses were transferred from face-to-face delivery to online delivery due to the Covid-19 pandemic. Colleges were at different levels of readiness for such a transformation. This book's purpose is to help institutions be prepared for online learning, whether or not in response to a crisis, by clarifying the tasks required by administrators to support online learning experiences offered to students at geological distances from the brick and mortar of an institution. As Ormond Simpson says in Chapter 13, "Everything in this book is ultimately aimed at turning out successful students." Undeniably, educational institutions are complicated and supporting student success with online learning involves managing multiple tasks that require collaboration and cooperation with people in departments across an institution from academic units and Information Technology to the Registrar's office. Distance learning policies, processes, evaluation systems, and business models frequently evolve, making adaptability and flexibility critical attributes of distance learning administrators.

To manage the complexity, educational institutions across the nation are creating new positions in e-learning leadership, often at the vice-president or vice-provost levels. Frequently, as with me in 2011, those applying for such positions have been faculty members and researchers who have never served in administration. They need rapid access to an overview of perspectives to consider and tasks to be accomplished or maintained. To gain the administrative skills I needed to build an effective office, I studied a number of invaluable books and articles: Kaye Shelton, and George Saltsman's book, *An Administrator's Guide to Online Education* (2005) served as my indispensable guide and helped me prioritize tasks and challenges.

That book needs an update. Much has evolved in the realm of distance learning since 2005, including policies, technologies, professional development programs, and design and evaluation approaches. Although other books have addressed advances made since that book was published, no single book has systematically compiled comprehensive guidelines for addressing the issues that distance learning administrators currently face. This book was compiled to do just that by providing up-to-date theoretical insights as well as practical guidance regarding how leaders in distance learning might affect positive change.

The book is designed to benefit a broad readership of those interested in educational leadership, be they students, e-learning instructors and administrators, or those who supervise e-learning administrators. Graduate students studying educational technology and/or educational administration and leadership are sure to benefit from its contents. The book will also provide guidance to those who are already in or are moving into administration of e-learning in colleges, universities, or PreK-12. Chief information officers (CIOs), provosts, school superintendents, and K-12 principals might refer to the recommendations in order to lead those in charge of distance learning at their institutions.

The pioneers who, in the 1990's jumped onboard as explorers and developers of the new paradigm in education were the first to design, develop, and teach online courses and build online degree programs. Some later stepped into administering institutional transformation as change agents. And now, in large part due to the Covid-19 crisis, we see that our hard work as pioneers and change agents put online-education solidly in the mainstream.

This book is useful due to contributions by those pioneers of the first generation to deliver or administer distance learning through online delivery as instructors, practitioners, leaders on a campus, or administrators of learning technologies. They share their experiences and wisdom here regarding what it takes to lead a campus in planning, delivering, and managing quality online courses and programs. Most are leading scholars and administrators who have invested their passion in quality education in higher education institutions. Each of the authors in this book informed each other and other distance educators as distance learning entered the mainstream. They contribute their insights based on years of experience as they broke ground in the new field of online learning. They provide comprehensive guidance to a person stepping into administration who needs to have access to an overview of all that is involved in distance learning administration.

Authors provide advice regarding what needs to be done to effectively administer online learning. Each chapter includes stories from personal experiences and activities that stimulate thought for current and future distance learning administrators. Authors have embedded questions, self-checks, prompts, or activities to help readers relate the concepts covered to their current or hypothetical experiences.

A special thanks must go to Yusra Visser and Ray Amirault who were to write the chapter on foundational theories. However, during the writing of this book, Yusra died. She was a distance learning pioneer whose contributions to the field and cheerful, loving nature will be long remembered. Regretfully and with sorrow we do not share her contribution which was incomplete at her passing. A previously published chapter on the topic by Anthony Picciano, another pioneer in the field, provides an overview of foundational theories for online education in Chapter 5.

Chapter 1, "Status of Online Learning," introduces the story of growth of online learning and different modalities and formats involved. It informs readers of issues of institutional and faculty readiness as well as predatory practices that highlight the important role that online program management currently plays.

Chapter 2, "Leadership for Online Learning," describes in detail specific skills of operational and strategic leadership. In addition, the importance of leading with knowledge, humility, and a broad perspective are emphasized and operationalized.

Chapter 3, "Barriers in Online Education and Strategies for Overcoming Them," enumerates interpersonal, pedagogical, and technological barriers to adoption of online education that must be addressed by distance learning administrators. It then describes strategies for overcoming barriers.

Chapter 4, "Legalities, Policies, Ethics, Accreditation, and Institutional Support," provides multiple links to resources for becoming knowledgeable regarding the government mandated rulings such the Higher Education Act, the Clery Act, and the Online State Authorization Rule. The importance of familiarity with accreditation standards is also emphasized.

Chapter 5, "Foundational Theories," introduces a theoretical, multimodal model integrating the principles of social constructivism, the community of inquiry model, connectivism, and online collaborative learning. The chapter provides examples of which aspects of the model would or would not be used under certain circumstances.

Chapter 6, "Analyzing Your Context," provides a detailed account of key components in distance learning systems and shows how they align with distance learning functions. Authors distinguish five levels of organizational effort for analyzing gaps, desired results, and needs of faculty members to encourage improvement and innovation.

Chapter 7, "Managing the Course Development Process," identifies components of the administrative process for developing online courses: Environment, Standards and Evaluation, Roles and Responsibilities, and Operations. Within each of these components are specific decision items with examples to allow online/distance administrators to create and manage a course development process that is appropriate for their institution.

Chapter 8, "Course Designs for Distance Teaching and Learning," describes administrative strategies for working with faculty members to grow distance learning offerings of courses and programs. Professional development offerings in course design for instructors are described.

Chapter 9, "Engaging Faculty in Online Education," provides guidance for engaging instructors, including ways to identify faculty readiness standards and key indicators of excellent online teaching. The chapter describes different professional development strategies and models and discusses ways to incentivize and compensate course developers and instructors.

Chapter 10, "Quality Assurance," describes how Sloan-C's five quality pillars for online education help to assure that online education is at least equal to the quality of education in face-to-face courses. The pillars are access, learning effectiveness, student satisfaction, faculty satisfaction, and cost effectiveness.

Chapter 11, "Recruitment and Marketing," provides proven, detailed, concrete steps for your institution to follow to recruit students and market programs, including how to (a) get support and funding, (b) identify your prospective student audience, (c) establish your brand and archetype, (d) engage with your target audience, (e) plan and execute changes to your website and marketing strategy, and (f) test, measure, refine, and improve your marketing strategy.

Chapter 12, "Student Support," explores the role of student affairs and support services in distance learning environments including students' support needs; the importance of on-boarding students; the role of the library and librarians; and the role of financial aid, tutoring, career services, and co-curricular programming.

Chapter 13, "Student Success," describes the problem of high drop-out rates in higher education and the roles that course design and academic and non-academic student supports play in student retention and success. Specifically, appropriate course workload and structure are discussed as well as strategies to motivate students and provide for learning readiness.

Chapter 14, "Support Technologies," provides distance learning administrators with guidance in selecting relevant technologies to design, organize, and deliver an engaging distance learning experience, use authentic tools and strategies to design and assess learning, curate and produce media, and apply technologies to personalize learners' experiences.

Chapter 15, "Your Distance Learning Community," emphasizes networking and connecting with other online educators. The chapter lists, describes, and provides contact information for the major professional associations, scholarly and trade journals, and social media sites for those interested in online/distance learning, teaching, design, and management.

Chapter 16, "Ramping up Distance Learning in a Crisis: Lessons Learned from Covid-19," shares the New Mexico State University Academic Technology team's model for anticipating needs and providing support during the Pandemic response to emergency campus closure and rapid transfer of face-to-face courses to online course delivery.

Chapter 17, "Conclusions," reiterates the motivating purpose for the book. The chapter highlights overarching themes discussed by several authors. enumerates many of the tasks that authors recommend focusing on, and introduces important tasks not covered in depth.

Figures and Tables

Figures

Tables

Notes on Contributors

Lauren Cifuentes

is a College Professor in the Educational Design and Learning Technologies program at NMSU where she teaches Critical Digital Literacy, Technology and Pedagogy; Foundations of Learning Design; and Design and Development Research to graduate students who are primarily early preK-16 teachers. Her expertise lies in distance learning, cognition, and learning design. Prior to her position at NMSU she directed distance learning initiatives at Texas A&M University-Corpus Christi and taught for 23 years at Texas A&M University, College Station. She has conducted countless workshops on technology applications for K-12 teachers in schools and universities and has over 100 publications primarily focused on distance learning.

Hannah Digges Elliott

is an Instructional Designer in the Center for Innovative Teaching & Learning at Western Kentucky University. She holds a B.A. in History, an M.A.E. in Adult Education, and a Graduate Certificate in Instructional Design from Western Kentucky University. She is currently a doctoral candidate in the Ed.D. program in Educational Leadership at Morehead State University. She is a 2020 Cochran Intern for the Association for Educational Communications and Technology (AECT), current Graduate Student Assembly Representative to the Systems Thinking & Change Division, and the Communications Officer-Elect for the Graduate Student Assembly.

Tonia A. Dousay

is an Associate Professor of Learning Sciences at the University of Idaho. She previously taught at the University of Wyoming and James Madison University, and often consults with other institutions and government agencies on distance learning and using technology equitably. She actively collaborates with STEM disciplines to brainstorm innovative ways to use, teach, and create with technology, impacting education at all levels and in all contexts. Her current research focuses on reducing barriers to STEM disciplines with virtual learning experiences, the role of self perceptions of creativity and skill proficiency on engagement, and innovative practicum experiences for preservice teachers.

Duane M. Dunn

 is assistant dean of academic programs for the College of Agriculture at Kansas State University. Prior to joining the College of Agriculture, Dunn served as associate dean with K-State's Global Campus, the distance learning arm of the university. His responsibilities encompassed program development, quality of design, policy and procedures, and outreach services. He has over 30 years of administration serving as a technical college president, a community college president and teaching. He enjoys the opportunities as a peer evaluator for the Higher Learning Commission and as consultant evaluator for a number of institutions.

Robbie Grant

 joined Academic Technology in 2004 (known as ICT Training Services at that time) as a Systems Analyst. In 2006 he was promoted to the position of LMS Administrator and has been the lead LMS Administrator since that time. In 2017 Robbie was named manager of the Academic Technology unit and in September of 2020 he was named Director of Academic Technology at NMSU. He received his Bachelor's degree in Marketing and his Master's in Business Administrator from New Mexico State University. Robbie also served as a Canvas Coach for the public facing Canvas user's community from 2013-June 2020.

Cassidy S. Hall

 is an Associate Clinical Professor of Educational Technologies and the Director of the Doceo Center for Innovation + Learning at the University of Idaho. She works closely with Classroom Technology Services and the Center for Excellence in Teaching and Learning to support technology integration and offer faculty training on all UI campuses. She also provides technology integration support and professional development to K-12 educators throughout the state of Idaho. She previously dedicated 15 years to working in public education in Pennsylvania as a library media specialist, teacher, technology coach, and instructional coach.

Atsusi "2c" Hirumi

currently holds a joint appointment with the Department of Learning Sciences in the College of Community Innovation and Education, and the Department of Medical Education in the College of Medicine at UCF. For the past 25 years, Dr. Hirumi has centered his teaching, research and service on the design of online and hybrid learning experiences. He has worked with faculty, staff, students and administrators in K12 and higher education, medical centers, and the military across North and South America, Asia, and the Middle East to improve eLearning. Dr. Hirumi's research now focuses on advancing medical education and fostering transdisciplinary collaboration among instructional designers and educators in the health professions. Awards include: The David H. Jonassen Excellence in Research Award presented by the Association for Educational Communication and Technology for long-term record of excellence in research and impact in ID&T, the US Army Training Maverick Award for leadership in distance learning, the Texas Distance Learning Association Award for commitment to excellence and innovation, AERA Studying and Self-Regulated Learning SIG Poster Award, the Outstanding Research Proposal awarded by the Research and Theory Division of AECT, UCF's Scholarship for Teaching and Learning Award, the WebCT Exemplary Online Course Award, and the Phi Delta Kappa Outstanding University Practitioner Award.

Swapna Kumar

is a Clinical Associate Professor of Educational Technology at the College of Education, University of Florida, USA. She coordinates the online doctoral program in Educational Technology at the College of Education. Her current research is focused on quality assurance in online programs and online mentoring/supervision. Details of her publications can be found at http://www.swapnakumar.com

Michelle Lebsock

joined Academic Technology in 2014 and is an Enterprise Applications Administrator. She is a co-administrator for Canvas, the lead administrator for Zoom, Canvas Studio, and Adobe Connect, and supports the Panopto integration with Canvas. She collaborates with Classroom Technology and Instructional Media Services to provide faculty training for simulcast classrooms using Zoom and Adobe Connect and partners with the Teaching

Academy to support NMSU's flagship Technology Enhanced Active Learning (TEAL) classroom. Michelle received her bachelor's degree in Journalism and Mass Communications with a minor in Economics from NMSU, her master's in Film Production from Chapman University, and is a doctoral candidate in the department of Educational Leadership and Administration at NMSU. She is a Quality Matters Master Reviewer and has completed NMSU's Course Design Summer Institute. Michelle has served as online adjunct faculty for the Journalism and Media Studies department since 2017.

Florence Martin

is a Professor of Learning, Design and Technology at University of North Carolina Charlotte. She teaches 100% online and engages in research focusing on the effective design of instruction and integration of digital technology to improve learning and performance. She has conducted several studies focusing on designing and integrating online learning environments to improve learner achievement and engagement. For more details, visit https://www.florencemartin.net

Christopher T. Miller

is a Professor of Education and Director of Morehead State University at Mt. Sterling. He has served as the Interim Dean of the College of Education and as chair of the Department of Foundational and Graduate Studies in Education at Morehead State University. He holds a B.S. in Applied Science and Technology from Morehead State University, a Master's in Interior Design, Merchandising and Textiles and an Ed.D. in Instructional Systems Design from the University of Kentucky. He was a 2000 Cochran Intern for the Association for Educational Communications and Technology (AECT), Past-President of the AECT Foundation, and is currently serving as the Technology Integrated Learning Division Representative on the AECT Board of Directors. He recently co-edited, with Dr. Anthony A. Piña, *Lessons in Leadership in the Field of Educational Technology.*

Efrén de la Mora Velasco

is a post-doctoral scholar at the Rosen College of Hospi-tality Management at the University of Central Florida. He received his B.S. in information systems and his M.A. in Learning Technologies from the University of Guadala-jara, Jalisco, Mexico. He was an associate professor of ed-ucational technology and multimedia programming and design at the University of Guadalajara for 8 years. For the past 4 years, Dr. De la Mora Velasco investigated the im-plementation of technologies to facilitate motivation, engagement and learning, as well as factors related to higher education students' academic achievements. Dr. De la Mora Velasco's research now focuses on information systems, consum-er behavior, and learning technologies. Awards include the Desirable Profile for Associate Professors by the Secretariat of Public Education of Mexico, and the Latin American Academy Fellowship by the State University of New York.

Rachel Mork

is a writer, editor, and partner at Verified Studios, a higher education marketing consultancy. In addition to almost a decade writing marketing copy for col-leges and universities through Verified Studios, she has consulted for a variety of clients providing advice, analysis, and content to support marketing efforts. Her clients include therapists, self-help gurus, execu-tive coaches, trainers, medical advisors, planned giv-ing facilitators, and nonprofit organizations.

Daniel Olsson

joined Academic Technology in early 2018 as an Instruc-tional Technology Consultant. Dan regularly provides professional development, consulting services, and tech-nical support for NMSU faculty. He is a co-administrator of the Canvas Learning Management System and the lead administrator for EvaluationKit (NMSU's enterprise course evaluation software). Dan received his Bachelor's degree in Electrical Engineering from New Mexico State University. He also holds a Master's in Business Adminis-tration also from NMSU. Dan worked in multiple engineering roles within the U.S. federal civil service for most of his early career prior to returning to his alma mater. He has also served as an adjunct faculty member teaching online with the Student Success Center and First Year Initiatives program.

Anthony G. Picciano

holds multiple faculty appointments at the City University of New York's Hunter College, Graduate Center; and the School of Professional Studies. He has also held administrative appointments at the City University and State University of New York including that of Vice President and Deputy to the President at Hunter College. He assisted in the establishment of the CUNY PhD Program in Urban Education and served as its Executive Officer for ten years (2007–2018). Dr. Picciano's research interests include education leadership, education policy, online and blended learning, multimedia instructional models, and research methods. He has authored seventeen books and numerous articles including *Educational Leadership and Planning for Technology* which currently is in its fifth edition (Pearson Education). His latest book is *Blended Learning: Research Perspectives, Volume 3* (with C. Dziuban, C. Graham & P. Moskal, Routledge/Taylor & Francis Publishers, in press). He has been involved in major grants from the U.S. Department of Education, the National Science Foundation, IBM, and the Alfred P. Sloan Foundation. He was a member of a research project funded by the U.S. Department of Education – Institute for Education Sciences, the purpose of which was to conduct a meta-analysis on "what works" in postsecondary online education (2017–2019). In 1998, Dr. Picciano co-founded CUNY Online, a multi-million dollar initiative funded by the Alfred P. Sloan Foundation that provides support services to faculty using the Internet for course development. He was a founding member and continues to serve on the Board of Directors of the Online Learning Consortium (formerly the Sloan Consortium). His blog started in 2009 has averaged over 600,000 visitors per year. Dr. Picciano has received wide recognition for his scholarship and research including being named the 2010 recipient of the Alfred P. Sloan Consortium's (now the Online Learning Consortium) National Award for Outstanding Achievement in Online Education by an Individual. Visit his website at: anthonypicciano.com

Anthony A. Piña

is Associate Provost for Teaching and Learning and Distinguished Lecturer at Sullivan University. Tony has been a consultant to Fortune 500 corporations, small businesses, local government agencies, non-profit organizations, the U.S. Department of Defense and to educational institutions across the country. He was the recipient of the 2019 Wagner Award for Leadership in Online Learning and has published 6 books on distance education and leadership – including the award-winning

Leading and Managing e-Learning: What the e-Learning Leader Needs to Know (Springer). Tony has developed and taught numerous online courses and developed online degrees from associate to doctorate. He has overseen instructional design teams for hundreds of online courses.

Meredith Ratliff

received her B.S. and M.A.T. in Mathematics at the University of Florida. She has been Associate Faculty in the mathematics department at Valencia College in Kissimmee, Florida for the past eight years. Ms. Ratliff is currently a doctoral candidate in Instructional Design and Technology program at the University of Central Florida.

Ray Schroeder

is a senior fellow of the University Professional and Continuing Education Association (UPCEA), as well as a professor emeritus and associate vice chancellor at the University of Illinois Springfield (UIS). He launched the UIS online learning program in 1997; founded the university's Center for Online Learning Research and Service; and became associate vice chancellor for online learning in 2013 – a position he still holds. Schroeder regularly publishes articles, book chapters, and presents nationally on emerging topics in online and technology-enhanced learning. He is the recipient of numerous national awards and citations for individual excellence and leadership from various associations and entities, including the Sloan Consortium, the U.S. Distance Learning Association, the *American Journal of Distance Education*, the Illinois Council for Continuing Higher Education, the University of Wisconsin, and the University of Illinois.

Adam Schultz

is the founder and CEO of Verified Studios, a digital agency that's been building and marketing highly effective digital experiences for Higher Ed clients since 2006.

Renay M. Scott

serves as Vice President of Student Success for New Mexico State University and Professor of Education. Dr. Scott has also served as President, Provost, and Dean of Arts and Sciences at two community colleges and Associate Professor of Education at Central Michigan University where she taught in the Masters of Educational Technology program and undergraduate teacher preparation program. She lives in New Mexico and enjoys bicycling, camping and reading.

Ormond Simpson

is a consultant in distance and online education, working recently as Visiting Fellow at the London University International Programmes. He was previously Visiting Professor at the Open Polytechnic of New Zealand, and Director of the Centre for Educational Guidance and Student Support at the UK Open University. He has worked, given keynote presentations and run workshops in 17 countries in Africa, South America, India, China, the West Indies, South Korea, and Europe. His next keynote will shortly be to the Open University of Nepal. His interests are in student support and retention, cost-benefits of retention activities, ethics, and learning motivation. His latest book is *Supporting Students for Success in Online and Distance Education* (2012, Routledge). He has written many book chapters and journal articles, which are freely available from his website www.ormondsimpson.com He originally graduated with a degree in theoretical physics, but believes that the task of developing really effective distance student support is just as challenging as finding a Theory of Everything...

Timothy Strasser

(University of Pittsburgh, 2019) has worked as an Instructional Consultant for both New Mexico State University and the University of Pittsburgh, focusing on online teaching and learning. At NMSU, he was part of a small team that provided university-wide support to NMSU faculty in using Canvas to teach both synchronous and asynchronous formats. He also was the main faculty contact for support of the polling software i>Clicker and the anti-plagiarism software Turnitin. At the University of Pittsburgh, he assisted faculty with instructional design of courses while using the Blackboard Learning Management System. His teaching experience includes approximately 10 years, including eight years of online teaching experience, instructing various courses for NMSU's College of Education and for Doña Ana Community College's Education Program.

Josh Strigle

began serving online students and faculty in 1998, as the first distance learning help desk employee at the College of Central Florida. He has experienced the pains associated with the growth of online learning from the administrative, as well as the student perspective. He has served as his college's representative to the Members Council for Distance Learning and Student Support, of the Florida Virtual Campus, since 2010 and recently completed a term as chair. This combination of student, administrative and policy experience serves him well, as he seeks to continually improve the learning experience for online students.

Karen Swan

is the Stukel Distinguished Professor of Educational Leadership and a Research Associate in the Center for Online Learning, Research and Service at the University of Illinois Springfield. Dr. Swan has been teaching online for over twenty years and researching online learning for almost as long. Her current research focuses on interactivity, social presence, person-centered education, and undergraduate retention and progression in online and blended programs. Dr. Swan is a Fellow of the Online Learning Consortium (OLC), a member of the International Adult and Continuing Education Hall of Fame, and a founding member of the OLC Board of Directors. She received the OLC award for Outstanding Achievement by an Individual, the National University Technology Network (NUTN) award for Outstanding Service, the Distinguished Alumnus Award from Teachers College, Columbia University, the Springfield University Burks Oakley II Distinguished Online Teaching Award, and the Association for Educational Communications and Technology (AECT) 2020 Distance Education Book Award.

Jennifer Veloff

 is an Online Program Manager assisting departments in their efforts to provide a strong foundation for the online initiative at the Colorado School of Mines. She earned her M.Ed. in Curriculum and Instruction with an emphasis in Instructional Technology from the University of South Florida and also has her Project Management Professional (PMP) certification. She has experience in higher education teaching as an adjunct professor and has practical hands-on experience with multiple instructional modalities. During the last 14 years, she has provided leadership for online and distance education programs as well as managed resources and personnel for several large government contracts and an instructional design team.

CHAPTER 1

Status of Online Learning

Christopher T. Miller and Hannah Digges-Elliott

Abstract

This chapter is designed to provide background information on the status of online learning. While many other chapters in this book will focus in greater details on topics related to administering distance learning, this chapter will provide an introduction to some of those topics.

Keywords

online learning – evolution of online learning – online learning challenges

1 Introduction

Distance learning is a concept that encompasses many forms of remote learning. It has been a form of learning for a significant number of years that includes televised courses, correspondence courses, and interactive television (ITV). Online learning is a more recent aspect of distance learning that occurs via the Internet. Online learning can be conducted through both synchronous (same time, any place) or asynchronous (any time, any place). Online learning can also happen in a variety of formats that include content presented in a standard web page format, through a learning management system (LMS) such as Blackboard or Canvas, or even through video-based conferencing systems such as Zoom or WebEx.

The focus of this chapter will be on background of online learning and its growth, the changes that have occurred over the years, and problems with online learning. At the conclusion of this chapter, you will address the following objectives:
– Provide a description of the evolution of online learning.
– Address the changes in online learning over the years.
– Identify various challenges to online learning.

© KONINKLIJKE BRILL NV, LEIDEN, 2021 | DOI: 10.1163/9789004471382_001

2   Purpose Behind Online Learning as a Transition from Previous
       Distance Learning Concepts

Online learning is a constantly evolving concept in both content and delivery. The delivery of opportunities has also evolved over the years. Learning has evolved from an oral tradition and apprentice model to highly structured processes that progress from traditional face-to-face instruction to online learning. Some of the fastest changes in education have occurred over the last two centuries with the advent of distance learning, which encompassed a variety of forms of delivery. Distance learning is a form of learning content that is delivered with physical separation between the teacher and the learners. Distance learning has evolved from a slow process of correspondence education that relied on instruction, completed assignments, and feedback being sent back and forth through mail between the instructor and the student. With the advent of radio and television, the process became somewhat faster as the content was delivered over the airwaves, but it was a one-way form of communication. Much of the interactions that occurred were focused on instructor-to-student and student-to-content learning. Additionally, the instructor-to-student interaction was delayed due to the one-way communication.

Various technology advancements leading to the advent of personal computers and the rise of the Internet during the 1980s created the possibility for teaching face-to-face from a distance (Keegan, 1996). This created an opportunity for not only instructor-to-student interactions and student-to-content learning but now opportunities were open for student-to-student interactions and student-to-instructor interactions all in real time. As the technology progressed the learning opportunities increased, and online learning became more appealing for learners. To better understand the changes, a brief historical background is provided to show the changes over time with the technology.

3   Brief Background on Online Learning

Distance learning was already occurring all the way back to 1728 with mail-based correspondence courses being advertised by Caleb Phillips in the Boston Gazette (Ferrer, 2017; Graduate Educational Information Services, 2020). By the 1920s distance learning was utilizing telephones, radio, and even phonograph recorded materials and lectures to distance-based learners. Over time distance learning evolved to content being provided via television with the 1970s bringing about broadcast over satellite or cable (Graduate Educational Information

Services, 2020). While there had been early implementation of providing learning resources online by different groups it was not until the mid-eighties that universities began offering accredited graduate degrees through online courses with the first in 1985 through Nova Southeastern University (G. Miller, 2014).

Significant changes occurred in the realm of online learning during the 1990s starting with the 1990 development of the first web browser by Tim Berners-Lee called WorldWideWeb or eventually Nexus (Berners-Lee, n.d.) and in 1991 the first webpage (Berners-Lee, 1991). Over time other browsers developed that shifted internet access to a more robust graphical look with color compared to the earlier text-based internet access. The quickly developing internet web browsers helped online learning grow further with online programs developing such as Western Governor's University, Jones International University and others (G. E. Miller et al., 2013). While many universities offer online courses and online programs, a number of fully online universities were quickly established. One of the first online universities was the University of Phoenix, established in 1989. Jones International University became the first accredited fully online university in 1996 (History and Trends of Learning Management System, 2016).

While online learning was occurring through text-based systems, email, and early webpages, one of the largest game changers for institutional online learning via courses and programs was the learning management system or LMS. The purpose of the LMS as a software application was to automate the administration, tracking, and reporting of training events (Ellis, 2009). The first of many LMSs that were developed was FirstClass by SoftArc (History and Trends of Learning Management System, 2016) with many others developing over time including Blackboard, Canvas, Angel, Desire2Learn, and Sakai. While the majority of LMSs are purchased through software contracts, some LMS products have been free or open source such as Sakai and Moodle. Moodle as an example, is a free and open-source learning management system supported through a variety of plug-in options that learning management administrators can select to incorporate into their institution's system.

As online learning continues to increase, it is important to understand how important LMS services have grown for use by higher education institutions. Currently there are 4,298 degree-granting institutions in the United States (Moody, 2019). Annual data collected shows that there are 3,386 institutions in 2019 with more than 500 full-time equivalent students. Based on those institutions there were three top LMS products being used that included Canvas with 1,094 institutions using (31.9%), Blackboard with 1,013 institutions using

(29.5%), and Moodle with 588 institutions using (17.1%) (edutechnica, 2019). The report also showed that an additional 691 institutions (20.1%) used Desire-2Learn, Sakai, or another LMS. This data is significant in understanding the prevalence of online learning in today's education. The edutechnica report shows that approximately 79% of US higher education institutions use an LMS to support their online learning courses. It should be noted that the number could be higher as this data does not take into consideration institutions with fewer than 500 full-time equivalent students.

Online learning continued to evolve along with technological advances such as the capability to create and access open educational resources (OER). OERs are free resources made legally available online. They usually include copyright licenses that allow for sharing, reproduction, and making derivative works, and access is not restricted by geography, or subscriptions. OERs, include images, books, articles, videos, podcasts, software, educational kits, etc. OERs expand the opportunity of open education with resources and practices (Littlejohn & Hood, 2017). One of the best descriptions of open educational resources and their purpose can be found in the Cape Town Open Education Declaration, which is a world-wide signed declaration of support for open education resources (CTOED, 2008). Open Content Licence (OCL) by David Wiley (Wiley, 1998) allowed for the free distribution of content that could be modified, used, and redistributed under a license similar to what was used in open source software. Open content continued until mid-2003 when it was closed in favor of the newly established Creative Commons (Wiley, 2003). Creative Commons was created in 2001 (DomainTools, n.d.) with an expanded focus on copyright licensing with a core set of six attribution licenses with limits regarding adapting/not-adapting, sharing/non-sharing of modified versions of the original work, and commercial/non-commercial use of the work (Creative Commons, 2017, 2020).

The rise of open educational content lead to a new aspect of online learning known as massive open online courses or MOOCs. The purpose of a MOOC was to expand the learning opportunity of an online course beyond the paying students by opening the course as a non-credit course. The first course that created this opportunity was a University of Manitoba course on learning theory taught by Stephen Downes and George Siemens (Parry, 2010) in 2008. The course had 25 paying students, but over 2,300 people participated in the course for free with access to all of the course materials. Since this course was first offered, there has been tremendous growth of MOOCs offered by traditional universities through, for instance, Coursera and edX, as well as a variety of non-profit providers such as Khan Academy, and for-profit companies such as Udacity.

4   Growth of Online Learning Over Three Decades

From the early beginnings of online learning to 2020 there have been significant changes to technologies, the development of online courses and then programs, and finally to online institutions. Based on recent data it is obvious that there has been exponential growth over the years. Using IPEDS data (Integrated Postsecondary Education Data System) the National Center for Educational Statistics (NCES) found that during fall 2018 35.3% of over 19 million students, took online courses that were offered across public and private universities (National Center for Educational Statistics, 2018). The data remains consistent on the percentage of students taking online courses with a slightly higher percentage in graduate level online courses. Table 1.1 using the NCES (2018) data shows a breakdown of enrollments by degree type.

TABLE 1.1   2018 enrollments in online courses

	Total number of students	Total of students not taking distance education courses	Total of students taking distance education courses
Total of all students	19,645,918	12,713,844 (64.7%)	6,932,074 (35.3%)
Total Postbaccalaureate	3,035,683	1,828,318 (60.2%)	1,207,365 (39.8%)
Total Undergraduate	16,610,235	10,885,526 (65.5%)	5,724,709 (34.5%)
Undergraduate 4-year	10,865027	7,112,844 (65.5%)	3,752,183 (34.5%)

When considering the growth of online learning over the past 30 years it is important to also consider the benefits and pitfalls of online learning. There have been various standpoints regarding online learning vs. face-to-face learning with each side stating that their format is superior. Some have described online learning as no better than correspondence courses and the increase of online degrees impacts the credibility of education (Angiello, 2010). At an earlier date this claim could easily have been made when online instruction was primarily asynchronous and the synchronous components were essentially text-based chats. It could be argued that with the proliferation of video chat software programs such as Skype, WebEx, Microsoft Teams, and Zoom, that a closer level of personal communication can be held within an online course.

5   Modalities of Online Learning

Modalities of learning lie along a continuum with fully online learning on one end and fully face-to-face learning on the other. Between the two, you will find hybrid (or blended) learning. Online learning in its most pure form is a modality that requires no physical in-class seat time of the students and relies heavily on technology for the educational experience. As you move towards face-to-face learning, you will find hybrid modalities of instruction where students experience both online and in-class instruction (Means et al., 2009). For hybrid learning, the amount of in-class instruction versus online instruction varies wildly and depends on how an institution conceptualizes the modality. While some institutions rely on quality as a driver as to how to define the different modes of online learning such as hybrid or fully online, most rely on the quantity of the instruction that takes place in a given environment meaning the percentage that a class is online versus face-to-face (Hrastinski, 2019).

Within online and hybrid/blended modalities, there are further subclassifications that include the use of asynchronous and/or synchronous instruction. Asynchronous instruction takes place non-simultaneously at the students' discretion. Synchronous instruction is a computer mediated simultaneous experience with communication occurring in real-time similar to a conversation occurring in physical space (O'Byrne & Pytash, 2015). Depending on the mix of modalities, hybrid and online courses may look very different from one another. The variability in modalities of online learning mirror the variability in face-to-face courses. Some face-to-face courses are lecture based, others focus more on project-based learning, others still are writing-intensive, and so on. Due to the variability, there can be no direct comparison between modalities focused solely on the mediums used (Hodges et al., 2020). Instructional strategies and teaching play a larger role in the effectiveness in instruction than the modality used.

6   Program Formats (Individual Learning, Traditional Course and Programs, Microcredentials, Etc.)

As online learning took hold historically, most of the programmatic offerings focused on traditional baccalaureate and master's degree procurement. The goal for institutions may be to provide online offerings to (1) attract students, and (2) confer degrees. As a result of these goals as well as demand, institutions report that online learning is important to their strategies as they move forward which is due to the rising numbers of students taking online courses (Allen & Seaman, 2014).

While online degrees were not preferred by employers due to a perception of reduced standards, as the ubiquity and quality of online learning options increased, so did occupational acceptance (Gallagher, 2019). This is further seen in the proliferation of micro credentials such as standalone certifications or digital badges from organizations or even higher education institutions. Institutions such as Harvard Extension, Stanford, and MIT among others have all stepped forward to offer courses and certificates in various topics or competency areas without the requirement of admission. While many of these courses are offered as massively open online courses, many educational providers have offered paid credential alternatives as well (Gallagher, 2019). In addition to generating revenue for the institutions, such offerings allow access to education for those who are unable to afford a traditional four-year education, are in need of additional credentialing for the workforce, or have a desire for continuing and professional education (Horton, 2020). While there is the possibility of stacking micro credentials to show expertise in place of a degree on a resume, it remains to be seen if traditional degree programs could be replaced fully by alternative program formats and/or microcredentials (Horton, 2020).

The flexibility desired with microcredentials is also mirrored in the emergence of competency-based instruction. While competency-based education has been around for well over a century we have seen the ties being made to online learning over the last twenty years. A prime example is Western Governor's University, a competency-based institution created in the 1990s, that had over 120,000 enrollments in 2018, all of which were online students (Lederman, 2019).

The move towards competency-based seems to be predicated on the emerging emphasis on tangible learning objectives that are tightly defined, the clear connection between assessments and objectives and showing mastery therein, as well as the demand for flexibility and personalization in both instruction and time to completion (Nodine, 2016). Many of these programs allow students who come into a course with previous skills and knowledge to bypass instruction through direct assessment and earn credit for these skills. This lack of "seat time" flies in the face of the traditional credit hour model (Burnette, 2016). While not necessarily cheaper than a traditional degree or certificate, competency-based education programs allow students to garner more credit hours quicker. Also, competency-based education models tend to lean towards more individualized and adaptive learning experiences. By gaining credit for prior knowledge through direct assessment, students can regulate their own pace both within specific courses and programmatically. Further, if the program has the technical ability, students can receive feedback in the form of remediation assignments as needed based on their responses to an assignment or quiz.

7   Mass Migration to Online Learning Due to 2020 Global Pandemic

In Spring 2020, PreK-12 to graduate level education institutions experienced a radical disruption with the cancelling of in-person classes due to the COVID-19 global pandemic. This required both instructors and students with differing experiences with distance education and technology to move to a remote teaching environment. Institutions of all types experienced the need to scale their technology and support services within weeks to different degrees based on the ubiquity of online learning and associated modalities at that institution. Despite educational technologies and support availability being high at many institutions, it is likely that many instructors who moved to remote instruction may have had little experience with many of these technologies and support services (Brooks et al., 2020). The importance of the phrase "remote teaching" cannot be underscored enough. Despite studies that have shown that online learning is as effective as face-to-face learning, there is still an ongoing belief among many that it is less effective. The immediacy of action needed as part of the COVID-19 migration to remote learning did not allow for the careful, methodical design and development that effective online learning requires. The Johnson et al. (2020) study surveyed 897 faculty members and administrators at 672 higher education institutions from early to mid April 2020 regarding their rapid transition from face-to-face to online in response to the COVID-19 pandemic. In that study, it was reported that 32% of faculty surveyed indicated that they had lowered their expectations regarding student work quality and 48% lowered their expectations as to the amount of work that could be done by students as compared to their expectations before the pandemic transition. However, this may be due to issues associated with the remote teaching migration, experience and resources available to all parties, and other issues and not based on modality alone. As a result, the remote learning experience due to the COVID-19 migration should not be equated to online learning experiences that have been thoughtfully designed (Hodges et al., 2020). This sort of description would bring the reputation of online learning down even further in the estimation of those already skeptical of its efficacy.

8   Issues to Consider with Online Learning

Although there has been an increased number of online courses and programs offered since online learning began developing, there are still issues that need to be considered. These issues focus on three primary areas. These areas include online course and program issues, problems with online learning, and quality issues in online learning and programs.

9   **Online Course and Program Issues**

Central to the success and effectiveness of the online course and program is the faculty member as a course designer, subject matter expert, and/or instructor. The simple application of face-to-face teaching instructional strategies and techniques does not always translate to the online environment. Traditional face-to-face class instructional strategies may be more instructor-centered and focused on the transmission of information from the instructor to the student. In an online environment where students are more self-regulated and the structure of the actual classroom is not present, it is imperative to move to student centered strategies (Keengwe & Kidd, 2010). As a result, to ensure success in the online environment, it is not enough to conquer the technology, they must also transform the way they approach teaching.

10   **Problems with Online Learning**

There are several problems facing institutions who offer online learning including academic honesty, equity, and assessment and evaluation. Academic honesty in the online environment including plagiarism and other forms of cheating is a concern for stakeholders in higher education. While fairly prevalent in post-secondary institutions, the prevalence seems to be higher in the online environment (McGee, 2013). There are companies who have created or are looking to create and implement technologies to help deter cheating in the online environment such as online proctoring and plagiarism checking tools. It is up to the institution, however, to help connect faculty with the resources needed whether that be information through professional development or access to tools and technology.

Another problem with online learning is the perception of equity. While online learning has been heralded as bringing education to the masses, it also does have a cost to entry. Students must have access to technology capable of streaming audio and video in some cases and internet access at least, and they must be able to traverse the digital environment in both skill and ability. The cost of and access to technology in addition to the cost of tuition can be barriers to entry (Bell & Federman, 2013). These issues can also affect the success of students who do overcome those initial barriers to entry. Students who are not confident in their technological skills, are underprepared, or face other associated issues may drop out of their online classes due to the lack of guidance and support (Bell & Federman, 2013). This could happen after they have spent money they cannot afford to lose.

Further, there are problems with the assessment and evaluation of online learning including a lack of online specific student evaluations as well as the lack of data as to long term achievement results. Many institutions are relying on uniform student evaluations that are given to online, hybrid, and face-to-face students. This lack of specific evaluation measures makes it difficult to know what needs to be specifically addressed in the online environment. Also, much of the research on online learning is immediate to the completion of a course or program. However, there needs to be more longitudinal research to explore skill transfer from online course to practice (Bell & Federman, 2013).

11   Quality Issues of Online Courses and Programs

The quality of an online course or program is contingent on quality of the design and teaching of the course. There are two primary considerations that guide the creation and scaling of online learning programs: institutional readiness and faculty readiness. First, there are institutional readiness considerations such as attitudes regarding effectiveness, technological and pedagogical infrastructure, and cost and revenue. Second, there are faculty readiness considerations such as course design, instructor preparedness, course quality, and efficacy of teaching.

11.1   *Institutional Readiness Considerations*
Institutional issues to be dealt with in the creation and scaling of online programs include the pervasive belief that online learning is inferior to face-to-face instruction. As noted in the Means et al. (2009) meta-analysis of 27 Department of Education studies of online learning versus face-to-face learning, this belief has not been borne out in the literature. Online learning experiences were found to be as effective as face-to-face learning experiences. Further, blended learning experiences were found to have better outcomes than face-to-face learning experiences. It should be noted, however, that instructional strategies are more telling of effectiveness than modality (Hodges et al., 2020). Despite the issues of studying effectiveness of modalities focused on the mediums, institutions must be ready and willing to challenge this notion of the supremacy of the face-to-face modality through the dissemination of research, a focus on instructional design and strategies, and a concrete plan for creating and scaling courses and programs.

Another area of concern for institutions looking to scale online courses and programs is that of policy and support. Institutions should create policies that govern the creation and proliferation of online courses. Policies should include definitions of terms specific to their institutions, expectations for instructors and students in the online environment, and support for both faculty and students (Meyer & Barefield, 2010). Associated technologies and systems should guide these policies in addition to spurring a culture of support. Further, institutions should identify support needs beyond technical resources such as instructional design support, financial support, personnel such as additional faculty, online advisers, student support specialists, and online tutors among others.

Finally, institutions tend to consider a cost and revenue calculus in the creation of online courses and programs (Bell & Federman, 2013). The cost to entry and maintenance for online learning from an institutional perspective is very high due to the pricing of learning management systems, supportive applications, and institutional applications for student tracking, policy creation, and personnel among other considerations. There are additional concerns about increased course development time and faculty workload (Appana, 2008). Despite this cost to entry for institutions, that cost does reduce overtime, and online learning generates a large amount of much needed revenue for institutions that face declining state dollars and attendance numbers due to the ability to tap into markets previously unavailable to institutions (Appana, 2008).

11.2 *Faculty Readiness Considerations*

Faculty readiness is central to the success and effectiveness of online courses. As an example, the 2020 COVID-19 pandemic resulted not in traditional learning experiences but a newer form of remote learning due to the lack of faculty readiness. Due to a lack of online teaching preparedness, faculty were faced with shifting content and instruction online with a short turnaround rather than allowing for the development of authentic online learning experiences. While faculty do require the administrative support and infrastructure to embark on this endeavor, they also must be able to create, teach, and manage the courses and programs. This requires knowledge of online course design, ability to apply best practices, technological preparedness, and the application of pedagogical strategies appropriate for the online environment, while keeping in mind that the goal is to provide a quality learning experience for their online students.

Institutions must be prepared to provide support for faculty to ready them for the online environment. Many institutions offer support in the form of professional development opportunities, access to instructional designers, technological support, and mechanisms for course evaluation of best practices. These support mechanisms for faculty cannot focus only on the technology or only on the pedagogy, they must instead focus on the entire online teaching and learning process online and include technology, pedagogy, course supervision, and facilitation of interaction (Keengwe & Kidd, 2010). The 2020 COVID-19 experience highlights the need for institutional support particularly as most faculty are having to prepare contingency plans for future courses. Many institutions have implemented mass trainings, course development, and purchase of resources to support and supplement instruction (Brooks et al., 2020). Various institutions focus on professional development as a means to improving the quality of instruction in the online environment. While this can occur in distributed support models, it is not a rarity to see a centralized support office for online learning (Britto et al., 2013).

To evaluate both readiness and success of supports and implementation of online learning, there is a need to provide evaluation of both the design of the course and the delivery or instruction of the content. Doing so allows for the identification of institutional and instructional shortcomings in the support of online teaching and learning. With regard to evaluating the course design, there are no ubiquitous quality measures for evaluating online and/or hybrid course design (Allen et al., 2016). Many institutions will develop their own quality online course evaluation processes and/or they will use well-established quality models such as Blackboard's Exemplary Course Program Rubric, Quality Matters, and others to drive their decision making (Baldwin et al., 2018). Despite this lack of uniformity in overall quality evaluation and best practices, the Baldwin et al. (2018) study noted that in their review of six national and state-wide quality assessment measures, there were best practices in online course design that spanned the measures. These included the following:

- Objectives are available.
- Navigation is intuitive.
- Technology is used to promote learner engagement/facilitate learning.
- Student-to-student interaction is supported.
- Communication and activities are used to build community.
- Instructor contact information is stated.
- Expectations regarding quality of communication/participation are provided.
- Assessment rubrics for graded assignments are provided.
- Assessments align with objectives.
- Links to institutional services are provided.
- Course has accommodations for disabilities.
- Course policies are stated for behavior expectations. (p. 56)

In addition to evaluating a course's design based on best practices as defined by the institution and/or other organizations, teaching also should be assessed. This has been done traditionally by examining student grades and attitudes.

Many institutions conduct student evaluations of online courses using the same instrument used in face-to-face courses despite the potential differences in the teaching and design of each modality (Bangert, 2008).

12   Rise of Online Program Management

There is a current push for high-level administrators focused on online learning and related initiatives such as a "Chief Online Learning Officer," "Vice-Chancellor of ELearning," or a "Dean of Online Education" (Herron et al., 2016). The goal of these positions is to foster collaboration and buy-in across departments and disciplines while upholding the value of effective teaching and learning strategies and practices and bridging the expanse between technology and education. Compared to program managers, these administrative positions work on less minutiae associated with the nuts and bolts of creating and managing online courses and programs, but instead create high-level reports, guide policy making, and ensure regulation compliance.

Program managers, however, may include not only the creation and maintenance of programs and courses, but also the management of resources and support. Unlike the high-level administrators such as a "Chief Learning Officer" who is often located with other administrators, the program managers are usually within non-academic/non-teaching units, but this varies by institution. Some program managers and their accompanying units are integrated into the current organizational structure, other institutions create new units or departments, and others still will create entire separate colleges to manage and support the online learning undertakings not limited to programmatic and course development (Gellman-Danley & Fetzner, 1998). No matter their location, ideally these leaders typically understand both higher education and business with an eye towards marketing, business, and operations. Further, they must have the ability to transcend typical academic silos within an institution to identify partners from multiple areas (Portugal, 2006).

A criticism is that distance learning programs and their management rely primarily on part-time adjunct faculty and due to a lack of training requirements and oversight, that that practice negatively affects the online programs and courses. Some institutions are combatting this by attempting to integrate the full-time faculty with the part-time adjunct faculty to help breed familiarity and faculty learning communities. Others have created online faculty professional development programs that require participation as a gateway to teaching online (Gaillard-Kenney, 2006). The issue is that there is not one consistent solution.

A recent trend is the partnership of online program management companies with higher education institutions. These companies offer services in marketing, design, and even subject matter expert content in some cases with an ala carte menu of services. The use of such services allows for the scaling of online courses and programs quickly to meet the demand for such in a way that institutions could not do on their own (Pelletier, 2018). However, the use of such programs is not without controversy. Some criticisms involve the financial model of these companies that employ revenue sharing with the higher education institution. This financial intertangling can actually give the companies stake in raising tuition (Pelletier, 2018).

13   Rise of Predatory Programs

As online programs have grown and developed so has the development of predatory programs or diploma mills. As the Internet has grown with opportunities for education, so have opportunities for scammers and predators. A diploma mill is essentially considered a substandard or fraudulent college that offers potential students degrees with little or no serious work (Piña, 2009). There are several hallmarks of a diploma mill that prospective students and educators can identify that include limited admissions processes likely focused on a credit card, institutional accreditation that is not recognized by the Council on Higher Education Accreditation (CHEA) or the U.S. Department of Education, degrees offered based on a review of work experience, resume, limited time needed to complete a program, or promise degrees in exchange for specific amounts of money (Phillips, n.d.; Simonson, 2011).

While it is important for consumers to beware of diploma mills it is especially important for distance learning and institutional administrators to verify the degrees and coursework submitted by potential faculty. It is important that academic credentials are verified prior to an instructor beginning to teach for an institution. One of the most important ways is for the institution to only accept official transcripts that are submitted by the faculty member's degree granting institution. It is also important for institution administrators to ensure that degrees being presented by faculty applicants are from recognized accreditors and/or the U.S. Department of Education. While there are many examples, a recent case involved a professor in West Virginia University's Department of Community Medicine in which the individual falsified his credentials for employment, obtaining grants, and immigration status (Ove, 2018).

14   Status of DL Admin and Emerging Initiatives

The history of online learning shows the power and limitations of innovation in education. Online learning has the power to bring quality educational opportunities to spaces, times, and populations not previously reached with traditional modalities when done thoughtfully with sound pedagogical strategies. Unchecked proliferation not beholden to quality measures, regulation, and best practices has a chilling effect on attitudes, positive proliferation, and/or educational experience. Higher education institutions that consider online learning part of their long-term strategic plans are creating new high-level administrative positions meant to help guide the institutional plans, policies, and relationships. These new administrative positions expand the role of the online program manager to include the development of new online programs, creating partnerships with external agencies, and exploring new avenues for online programming. This is becoming increasingly important in light of the changes to jobs, job training, and the creation of new innovations due to the 2020 COVID-19 pandemic. Some of these changes include increased remote work, changes in job roles, responsibilities, and organizational knowledge.

As we look towards the future, we are on the cusp of major changes in online learning that hold the opportunity for forward, positive progression. As we see the rise of microcredentials and competency-based education, more conversations about the efficacy of seat time and the Carnegie hour will need to continue. As higher education institutions continue to partner with online program management companies along with the continuing impact of predatory programs and practices, regulations on an institutional, state, regional, and/or federal level may need to be explored to ensure that student learning is protected.

Finally, a new chapter of evaluation and assessment of online learning is upon us. In the aftermath of remote teaching and the equivocation of remote teaching with online learning, there are calls for increased scrutiny. However, we should not fall victim to focusing only on the efficacy of the technology and outcomes, but instead we must focus on the pedagogical strategies that make modalities effective. As an example, students that succeed in online learning environments and are used to self-regulation of learning are more apt to be successful in the face-to-face environment as well. Interestingly, the act of teaching online in a learner-centered environment has been shown to lead to a transfer of the same pedagogical strategies in the face-to-face classroom environment (Andrews-Graham, 2018).

As you progress through this book, many of the topics introduced will be explored further. Important topics that have been touched upon in this chapter will be discussed in more depth and provide actionable recommendations to evolve your practice. Some of those topics include quality assurance, online learning success, managing course development, and support technologies. Each of these topics help to frame the distance learning administrator to not only support online learning, but to explore the new and developing potentials as online learning expands.

In small group discussion, address the objectives at the beginning of this chapter.

References

Allen, I. E., & Seaman, J. (2014). *2013 – Grade change: Tracking online education in the United States*. Babson Survey Research Group. https://onlinelearningconsortium.org/survey_report/2013-survey-online-learning-report/

Allen, I. E., Seaman, J., Poulin, R., & Straut, T. T. (2016). *Tracking online education in the United States* (p. 62). Babson Survey Research Group. https://onlinelearningsurvey.com/reports/onlinereportcard.pdf

Andrews-Graham, D. A. (2018). The effect of online teaching on faculty after returning to the traditional classroom. *Online Journal of Distance Learning Administration, 21*(4). https://www.westga.edu/~distance/ojdla/winter214/andrewsgraham214.html

Angiello, R. (2010). Study looks at online learning vs. traditional instruction. *Education Digest, 76*(2), 56–59.

Appana, S. (2008). A review of benefits and limitations of online learning in the context of the student, the instructor, and the tenured faculty. *International Journal on E-Learning, 7*(1), 5–22.

Baldwin, S., Ching, Y.-H., & Hsu, Y.-C. (2018). Online course design in higher education: A review of national and statewide evaluation instruments. *TechTrends: Linking Research & Practice to Improve Learning, 62*(1), 46–57.

Bangert, A. W. (2008). The development and validation of the student evaluation of online teaching effectiveness. *Computers in the Schools, 25*(1–2), 25–47.

Bell, B. S., & Federman, J. E. (2013). E-learning in postsecondary education. *The Future of Children, 23*(1), 165–185.

Berners-Lee, T. (n.d.). *Tim Berners-Lee: WorldWideWeb, the first Web client*. W3C. Retrieved June 5, 2020, from https://www.w3.org/People/Berners-Lee/WorldWideWeb.html

Berners-Lee, T. (1991, August 6). *The World Wide Web project*. World Wide Web. http://info.cern.ch/hypertext/WWW/TheProject.html

Britto, M., Ford, C., & Wise, J.-M. (2013). Three institutions, three approaches, one goal: Addressing quality assurance in online learning. *Online Learning Journal*, *17*(4). https://www.learntechlib.org/p/183757/

Brooks, C., Grajek, S., & Lang, L. (2020). Institutional readiness to adopt fully remote learning. *EDUCAUSE Review*. https://er.educause.edu/blogs/2020/4/institutional-readiness-to-adopt-fully-remote-learning

Burnette, D. M. (2016). The renewal of competency-based education: A review of the literature. *Journal of Continuing Higher Education*, *64*(2), 84–93.

Creative Commons. (2017, November 7). *About the licenses*. Creative Commons. https://creativecommons.org/licenses/

Creative Commons. (2020, January 24). *Frequently asked questions*. Creative Commons. https://creativecommons.org/faq/#what-is-creative-commons-and-what-do-you-do

CTOED. (2008, January 22). *The Cape Town Open Education Declaration: Unlocking the promise of open educational resources*. The Cape Town Open Education Declaration. https://www.capetowndeclaration.org/read-the-declaration

DomainTools. (n.d.). *CreativeCommons.org WHOIS, DNS, & Domain Info – DomainTools*. Retrieved June 13, 2020, from https://whois.domaintools.com/creativecommons.org

edutechnica. (2019, October 7). 7th Annual LMS data update | edutechnica. *EdTech Talk and Analysis*. https://edutechnica.com/2019/10/07/7th-annual-lms-data-update/

Ellis, R. K. (2009). *A field guide to learning management systems* (Learning Circuits, p. 8). American Society for Training and Development.

Ferrer, D. (2017, December 13). *History of online education*. TheBestSchools.Org. https://thebestschools.org/magazine/online-education-history/

Gaillard-Kenney, S. (2006). Adjunct faculty in distance education: What program managers should know. *Distance Learning*, *3*(1), 9–16.

Gallagher, S. (2019). *Employer demand shaping the future of microcredential market: Insights from a national survey | UNBOUND*. https://unbound.upcea.edu/innovation/alternative-credentialing/microdegrees/national-survey-suggests-that-employers-will-lead-way-on-digital-badging/

Gellman-Danley, B., & Fetzner, M. J. (1998). Asking the really tough questions: Policy issues for distance learning. *Journal of Distance Learning Advmination*, *1*(1). https://www.westga.edu/~distance/danley11.html

Graduate Educational Information Services. (2020). *History of distance learning*. http://www.godistancelearning.com/history-of-distance-learning.html

Herron, J., Lashley, J., Salley, W., & Shaw, M. (2016). The chief online learning officer: Competencies, roles, and trajectories. *Unbound: Reinventing Higher Education*. https://unbound.upcea.edu/online-2/online-education/the-chief-online-learning-officer-competencies-roles-and-trajectories/

History and Trends of Learning Management System [Infographic]. (2016, April 12). *Oxagile*. https://www.oxagile.com/article/history-and-trends-of-learning-management-system-infographics/

Hodges, C., Moore, S., Lockee, B., Trust, T., & Bond, A. (2020, March 27). The difference between emergency remote teaching and online learning. *Educause Review.* https://er.educause.edu/articles/2020/3/the-difference-between-emergency-remote-teaching-and-online-learning

Horton, A. P. (2020, February 17). *Could micro-credentials compete with traditional degrees?* https://www.bbc.com/worklife/article/20200212-could-micro-credentials-compete-with-traditional-degrees

Hrastinski, S. (2019). What do we mean by blended learning? *TechTrends, 63*(5), 564–569. https://doi.org/10.1007/s11528-019-00375-5

Johnson, N., Veletsianos, G., & Seaman, J. (2020). U.S. faculty and administrators' experiences and approaches in the early weeks of the COVID-19 pandemic. *Online Learning, 24*(2), Article 2. https://doi.org/10.24059/olj.v24i2.2285

Keegan, D. (1996). *Foundations of distance education* (3rd ed.). Routledge.

Keengwe, J., & Kidd, T. T. (2010). Towards best practices in online learning and teaching in higher education. *MERLOT Journal of Online Learning and Teaching, 6*(2), 533–541.

Lederman, D. (2019, December 17). *The biggest movers online.* Inside Higher Ed. https://www.insidehighered.com/digital-learning/article/2019/12/17/colleges-and-universities-most-online-students-2018

Littlejohn, A., & Hood, N. (2017). How educators build knowledge and expand their practice: The case of open education resources. *British Journal of Educational Technology, 48*(2), 499–510.

McGee, P. (2013). Supporting academic honesty in online courses. *Journal of Educators Online, 10*(1).

Means, B., Toyama, Y., Murphy, R., Bakia, M., & Jones, K. (2009). *Evaluation of evidence-based practices in online learning: A meta-analysis and review of online learning studies.* US Department of Education. https://eric.ed.gov/?id=ED505824

Meyer, J. D., & Barefield, A. C. (2010). Infrastructure and administrative support for online programs. *Online Journal of Distance Learning Administration, 13*(3). https://msu.idm.oclc.org/login?url=http://search.ebscohost.com/login.aspx?direct=true&db=eft&AN=508190039

Miller, G. (2014). *History of distance learning.* Worldwidelearn.com. https://www.worldwidelearn.com/education-articles/history-of-distance-learning.html

Miller, G. E., Benke, M., Chalous, B., Ragan, L. C., Schroeder, R., Smutz, W., & Swan, K. (2013). *Leading the e-learning transformation of higher education.* Stylus Publishing.

Moody, J. (2019, February 15). *A guide to the changing number of U.S. universities.* US News & World Report. https://www.usnews.com/education/best-colleges/articles/2019-02-15/how-many-universities-are-in-the-us-and-why-that-number-is-changing

National Center for Educational Statistics. (2018). *Number and percentage of students enrolled in degree-granting postsecondary institutions, by distance education participation, location of student, level of enrollment, and control and level of institution: Fall 2017 and fall 2018*. Digest of Education Statistics, 2019; National Center for Education Statistics. https://nces.ed.gov/programs/digest/d19/tables/dt19_311.15.asp

Nodine, T. R. (2016). How did we get here? A brief history of competency-based higher education in the United States. *The Journal of Competency-Based Education*, *1*(1), 5–11. https://doi.org/10.1002/cbe2.1004

O'Byrne, W. I., & Pytash, K. E. (2015). Hybrid and blended learning. *Journal of Adolescent & Adult Literacy*, *59*(2), 137–140.

Ove. (2018, UGUST). Federal agents hunting for ex-WVU professor accused of faking credentials, immigration fraud. *Pittsburgh Post-Gazette*. https://www.post-gazette.com/news/crime-courts/2018/08/20/Federal-agents-hunting-for-ex-WVU-professor-accused-of-faking-credentials-immigration-fraud/stories/201808200129

Parry, M. (2010). Online, bigger classes may be better classes. *Chronicle of Higher Education*, *57*(2), A1–A22.

Pelletier, S. G. (2018). The evolution of online program management. *Unbound: Reinventing Higher Education*. https://unbound.upcea.edu/leadership-strategy/continuing-education/the-evolution-of-online-program-management/

Phillips, V. (n.d.). *10 ways to spot a diploma mill*. GetEducated. https://www.geteducated.com/college-degree-mills/161-college-degree-or-diploma-mill/

Piña, A. A. (2009). E-mentor: How online diploma mills hurt e-learning. *E-Mentor*, *5*(32). http://www.e-mentor.edu.pl/artykul/index/numer/32/id/702

Portugal, L. M. (2006). Emerging leadership roles in distance education: Current state of affairs and forecasting future trends. *Online Journal of Distance Learning Administration*, *9*(3), 1–11.

Simonson, M. (2011). What diploma mills are not. *Distance Learning*, *8*(2), 72–71.

Wiley, D. A. (1998, July 14). *OpenContent License (OPL)*. OpenContent. https://web.archive.org/web/19990129013417/http://www.opencontent.org/opl.shtml

Wiley, D. A. (2003, June 30). *OpenContent is officially closed*. OpenContent. https://web.archive.org/web/20030802222546/http://opencontent.org/

CHAPTER 2

Leadership for Online Learning

Ray Schroeder

Abstract

The objectives of this chapter are to establish a foundation for a deeper dive into the many aspects of leadership for distance learning that are detailed in this book. The reader will build an understanding of the roles and requirements of effective operational leadership in the day-to-day operations of distance learning. Further, it is the objective of this chapter to explain the multifaceted roles of the strategic leader within the institution to advance the distance learning program within the institution as well as the broader field worldwide. Tools, techniques, examples, and resources will be shared to accomplish these objectives. Finally, it is intended that the reader will assimilate an understanding and appreciation of the importance of leading with knowledge, humility, and wide perspective.

Keywords

advocacy – entrepreneurship – leadership – operational leadership – professionalism – strategic leadership – team building – technologies

1   Leadership

The leadership role is a particularly human one in what is often considered a technological field. In the broadest sense, this is the leadership that is driving the advancement of higher education into the fourth industrial revolution. It requires an array of skills and knowledge spanning the relevant pedagogies, emerging technologies; interpersonal skills; intrinsic qualities such as empathy; teaching abilities; and visioning. Collectively, these and associated qualities enable leaders to effectively implement the mission of the institution online. Through technology, we bring the essence of the college or university to the student rather than requiring the student to come to campus.

In this chapter, the reader will learn about the qualities of effective operational leadership, including the skills and abilities that must be honed to be successful in leading on the front lines of distance education. Also, we will examine the qualities of strategic leadership, which is different in important ways from the day-to-day operational leadership. The pathway from operational to strategic leadership will be discussed in detail because this is the common route from front-line leadership and maintenance of the online enterprise to institution-wide visioning and leading. Finally, we will examine leading beyond the institution. In higher education, there is a long tradition and expectation that leaders will contribute to the broader field, both nationally and internationally. In doing so, as we will see, significant benefits will return to the institution and to the individual.

2   Operational Leadership

Leaders in this field most commonly begin either as an instructional designer or as a faculty member who becomes enamored with mediated teaching. In either case successful leaders have a personal commitment to serve distant students by facilitating and enabling the most effective learning modes and methods. Others enter the track to online distance learning leadership from electronic media and computer services. They too share this mission to serve learning at a distance.

After performing in a direct service role for some time – either assisting subject matter experts and faculty members to develop online classes or students in succeeding in those classes – these professionals advance in their careers to operational leadership positions. These positions are the ones that are leading the teams who put pedagogy into practice to build successful courses and programs. They engage faculty members and subject area experts in shaping the pathway to learning outcomes and ultimately to careers for students. Operational leaders work with deans and directors to assure that programs are deployed successfully and student satisfaction is addressed. They impact the success of others up and down the leadership chain (Maxwell, 2004).

The work of the operational leader is at the front line of leading teams that are directly developing, deploying and supporting classes. Deep knowledge of the constantly evolving pedagogies, technologies and best leadership practices is required to succeed as an operational leader in this field. This knowledge taps education theory; scientific foundations of networking technologies; and social science principles of leadership, interpersonal engagement, and client empowerment.

2.1   *Knowledge of Pedagogies*

The pedagogies of online distance learning span pedagogy (principles and practices of teaching youth), andragogy (principles and practices of teaching adults), and heutagogy (principles and practices of teaching the self-directed learner) (Blaschke, 2018).

For online learning at the pre-K, elementary and secondary levels, appropriate online pedagogy is most relevant in the design and development of modules and classes. Increasing pressure on state education budgets and demands from parents for broader curricula have led to an increase in online programs in most states. Online classes offer flexibility in scheduling and are especially popular in summer K/12 programs. The practices and principles governing online teaching and learning at this level are somewhat different from face-to-face offerings since the students are at a distance. Practitioners and leaders in elementary and secondary fields must become well-familiar with the pedagogy of teaching and learning at this level in order to best serve the students. Much has been written on this topic as K/12 schools expand their online teaching (Shattuck & Burch, 2018).

In the post-secondary environment, knowledge and implementation of best practices in andragogy are also essential. These differ from those engaged in teaching children. The relative intellectual maturity of the post-secondary students and the added goal of career preparation are among the factors that prescribe different principles and practices in teaching this group. The growth of online learning in the post-secondary field has been especially strong with more than one-third of all students taking at least one online class in 2018 (Lederman, 2019). Effective practices and principles continue to evolve as colleges and universities drive innovation in higher education (Contact North, 2017).

The lifelong learner is increasingly well-versed in using the Internet to meet their own needs. They are mature, and in many regards, self-sufficient in their learning. Yet, this group also needs the support of professionals and the leadership of online learning. Heutagogy describes the principles and best practices in this emerging field. This newcomer to the "gogy" group is growing rapidly and becoming more and more important as colleges and universities seek to sustain the mature lifelong learner (Davis, 2018).

Pedagogy Self-Review – where will you specialize?
Consider how principles and practices vary among the maturity and goals of learners, though they are certainly not mutually-exclusive, each area carries different emphases. Refer to the cited sources:
– Pedagogy serves which learner group?
– Andragogy serves which learner group?
– Heutagogy serves which learner group?

2.2   *Knowledge of Technologies*

The second key area of knowledge for operational leaders is the technology of delivery modes for distance education. Over time, these modes have evolved as learning management systems have become more sophisticated; virtual reality and augmented reality have brought new dimensions to online learning; and adaptive learning offers more refined outcomes-driven approaches. Knowledge of emerging and developing technologies is a difficult, but essential role of the operational leader. Responsibility for keeping technologies current and anticipating the advent of new technologies is a vital function in institutions.

The premier online distance learning tool, the learning management system (LMS) has become a key organizational tool in today's online learning. The LMS provides the framework within which learning content is delivered, interaction is hosted, grades are assigned, and the learning process is monitored. The operational leader is charged with assuring the LMS is up-to-date and meeting the needs of both learners and instructors. The LMS is the source of rich data that can inform faculty and administrators of the engagement and progress of students in their classes. Tracking the paths that learners follow through their online classes and recording the number of minutes spent on each task can inform decisions on how to best streamline and optimize their learning paths. The operational leader assists front-line staff members, faculty, and administrators in extracting and applying this valuable information from the LMS. A whole host of features and functions are held within the LMS today, including those previously mentioned as well as assuring accessibility, transparency, and ease of navigation through the online classroom (Pappas, 2017).

Virtual Reality (VR), Augmented Reality (AR) and Mixed Reality (XR) are emerging to provide immersive environments in online distance learning. These technologies must be on the radar of the successful operational leader. Advances in this field enable virtual laboratories and collaborative work on real-life structures. Anatomy and physiology are greatly enhanced for the distant online learner by using these three-dimensional immersive technologies. They are at the forefront of the future of the field (Merry, 2016).

Though neither a pedagogy or a technology per se, gamification has become a successful online learning strategy that requires the attention of the operational leader of online learning. Gamification is recognized as an effective approach to learning that emphasizes scaffolding of learning and reinforcement for knowledge and skill acquisition. Much like a video game, learners can become highly engaged in gamified learning, seeking new levels of understanding and acquisition of insights (Pandey, 2015). Operational leaders are positioned to commission models of gamification and put in place the support structures for faculty and programs to experiment with this promising emerging online learning approach.

There is a virtual firehose spouting new and emerging technologies. One of the key challenges for the operational leader is to stay on top of these developments in order to best inform upper administration, faculty, and other campus leaders about the potential for forms of competition and expectations for the near future. Social media are among the best sources of early announcements of emerging technologies and applications in online learning. The savvy operational leader will create a daily reading list to assure updates do not escape attention.

Technologies Self-Review – where will you go to keep up to date?
- Identify at least one blog that will help you follow the emerging technologies (hint: MIT has some great resources; I also publish daily blogs on the topic)
- Identify at least one Twitter persona to follow on this topic
- Identify at least one LinkedIn persona to follow on this topic

2.3   *Team Building, Hiring and Budgeting*

The work of the operational leader is much about team leadership and development. The leader cannot do all of the required tasks of supporting the distance education program. In order to thrive in the position, one has to excel in inter-personal skills. This requires an understanding – whether naturally intuitive or more reasoned and calculated – the "knowing" of when to challenge workers; when to support them; and how to motivate the team members is at the heart of success in leading a successful team (University of Scranton, n.d.).

Knowing the right person to hire is much more than simply counting skills and experiences on a resume. It is about understanding the qualities of the applicants. Who fits into the team? Who has the drive to succeed? Who will come through when the going gets tough? I like to remind mentees that in the hiring process, you are hiring the entire person, not the resume. Many times in my career I have hired people who had fewer credentials beyond those that were minimally required, but who had the "heart" and commitment that enabled them to excel and to move upward in their careers. Remember that sharp staff members can readily learn new facts, skills and techniques, but it is much harder for them to learn to care deeply about the instiution and their colleagues. Yet, this caring is a huge part of their – and your – success.

Budgeting is one more of the areas that is important to success in operational leadership. Commonly, one has an accountant or bookkeeper who assists in the actual tracking of day-to-day expenditures. But, the art of leadership is in the strategy of prioritizing expenditures through the year, assuring that funds remain for emergencies and also for new inititiaves. I have always found it most useful to include the team in planning the broad budget priorities. That engagement helps the leader to make better decisions by tapping the insight of those who care about the outcomes, and it further vests the team in the success of the overall distance education initiative.

> *Team Building Self-Review – how will you build the team?*
> – If you are currently working, consider the team on which you now serve; if you are a student, consider the classmates you know well
> – Identify who in your peer group is a morale-builder; who is a fact-builder, who takes criticism well; who criticizes others
> – Consider which one of your peers has the inter-personal skills, the dedication and commitment to best serve on a team

2.4   *Operational Leadership Skills*

A whole highly-refined skillset is necessary for effective operational leadership. These are the skills that enable the leader to achieve results even in times of crisis. The University of Scranton (n.d.) outlines five key skills that are essential for the successful operational leader:

– An Operations Manager is Realistic
– An Operations Manager Looks for Efficiency
– An Operations Manager Focuses on Quality
– Operations Leaders Are Effective at Logistics
– Operations Leaders Do Not Manage; They Lead

To achieve these standards, operational leaders need to pursue self-development and professional and continuing education. They are called upon to develop these skills in a variety of ways. While the acquisition of knowledge of pedagogics and technologies is a concrete regular routine, the achievement of soft skills is equally, and perhaps more important.

At all levels of leadership, communication is key. Think of great leaders whom you admire. Abraham Lincoln, Martin Luther King Jr., Benjamin Franklin, and Mahatma Gandhi come immediately to my mind. They all communicated exceptionally well. They all maintained a measure of respect for all people. They were compassionate and thoughtful. When they spoke or wrote, it seemed as though they were speaking directly to me, not to a large, undefined audience. Their messages were personal. They were genuine in their regard and empathy for others. These leaders listened first, and spoke only after considering what others had to say. These are the very characteristics that made them great leaders (Myatt, 2012).

The TBM consulting group suggests "The greatest opportunity for improvement in the operations organization is the development of 'soft skills.'" (Pate, 2016). These interpersonal leadership skills are essential to engendering confidence, mentoring, and inspiring the online distance learning support and instructional design team to achieve their best. They are the essence of excellence that advance a leader to the role of strategic leadership.

Leadership Skills Review – Who is your "ideal" leader?
Consider the attributes of great leaders. Who personifies those attributes to you? What attributes have you identified in your selection? How will you cultivate those attributes as you advance your leadership career?

3   Strategic Leadership

Over time, some operational leaders advance to strategic leadership. In a large university there may be half a dozen operational leaders in the online distance learning initiative serving in different colleges, directing various aspects of initiatives such as instructional design, media, online student support, and online faculty development. However, there are generally only one or two strategic leaders focused on the online initiative in the broad context of the institution-wide mission. Commonly, these carry the title of associate vice chancellor or associate provost for online learning. The positions may be grouped with other c-suite leaders including the chief information officer; the chief business officer; the associate vice chancellor (or vice president) for graduate or undergraduate studies; and the associate vice chancellor for research. As a group these leaders report to the provost or vice president of the university. In these positions, successful professionals lead the enterprise in their areas. They create the vision for the university and articulate it to the broader community. Strategic leaders engage governing boards, and accrediting bodies to assure success of programs and plans of the university. Skills and tools of strategic leadership build upon, and add to, those of operational leadership.

Strategic leaders of institutions set the mandate for development and expansion of online distance learning. Increasingly, that is occurring as higher education moves away from the more restrictive four-years-on-campus-and-out model of the baccalaureate to the lifelong learning of the "60-year curriculum" in which learners return to taking university classes and modules over an entire professional life (Tugend, 2019). This has accelerated at some institutions by the advent of the COVID-19 pandemic. The response of students to the flexibility of online learning has generated a new demand for online delivery of the curriculum.

Online enrollments have grown from 31.1% in 2016 to 33.1% in 2017 and 34.7% in 2018 (Lederman, 2019). With that growth, the role of the online strategic leader has moved from the fringes of the institution. Leadership of online and distance initiatives that began as a nascent movement serving a very small number of students enrolled in continuing education units some twenty years ago have moved to the Provost and C-suite center of the institution. The facets of strategic distance learning leadership are many. They include the full range of areas covered by operational leaders associated with the enterprise of supporting online learning. In addition, the strategic leader addresses advocacy, entrepreneurism, professionalism, and innovation.

In 2016, the University Professional and Continuing Education Association began an ambitious effort to identify the "Hallmarks of Excellence in Online Leadership" (University Professional and Continuing Education Association, 2016). The task force of leaders at colleges and universities across the United States identified and articulated hallmarks of excellence in leadership in our field. These aspirational hallmarks have been endorsed across higher education with specific endorsements from the American Council on Education (ACE); the Association of College and Research Libraries (ACRL); the largest information technology association in education (EDUCAUSE); Multimedia Educational Resources for Learning and Online Teaching (MERLOT); National Association of College and University Chief Business Officers (NACUBO); National Association of Student Personnel Administrators (NASPA); and the faculty-driven peer-review association promoting quality of online and blended course design Quality Matters. These seven hallmarks are freely available through Creative Commons licensing and serve as a framework to consider the role of the strategic online leader.

3.1 Internal Advocacy Leadership

In the forefront of the minds of college and university c-suite leaders is leading the institution in recognizing the value and ever-expanding potential of online distance learning. For the past two decades we have been in the transition from a solely face-to-face enterprise to one that extends beyond the campus to reach students where they work and reside. National statistics confirm the insuppressible rise of the number and overall percentage of post-secondary students enrolled online (Bastrikin, 2020). Year by year, the numbers of students choosing to have their learning delivered online rise, even at a time when overall college enrollments have been dropping. Online college enrollments increased every year while overall enrollments dropped more than two million students last decade (Nietzel, 2019). The trend is clear. However, for a variety of reasons, many in academe fail to acknowledge the steady growth in preferences for online delivery among learners. Even as on-campus enrollments decline, college committees continue to plan for expansive growth of residential programs. Many of these programs will fail to draw enrollments in sufficient size to sustain the costs of faculty and facilities. The online strategic leader is responsible for re-directing – as appropriate – these initiatives to delivery through 21st century, fourth industrial revolution modes.

Day-to-day the strategic leader works side-by-side with others in the leadership team: the associate vice chancellors/vice presidents; the c-suite staff; and the provost/vice president. This leadership team coordinates goals, strategies and milestones for advancing the institution. Coordination and cooperation are essential to assure that goals are accomplished in an organized and timely fashion. Conflicting or confused messaging is not acceptable. Everyone on the leadership team must communicate often and support one another.

Leading the distance learning strategic initiative includes building an understanding of the realities of the need and value shift among learners in our society that results in continuing growth of online distance learning, while campus enrollments have declined steadily in the past decade. Internal to the institution, the strategic online leader is responsible for advocating for the online delivery of new programs that are in-demand and relevant to employers and prospective students. Much of this work is done with department chairs and deans. It involves continuously informing academic program leaders about the opportunities and online competition in their disciplines.

The heart of every institution is the faculty. It is important that they are informed and engaged in the vision of online delivery of the curriculum to students who are seeking to build on that learning to launch and to advance careers. The online strategic leader often engages faculty senate and faculty union leaders. No online initiative will thrive without the faculty understanding the context and the goals of online initiatives. It is wise to engage blogs and other social media to provide a steady stream of updated information to the faculty. Personal contact with faculty leaders is an important part of strategic leaders' daily work.

The foundation of the work of the strategic leader is up-to-date knowledge and information. It is essential that the leader can drink from the "firehose" of new technology, practices and applications across academic fields. The online leader must be able to filter the massive flow to provide relevant updates to academic leaders. Tapping that flow must be done through a variety of sources: social media, technical journals, educational publications, economic forecasting sources, and more.

Knowledge and information, however, is not enough. The online strategic leader must have a deep understanding of the mission and vision of the institution as well as higher education as a whole. It is only with a reservoir of knowledge about the changing field of higher education and the evolving economy that strategic leaders can offer sound advice to campus leaders.

Internal Leadership Review – three elevator speeches
In each of the following three instances, imagine you are entering an elevator for a 6o-second ride with the designated person. How would you succinctly describe the need to establish an online Blockchain Developer Certificate program. (Hint: consider workforce demand, links to industry and placement.)
– Dean of Engineering (where computer science is located)
– Dean of Business (where accounting and information systems are located)
– Chair of the faculty senate

3.2   *Entrepreneurial Leadership*

Distance learning is entrepreneurial in and of itself. Moving beyond the campus entails the risks and innovation of an entrepreneur. It is new, and by definition, brings the challenges of doing things differently than they had been done in the past. At the core of the activity of the distance learning leader is to envision, advocate, and support entrepreneurial activities and personnel at the institution. These entrepreneurial initiatives are the ones that are transforming higher education from the centuries-old model of students coming to a campus into a model in which the resources of the university are virtually delivered to the students through technology.

Entrepreneurism in distance education can take many forms. Some center on new technologies. Others are innovations in pedagogies and practices. All have the potential to advance teaching and learning. Teaching efficiencies, engagement enhancements, and visualization advances are all current examples that need nurturing and support from the strategic leader. And, of course, many of these require financial support as well.

The role of the online distance education leader in promoting, advocating and supporting productive entrepreneurism is one that begins with a clear and constantly-updated understanding of the evolving landscape of distance education. This requires daily readings of credible journals, social media, and proceedings papers in the field. These readings are also best supplemented with frequent engagements in-person or online with the thought leaders in the field. Such engagement can come in conferences, symposia and, as relationships build, through direct email and face-to-face discussions with colleagues.

Some current examples of areas for entrepreneurial activity include the multiple mode delivery of classes, sometimes called variously by the names of hyflex, blendflex, or dual mode approach (Soesmanto & Bonner, 2020). These approaches gained some momentum in the COVID-19 pandemic. They entail concurrently offering classes in both online and face-to-face modes enabling students to choose day-by-day, week-by-week whether to attend online or face-to-face sessions. To offer a single section of a class in multiple delivery modes in this way is not normally within the institutional guidelines for workload and course listings. The distance education leader is cast into the role of advocating such a deviation with other top administrators including the Provost, Registrar, and others. It may be that this will require presentations and evidence-sharing with the faculty union or academic senate, various other governance committees, and even the governing board of the institution.

In other cases, entrepreneurial leadership involves gaining administrative as well as financial support for the use of emerging technologies in enhancing the delivery of the curriculum via distance education. An example of this comes from the challenge to provide shared experiences with students. In the earlier years of distance education, it was difficult, if not impossible in some cases to access realistic, three-dimensional and contextual experiences for students who were located remotely at a distance. However, rapidly-advancing technologies in augmented and virtual reality now offer opportunities for providing rich media experiences in laboratory simulations, virtual historical and archeological visits, and artistic and immersive learning. These experiences are rapidly becoming available at a distance through the advent of 5G wireless technologies (Schroeder, 2020b).

Leadership and advocacy for specific technologies often involves acquiring funding through grant or gift sources to enable faculty members to experiment and refine practices in using the technologies to enhance teaching and learning. Fund-raising abilities and grantsmanship are two of the key tools of entrepreneurial leadership. Without funds, many projects remain pipe dreams and never come to fruition. In some cases, the funding must cover not only the hardware and software, but also upskilling of current staff or the hiring of new staff members to utilize the technology. Creating interactive augmented and virtual reality videos requires working with a programming as well as video recording team.

Entrepreneurial Leadership Exercise
Imagine that you have a faculty member who is most interested in creating virtual reality simulations of micro-counseling sessions. She would like to create realistic three-dimensional interactive videos in which the virtual subject responds to a wide variety of questions that might be posed by the student. How might you support this entrepreneurial request? How would you:
– Seek funding for hardware and software – for what items?
– Seek re-training or hiring of new staff – for what services?
– Seek policy approvals – for what new unique activities?
– Seek faculty non-instructional development release time?

3.3   *Faculty Support Leadership*

The faculty are the ones who reach out to students, who through their teaching, mentoring, and examples catalyze change in students and through them, society at large. It is essential that the leader of online distance education initiatives is connected closely to faculty members of the institution. In many cases, our leaders come from faculty lines. In that way, they are steeped in the three-part mission of faculty: teaching, research, and service. These leaders have a strong affinity to the pressures and aspirations of the faculty at large. However, it is not requisite that leaders of distance education programs come directly from faculty lines. Yet, it is necessary that they understand well and appreciate, the duties and roles of the faculty. This understanding is best used to build a bridge of appreciation and trust with those who teach, research, and serve on behalf of the institution.

In the field of higher education, the preparation for faculty positions have in the past – and for the most part, continue to be – comprised of doctoral education solely in the academic discipline to be taught. Unlike teachers at the elementary and secondary levels who are schooled in the theoretical foundations of education, the psychology of education, and effective practices and pedagogies, faculty at the post-secondary level most generally have none of that background. Faculty members, until the advent of online learning, most generally came from traditional campuses. They were taught in classrooms, lecture halls and seminar rooms. So it is that most of the faculty members teach the way that they were taught. Generation after generation of professors emulated the teaching practices of their teachers. Lectures have been the common mode of delivery of information for learning over the centuries. It is a one-way communication mode that does not inherently encourage engagement and interaction that researchers and practitioners of this century find to be most effective in the transferring of knowledge, insight, and motivation. These are among the values held highly in teaching all students, but especially those who are at a distance.

Since our faculty members have not been schooled in best teaching practices, let alone the use of technology, to teach distant students, it is imperative that institutions provide on-going development and training in these areas. An important role of the strategic leader is to envision, advocate for, and assure efficient, effective faculty development programs are instituted to support the faculty.

One approach taken by thousands of institutions is to utilize the renowned rubric and services non-profit, quality assurance organization that delivers a system to help review, track improvement and certify the quality of instructional design and practices (Quality Matters, 2020). There are many other high-quality rubric-based online learning design programs. Some universities build their own standards for certification of design and delivery practices in online distance learning. A key indicator of success is to engage peer review among faculty members at the institution. Using this approach helps to assure broad acceptance among the faculty by engaging them directly in the certification process.

The faculty members of the institution have many time-consuming obligations. These include the broad categories of teaching, research and service. However, most institutions employ a shared-governance approach. "Shared governance is decision-making authority that incorporates input from staff, faculty and sometimes special interest groups. All parties have well-defined responsibilities and, as a group, they share accountability for their decisions" (Eisenstein, 2019). Committee activities involved in shared governance can amount to the equivalent of a full day of work every week.

Given the long work days and weeks of faculty members, it is particularly welcome if the strategic leader can provide forms of recognition for faculty members' added workload in learning new teaching practices for the distant students and revising their course offerings to meet new standards. Such recognition can come in the form of a stipend, modest release time from other duties (such as one of the several courses scheduled for a semester), or an overload payment in an amount equal to compensation received for a course, or part of a course. Additionally, creating an awards program to recognize outstanding courses and official recognition from the leader submitted into the personnel file of the faculty member can help to increase morale and provide an incentive to excel. Such letters can be determining factors in the promotion and tenure process of a faculty member.

In many institutions, funds for traveling to professional conferences are tightly controlled. It can be especially beneficial to secure funding to subsidize faculty members attending professional conferences. Travel and associated connections with colleagues at other institutions are valued by faculty members, and the practices and strategies learned by faculty members in attending those conferences can enhance their offerings and help colleagues to implement improvements as well. These travel stipends can be distributed by way of an internal competition based on performance.

Faculty Support Leadership Exercise
Instructional design and teaching practices can most directly affect student learning and perceived quality of the online distance education program. What approaches might you consider to enhance faculty engagement in development in these instances?
– A faculty leader is unconvinced that renovating his or her class to better engage students will advance learning outcomes in the class.
– A department as a whole has experienced a slow decline in student evaluations and in enrollments in their department. The department is staffed with more senior faculty members who have not been exposed to Quality Matters or other such programs.
– A group of newly-hired professors is slated to start employment in mid-August, two weeks before the start of the fall term. As a whole, they do not have any high-level development in teaching online, but they have online classes beginning in just two weeks.

3.4   *Student Support Leadership*

Learners are the raison d'être for our institutions. Our service to students is the measure of our success. Best practices in higher education stress student-centeredness; that is, that we serve the students' interest first and foremost, not the convenience or preference of employees of the university. Assuring this student centeredness is very high on the priority list of the strategic leader.

Strategic leadership in student support should require pro-active efforts on behalf of students taking online classes. To best provide leadership in this area, it is important to experience an online class and sit in the virtual seat of the distant students. Successful leaders periodically enroll in classes to get the full experience of an online student. Only as a student can we fully understand the student-centeredness (or lack thereof) in our classes; sample the relevance of classes; experience the responsiveness of faculty members; even contact the registrar's office to determine practices in responding to student questions and problems. Through those experiences, a leader can determine how to best represent student interests.

Armed with these experiences, as well as candid conversations with student focus groups and student representatives, the strategic leader should vision the standards and practices that will best meet student needs. This is such a critical topic that leaders should seek out best and emerging practices at other institutions. Where possible, innovative practices to facilitate student participation and to promote access to services for distant students should be pursued. This is a never-ending task. We can always improve access and services through new policies and even using new technologies, such as sophisticated chat boxes that provide satisfying, not frustrating, answers to questions and inquiries.

Unfortunately, because distant online students are often a minority of those at a university, they are under-represented in student government, student newspaper reporting, and in student organizations. It falls to the online strategic leader to draw these under representations to the attention of those who can make a difference in assuring that the voice of the distant student is heard as distinctly and loudly as those students who are attending on-campus classes. Remember always that the distant online student pays tuition and fees analogous to, and sometimes more, than on-campus students. They have the right to be heard and served.

Student Support Leadership Exercise
– How would you go about assessing student-centeredness in your online classes?
– With whom would you advocate for greater coverage of distant students in the student newspaper?
– How would you go about seeking better services for distant students in the Registrar and Student Financial Aid offices?

3.5   *Digital Technology Leadership*

Digital technology has transformed the world. We are connected in ways that were impossible before the advent of wireless cellular technology; virtual and augmented reality; remote monitoring; and the associated technologies of big data collection and visualization. These technologies have evolved and overtaken our everyday lives in the past few decades, and higher education is no exception. There are more than 10 billion mobile devices in use in the world with more than three-fourths of all Americans owning smart phones and every third person in the world owning a mobile device (Georgiev, 2020). The numbers continue to grow each year, and are expected to accelerate with the advent of high bandwidth 5G networks.

The President and CEO of EDUCAUSE, John O'Brien, in the wake of the COVID-19 pandemic that forced thousands of universities to close their campuses and deliver their curriculum online, stated the importance and role of technology so well:

> And let's also dedicate ourselves to the more nuanced but critical message that technology is not a utility. It is a strategic asset, a differentiating value, and a path to achieving institutional goals and stability. It is not just a lifeline that got us through a tricky situation. It is and must increasingly be understood as an integral, strategic part of the successful college or university. Not in the future. Now. (O'Brien, 2020)

This strategic asset plays a key role in the work of the online distance education program leader.

As technologies proliferate, change, and advance at an incredibly rapid rate, the leader of the online distance education program is expected to keep up to date with the advancements and to assess the predictions for the future. Often compared to "drinking from a firehose," keeping up with these developments and preparing for the future is one of the daunting aspects of leadership in our field.

While there are many new technologies that flourish, many more emerge that quickly fade and are no longer supported. One example is "Google Wave" – an array of technologies supported by industry giant Google, Wave made its much-heralded debut in 2009, but in August 2010, Google announced it was shutting down the project and leaving many early adopters without an alternative (Clifton, 2020). I recall that I was presenting a workshop on Wave technology at the annual Distance Teaching and Learning Conference in Madison on the day the announcement came out that it would no longer by supported by Google. Embarrassment aside, this provided an opportunity to review the important process of vetting new and emerging technologies before making an institutional commitment to their use.

The online distance education leader is positioned to inform the university community of new and emerging technologies that are ready, or may soon be ready, for meaningful adoption as a "strategic asset" for the delivery of learning opportunities to distant students. In order to inform the community, the leader has to be informed on a daily basis. One of the best ways to keep up with the technologies is to closely monitor validated social media sites. I currently produce a number of blogs as well as Twitter and LinkedIn feeds that provide daily updates of the technologies, policies and emerging practices in our field (Schroeder, 2020a). There are other such sites online that are most useful in filtering the firehose stream of new and emerging technologies and practices. The impact of leadership in the area of digital technology, of course, extends beyond the distance learning initiative; it impacts all aspects of the university.

Digital Technology Leadership Exercise

As a leader, it is important that you develop a personal learning network that will keep you up to date on the current and emerging trends in digital technology.

- Identify and follow three blogs that you feel are valuable in tracking digital technology – and add them to bookmarks that you will visit often.
- Identify and follow three technology leaders on Twitter whom you will add to your network.
- Identify and follow three technology leaders on LinkedIn whom you will add to your network.

3.6   *Professionalism of the Leader*

For many of us, defining professionalism may be difficult, but recognizing it in action is not. The U.S. Department of Labor describes it well:

> Professionalism does not mean wearing a suit or carrying a briefcase; rather, it means conducting oneself with responsibility, integrity, accountability, and excellence. It means communicating effectively and appropriately and always finding a way to be productive. (n.d.)

It is just so in the leadership of the distance education initiative.

Professionalism in our field is especially important in part because online distance education is new in the very old field of academe. No more than a mere quarter of century has passed since online learning began to gain traction among universities. As relative newcomers, we must prove ourselves to be as professional and credible as the arts, humanities, and sciences. In earlier years, online learning was considered as a "passing fad" in higher education; it was expected to fade with time. Of course, that is not the case, and most leaders in higher education recognize that online distance learning is a credible and important part of the enterprise of the university. Nevertheless, we must conduct ourselves as professionals if we are to be taken seriously and have the impact to which we aspire.

Practically, this means treating all of our colleagues with respect. We must recognize that nearly all of those in higher education are committed to quality and inclusiveness in the service of students and the mission of the university. We should enthusiastically endorse and support the diversity of interests and approaches to reaching those goals.

There is another characteristic of professionalism that leads to success and fulfillment. It is one that may not immediately come to mind. Dave Robson of the BBC recognizes it:

> It's more than two millennia since the philosopher Socrates argued that humility is the greatest of all virtues. His timeless observation was that the wisest people are the first to admit how little they really know .... The latest findings suggest that the trait is especially important for leaders, with evidence that displays of humility can improve strategic thinking and boost the performance of colleagues across an organization. (Robson, 2020)

It is with humility that we are most inclined to listen to others, to pay respect to others, and to receive their insights and wisdom to enlighten our own actions. This is a key aspect of professionalism. It is something to remember every day as you encounter others and plan for the future.

Professionalism in Leadership Exercise
Building professionalism requires a good bit of looking in the mirror each day. And, this means looking not just the silvery physical mirror, but the virtual mirror of your intention, respect for others, and personal integrity. Consider taping a short list of non-physical characteristics to the mirror you use before going out the door. Put on that list those intangible characteristics such as humility that you want to express in your behavior that day.

Add to your list from the last exercise three leaders from Twitter and three from LinkedIn whom you consider to be consummate professionals in our field. Read their postings daily. This will help to reinforce those values in your work each day.

Read and complete the exercises, with colleagues as appropriate, at the United States Department of Labor site in the bibliography below.

3.7   *Advocacy and Leadership beyond the Institution*

Our discussions in this chapter have focused on leading within the institution. However, in our field of distance education, there is much to be done beyond the institution on a national and international level. Teaching the distant student is an integral component of higher education. As we have seen through hurricanes, pandemics, and a variety of other natural disasters, distance learning is essential to keep the semesters going. Increasingly, as we have discussed, we are seeing the emergence of lifelong learners pursuing a 60-year curriculum of continuing professional education in keeping current and advancing in their careers (Tugend, 2019). At the same time, many thousands of MOOCs are serving millions of students worldwide through large scale online learning (Class Central, n.d.).

Many journalists, legislators and government administrators do not fully understand the distance education movement and magnitude of our field. They recall, fondly, their days on a small or large college or university campus with large lecture halls and in-person laboratories. These external leaders have a misperception of higher education today and in the future. They do not fully recognize the impact of both the technological and societal changes that are propelling our field. Just as business and industry has leveraged the technologies that are driving the fourth industrial revolution, so too are we applying those technologies and addressing those societal changes as EDUCAUSE's President and CEO John O'Brien suggests these are the "integral, strategic part of the successful college or university." These are not just future dreams, but they are the reality of today.

The online distance education leader is often put in the role of explaining the new traditional student – one who is a lifelong learner, taking classes from home or work. The leader is called upon to describe these changes through news interviews, public speeches and professional conference presentations. We must prepare to explain the advent of technologically-enhanced distance education to a broad audience in many forums. Conducting research and publication in our field to enlighten the impact of our practices is a very valuable contribution.

Speaking to the media is a common event. It is important to respond promptly to interview requests; reporters have deadlines to submit their reports for publication or broadcast, frequently on the same day. Offering your knowledge and perspectives on topics relevant to higher education is a great opportunity to reach many thousands of people. In such interviews, you can dispel myths and share more accurate descriptions of realities and expectations in our field both today and for the near future.

Less common, but perhaps even more important, is speaking to governmental agencies and committees. It is incumbent on the leader to guide public policy, rules, and regulations to best serve distant students. Even today, many state and federal regulations assume that students in higher education are right out of high school and living on the campus. Increasingly, those "traditional" students are becoming the minority of college students. State and federal financial aid must change to embrace the ever-growing percentage of adult students. For example, public programs for student loan forgiveness in exchange for public service must be friendly to the adult student. In sum, all programs and policies must be reviewed from the perspective of the lifelong learner.

Colleges and universities are well-served by enterprising distance education leaders who step up to take leadership positions in professional associations such as the Online Learning Consortium (OLC); the University Professional and Continuing Education Association (UPCEA); the WICHE Cooperative for Educational Technologies (WCET); the United States Distance Learning Association (USDLA) and other national and regional associations. Leading your peers in this field is very important. Also, participating in development programs and activities are an important service for the future. Such programs as the OLC-supported Institute for Emerging Leaders in Online Learning – IELOL (Online Learning Consortium, 2020) are programs that help to advance the credentials and experiences of those who seek to move forward into leadership positions in our field. Serving as a faculty member in IELOL or any of the many professional development continuing education programs offered by entities such as Quality Matters and colleges and universities nationwide, is important to extending the knowledge, values, and principles of leadership to the next generation of leaders.

Advocacy and Leadership Exercise

True leaders in this field welcome the opportunity to speak or exchange email with aspiring leaders. For this exercise, review your responses to the exercises for digital technology and professionalism, and identify one leader you feel has the qualities you admire. Contact the leader and ask a few questions that you have after reading this chapter. Consider keeping in contact with your chosen leader as you move forward in your career.

3.8   *In Sum*

Strive to lead with knowledge, humility, and a wide perspective. Listen before you talk. Learn from others; they will inform your leadership. Guide your institution carefully with insights grown from wide experience, conversations, and reading. Remember that leadership is a seven-day-a-week job. Be sure to read daily to keep up with the advancements and predictions for online distance learning. Disseminate knowledge widely through publication, traditional media, and social media. Give back to the field through cultivating the careers and perspectives of those who are entering the field. I have discovered through a quarter century of leading a university distance education program and two decades of leadership in national associations dedicated to development and excellence in online distance education that this field is a fertile field for a truly rewarding career where you can make a difference in the lives of countless students.

3.8.1   Resources

I am a strong advocate of Personal Learning Networks (PLNS) in which you develop a network of professionals in your field and related areas who help you to thrive and rise in your endeavors (Gutierrez, 2016). I encourage you to build your own personal learning network. This PLN will keep you up to date through your contacts, their postings and other interactions on the current and future developments in our field.

The citation list for this chapter is filled with valuable information that you may find useful as you advance in this field. Many will become outdated over time. Some have durable advice and information. In particular, I recommend you refer to the Handbook of Distance Education (Moore & Diehl, 2018) often. It is a larger compilation of important information for our field. I also recommend Leading the eLearning Transformation of Higher Education, 2nd edition (Miller & Ives, 2020), that draws upon experienced leaders in our field.

References

Bastrikin, A. (2020, April 12). *Online education statistics*. Retrieved May 17, 2020, from https://educationdata.org/online-education-statistics/

Blaschke L. M. (2018). Self-determined learning (heutagogy) and digital media creating integrated educational environments for developing lifelong learning skills. In D. Kergel, B. Heidkamp, P. Telléus, T. Rachwal, & S. Nowakowski (Eds.), *The digital turn in higher education*. Springer VS. https://doi.org/10.1007/978-3-658-19925-8_10

Class Central. (n.d.). *Class central: #1 search engine for free online courses & MOOCs*. Retrieved June 6, 2020, from https://www.classcentral.com/

Clifton, J. (2020, January 27). *10 failed Google projects*. Retrieved June 6, 2020, from https://computer.howstuffworks.com/10-failed-google-projects10.htm

Contact North. (2017, March 7). *A new pedagogy is emerging ... and online learning is a key contributing factor*. Retrieved May 3, 2020, from https://teachonline.ca/tools-trends/how-teach-online-student-success/new-pedagogy-emerging-and-online-learning-key-contributing-factor

Davis, L. (2018, April 18). *Heutagogy explained: Self-determined learning in education*. Retrieved May 3, 2020, from https://www.schoology.com/blog/heutagogy-explained-self-determined-learning-education

Eisenstein, L. (2019, July 11). *Shared governance model for higher education boards.* Retrieved June 1, 2020, from https://www.boardeffect.com/blog/shared-governance-model-higher-education-boards/

Georgiev, D. (2020, June 2). *60+ revealing statistics about smartphone usage in 2020.* Retrieved June 6, 2020, from https://techjury.net/blog/smartphone-usage-statistics/#:%7E:text=There%20are%203.5%20billion%20smartphone,the%20world%20today%20(2020).&text=Almost%20every%20third%20person%20worldwide%20owns%20a%20smartphone

Gutierrez, K. (2016, June 21). *What are personal learning networks?* Retrieved June 16, 2020, from https://www.shiftelearning.com/blog/personal-learning-networks

Lederman, D. (2019, December 11). *Online enrollments grow, but pace slows.* Retrieved May 3, 2020, from https://www.insidehighered.com/digital-learning/article/2019/12/11/more-students-study-online-rate-growth-slowed-2018

Maxwell, J. (2004, February 15). *The operational leader often influences success of others.* Retrieved May 3, 2020, from https://www.bizjournals.com/houston/stories/2004/02/16/smallb3.html

Merry, P. (2016, September 28). *Immersive virtual reality: Online Education for the next generation.* Retrieved May 3, 2020, from https://www.govtech.com/education/immersive-virtual-reality-online-education-for-the-next-generation.html

Miller, G., & Ives, K. (Eds.). (2020). *Leading the elearning transformation of higher education* (2nd ed.). Stylus Publishing.

Moore, M., & Diehl, W. (Eds.). (2018). *Handbook of distance education* (4th ed.). Routledge.

Myatt, M. (2012, April 2). *10 Communication secrets of great leaders.* Retrieved May 4, 2020, from https://www.forbes.com/sites/mikemyatt/2012/04/04/10-communication-secrets-of-great-leaders/#18ea698b22fe

Nietzel, M. T. (2019, December 16). *College enrollment declines again. It's down more than two million students in this decade.* Retrieved May 17, 2020, from https://www.forbes.com/sites/michaeltnietzel/2019/12/16/college-enrollment-declines-again-its-down-more-than-two-million-students-in-this-decade/#1a4479f33d95

O'Brien, J. (2020, May 18). *Not in the future – Now.* Retrieved June 5, 2020, from https://er.educause.edu/articles/2020/5/not-in-the-future-now

Online Learning Consortium. (2020). *Institute for Emerging Leadership in Online Learning (IELOL).* Retrieved June 6, 2020, from https://onlinelearningconsortium.org/learn/ielol/

Pandey, A. (2015, October 6). *6 killer examples of gamification in elearning* [Updated 2020]. Retrieved May 3, 2020, from https://elearningindustry.com/6-killer-examples-gamification-in-elearning

Pappas, C. (2017, December 17). *What is a learning management system? LMS basic functions and features you must know* [2019 update]. Retrieved May 3, 2020, from https://elearningindustry.com/what-is-an-lms-learning-management-system-basic-functions-features

Pate, D. (2016, March 22). *Operational leadership: The required skill sets at every level.* Retrieved May 4, 2020, from https://www.tbmcg.com/resources/blog/operational-leadership-the-required-skill-sets-at-every-level/

Quality Matters. (2020). *Home.* Retrieved June 1, 2020, from https://www.qualitymatters.org/

Robson, D. (2020, May 31). *Is this the secret of smart leadership?* Retrieved June 1, 2020, from https://www.bbc.com/worklife/article/20200528-is-this-the-secret-of-smart-leadership?ocid=ww.social.link.email

Schroeder, R. (2020a, June 6). *Ray Schroeder online learning.* Retrieved June 6, 2020, from https://rayschroeder.com/

Schroeder, R. (2020b). Dawn of 5G: Empowering VR, AR and much more. *Inside Higher Ed.* Retrieved May 30, 2020, from https://www.insidehighered.com/digital-learning/blogs/online-trending-now/dawn-5g-empowering-vr-ar-and-much-more

Shattuck, K., & Burch, B. (2018, May 2). *Quality matters: National standards for quality online teaching (K-12) literature review.* Retrieved May 3, 2020, from https://www.qualitymatters.org/sites/default/files/research-docs-pdfs/National-Standards-for-Quality-Online-Teaching-Lit-Review-050418.pdf

Soesmanto, T., & Bonner, S. (2020). *Dual mode delivery in an introductory statistics course: Design and evaluation.* Taylor & Francis. Retrieved May 30, 2020, from https://amstat.tandfonline.com/doi/full/10.1080/10691898.2019.1608874

Tugend, A. (2019, October 10). *60 years of higher ed – Really?* Retrieved June 6, 2020, from https://www.nytimes.com/2019/10/10/education/learning/60-year-curriculum-higher-education.html

United States Department of Labor. (n.d.). *Professionalism.* Retrieved June 6, 2020, from https://www.dol.gov/odep/topics/youth/softskills/Professionalism.pdf

University of Scranton. (n.d.). *5 necessary management traits of operations leaders.* Retrieved May 3, 2020, from https://elearning.scranton.edu/resource/business-leadership/5-management-traits-of-operations-leaders

University Professional and Continuing Education Association. (2016, March 7). *Hallmarks of excellence in online leadership.* Retrieved May 5, 2020, from https://upcea.edu/resources/hallmarks-online/

CHAPTER 3

Barriers in Online Education and Strategies for Overcoming Them

Florence Martin and Swapna Kumar

Abstract

At the conclusion of this chapter, you will be able to:
- Identify and discuss different types of barriers (institutional barriers, technology and technical barriers, pedagogical barriers, and interpersonal barriers) that exist in the adoption of online education.
- Describe strategies for instructors, learners, and administrators to overcome barriers in online education.

Keywords

online education barriers – interpersonal barriers – pedagogical barriers – technology and technical barriers – institutional barriers – strategies for overcoming barriers

1 Introduction

Online education has dramatically grown at higher education institutions over the last two decades, and we have more than 6 million students taking at least one online course in higher education (Seaman, Allen, & Seaman, 2018). Institutions have adopted online education in various ways, depending on the type of institution, the communities that they serve, and the level of courses they offer to undergraduate and graduate students. During COVID-19, the entire world had to quickly shift to online education irrespective of their existing infrastructure and preparation for online teaching. There is a need to examine what needs to be in place for online education to be not only implemented but implemented successfully.

In this chapter we identify barriers in online education and provide strategies on how administrators, faculty and students can overcome them. Most institutions have created conditions and resources for successful instruction

© KONINKLIJKE BRILL NV, LEIDEN, 2021 | DOI: 10.1163/9789004471382_003

and student support on their campuses over years and decades. Online teaching and learning also require a supportive larger institutional context and the provision of various types of resources for faculty and students. In the absence of such conditions, barriers are faced by institutions, administrators, faculty, and students. Institutions might also face different types of barriers based on their phase of online education implementation – ranging from whether they are just embarking on online education to contexts where they might have already offered online education for several years. Additionally, leaders' or institutions' priorities regarding what barriers to overcome depend on their phase of online education adoption. In the 2020 CHLOE report, some of the challenges reported by administrators include requiring student orientations, mandating training before faculty teach online, and costs involved in offering online education (Legon, Garrett, & Fredericksen, 2020). Therefore, we begin this chapter with barriers identified when institutions initially adopted online learning that might be helpful to those new to it followed by technical, pedagogical, and interpersonal barriers. In the final section, we propose strategies for administrators, instructors, and students to overcome these barriers.

What type of barriers have you encountered in online education, and what strategies did you use to resolve the barrier?

2   Barriers in 2020

In this chapter, while examining barriers in 2020, we classify them into four categories, institutional barriers, technology and technical barriers, pedagogical barriers, and interpersonal barriers.

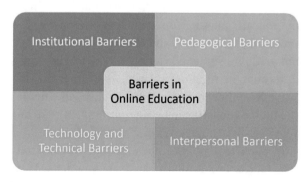

FIGURE 3.1
Barriers in online learning

3   Institutional Barriers

A number of barriers for online education exist at the institutional level. Institutions face different types of barriers based on whether they are just embarking on online education, have already integrated blended learning, or have already implemented some online education. In 2020, most institutions of higher education already have different types of technologies available to on-campus students and faculty. For example, aligning technology systems across a university (e.g., student information system and learning management system), and multiple campuses of a university system might already be in place. However, such infrastructure might not always be sufficient for online education offerings, and accessible to faculty and students at a distance. Additionally, trained staff who are available 24/7 to support online faculty and students, instructional designers who can help faculty create online course offerings, professional development or training that is offered completely online for online faculty and students, and administrative resources to support online students are often missing at institutions of higher education. A multitude of on-campus resources already exist in higher education institutions that support on-campus students. These have to be created and made available to online students, so that they are supported during all academic processes related to online education (Berge, 1998). These processes encompass registration, administration, paperwork, graduation, and other areas of an academic program, not only during teaching and learning interactions within online courses. Finally, online education is often adopted in certain parts of an institution or by specific programs in an institution. The lack of resources and support that are institution-wide can be a significant barrier for those specific programs or faculty trying to engage in online education. It is difficult for programs, faculty, and students to succeed in the absence of an institutional strategic plan, policies, various funding models, and standards for online education, and leadership and champions who understand online education management.

Literature across the last two decades indicates that instructors consider lack of administrative support a barrier to online teaching (Martin, Wang, Budhrani, Moore, & Jokiaho, 2019). This pertains to incentives and resources provided, the training instructors need to teach online, or acknowledgment of the effort required to create and teach an online course. Research has shown that online teaching is time consuming, primarily when the course is first designed (Oyarzun, Martin, & Moore, 2020), and secondly, due to the time taken to facilitate an online course effectively. Institutions and administrators do not always recognize the time and effort that goes into online course design and facilitation, or the resources (e.g. instructional designers, help with multimedia, etc.) needed to create an online course. Faculty consider this a barrier because they are not provided with incentives or recognition, and their workload is not adjusted when they have to teach online (Maguire, 2005; Shea, 2007).

Another aspect of the faculty workload barrier is the lack of enrollment limits on online courses since there is no restriction on physical space, and often, online courses are perceived as ways to increase student revenue. The scalability of online courses is a barrier for instructors who deal with large class sizes, and the challenges of increased grading and feedback that they have to provide with every additional student enrolled (Tomei, 2006). Policies for teaching assistants that are common in on-campus courses are often missing or considered unnecessary in online courses, posing an additional barrier for faculty. Additionally, at some institutions, online teaching is still not valued for promotion and tenure, and there is a general notion that online courses are not of equal quality as face to face courses.

Administrators on the other hand, also experience barriers when embarking on online program offerings, and when getting faculty buy-in to teach online. Not all faculty are motivated to teach online even if there is a need at the institution, and many are resistant to changing their pedagogical practices, especially when these have worked well for them in an on-campus environment. The organizational change that is needed for online education to be successful can lead to resistance at multiple levels. Online education also necessitates marketing and recruitment in different channels and to a diverse and wider geographical audience than on-campus education, which can be a challenge for administrators. The accreditation of online programs and relevance of program content for non-traditional populations who might not appreciate content that is traditionally taught in on-campus programs can also pose a barrier for administrators trying to increase online program offerings at their institution.

The absence of policies and standards for teaching online is also a barrier for institutions (Haber & Mills, 2008). Although professional organizations such as Quality Matters and Online Learning Consortium have created guidelines for online course design, online program design, and online facilitation, not all institutions have adopted guidelines for online education quality or created their own standards. Likewise, within an institution, student evaluations, or peer evaluations that are specific to online courses or to those who teach online often do not exist. For example, institutions often use the same rubric for face-to-face student evaluation and online evaluation when it is evident that the requirements and standards for online courses are very different from face-to-face courses.

Examine what institutional barriers exist in your organization.

4   Technology and Technical Barriers

As stated in the institutional barriers section, institutions with online education offerings require different types of infrastructure for instruction to take place seamlessly, and also need dedicated staff who can support faculty and students in this endeavor. Regularly updated hardware and software, network administration, connectivity, security, and maintenance of all these, form the backbone of online education offerings. Online students will not be able to learn if they are unable to access systems and information provided using any device that they have available to them and choose to study with. They also cannot learn or access their courses if they do not receive enough technical support to do so. Likewise, institutions might not have technologies and resources in place for online students with special needs, thus hindering the participation and success of certain populations. In addition, institutions need to have technology in place for instructors to design and teach online courses. Learning Management Systems are the backbone of online courses (LMS). Through the LMS, instructors are able to send announcements, load instructional material, create activities and assignments and provide feedback on student activities. In addition to the LMS, online synchronous tools are used for real-time communication (Martin & Parker, 2014). Online instructors also use video development tools to create videos for students. Institutions have to make these tools available for their instructors to use.

Even in the presence of hardware and software that enable integration between academic, information, and financial systems, institutions often lack discipline-specific technologies or research technologies that can be made available to students at a distance. Instructors might not have access to all the hardware and software they need to teach online. For example, if they are teaching subjects that involve equations, instructors have to teach students complex equations online, and having technology with the capability to demonstrate writing equations is important. If instructors do not have access to the hardware they need or software to create and demonstrate writing equations, this is a significant hindrance to student learning. Another example is the use of software for data analysis (e.g., SAS and SPSS) or for experiments (e.g., simulations)

Additionally, the absence of proctoring software and plagiarism software can be a barrier for institutions wanting to offer certain programs online, if assessments and exams are integral to those offerings (Berge, 1998).

Instructors consider the lack of training to use technology skills as a barrier (Muilenburg & Berge, 2001). Not all institutions might have centers for teaching and learning or adequate instructional designers and staff to support faculty in their use of technology and creation of online courses. Even in the case that institutions provide a variety of training, these are not always offered online to serve online instructors at a distance from the institution, and are often not offered to adjunct instructors or teaching assistants. When they are offered, instructors sometimes do not have the time to participate (Schmidt, Tschida, & Hodge, 2016).

While teaching, technology glitches can occur, which can interrupt an online course. In online courses, technical support is not always immediately available, and instructors consider both the occurrence of technical problems and the lack of technical support as a barrier. With the advancement in technology also comes the challenge of rapidly changing software and delivery systems. There are a number of instructional technologies introduced on the market each day. The learning curve associated with such changes is a barrier for online instructors (Panda & Mishra, 2007).

Technology access for students is another barrier that can impact institutional enrollment and student participation as well as learning in online courses. Not all students have access to the Internet or devices to participate in online courses. The cost to access the Internet, lack of bandwidth that supports certain types of online learning, and the cost of technology that is needed to study online can be a barrier for students. Additionally, orientations or training might not be provided to online students embarking on online education under the assumption that certain generations or those choosing to learn online are already comfortable with technology. Despite the availability of technology and its use for social purposes, technology literacy and the lack of knowledge to use technologies for learning and academic purposes can be a significant barrier for students in online education (Gutiérrez-Santiuste, Gallego-Arrufat, & Simone, 2016). Finally, both students and instructors consider privacy and security concerns a barrier in online learning. When students write or post online, especially using various technologies that are outside the LMS, not all the data is secure. While several technologies take the user's privacy into consideration, and have privacy policies developed, some technologies do not. Hence instructors must be sure that student data from the use of technologies outside of the LMS cannot be shared with anyone (Singh, Mangalaraj, & Taneja, 2010).

Examine what technology and technical barriers exist in your organization.

5   Pedagogical Barriers

The dramatic increase in online education offerings over the last decade has resulted in the need for large numbers of faculty to teach online. Undergraduate and graduate online courses and programs, online certificates, and open online courses have necessitated the transfer of content and adaptation of pedagogy to a completely online environment. Most faculty who have terminal degrees have usually not formally learned to teach and they draw on their own experiences as students and learn how to teach on the job when they become instructors. Teaching online is a challenge because many have not been online students themselves or had online learning experiences to draw upon. Lack of instructor training to teach online is a significant barrier in the implementation of online education.

It is important for faculty to take the time to learn how to design and facilitate online courses before they teach them. Typically, faculty are not familiar with instructional design or the systematic approach to designing instruction. Knowledge of instructional design is key to designing an effective online course, especially including measurable goals and objectives, and including aligned activities, instructional material, and assessment. Hence, lack of training on online learning and knowledge of instructional design is considered a barrier. From a student perspective, poorly designed online courses are a barrier to their learning, especially because they do not have real-time access to an instructor who can clarify or explain anything they do not understand. Students can have challenges with navigation, unclear expectations, and unclear instructions for assessments that pose as barriers in their online learning success.

Sometimes instructors simply load content from face-to-face courses into an LMS with little adaptation for online delivery. The resulting course that has not been conceptualized for an online environment can be a barrier for student learning in the new environment. Rethinking course design (e.g., activities and assessments) for the online environment and for students at a distance is essential for successful online learning. Faculty expend tremendous effort in the creation, design, and facilitation of an online course. For example the creation of online videos and online materials can be likened to the writing of a book, involving research, conceptualization, and writing on the part of the faculty. These lead to questions of intellectual property and course ownership by faculty and universities that are barriers to online teaching (see Chapter 8 for more on the important issue of course ownership).

An additional problem with online course design is the need to adapt it based on the disciplines, knowledge, skills (e.g., conceptual knowledge or hands-on skills), and the level of course being taught (e.g., beginners versus advanced courses). The adoption of a 'one size fits all' can be a pedagogical barrier to student learning of disciplinary knowledge and skills, reinforcing the need for faculty training in online teaching and time to develop course materials that align with the larger goals of a program. Online courses might also lack adaptation of content for cultural or social differences, which can be a significant barrier for online students located in other cultures or geographies.

The lack of accessible instructional material that meets the needs for all students is a barrier for students with special needs. When students with special needs take on-campus courses, they are usually provided special accommodations by the office of disability on campus. This should also be the case for online courses, and is often practiced at institutions of higher education. However, it is often the case that when students with special needs take online courses, their instructors are expected to make special accommodations in the online courses. For example, if students with vision or hearing impairment take online courses, videos are expected to be closed-captioned and transcripted, tables are expected to include headers, and images are expected to include alternative text. These additional requirements take extra work, and instructors might lack the time or resources to implement them, might not be aware of how to make content accessible online, and can consider creating accessible instructional material a challenge. Support for instructors should be provided in order for them to make their courses accessible to all learners. Faculty consider their limited knowledge of copyright policies and intellectual property rights as a barrier. They fear inadvertently breaking copyright laws. When faculty teach online, they use electronic resources, and it is important for them to have a clear understanding of copyright policies. Faculty are also concerned regarding intellectual property because once they create online course content, universities have access to the resources even after they leave the institution.

Online teaching includes both course design and facilitation. Online facilitation presumes that instructors are familiar and competent in communicating online, conveying their teaching personality in the online environment, and are able to manage the online environment, both to interact with students and to assess their learning (Martin, Wang, & Sadaf, 2020). Beginning instructors often struggle in these areas and find the inflexibility of the online environment to be a barrier. Furthermore, online courses often include online discussions that instructors have to facilitate throughout the week, which can be a barrier for those used to facilitating on-campus discussions in their courses during class time. Emails and messages are often the main means of communication in online courses, which instructors have to address individually. They can be a barrier because of the time taken to communicate with students and the fact that such communications are not limited to a specific time or space. Online synchronous sessions where instructors meet with groups of students in real-time require competence to manage the software and conversations in the online environment.

As part of the facilitation process, online instructors spend a considerable amount of time grading and providing feedback to online students (Oyarzun, Martin, & Moore, 2020). In a face to face course, instructors can give immediate feedback on discussions and activities in class. However, in an online course, instructors have to often set aside dedicated time each week for grading the various activities and discussions and providing constructive feedback to the learners, in addition to the assessments that instructors might include. Instructors consider this as a barrier in managing their workload because in online courses, there is additional time involved in providing feedback and completing grading.

Lack of access to the institutional library and scarce online resources to help students with information literacy skills can also be a barrier for online students in research-oriented courses or programs. On-campus students have access to student advisors to plan their programs of study, register, discuss financial resources, etc. Students can find it difficult to understand expectations in online programs and succeed when online programs lack library access and advising.

What pedagogical barriers do students and instructors face in your organization?

6 Interpersonal Barriers

One of the main barriers in online education is the lack of personal relationships between students and faculty (Llyod, Byrne, & McCoy, 2012). In a face-to-face classroom, instructors and students are able to see each other at every class meeting and also have informal conversations in other settings on campus. In the online environment, courses are planned in advance and are largely delivered in an asynchronous format. This leads to conversations that are usually very structured and intentional, stifling opportunities for relationship building. The absence of spontaneous and informal conversations where students and instructors can get to know each other, and where students can get to know their peers is a significant barrier in the online environment. Both faculty and students have reported this lack of interaction and the challenges with building personal relationships as a barrier in online education.

Learner to learner interactions are typically very structured in online courses when compared to face-to-face classrooms. The lack of face-to-face interactions and the lack of personal relationship with the instructor and with the peers is one the major barriers for online students (Kebritchi et al., 2017). This leads to a sense of isolation and a sense of disconnectedness from the online course and the university, which is a barrier to student learning. Furthermore, this decreases learner motivation and increases learner anxiety, which prevents students from succeeding in the online environment. Some students also experience anxiety and self-efficacy problems with online technologies as well as their academic abilities, which becomes a barrier. Cultural and social diversity can also lead to student anxiety and inability to fulfill expectations in online courses where personal relationships are lacking. Finally, online courses require students to manage their own learning, requiring self-regulation and time management to complete all the activities. This is a barrier for online students especially if they are not efficient in time management. Online students are often non-traditional learners with multiple commitments, which is also a barrier to their successful completion of online courses.

Similar to online students, instructors who might not be located on campus and only teach online can face isolation and a sense of disconnectedness that is a barrier to online teaching. Faculty motivation is a significant barrier in online learning for several reasons. Instructors must learn a new way of delivering instruction, which involves different course design and facilitation strategies. Several instructors lack the motivation to switch to the new modality of course delivery. Some faculty are also still resistant to innovation and are of the opinion that this new modality does not result in the same learning as traditional face to face instruction. The challenges of building relationships with students or lack of dynamic conversations also cause a decrease in faculty motivation to teach online, as they miss the experience of classroom interactions, where they receive immediate feedback on their teaching in students' non-verbal cues. Similar to students, some faculty might experience anxiety with learning new technologies, and low self-efficacy in the technologies or teaching online that serve as barriers to online instruction.

Instructor and administrators' beliefs about the lower quality of online education compared to on-campus education, and the lack of efficacy of online education can pose as significant barriers in the implementation of online education (Cifuentes, Suryavanshi, & Janney, 2018). Instructors and administrators often believe that online instruction does not result in student learning in the same way that on-campus teaching does. Some might fear insufficient enrollment and retention, while others might also worry about the reputation or ranking of their institution and programs.

What interpersonal barriers do online students, and instructors face in your organization?

Thus, various barriers exist for administrators, instructors and students when teaching online. In the section below, we outline strategies for overcoming these challenges.

7 Strategies for Overcoming Barriers in Online Learning and Teaching

7.1 *Administrators and Institutions*

Various strategies can be used by administrators to overcome barriers in online education. It is important for administrators to have a strategic plan, institutional wide policies, and standards for online education at their institution. Administrators should take alternative funding models into account for the delivery of online programs and have a budget for online education (Rumble, 2019). Implementing organizational change is critical for the success of online education, and administrators have to encourage buy-in from various stakeholders, including various institutional leaders and faculty. As an administrator, it is important to provide department chairs, and other leaders resources to implement change in addition to providing infrastructures, technologies, support services, and support personnel. Additionally, administrators should be prepared to provide training opportunities, incentives, release time, and resources to faculty members for online course design and delivery. It is also imperative for administrators to work towards delivering quality online education, by setting enrolling limits, providing evaluation measures (Jung & Latchem, 2012; Jung, 2003) specific for online education and continuing to provide support for both faculty and students and valuing online education.

7.2 *Recommendations for Administrators and Institutions*
– Create a strategic plan and budget for online learning.
– Create institution-wide policies and standards for online courses.
– Align online offerings with accreditation processes for online programs.
– Consider alternative funding models for online programs.
– Ensure buy-in from institutional leaders and faculty.

- Encourage change agents and provide resources for implementing organizational change.
- Provide administrators with time and opportunities to align their management strategies to online education.
- Provide infrastructure, technology, and systems that facilitate academic processes.
- Provide student support services for online students (e.g., registration, financial aid, etc.).
- Provide academic support services for online students (e.g., writing center, disability services).
- Ensure adequate staff to maintain networks and technology.
- Ensure faculty have access to hardware and software necessary for online teaching.
- Support online programs in recruitment and marketing efforts.
- Provide training opportunities for faculty on both pedagogical and technological skills.
- Provide resources for faculty for course design and development.
- Provide opportunities for faculty to align their teaching beliefs and strategies to online teaching.
- Provide release time or adjust faculty workload for course development and teaching.
- Provide incentives and recognition for faculty (e.g., awards for online teaching).
- Value online teaching during the tenure and promotion process.
- Create or adopt evaluation instruments for online teaching.
- Set enrollment limits in online courses.
- Provide technical support for both faculty and students.
- Keep up with technology changes and adopt technology that benefits students.

Reflect to identify what strategies do you use as an administrator to overcome barriers for online education.

8   Instructors

Various strategies can be used by faculty to overcome the barriers they face with online teaching, in addition to the resources and support that their institution has to provide. It is important for faculty to participate in professional development and be prepared with both technology and pedagogical skills both for course design and delivery, given the paradigm shift that is involved in teaching online. It is important for faculty to design quality online courses where they engage their students in the learning and provide opportunities for interaction between learner-learner, learner-instructor and learner-content (Bolliger & Martin, 2019; Moore, 1989). Faculty have to be familiar with the support available to them on campus and know who to reach out to for technical and pedagogical support when challenges arise. It is essential for faculty to be familiar with the policies and standards regarding online learning, and intellectual property rights and copyright laws and guidelines (Lipinsky & Brennan, 2013). Finally, time is a big barrier, and faculty have to make the time to design their online courses and also use various time management strategies when teaching online (Martin, Budhrani, & Wang, 2019: Oyarzun, Martin, & Moore, 2020).

8.1 *Recommendations for Instructors*
– participate in training on both technology and pedagogical aspects for online teaching,
– become familiar with basic computer operations and software or hardware used for online teaching,
– use sound instructional design principles to create online courses,
– use online course facilitation strategies to effectively facilitate the online course,
– use time management strategies to effectively manage time when required to spend more time on grading and feedback,
– create engaging online courses with opportunities for learner-learner, learner-instructor, and learner-content interaction,
– learn how to create accessible online learning,
– schedule time to design the course prior to delivery,
– reach out to technical support staff when a technical challenge exists,
– provide guidance for students to reach out to technical support when they need assistance,
– be familiar with quality standards and policies on online learning,
– be familiar with intellectual property rights and copyright of electronic materials, and
– keep students' privacy and security in mind when creating online courses.

Reflect to identify what strategies instructors use to overcome barriers for online education.

9   Learners

Various strategies can be used by learners to overcome barriers in online learning. Students have to ensure access to the technology, and also be ready to use
the technology to be successful in online learning. They can be prepared for
online learning by participating in the orientation provided to them by the
university, program, and/or the course. To be a successful online learner, they
have to be self-disciplined, stay on task, learn from a variety of formats, follow instructions online, use various technologies and manage their time well,
and complete activities and assignments by the due date (Martin, Stamper, &
Flowers, 2020). Communicating in the online environment is different from
the face to face setting. Learners need to use various technologies for communication, as well as reach out to the instructor for assistance or to discuss
feedback or ask clarification questions. They also need to be prepared to use
different tools to communicate with their peers.

9.1   *Recommendations for Students*
- access hardware and software needed to be successful when enrolling in
  online courses,
- participate in an orientation for online learning,
- familiarize themselves with basic computer operations and software or
  hardware needed in online courses,
- access online help desk/tech support for assistance,
- devote the appropriate number of hours for the online course and plan time
  for course activities,
- stay on task and avoid distractions while studying,
- contact the instructor with any challenges or difficulties faced during the
  course,
- learn from a variety of formats (lectures, videos, podcasts, online discus-
  sion/conferencing),
- follow instructions in various formats (written, video, audio etc),
- use asynchronous technologies (discussion boards, e-mail, etc.),
- use synchronous technologies (Webex, Collaborate, Adobe Connect, Zoom,
  etc.) to communicate, and
- complete activities and assignments by the due date assigned by the instructor.

Reflect to identify what strategies learners use to overcome barriers to be
successful online learners.

10 Summary

In this chapter, we discuss four different types of barriers in online education, institutional barriers, technology and technical barriers, pedagogical barriers, and interpersonal barriers. To overcome the barriers, we propose what a distance learning administrator needs to facilitate so that other administrators, instructors, and students can be successful in online education. The following two objectives were covered in this chapter.

- Identify and discuss different types of barriers (institutional barriers, technology and technical barriers, pedagogical barriers, and interpersonal barriers) that exist in the adoption of online education
- Describe strategies for instructors, learners, and administrators to overcome barriers in online education

11 Conclusion

Online education has continued to increase, and barriers exists at all levels in online education. It is important for distance learning administrators, faculty, and students to identify these barriers and use various strategies to overcome them. Also, there is a need for more research to examine barriers both from quantitative surveys and qualitative interviews to add to the literature on what barriers exist in different types of institutions across the world. Barriers faced by an institution might depend on the phase of online education at the institution, the disciplines or types of programs that are offered online, and the students who enroll in the online offerings. Overcoming barriers at an institutional level can greatly contribute to the lessening of barriers for faculty and students. Communication between faculty and administrators is also essential to overcome barriers for faculty. Likewise, communication with students is important for overcoming student barriers.

12 Self-Check

Examine which of the following barriers exist in your instructional setting and think about strategies you can use to overcome them.

References

Berge, Z. L. (1998). Barriers to online teaching in post-secondary institutions: Can policy changes fix it. *Online Journal of Distance Learning Administration, 1*(2), 2.

Berge, Z. L., & Muilenburg, L. (2001). Obstacles faced at various stages of capability regarding distance education in institutions of higher education. *TechTrends, 45*, 40. https://doi.org/10.1007/BF02784824

Bolliger, D. U., & Martin, F. (2018). Instructor and student perceptions of online student engagement strategies. *Distance Education, 39*(4), 568–583.

Cifuentes, L., Suryavanshi, R., & Janney, A. (2018). Motivating instructors and administrators to adopt e-learning. In A. A. Piña, V. L. Lowell, & B. R. Harris (Eds.), *Leading and managing e-learning: What the e-learning leader needs to know*. Springer.

Gutiérrez-Santiuste, E., Gallego-Arrufat, M. J., & Simone, A. (2016). Barriers in computer-mediated communication: Typology and evolution over time. *Journal of e-Learning and Knowledge Society, 12*(1), 107–119.

Haber, J., & Mills, M. (2008). Perceptions of barriers concerning effective online teaching and policies: Florida community college faculty. *Community College Journal of Research and Practice, 32*(4–6), 266–283.

Jung, I. (2003). Cost-effectiveness of online education. In M. G. Moore & W. G. Anderson (Eds.), *Handbook of distance education* (pp. 717–726). Routledge.

Jung, I., & Latchem, C. (2012). *Quality assurance and accreditation in distance education: Models, policies and research*. Routledge.

Kebritchi, M., Lipschuetz, A., & Santiague, L. (2017). Issues and challenges for teaching successful online courses in higher education: A literature review. *Journal of Educational Technology Systems, 46*(1), 4–29.

Legon, R., Garrett, R., & Fredericksen, E. E. (2020). *The Changing Landscape of Online Education (CHLOE): Navigating the mainstream*. Quality Matters and Eduventures.

Lipinkski, T. A., & Brennan, M. J. (2013). Legal and recent copyright issues. In M. G. Moore & W. C. Diehl (Eds.), *Handbook of distance education* (pp. 551–568). Routledge.

Lloyd, S. A., Byrne, M. M., & McCoy, T. S. (2012). Faculty-perceived barriers of online education. *Journal of Online Learning and Teaching, 8*(1).

Maguire, L. L. (2005). Literature review–faculty participation in online distance education: Barriers and motivators. *Online Journal of Distance Learning Administration, 8*(1), 1–16.

Martin, F., Budhrani, K., & Wang, C. (2019). Examining faculty perception of their readiness to teach online. *Online Learning Journal, 23*(3), 97–119.

Martin, F., & Parker, M. A. (2014). Use of synchronous virtual classrooms: Why, who and how? *MERLOT Journal of Online Learning and Teaching, 10*(2), 192–210.

Martin, F., Stamper, B., & Flowers, C. (2020). Examining student perception of their readiness for online learning in 2018. *Online Learning, 20*(2), 38–58.

Martin, F., Wang, C., Budhrani, K., Moore, R. L., & Jokiaho, A. (2019). Professional development support for the online instructor: Perspectives of U.S. and German instructors. *Online Journal of Distance Learning Administration, 22*(3).

Martin, F., Wang, C., & Sadaf. A. (2020). Facilitation matters: Instructor perception of helpfulness of facilitation strategies in online courses. *Online Learning, 24*(1), 28–49.

Moore, M. (1989). Editorial: Three types of interaction. *American Journal of Distance Education, 3*(2), 1–7.

Muilenburg, L., & Berge, Z. L. (2001). Barriers to distance education: A factor-analytic study. *American Journal of Distance Education, 15*(2), 7–22.

Oyarzun, B., Martin, F., & Moore, R. (2020). Time management matters: Online faculty perceptions of helpfulness of time. *Distance Education, 41*(1), 106–127.

Panda, S., & Mishra, S. (2007). E-learning in a Mega Open University: Faculty attitude, barriers and motivators. *Educational Media International, 44*(4), 323–338.

Rumble, G. (2019). *The planning and management of distance education.* Routledge.

Schmidt, S. W., Tschida, C. M., & Hodge, E. M. (2016). How faculty learn to teach online: What administrators need to know. *Online Journal of Distance Learning Administration, 19*(1), 1–10.

Seaman, J. E., Allen, I. E., & Seaman, J. (2018). *Grade increase: Tracking distance education in the United States.* Babson Survey Research Group.

Shea, P. (2007). Bridges and barriers to teaching online college courses: A study of experienced online faculty in thirty-six colleges. *Journal of Asynchronous Learning Networks, 11*(2). http://citeseerx.ist.psu.edu/viewdoc/download?doi=10.1.1.453.4788&rep=rep1&type=pdf

Singh, A., Mangalaraj, G., & Taneja, A. (2010). Bolstering teaching through online tools. *Journal of Information Systems Education, 21*(3), 299.

Tomei, L. (2006). The impact of online teaching on faculty load: Computing the ideal class size for online courses. *Journal of Technology and Teacher Education, 14*(3), 531–541.

Appendix: Recommended Support Materials

Downloadable list of barriers

Institutional barriers
Lack of administrative support
Lack of resources for course design and development
Lack of release time or faculty workload
Clarity on intellectual property rights
Lack of incentives and recognition
Online teaching not valued for promotion and tenure
Limited knowledge on copyright of electronic materials
Lack of enrollment limits
Faculty buy-in for online teaching
Lack of evaluation instruments for online teaching
Lack of policies or standards for online courses
Accreditation processes

Technology and technical barriers
Lack of training on technology skills
Frequent technical problems
Lack of technical support
Rapidly changing software or delivery systems
Concern of access to students
Inadequate hardware and software
Concern of access to students
Cost and access to the Internet
Privacy and security concerns

Pedagogical barriers
Lack of training on online teaching
Lack of instructional design for online learning
Creating accessible instructional material
Perception of quality in online courses
Increased time for grading and feedback
Poorly designed online courses
Inaccessible course material

Interpersonal barriers
Lack of personal relationship with students and faculty
Faculty motivation
Resistance to innovation
Personal anxiety with online technologies
Lack of peer interaction
Student self-regulation in completing online activities

CHAPTER 4

Legalities, Policies, Ethics, Accreditation, and Institutional Support

Duane M. Dunn

Abstract

At the conclusion of this chapter, you will be aware of the need to administer the following: (1) identification of institutional policies regarding distance education; (2) a comparison of those institutional policies to accrediting agency standards for distance education; (3) a review of institutional policies and procedures with the state agency providing oversight of higher education; (4) a review of institutional procedures for assurance of US Department of Education regulations; (5) strategies for regular review and communication of distance education policies and procedures; and (6) a communication plan which emphasizes the ethical standards of distance education policy compliance.

Keywords

accreditation – accrediting agencies – state authorization – ethical behavior – compliance – regulations – Higher Education Act

1 Introduction

The Higher Education Act (HEA) of 1965 includes rules regarding Title IV federal student aid programs, the Clery Act requiring reporting of campus crime, institutional accreditation processes, and financial responsibility of institutions of higher education. Although the Act was passed in 1965 and is intended to be renewed every five years, the last reauthorization occurred in 2008. Subsequent extensions have occurred which provide continuation of Title IV, Cleary Act, accreditation, and financial expectations of institutions. In order to provide federal aid to students, institutions must meet those legal aspects of the HEA including the associated regulations. Those regulations may include specific aspects of distance education as well as the overall institutional operation.

© KONINKLIJKE BRILL NV, LEIDEN, 2021 | DOI: 10.1163/9789004471382_004

Distance education administrators should be familiar with the HEA as well as regulations specific to distance education including the application of those regulations to institutional policies (see Chapter 14 for more on the HEA).

As federal law, HEA requirements establish the legal responsibility of institutions in providing higher education to students. Violation of the HEA and regulations as well as failure to meet accreditation standards may lead to the institution's loss of Title IV eligibility. Some HEA regulations are specific to distance education as the growth and utilization of online and distance delivery has increased since 1965.

In addition, institutions are held responsible for a number of federal and state laws and regulations. Those include laws regarding accessibility, copywrite, privacy, and financial and constitutional protections. Institutional policies must address these broad legal requirements and administrators should be familiar with the policies as a means of assuring the legal requirements are fulfilled. Many of these broad legal requirements are addressed in other chapters, with this chapter having a focus on the HEA regulations including distance education authorization and the most recent changes to regulations. Institutions and individual faculty members can be, and sometimes are, fined for violations of any of the laws or regulations.

At the conclusion of this chapter, you will be aware of the need to administer the following: (1) identification of institutional policies regarding distance education; (2) a comparison of those institutional policies to accrediting agency standards for distance education; (3) a review of institutional policies and procedures with the state agency providing oversight of higher education; (4) a review of institutional procedures for assurance of US Department of Education regulations; (5) strategies for regular review and communication of distance education policies and procedures; and (6) a communication plan which emphasizes the ethical standards of distance education policy compliance.

Depending on the organization and governance structure of your institution the policies regarding distance education may have been or will be developed from a number of different aspects. A private university may be able to design its own policies while a public university may operate under the governance of a higher education governing or coordinating board which establishes policies for a number of different universities within its designated legislative authority. A locally governed community college may have authority to establish its own individual policies while a community college governed by a state system would need policies adopted by that state system. Regardless of the governance structure of the individual institution, distance education policies are primarily based upon the United States Department of Education (DOE) regulations found in the Higher Education Act (HEA) and further designated by the institution's accrediting agencies. These agencies are authorized by the DOE as part of the HEA Title IV act establishing eligibility of institutions to provide federal financial aid to attending students.

Walcutt and Schatz (2019) provide a historical perspective of the use of technology and distance education as educational delivery systems evolved. They cite a 2000 report from the Web-based Education Commission which indicated that 84% of four-year colleges expected to offer distance learning courses in 2002. In considering the growth and advancement of Learning Management Systems (LMS) and student interest since 2002 it becomes evident that attention to the ethical values of learning should then be appropriately addressed in the institutional policy and procedures.

Mannapperuma (2015) further cited the growth in student participation in distance education using information from the National Center of Education and Statistics, and she indicated that in 2007–08, 20% of all undergraduates took at least one distance education courses. Additionally, 9% of postbaccalaureate students completed their entire program through distance education. Manapperuma's report revealed that the DOE had recognized an increasing concern for oversight of institutions offering distance learning and the complexity of state oversight with federal authorization. The DOE established the Online State Authorization Rule in 2010 to provide guidance in state policy and subsequent institutional policy development with a focus on assuring integrity and ethics are considered in procedures and practices for distance education. The rule required states to obtain authorization to provide distance education to residents outside of the institution's location. However, since the initial development of the Online State Authorization Rule, many adjustments have been made and the DOE implementation continues to address concerns expressed by the states.

Because of the different governing structures and accrediting agency standards, a challenge often exists for distance education administrators to navigate varying institutional policies and communicate the importance of policy revisions to institutional leaders. When administrators move among colleges or universities they often find that distance education policies are different among those institutions. Furthermore, depending on each institution's organizational structure, the distance education administrator may or may not have direct access to the President or Provost responsible for leading efforts toward policy revisions.

A number of key indicators of whether institutional policies and procedures appropriately address distance education were identified in a DOE Office of Postsecondary Education's report of 2006, "Evidence of Quality in Distance Education Programs Drawn from Interviews with the Accreditation

Community." The report was based on discussions with accrediting organization staff and higher education experts for the purpose of identifying best practices in the accreditation of distance education. Peter Ewell, then vice president of the National Center for Higher Education Management Systems, provided an observation in the report that was supported by other participants in the discussions. His observation was that "... distance education is often held to a higher standard than traditional education when judging quality." Perhaps it is that higher standard that elicits the critical need to assure policy and procedures of the institution are clear, align with accreditation standards, and meet the mission and expectations of the institution.

Throughout this chapter aspects of distance education policies are provided to assist you in reviewing your institutional policies and navigating communications with your institutional leaders who are responsible for developing, adopting, and implementing policies.

2   Policy Factors

Institutional policies are designed to provide guidance to operational aspects of the college or university. Clarity of those policies reduce confusion and provide constituents with an understanding of how the institution will meet expectations. Distance education constituents may have different expectations than other constituents; therefore, specific policies regarding distance education are often included in policy and procedure manuals.

In his column in *Distance Learning*, Michael Simonson (2015) summarizes the positive indicators identified in the 2006 DOE report on evidence of quality ranging from instructional design support, faculty oversight of curriculum and involvement in course design, and technical support to a systematic approach to growth and management of distance education. He suggests administrators should also be aware of concerns in how distance education students are provided student services, the direct conversion of face-to-face courses to a distant modality, separate course evaluations from face-to-face instruction and distance instruction, and analysis of high numbers of complaints and drop out of distance students. Although the DOE report identified more extensive factors, the general aspect of policy and procedures should provide evidence that the institution honors academic standards and student services for all students regardless of instructional modality.

Those same aspects of distance education in comparison to face-to-face instruction align with accrediting agencies in establishing expectations of colleges and universities as assurance of academic standards, providing appropriate services toward student success, and a systematic approach to enrollment and program growth. Without those expectations addressed in policy, distance education as a mode of delivery for higher education may be uncertain and unchecked.

Quick check:
- Does your institution have specific policies relative to the delivery, assessment, and academic oversight of distance education?
- What is the process by which distance education policies are developed, reviewed, and modified at your institution?

3   Accreditation

The Higher Education Act (HEA) requires institutions to be accredited by an agency or association recognized by the Secretary of the United States Department of Education if the institution intends to participate in Title IV federal student aid programs. Accreditation is voluntary for the institution but is a requirement in order for the institutions to award students federal financial aid including Pell Grants and student loans. The provisions that govern the recognition of accrediting agencies are found at Part G-Program integrity and Subpart 2 Accrediting Agency Recognition section 1099b.[1] Specific to the ability of accrediting agencies to enforcement of required HEA standards, section 496 indicates that neither the statute nor the regulations require the same application of resources for each institution or program or for each standard.

A 2006 Congressional Research Services Report for Congress, authored by Skinner and Feder, noted that a debate topic for the HEA reauthorization could possibly include whether accrediting agencies should require additional evidence of achievement for students in distance education programs. Subsequently, accrediting agencies have adopted a number of different criteria or expectations of institutions specific to the federal regulations. Lingering interpretations of those criteria and expectations remain in many institutional distance education policies.

The DOE recognizes a number of accrediting agencies, historically referred to as regional accrediting agencies, providing accreditation to the majority of public and private colleges and universities. Those agencies are the Higher Learning Commission (HLC), the Middle States Commission on Higher Education (MSCHE), the New England Commission on Higher Education (NEASC), the Northwest Commission on Colleges and Universities (NWCCU), the Southern

Association of Colleges and Schools Commission on Colleges (SACS COC), and the two WASC entities of WASC Senior College and University Commission and the WASC Accrediting Commission for Community and Junior Colleges. Historically these accrediting agencies provided accreditation criteria and standards for colleges and universities based on geographic boundaries of states; however, recent regulations adopted by the DOE in 2019 allow institutions to seek regional accreditation outside of the historical alignment of agencies to state boundaries. The Council of Regional Accrediting Commissions (C-RAC) represents the seven organizations in order that quality education is addressed by the institutions within those regional agencies. Additionally, the Distance Education Accrediting Commission (DEAC) is an accrediting agency specifically structured for distance education institutions with primarily private member institutions.[2]

Although each of the accrediting agencies have some variance in the criteria or standards for distance education delivery, those agencies utilize a common understanding of the concept of distance education. The NWCCU Distance Education Policy states that the U.S. Department of Education defines Distance Education as follows:

> Distance education means education that uses one or more of the technologies listed below to deliver instruction to students who are separated from the instructor and to support regular and substantive interaction between the students and the instructor, either synchronously or asynchronously. The technologies may include: (1) The internet; (2) One-way and two-way transmissions through open broadcast, closed circuit, cable, microwave, broadband lines, fiber optics, satellite, or wireless communications devices; (3) Audio conferencing; or (4) Video cassettes, DVDs, and CD-ROMs, if the cassettes, DVDs, or CD-ROMs are used in a course in conjunction with any of the technologies listed in paragraphs (1) through (3). (NWCCU, 2013)

Similarly, all accrediting agencies utilize that definition in developing standards and processes for evaluating the member institution's ability to meet those standards.

An important aspect of the challenges distance education administrators face in meeting accrediting agency and DOE expectations regards assessing course delivery and meeting the requirements for regular and substantive interaction. Elsewhere in this book are chapters related to quality assurance, managing course development, and aspects of effective course design. Within those chapters are aspects of regular and substantive interaction. However, defining and measuring interaction in order to meet accrediting agency and DOE regulations is a responsibility of the administrator. A collaborative white paper presented by Online Learning Consortium (OLC), WCET (WICHE Cooperative for Educational Technologies), and the University Professional and Continuing Education Association (UPCEA) described the importance of regular and substantive interaction as a primary differentiator of distance education as compared to correspondence courses. The paper identifies that there is no statutory definition of regular and substantive interaction. Among the cases cited is the 2017 DOE Office of Inspector General's (OIG) audit of Western Governor University in which the OIG indicated the general meaning of regular and substantive interaction is that the interaction is relevant to the subject matter and describes the student and instructor interaction in which evaluation of performed tasks are submitted. The OIG further indicated that this general meaning does not include computer generated feedback, recorded webinars, video, and reading materials which do not result in required interaction with the instructor, or instances in which the student's only contact is with someone who is not the instructor (Online Learning Consortium). The lack of clarity of defined regular and substantive interaction is evident in accrediting agency expectations or criteria. Accrediting agency policies may address the percentage of the course that utilizes technical modality for interaction and follow the credit hour definition for length of course, but the definition and measure of regular and substantive interaction follow the OIG general meaning.

Also, it is important to understand that accrediting agencies differ in their standards of distance education as compared to correspondence education. For instance, SACSCOC specifically states in its Distance and Correspondence Education Policy Statement that:

> Correspondence education is a formal educational process under which the institution provides instructional materials, by mail or electronic transmission, including examinations on the materials, to students who are separated from the instructor. Interaction between the instructor and the student is limited, is not regular and substantive, and is primarily initiated by the student; courses are typically self-paced. (SACSCOC, 2018)

Similar clarifications of distinctions between distance and correspondence learning can be found in other accrediting agency policies. As a distance education administrator, it is critical that an awareness of those differences is applied in the institutional policies and procedures, and that faculty are well aware of those differences.

Each of the accrediting agencies establish standards which address aspects of institutional policies including faculty credentials, student services, student verification, curriculum standards, financial resources, integrated planning, and public information. The institution is expected to have policies and procedures which verify that those standards are addressed.

Accrediting agencies utilize peer review processes to verify institutions meet the full accrediting standards established by the agency. Within that verification process are specific aspects of distance education operations including a review of the institution's distance education policies and procedures. The peer review process and the calendar cycle of those reviews varies by accrediting agency.

Specialized accrediting agencies which review programmatic areas of colleges and universities utilize specific criteria to ensure the curriculum within those programs meet the industry or other specific standards. The Council for Higher Education Accreditation (CHEA) completed a study in 2002 in which specialized accrediting agencies were surveyed regarding specific assurance of quality standards for distance learning (CHEA, 2002). Of interest in the findings of the report was that the specialized accreditors indicated a limited need to develop separate standards, policies, and procedures for distance learning. The report indicates that outcomes of learning were the primary aspects of accreditation rather than the processes in which the learning was provided. The CHEA report indicated there should be a well-defined rationale for utilizing distance learning within the program and assurance that the program continued to meet the objectives of the program through appropriate institutional resources for students and faculty as well as consistent assessment practices. Regardless of the specialized accrediting agencys' positions on distance learning, most did include guidance for the institutions in assuring distance education is reviewed as part of the accreditation process. That guidance might address faculty qualifications, utilization of appropriate technology, and student access to curriculum and course materials.

Quick check:
- With what agency is your institution accredited?
- When was the last accreditation review and when is the next review for your institution?
- Within the last review find the report on your institution's distance education.
- Were there any recommendations for change or adjustments to policy or procedures?
- If so, have those recommendations occurred?

4   Policy Development

Community colleges are often early adopters of academic modalities due to the ability to provide flexibility in courses design and approval processes. That flexibility comes with responsibility of assuring students are provided a learning experience which mirrors that of the face-to-face on campus student experience. Kovel-Jarboe (1997) found that the development of policies specific to delivery modalities for community colleges addressed five broad policy clusters: quality; student support; human and financial resources; governance, mission, and programs; and infrastructure. These factors are addressed specifically in other chapters in this book; however, it is important to determine if your institutional policies do address those aspects unique to your college or university. Although the DOE and accrediting agency expectations are necessary from a regulatory and federal compliance perspective, the policies should also align with the identity and mission of the individual institution.

Larger systems may have varying levels of process and approvals which also address the system's mission and institutional identity. Institutions may include distance education policies within their overall academic policies and those policies may be established at the system level rather than at the institutional level. Regardless of the system, the factors Kovel-Jarboe found are expected to be provided in policy development. A few examples of system policy language and guidance is provided.

The University System of Georgia provides policy guidance for the thirty institutions in the system. The policy states the definition of distance education and provides clarity as to the institutional program approval process. As noted in The University System of Georgia policy 3.3.3 Distance Education is defined as:

> ... a formal educational process in which the majority of the instruction in a course occurs when the student and instructor are not in the same place and the instruction is delivered using technology. Instruction may be synchronous or asynchronous. No institution may offer programs completely online prior to the Board of Regents' approval of the academic program or programs to be offered completely online.[3]

As indicated in the definition and within the policy, this reflects the DOE definition of distance education but continues to address the system expectations for program approval. Also, the University System of Georgia coordinates Georgia On My Line as a means in which the twenty-six individual institutions which offer online courses and degrees utilize the system policies for guidance on delivery of distance programming.[4]

The Kansas Board of Regents (2020) provides general guidance to the institutions of which it governs and coordinates regarding distance education. Its policy is found in the Kansas Board of Regents policy manual, Chapter III section A.8.b.iv and v. The policy includes the definition based on the DOE definition but further clarifies the measured time and clarifies what constitutes a course as well as a program. That policies states:

iv. A "distance education course" is one in which faculty and students are physically separated in place or time and in which at least seventy-five percent of the instruction and interaction are provided synchronously or asynchronously via some form of mediated delivery system (i.e., 11.25 or more hours of instruction per credit hour are delivered via audio or video recording, live interactive video, CD-ROM, the Internet or World Wide Web, etc.).

v. A "distance education program" is one in which fifty percent or more of the required courses for the program are delivered via distance education courses.[5]

The Kentucky Community and Technical College System (2014) provides specific guidance regarding distance education in Policy Number: 4.14. This policy addresses the specific institutional expectations related to the academic, student and financial aspects of each college within the system.

> In order to support the successful implementation of distance learning instruction by Internet and interactive television (ITV)/video conference network, the following definitions, policies, responsibilities, and procedures pertaining to Academic Affairs, Student Affairs, and Business Affairs are hereby established.[6]

Regardless of the system or size of the institution the policy structure and content should address the distance education definition as aligned with the DOE, address the institutional process for program approval and the expectation of how distance education will meet the academic, financial and student services standards of the institution.

Quick check:
- Utilize your institutional policy on distance education and determine if it addresses the components Kovel-Jarboe found as strong indicators.
- What factors within the system or state governance are expressly included in your institutional distance education policy?

5   **Ethics Addressed in Policy**

Perhaps a frequent concern expressed by educators, students, and other constituents regarding distance education is assurance of ethical participation by the student as well as by the teacher and administrator. Even casual conversations with constituents may lead to questions such as: How do you know if the student is really the participant? How can you assure the faculty that the students aren't cheating on the exam? How do I know if the professor is actually teaching the course? What assurance is provided that the student is actually reviewing all of the material? Many of these questions or concerns are addressed through advancement and improvements in the technology associated with the institution's choice of a learning management system (LMS). Factors regarding selection of LMS and other technology aspects are addressed within this book; however, there remains a need for the institutional policies to also address assurance of ethical standards for distance education.

Accrediting agencies address those ethical standards within their guidelines and standards as does the DOE in its regulations within the Higher Education Act. The specific policy and procedural standards of an institution should be included in the university policy, the faculty handbook, and student handbook or the appropriate manuals specific to the institution.

Recognition of the need for ethical behavior is not a recent development for distance education administrators. Parisot (1997) provided an overview of the importance of faculty development including the importance of conveying the value of appropriate use of technology in teaching and learning processes. Parisot's study focused on various aspects which faculty face in utilizing distance education. Consistent within her findings is the importance of institutional value placed on student learning and the use of technology in maintaining that value. Within the institutional policy of distance education is the importance of consistent expectations of the value of outcomes for the student regardless of the modality of instruction. The increase in distance education since Parisot's study perhaps heightens the importance of specifically addressing the ethics, integrity, and honor aspects of distance education as those relate within the institutional mission.

Early recognition of the need to address ethics and integrity is found in Gearhart's 2001 article. She addresses the need for policies and procedures to include aspects related to harassment, privacy, plagiarism, and security as well as use of institutional resources for personal gain. A recommendation is to ensure constituent demographics and accessibility are included in the ethical framework of the policies. Additionally, the importance of addressing faculty development and communication of policy and procedures is recognized as important in policy and procedural development. For instance, faculty and staff should receive professional development in ensuring that content in online courses is accessible, following copyright law, and protecting student's privacy.

The manner in which aspects of ethics, integrity, and honesty are addressed specifically in policy or procedures of an institution may depend on the environment or structure in which distance education is administered within the institution. Aspects of ethics include privacy, data security, and adherence to the general expectations that students or constituents have of any higher education experience. General policies address those aspects however it is also appropriate to include reference to those policies within the handbooks or procedures specific to distance education. Additional layers of distance education policy and procedure may need to include use of Open Education Resource (OER), plagiarism, proctored exams, student verification, and length of course equivalent to the institutional definition of a credit hour. Walcutt and Schatz provide extensive aspects of the factors relative to the impact of technology and distance education on the education and specifically address ethics, accountability, and appropriate behavior of institutions.

Institutions often utilize an honor code as a means of addressing academic integrity and those may be referenced in the distance education policy and procedures. Implementation and adherence to the honor code may be a challenge for distance education administrators due to the remote nature of the student location and the application of appropriate technology to verify integrity. In their review of the use of honor codes, LoSchaivo and Shatz (2011) indicate that social and contextual factors do influence the effectiveness of honor codes for online instruction. Their report recommends that honor codes should be used but enhanced with other strategies including proctored exams when possible.

The aspect of ethics is also addressed as a key issue in artificial intelligence such that an acronym for Fairness, Accountability, Transparency, and Ethics (FATE) has become a recognized aspect of research and expectation for technology development.

Administrators should have regular interaction with institutional policy leaders as well as the units which implement those policies. Those interactions could include institutional committee or other organizational structures that create opportunities for interaction and codifying decisions leading to policy and procedural change. A committee structure specific to distance education may include institutional representation of units that impact the implementation of policies. These include admissions, Registrars office, office of assessment, technology, and other units according to the institution's organizational structure.

Quick check:
- Does your institutional honor code address distance education?
- Does your institution provide proctoring guidelines specific to distance education students?
- What institutional committees include distance education administrators in order to bring forward recommendations for policy and procedures?
- When was the most recent discussion at that committee regarding distance education policies and procedures which specifically address ethical teaching and learning standards?

6   Regulatory Compliance

The DOE provides regulatory oversight of higher education for those institutions that seek to utilize federal funding. The evolution and growth of distance and online education requires additional review of those regulations. Gellman-Deanley and Fetzner found that distance learning policy received marginal attention in their study conducted in 1998. However, as technical advancements occurred and students became more interested in distance and online learning as an avenue to higher education, the need for close alignment of policies to DOE regulations becomes more critical.

DOE regulations are not institutionally specific but rather provide directives of expectations. These regulations are often reviewed and modified by the DOE. That entails a process of publishing proposals in the Federal Register, a comment period, and inclusion of those comments by the DOE in consideration of regulatory change. Recently, a negotiated rulemaking process was utilized for the regulations of programs under Title IV of the HEA.[7] The process began in July 2018 with publication in the Federal Register of a notice of intent to establish a committee. In January 2019 committee members representing various sectors of higher education as well as constituent groups of students, professional associations, and public agencies convened to discuss proposed regulatory changes. Consensus language for the regulations was adopted in April 2019 with the regulations designated for implementation in July 2020.

Among the modifications to the regulations are the inclusion of face-to-face as well as distance delivery modalities in the regulations. This is a change from previously published regulations in which distance modality had separate standards differing from face-to-face instruction. Specifically related to this are regulations regarding disclosure to students regarding professional licensure and cost of attendance. The regulations specific to distance education also address regular and substantive interaction between student and instructor (discussed more broadly in Chapter 8), verification of student identity, and disclosure of licensure requirements based upon the location of the student.

As published in the Federal Register (C.F.R. 668.43, 2019) a number of regulations are identified for Section 668.43 under Title IV of the Higher Education Act of 1965 as amended. The regulations require institutions to meet several items regarding institutional information. Among those are:

- 668.43(a)(5) – disclosure as to whether the program meets the educational requirements for licensure or certification required for employment in the career;
- 668.43(a)(11) – information on the institution's policies regarding transfer of credit;
- 668.43(a)(12) – information on programs including courses provided by another institution;
- 668.43(a)(13–17) – information on program enrollment, placement, and retention.

Institutions have a legal obligation to meet these and other regulations provided in the HEA in order to fulfill their eligibility to provide Title IV federal financial aid to students. The distance education administrator, in collaboration with the appropriate administrative offices within the institution such as the Provost, Registrar, Financial Aid Administrator, and Admissions Administrator, is obligated to remain current on federal regulations and provide recommendations on policy revisions.

7   Summary and Conclusions

Policy development and implementation at the institutional level is affected by the organizational/governance structure of the institution. Careful attention is required by the distance education administrator to ensure the institution policy development aligns with the procedures established by the governing body. However, the administrator must also be aware of the broad oversight of accrediting agencies and adherence to federal regulations established by the Department of Education and included in the DOE Higher Education Act (2006).

It is incumbent on the administrator to have a means of communication with the institutional leaders who guide policy development and ensure any changes in accreditation or federal regulations are therefore addressed in the institutional policies.

As described in the chapter it is important that distance education policies and procedures provide the same level of rigor and expectation that is provided to on-campus students or delivered in face-to-face instruction.

The historical and continued growth of distance education will necessitate close observation and awareness of the policies and procedures adopted and implemented at the institutional level. Advancements in technology and learning management systems are valuable for administrators to utilize in implementing and assessing the effectiveness and compliance of regulations, policies, and procedures. Additionally, the administrator should remain aware of developments and resources available for policy development and compliance.

8 Resources

Resource and infrastructure requirements are often addressed through institutional collaborations in consortia. Those consortia may provide dual enrollment opportunities for students resulting in maximized use of federal financial aid. Many of those consortia were established as a means to maximize technology investments, utilize qualified faculty in order to meet enrollment potential, pursue shared software pricing, or establish opportunities for students to complete degree requirements without changing institutions.

However, from a policy perspective perhaps the largest collaboration is the National Council for State Authorization and Reciprocity Agreements (NC-SARA).[8] The compact was established through involvement of a number of professional organizations focused on distance education that recognized the developing nature of distance education throughout the United States. Reciprocal agreements were negotiated between individual states, but slight differences among those agreements resulted in challenges when students enrolled in courses from different colleges in different states. Additionally, institutions, systems, and agencies sought to ensure standards of quality and services, and consistency of delivery were provided to the students. State Authorization Reciprocity Agreements (SARA) are voluntary for state agencies as well as individual institutions within a member state. The National Council serves as the oversite entity for support of the member states and institutions within SARA.

NC-SARA is not a federal agency or a governing body of institutions. It is a compact of member states and institutions that provides support towards policy implementation. SARA is administered by four regional education compacts: Midwestern Higher Education Compact, New England Board of Higher education, Sothern Regional Education Board, and the Western Interstate Commission for Higher Education. These regional compacts have historically provided collaboration opportunities including student exchange programs, collective purchasing, and regional analyses for policy and planning. As the growth of distance education developed, especially with the use of web-based learning management systems, the regional compacts identified the value of a national council to provide consistent support and resources toward distance delivery. NC-SARA assists members with policy development through regular discussions, webinars, and other resources which provide information on DOE regulations, reciprocity, and data.

Several professional organizations provide valuable assistance and resources for distance education administrators in policy and procedure development as well as information on federal regulations.

WCET is the WICHE Cooperative for Educational Technologies providing leadership in the areas of policy and leadership in distance delivered higher education. WCET holds conferences and webinars, and provides research documents related to distance education.[9]

A subgroup pf WCET is the State Authorization Network (SAN) which provides resources relative to the regulatory aspects of state authorization for member institutions.[10]

The University Professional and Continuing Education Association (UPCEA) is a national organization of higher education institutions and professionals with a focus on continuing education. Although not specific to distance education, UPCEA provides resources primarily focused on issues, best practices, professional development, as well as policy and regulatory aspects for professionals interested in various aspects of continuing education.[11]

The Online Learning Consortium is a national organization specifically focused on the use of online learning. Resources include professional development, research, and best practices for faculty and administrators who are involved in distance education.[12]

Although other professional organizations provide resources, research, and professional development in distance learning these three organizations represent over 1000 different member institutions. Those institutions include public, private, two-year, and four-year colleges and universities. Distance education administrators can utilize those and other professional organizations for guidance in developing policies as well as monitoring changes in accreditation and regulatory compliance.

Notes

1 https://www.govinfo.gov/content/pkg/USCODE-2007-title20/html/USCODE-2007-title20-chap28.htm
2 A complete list of all accrediting agencies is available at the DOE website https://ope.ed.gov/dapip/#/agency-list
3 https://www.usg.edu/policymanual/section3/C338/#p3.3.3_distance_education
4 https://www.georgiaonmyline.org/
5 https://www.kansasregents.org/about/policies-by-laws-missions/board_policy_manual_2/chapter_iii_coordination_of_institutions_2/chapter_iii_full_text#performance
6 https://policies.kctcs.edu/administrative-policies/4-14.aspx
7 Information on that process can be found at https://www2.ed.gov/policy/highered/reg/hearulemaking/2018/index.html
8 https://nc-sara.org/
9 https://wcet.wiche.edu/
10 https://wcetsan.wiche.edu/
11 https://upcea.edu/
12 https://onlinelearningconsortium.org/

References

Council on Higher Education Accreditation Institute for Research and Study of Accreditation and Quality Assurance, Council for Higher Education Accreditation. (2002, December). *Specialized accreditation and assuring quality in distance learning.* CHEA Monograph Series, Number 2.

C.F.R. 668.43. (2019). Student assistance general provisions, the secretary's recognition of accrediting agencies, the secretary's recognition procedures for state agencies, 34 C.F.R 668.43 (2019). *Federal Register, 84*(212), Friday, November 1, 2019, Rules and Regulations.

Gearhart, D. (2001). Ethics in distance education: Developing ethical policies. *Online Journal of Distance Learning Administration, IV*(I).

Gellman-Danley, B., & Fetzner, M. J. (1998). Asking the really tough questions: Policy issues for distance learning. *Online Journal of Distance Learning Administration, I*(1).

Kansas Board of Regents. (2020, April). *Board policy manual, chapter III.* Kansas Board of Regents. https://www.kansasregents.org/about/policies-by-laws-missions/board_policy_manual_2

Kentucky Community & Technical College System. (2014). *Administrative policies: Policies and procedures relating to implementation of distance learning instructional support in academic affairs, student affairs, and business affairs.* Kentucky Community & Technical College System. https://policies.kctcs.edu/administrative-policies/4-14.aspx

Kovel-Jarboe, P. (1997). From the margin to the mainstream: State-level policy and planning for distance education. *New Directions for Community Colleges, 99.*

LoSchiavo, F. M., & Shatz, M. A. (2011). The impact of an honor code on cheating in online courses. *MERLOT Journal of Online Learning and Teaching, 7*(2).

Mannapperuma, M. (2015). Protecting students, protecting consumers: A new federal regulation of the for-profit distance learning industry. *Journal of Law & Policy, 23.* https://brooklynworks.brooklaw.edu/jlp/vol23/iss2/2

NWCCU Distance Education Policy. (2013). *Northwest Commission on Colleges and Universities.* https://www.nwccu.org/wp-content/uploads/2017/05/Distance-Education-Policy.pdf

Online Learning Consortium. (2019). *Regular and substantive interaction: Background, concerns, and guiding principles.* Online Learning Consortium, ERIC number: ED593878.

Pariost, A. H. (1997). Distance education as a catalyst for changing teaching in the community college: Implications for institutional policy. *New Directions for Community Colleges, 99.*

SACSCOC. (2018). *Distance and correspondence education, policy statement.* Southern Association of Colleges and Schools Commission on Colleges.

Simonson, M. (2015). Accreditation and quality in distance education. *Distance Learning, 12*(1), 27. Gale Academic OneFile. https://link-gale-com.er.lib.k-state.edu/apps/doc/A437133024/AONE?u=ksu&sid=AONE&xid=89c77ab3

U.S. Congressional Research Services. Accreditation and the Reauthorization of the Higher Education Act (RL32989; March 27, 2006).

U.S. Department of Education Office of Postsecondary Education. (2006). *Evidence of quality in distance education programs drawn from interviews with the accreditation community.* http://online.pasadena.edu/docs/Adminstration%20Page/Federal/Accreditation-Evidence-of-Quality-in-DE-Programs.pdf

Walcutt, J. J., & Schatz, S. (Eds.). (2019). *Modernizing learning: Building the future learning ecosystem.* Government Publishing Office.

CHAPTER 5

Theories and Frameworks for Online Education

Seeking an Integrated Model

Anthony G. Picciano

Abstract

In this chapter you will examine theoretical frameworks and models that focus on the pedagogical aspects of online education. After a review of learning theory as applied to online education, a proposal for an integrated Multimodal Model for Online Education is provided based on pedagogical purpose. The model attempts to integrate the work of several other major theorists and model builders such as Anderson (2011).

Keywords

online education – online learning – blended learning – learning theory – theoretical frameworks – model building – multimodal model

1   Introduction

In a provocative chapter of *The Theory and Practice of Online Learning*, Terry Anderson (2011) examines whether a common theory for online education can be developed. While recognizing that as a difficult, and perhaps fruitless, task, he nonetheless examines possibilities and proposes his own theory which he admits is not complete. The purpose of this article is to examine theoretical frameworks relevant to the pedagogical aspects of online education. It starts with a consideration of learning theories and funnels down to their specific application to online education. The article concludes with a proposal for an integrated model for online education based on pedagogical purpose.

2   Learning Theory

Learning theory is meant to explain and help us understand how people learn; however, the literature is complex and extensive enough to fill entire sections of a library. It involves multiple disciplines, including psychology, sociology, neuroscience, and of course, education. Three of the more popular learning theories – behaviorism, cognitivism, and social constructivism – will be highlighted to form the foundation for further discussion. Mention will also be made of several other learning theories that are relevant to online education. Before reviewing these theories, it will be worthwhile to have a brief discussion of the term *theory* itself.

Theory is defined as a set of statements, principles, or ideas that relate to a particular subject. A theory usually describes, explains, and/or predicts phenomena. The definition of theory also varies depending upon disciplines, especially when related to the term *model.* As noted by Graham, Henrie, and Gibbons (2013), the two terms are used interchangeably and generally refer to the same concept. However, a model is more frequently a visual representation of reality or a concept. In this discussion, the terms theory and model will be used interchangeably. The purpose of a theory or model is to propose the answers to basic questions associated with a phenomenon. Graham, Henrie and Gibbons (2013) reviewed this issue as related to instructional technology and recommended a three-part taxonomy first proposed by Gibbons and Bunderson (2005) that includes theories that:

- *Explore:* "What exists?" and attempts to define [describe] and categorize;
- *Explain:* "Why does this happen?" and looks for causality and correlation, and work with variables and relationships.
- *Design*: "How do I achieve this outcome?" and describes interventions for reaching targeted outcomes and operational principles (Graham, Henrie, & Gibbons, 2013, p. 13).

This taxonomy will serve as an overall guiding principle for the discussion of learning theories and models in this article.

3   Behaviorism

As its name implies, behaviorism focuses on how people behave. It evolved from a positivist worldview related to cause and effect. In simple terms, action produces reaction. In education, behaviorism examines how students behave while learning. More specifically, behaviorism focuses on observing how students respond to certain stimuli that, when repeated, can be evaluated, quantified, and eventually controlled for each individual. The emphasis in behaviorism is on that which is observable and not on the mind or cognitive processes. In sum, if you cannot observe it, it cannot be studied.

The development of behaviorism is frequently associated with Ivan Pavlov, famous for his experiments with dogs, food, and audible stimuli, such as a bell. In his experiments, dogs learned to associate food or feeding time with the sound of the bell and began to salivate. Pavlov conducted his experiments in the early 1900s and they were replicated by many other researchers throughout the 20th century. John B. Watson, among the first Americans to follow Pavlov's work, saw it as a branch of natural science. Watson became a major proponent of Pavlov and is generally credited with coining the term behaviorism. He argued that mind and consciousness are unimportant in the learning process and that everything can be studied in terms of stimulus and response.

Other major figures associated with behaviorism are B.F. Skinner and Edward Thorndike. Skinner is particularly well known, primarily because he introduced what he referred to as operant conditioning which emphasized the use of both positive and negative reinforcement to help individuals learn new behaviors. This was quite different from Pavlov, who relied on simple reflexive responses to specific stimuli although both Pavlov and Skinner promoted repetitive behavior that leads to habit formation. Skinner had a significant influence on early computer-assisted instructional (CAI) models as developed by Pat Suppes and others. A common aspect of early CAI programs was the reliance on encouragement and repetition to promote positive learning activities.

4   Cognitivism

Cognitivism has been considered a reaction to the "rigid" emphasis by behaviorists on predictive stimulus and response (Harasim, 2012, p. 58). Cognitive theorists promoted the concept that the mind has an important role in learning and sought to focus on what happens in between the occurrence of environmental stimulus and student response. They saw the cognitive processes of the mind, such as motivation and imagination, as critical elements of learning that bridge environmental stimuli and student responses. For example, Noam Chomsky (1959) wrote a critical review of Skinner's behaviorist work in which he raised the importance of creative mental processes that are not observable in the physical world. Although written mainly from the perspective of a linguist, Chomsky's view gained popularity in other fields, including psychology. Interdisciplinary in nature, cognitive science draws from psychology, biology, neuroscience, computer science, and philosophy to explain the workings of the brain as well as levels of cognitive development that form the foundation of learning and knowledge acquisition. As a result, cognitivism has evolved into one of the dominant learning theories. The future of cognitivism is particularly interesting as more advanced online software evolves into adaptive and personalized learning applications that seek to integrate artificial intelligence and learning analytics into instruction.

Behaviorism led to the development of taxonomies of learning because it emphasized the study and evaluation of multiple steps in the learning process. Behaviorists repeatedly studied learning activities to deconstruct and define the elements of learning. Benjamin Bloom (1956) was among the early psychologists to establish a taxonomy of learning that related to the development of intellectual skills and to stress the importance of problem solving as a higher order skill. Bloom's (1956) *Taxonomy of educational objectives handbook: Cognitive domains* remains a foundational text and essential reading within the educational community. Bloom's taxonomy is based on six key elements (see Figure 5.1) as follows:

- Creating: Putting elements together to form a coherent or functional whole, and reorganizing elements into a new pattern or structure through generating, planning, or producing.
- Evaluating: Making judgments based on criteria and standards through checking and critiquing.
- Analyzing: Breaking material into constituent parts, and determining how the parts relate to one another and to an overall structure or purpose through differentiating, organizing, and attributing.
- Applying: Carrying out or using a procedure through executing or implementing.
- Understanding: Constructing meaning from oral, written, and graphic messages through interpreting, exemplifying, classifying, summarizing, inferring, comparing, and explaining.

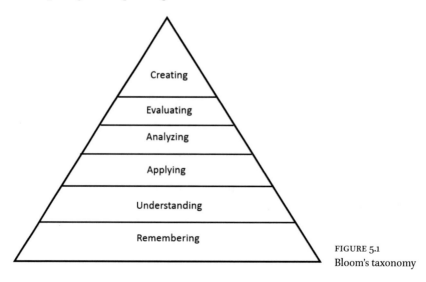

FIGURE 5.1
Bloom's taxonomy

– Remembering: Retrieving, recognizing, and recalling relevant knowledge from long-term memory.

Bloom, in developing his taxonomy, essentially helped to move learning theory toward issues of cognition and developmental psychology. Twenty years later, Robert Gagne, an educational psychologist, developed another taxonomy (events of instruction) that built on Bloom's and became the basis for cognitivist instructional design (Harasim, 2012). Gagne emphasized nine events in instruction that drive the definitions of objectives and strategies for the design of instructional material (see Figure 5.2).

1. **Gain attention:** Use media relevant to the topic.
2. **Describe the goal:** Provide clear objectives to the overall course goals.
3. **Stimulate prior knowledge:** Review previously presented material and concepts and connect them to the material to be addressed in the current module.
4. **Present the material to be learned:** Readings, presentations, demonstrations, multimedia, graphics, audio files, animations, etc.
5. **Provide guidance for learning:** Discussions to enable learners to actively reflect on new information in order to check their knowledge and understanding of content.
6. **Elicit performance:** Activity-based learning such as group research projects, discussion, homework, etc.
7. **Provide feedback:** Immediate, specific, and constructive feedback is provided to students.
8. **Assess performance:** Assessment activity such as a test, research project, essay, or presentation.
9. **Enhance retention and transfer:** Provide opportunities for additional guided practice or projects that might relate learning to other real-life activities.

FIGURE 5.2   Gagné's nine events of instruction

5   Social Constructivism

Parallel to behaviorism and cognitivism was the work of several education theorists, including Lev Vygotsky, John Dewey, and Jean Piaget. Their focus on social constructionism was to describe and explain teaching and learning as complex interactive social phenomena between teachers and students. Vygotsky posited that learning is problem solving and that the social construction of solutions to problems is the basis of the learning process. Vygotsky described the learning process as the establishment of a "zone of proximal development" in which the teacher, the learner, and a problem to be solved exist. The teacher provides a social environment in which the learner can assemble or construct with others the knowledge necessary to solve the problem. Likewise, John Dewey saw learning as a series of practical social experiences in which learners learn by doing, collaborating, and reflecting with others. While developed in the early part of the 20th century, Dewey's work is very much in evidence in a good deal of present-day social constructivist instructional design. The use of reflective practice by both learner and teacher is a pedagogical cornerstone for interactive discussions that replaces straight lecturing, whether in a face-to-face or online class. Jean Piaget, whose background was in psychology and biology, based his learning theory on four stages of cognitive development that begin at birth and continue through one's teen years and beyond. Seymour Papert, in designing the Logo programming language, drew from Jean Piaget the concept of creating social, interactive microworlds or communities where children, under the guidance of a teacher, solve problems while examining social issues, mathematical and science equations, or case studies. Papert's approach of integrating computer technology into problem solving is easily applied to many facets of instructional design.

6   Derivatives of the Major Learning Theories

A number of theories and models have roots in one or more of the above frameworks. In the latter part of the 20th century, the major learning theories, especially cognitive theory and social constructivism, began to overlap. For example, Wenger and Lave (1991) and Wenger (1998) promoted concepts such as "communities of practice" and situated learning. Their position was that learning involves a deepening process situated in, and derived from, participation in a learning community of practice. Their work is very evident in many studies, including those related to online education.

Information processing learning theory is a variation of cognitivism that views the human mind as a system that processes information according to a set of logical rules. In it, the mind is frequently compared to a computer that follows a set of rules or program. Research using this perspective attempts to describe and explain changes in the mental processes and strategies that lead to greater cognitive competence as children develop. Richard Atkinson and Richard Shiffrin (1968) are generally credited with proposing the first information processing model that deals with how students acquire, encode, store (in short-term or long-term memory), and retrieve information.

One of the more popular and controversial theories relates to learning styles and posits that individuals learn differently depending upon their propensities and personalities. Carl Jung argued that individual personality types influence various elements of human behavior, including learning. Jung's theory focuses on four basic psychological dimensions:

- Extroversion vs. Introversion
- Sensation vs. Intuition
- Thinking vs. Feeling
- Judging vs. Perceiving

While each unique dimension can influence an individual learning style, it is likely that learning styles are based on a combination of these dimensions. For example, a learning style might include elements of extroversion, sensation, feeling, and perception as personality dimensions. Readers may be familiar with the Myers-Briggs Type Inventory (MBTI) which has been used for decades to assist in determining personality types, including how personality relates to student learning. The MBTI is based extensively on Jung's theories and has been used to predict and develop different teaching methods and environments and to predict individual patterns of mental functioning, such as information processing, idea development, and judgment formation. It can also be used to foretell patterns of attitudes and interests that influence an individual's preferred learning environment and to predict a person's disposition to pursue certain learning circumstances and avoid others. Lin, Cranton, and Bridglall (2005) remind us that much of the work of Carl Jung and the MBTI is applicable to learning environments, whether face-to-face or online. For example, the extrovert may prefer active, highly collaborative environments while the introvert would prefer less interaction and less collaboration. This suggests that instruction should be designed to allow both types of individuals – the outgoing social organizer as well as the introspective reflective observer – to thrive.

Howard Gardner has developed a theory of "multiple intelligences" that proposes that intelligence is not merely a singular entity but consists of multiple entities used by individuals in different proportions to understand and to learn about the world. Gardner has identified nine basic intelligences: linguistic, logical/mathematical, spatial, musical, bodily kinesthetic, interpersonal, intrapersonal, naturalistic, and existential (see Figure 5.3).

Gardner's theory has received criticism from both psychologists and educators who view these "intelligences" as talents, personality traits, and abilities. His work has also been questioned by those who propose that there is, in fact, a root or base intelligence that drives the other "intelligences." Gardner does not necessarily disagree with this latter position but maintains that other intelligences can be viewed as main branches off the base root intelligence. This theory has important pedagogical implications and suggests the design of multiple learning modalities that allow learners to engage in ways they prefer, according to their interest or ability, and to challenge them to learn in other

1. **Verbal-linguistic intelligence:** well-developed verbal skills and sensitivity to the sounds, meanings, and rhythms of words
2. **Logical-mathematical intelligence:** ability to think conceptually and abstractly, and capacity to discern logical and numerical patterns
3. **Spatial-visual intelligence:** capacity to think in images and pictures, to visualize accurately and abstractly
4. **Bodily-kinesthetic intelligence:** ability to control one's body movements and to handle objects skillfully
5. **Musical intelligence:** ability to produce and appreciate rhythm, pitch, and timber
6. **Interpersonal intelligence:** capacity to detect and respond appropriately to the moods, motivations, and desires of others
7. **Intrapersonal intelligence:** capacity to be self-aware and in tune with inner feelings, values, beliefs, and thinking processes
8. **Naturalist intelligence:** ability to recognize and categorize plants, animals, and other objects in nature
9. **Existential intelligence:** sensitivity and capacity to tackle deep questions about human existence such as: What is the meaning of life? Why do we die? How did we get here?

FIGURE 5.3   Gardner's multiples intelligences (Source: Gardner, 1983)

ways that are less related to their preferences, interests, or abilities. Gardner's work also addresses the common concern that too much teaching and learning is linguistically based (reading, writing, and speaking) and that the other intelligences are underutilized.

Modern neuroscience research also suggests that students learn in different ways depending upon a number of factors including age, learning stimuli, and the pace of instruction. Willingham (2008) suggests that learning is a dynamic process that may evolve and change from one classroom to another, from one subject to another, and from one day to another. This research also supports the concept that multiple intelligences and mental abilities do not exist as mere "yes/no" entities but within continua which the mind blends in a manner consistent with the way it responds and learns from the external environment and instructional stimuli. Conceptually, this suggests a framework for a multimodal instructional design that relies on a variety of pedagogical techniques, delivery approaches, and media.

Lastly, Malcom Knowles (1998) deserves mention as the individual who distinguished between andragogy (adult learning) and pedagogy (child learning). Adults, whether seeking to enhance their professional skills or to satisfy curiosity about a subject, learn differently than children. Courses designed for adults should tap into their social contexts and experiences. Knowles' insights are especially important for higher education, where online technology is used extensively for adult students in traditional and continuing education programs, competency-based learning, and career/professional development.

In sum, a number of theories have been, and will continue to be, applied to instruction, including online and blended learning. Several theories specifically related to online education will now be examined.

7   Learning Theories for Online Education

Just as no single learning theory has emerged for instruction in general, the same is true for online education. A number of theories have evolved, most of which derive from the major learning theories discussed previously. In this section, several theories will be examined in terms of their appropriateness for the online environment.

7.1   *Community of Inquiry (CoI)*

The "community of inquiry" model for online learning environments developed by Garrison, Anderson, and Archer (2000) is based on the concept of three distinct "presences": cognitive, social, and teaching (see Figure 5.4). While recognizing the overlap and relationship among the three components, Anderson, Rourke, Garrison, and Archer (2001) advise further research on each component. Their model supports the design of online and blended courses as active learning environments or communities dependent on instructors and students sharing ideas, information, and opinions. Of particular note is that "presence" is a social phenomenon and manifests itself through interactions among students and instructors. The community of inquiry has become one of the more popular models for online and blended courses that are designed to be highly interactive among students and faculty using discussion boards, blogs, wikis, and videoconferencing.

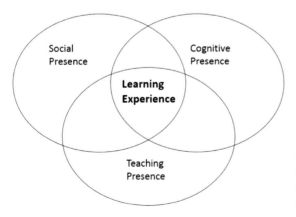

FIGURE 5.4
Community of inquiry (from Garrison, Anderson, Garrison, & Archer, 2000)

7.2   *Connectivism*

George Siemens (2004), one of the early MOOC pioneers, has been the main
proponent of connectivism, a learning model that acknowledges major shifts
in the way knowledge and information flows, grows, and changes because of
vast data communications networks. Internet technology has moved learning from internal, individualistic activities to group, community, and even
crowd activities. In developing the theory, Siemens acknowledged the work
of Alberto Barabasi and the power of networks. He also referenced an article
written by Karen Stephensen (1998) entitled "What Knowledge Tears Apart,
Networks Make Whole," which accurately identified how large-scale networks
become indispensable in helping people and organizations manage data and
information.
   Siemens describes connectivism as:

> the integration of principles explored by chaos, network, and complexity
> and self-organization theories [where] learning is a process that occurs
> within nebulous environments of shifting core elements – not entirely
> under the control of the individual. Learning (defined as actionable
> knowledge) can reside outside of ourselves (within an organization or a
> database), is focused on connecting specialized information sets, and the
> connections that enable us to learn more and are more important than
> our current state of knowing. (Siemens, 2004)

Siemens noted that connectivism as a theory is driven by the dynamic of
information flow. Students need to understand, and be provided with, experiences in navigating and recognizing oceans of constantly shifting and evolving
information. Siemens proposed eight principles of connectivism (see Figure
5.5). Connectivism is particularly appropriate for courses with very high enrollments and where the learning goal or objective is to develop and create knowledge rather than to disseminate it.

7.3   *Online Collaborative Learning (OCL)*

Online collaborative learning (OCL) is a theory proposed by Linda Harasim that
focuses on the facilities of the Internet to provide learning environments that
foster collaboration and knowledge building. Harasim (2012) describes OCL as:

> a new theory of learning that focuses on collaborative learning, knowl-
> edge building, and Internet use as a means to reshape formal, non-for-
> mal, and informal education for the Knowledge Age. (p. 81)

1. Learning and knowledge rests in diversity of opinions.
2. Learning is a process of connecting specialized nodes or information sources.
3. Learning may reside in non-human appliances.
4. Capacity to know more is more critical than what is currently known.
5. Nurturing and maintaining connections is needed to facilitate continual learning.
6. Ability to see connections between fields, ideas, and concepts is a core skill.
7. Currency (accurate, up-to-date knowledge) is the intent of all connectivist learning activities.
8. Decision making is itself a learning process. Choosing what to learn and the meaning of incoming information is seen through the lens of a shifting reality. While there is a right answer now, it may be wrong tomorrow due to alterations in the information climate affecting the decision.

FIGURE 5.5   Siemens' eight principles of connectivism

Like Siemens, Harasim sees the benefits of moving teaching and learning to the Internet and large-scale networked education. In some respects, Harasim utilizes Alberto Barabasi's position on the power of networks. In OCL, there exist three phases of knowledge construction through discourse in a group:

1. Idea generating: the brainstorming phase, where divergent thoughts are gathered
2. Idea organizing: the phase where ideas are compared, analyzed, and categorized through discussion and argument
3. Intellectual convergence: the phase where intellectual synthesis and consensus occurs, including agreeing to disagree, usually through an assignment, essay, or other joint piece of work (Harasim, 2012, p. 82).

OCL also derives from social constructivism, since students are encouraged to collaboratively solve problems through discourse and where the teacher plays the role of facilitator as well as learning community member. This is a major aspect of OCL but also of other constructivist theories where the teacher is not necessarily separate and apart but rather, an active facilitator of, knowledge building. Because of the importance of the role of the teacher, OCL is not easy to scale up. Unlike connectivism, which is suited for large-scale instruction, OCL is best situated in smaller instructional environments. This last issue becomes increasingly important when seeking commonality among online education theories.

Many other theories can be associated with online education but, rather than present more theories and in keeping with one of the major purposes of this article, it is appropriate to ask whether an integrated or unified theory of online education is possible.

8   Can We Build a Common Integrated Theory of Online Education?

As noted, Terry Anderson (2011) examined the possibility of building a theory of online education, starting with the assumption that it would be a difficult, and perhaps impossible, task. He approached this undertaking from a distance education perspective, having spent much of his career at Athabasca University, the major higher education distance education provider in Canada. While he acknowledged that many theorists and practitioners consider online learning as "a subset of learning in general" (Anderson, 2011, pp. 46–47), he also stated:

> online learning as a subset of distance education has always been concerned with provision of access to educational experience that is, at least more flexible in time and in space as campus-based education. (Anderson, 2011, p. 53)

These two perspectives (subset of learning in general and subset of distance education) complicate any attempt to build a common theory of online education. Blended learning models, for instance, do not easily fit into the distance education schema, even though they are evolving as a prevalent component of traditional face-to-face and online education environments.

Anderson considered a number of theories and models but focused on the well-respected work of Bransford, Brown, and Cocking (1999) who posited that effective learning environments are framed within the convergence of four overlapping lenses: community-centeredness, knowledge-centeredness, learner-centeredness, and assessment centeredness. These lenses provided the foundational framework for Anderson's approach to building an online education theory, as he examined in detail the characteristics and facilities that the Internet provides with regards to each of the four lenses. Second, he noted that the Internet had evolved from a text-based environment to one in which all forms of media are supported and readily available. He also accurately commented that the Internet's hyperlink capacity is most compatible with the way human knowledge is stored and accessed. In this regard, he referred to the work of Jonassen (1992) and Shank (1993) who associated hyperlinking with constructivism. Finally, Anderson extensively examined the importance of interaction in all forms of learning and referred to a number of mostly distance education theorists such as Holmberg (1989), Moore (1989), Moore and Kearsley (1996), and Garrison and Shale (1990). The essence of interaction among students, teachers, and content is well understood and is referenced in many theories of education, especially constructivism. Anderson's evaluation of interaction concludes that interactions are critical components of a theory.

With these three elements in mind (the Bransford, Brown, and Cocking lenses, the affordances and facilities of the Internet, and interaction), Anderson then proceeded to construct a model (see Figure 5.6). He did add one important element by distinguishing community/collaborative models from self-paced instructional models, commenting that community/collaborative models and self-paced instructional models are inherently incompatible. The community/collaborative models do not scale up easily because of the extensive interactions among teachers and students. On the other hand, the self-paced instructional models are designed for independent learning with much less interaction among students and teachers.

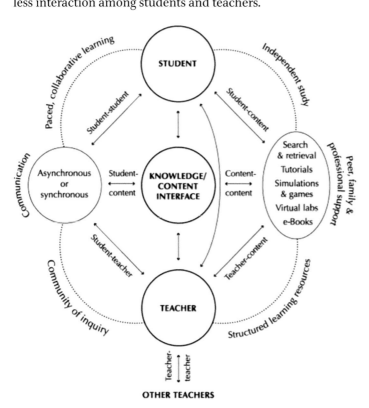

FIGURE 5.6   Anderson's online learning model (reprinted with permission from Anderson, 2011)

Figure 5.6 illustrates

the two major human actors, learners and teachers, and their interactions with each other and with content. Learners can of course interact directly with content that they find in multiple formats, and especially on the Web; however, many choose to have their learning sequenced, directed, and evaluated with the assistance of a teacher. This interaction can take place within a community of inquiry, using a variety of Net-based synchronous and asynchronous activities ... These environments are particularly rich, and allow for the learning of social skills, the collaborative learning of content, and the development of personal relationships among participants. However, the community binds learners in time, forcing regular sessions or at least group-paced learning. The second model of learning (on the right) illustrates the structured learning tools associated with independent learning. Common tools used in this mode include computer-assisted tutorials, drills, and simulations. (Anderson, 2011, pp. 61–62)

Figure 5.6 demonstrates the instructional flow within the two sides and represents the beginnings of a theory or model from the distance education perspective. Anderson concluded that his model "will help us to deepen our understanding of this complex educational context" (Anderson, 2011, p. 68), which he noted needs to measure more fully the direction and magnitude of each input variable on relevant outcome variables.

Anderson also commented about the potential of the Internet for education delivery, and that an online learning-based theory or model could subsume all other modes with the exception of the "rich face-to-face interaction in formal classrooms" (Anderson, 2011, p. 67). This becomes a quandary for Anderson in trying to develop a common theory of online education in that it does not provide for in-person, face-to-face activity and is problematic for those who see online education as a subset of education in general.

9   An Integrated Model

Anderson's model assumed that none of the instruction is delivered in traditional, face-to-face mode, and so excluded blended learning models that have some face-to-face component. Is it possible, therefore, to approach the search for an integrated model for online education from the face-to-face education in general or even the blended learning perspective?

Bosch (2016), in a review of instructional technology, identified and compared four blended learning models using twenty-one different design components. These models emphasized, to one degree or another, the integration of pedagogy and technology in course design. Among the models was a Blending with Pedagogical Purpose Model (see Figure 5.7), developed by this author, in which pedagogical objectives and activities drive the approaches, including the online technology that faculty members use in instruction. The model also suggests that blending the objectives, activities, and approaches within multiple

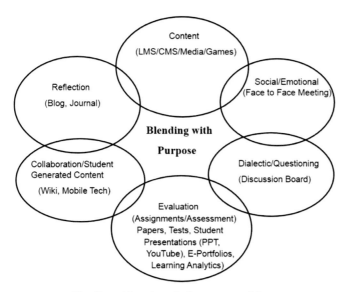

FIGURE 5.7   Blending with pedagogical purpose model

modalities might be most effective for, and appeal to, a wide range of students. The model contains six basic pedagogical goals, and approaches for achieving them, to form learning modules. The model is flexible and assumes that other modules can be added as needed and where appropriate. The most important feature of this model is that pedagogy drives the approaches that will work best to support student learning. The modules are also shown as intersecting but this is optional; they may or may not intersect or overlap depending upon the approaches used. For instance, some reflection can be incorporated into collaboration or not, depending upon how the collaborative activity is designed. It might be beneficial to have the collaborative groups reflect specifically on their activities. Similar scenarios are possible for the other modules. Ultimately important is that all the modules used blend together into a coherent whole. The following paragraphs briefly review each of these modules.

Content is one of the primary drivers of instruction and there are many ways in which content can be delivered and presented. While much of what is taught is delivered linguistically (teacher speaks/students listen or teacher writes/students write), this does not have to be the case, either in face-to-face or online environments. Mayer (2009) has done extensive reviews of the research and has concluded that learning is greatly enhanced by visualization. Certain subject areas, such as science, are highly dependent upon the use of visual simulations to demonstrate processes and systems. The humanities, especially art, history, and literature, can be greatly enhanced by rich digital images as well. Course/learning management systems (CMS/LMS) such as

Blackboard, Canvas, or *Moodle* provide basic content delivery mechanisms for blended learning and easily handle the delivery of a variety of media including text, video, and audio. Games have also evolved and now play a larger role in instructional content. In providing and presenting content, the Blending with Pedagogical Purpose model suggests that multiple technologies and media be utilized.

The Blending with Pedagogical Purpose model posits that instruction is not simply about learning content or a skill but also supports students *socially and emotionally.* As noted, constructivists view teaching and learning as inherently social activities. The physical presence of a teacher or tutor, in addition to providing instruction, is comforting and familiar. While perhaps more traditionally recognized as critical for K-12 students, social and emotional development must be acknowledged as important to education at all levels. Faculty members who have taught graduate courses know that students, even at this advanced level, frequently need someone with whom to speak, whether to help understand a complex concept or to provide advice about career and professional opportunities. While fully online courses and programs have evolved to the point where faculty members can provide some social and emotional support where possible and appropriate, in blended courses and programs this is more frequently provided in a face-to-face mode.

Dialectics or questioning is an important activity that allows faculty members to probe what students know and to help refine their knowledge. The Socratic Method remains one of the major techniques used in instruction, and many successful teachers are proud of their ability to stimulate discussion by asking the "right" questions to help students think critically about a topic or issue. In many cases, these questions serve to refine and narrow a discussion to very specific "points" or aspects of the topic at hand, and are not meant to be open-ended activities. For dialectic and questioning activities, a simple-to-use, threaded electronic discussion board or forum such as VoiceThread is an effective approach. A well-organized discussion board activity generally seeks to present a topic or issue and have students respond to questions and provide their own perspectives, while evaluating and responding to the opinions of others. The simple, direct visual of the "thread" also allows students to see how the entire discussion or lesson has evolved. In sum, for instructors who want to focus attention and dialogue on a specific topic, the main activity for many online courses has been, and continues to be, the electronic discussion board.

Reflection can be incorporated as a powerful pedagogical strategy under the right circumstances. There is an extensive body of scholarship on the "reflective teacher" and the "reflective learner" dating from the early 20th century (Dewey (1916), Schon (1983)). While reflection can be a deeply personal activity, the ability to share one's reflections with others can be beneficial. Pedagogical activities that require students to reflect on what they learn and to share their reflections with their teachers and fellow students extend and enrich reflection. Blogs and blogging, whether as group exercises or for individual journaling activities, have evolved into appropriate tools for student reflection and other aspects of course activities.

Collaborative learning has evolved over decades. In face-to-face classes, group work grew in popularity and became commonplace in many course activities. Many professional programs, such as business administration, education, health science, and social work, rely heavily on collaborative learning as a technique for group problem solving. In the past, the logistics and time needed for effective collaboration in face-to-face classes were sometimes problematic. Now, email, mobile technology, and other forms of electronic communication alleviate some of these logistical issues. Wikis, especially, have grown in popularity and are becoming a staple in group projects and writing assignments. They are seen as important vehicles for creating knowledge and content, as well as for generating peer-review and evaluation (Fredericksen, 2015). Unlike face-to-face group work that typically ended up on the instructor's desk when delivered in paper form, wikis allow students to generate content that can be shared with others during and beyond the end of a semester. Papers and projects developed through wikis can pass seamlessly from one group to another and from one class to another.

Evaluation of learning is perhaps the most important component of the model. CMSs/LMSs and other online tools and platforms provide a number of mechanisms to assist in this area. Papers, tests, assignments, and portfolios are among the major methods used for student learning assessment, and are easily done electronically. Essays and term projects pass back and forth between teacher and student without the need for paper. Oral classroom presentations are giving way to YouTube videos and podcasts. The portfolio is evolving into an electronic multimedia presentation of images, video, and audio that goes far beyond the three-inch, paper-filled binder. Weekly class discussions on discussion boards or blogs provide the instructor with an electronic record that can be reviewed over and over again to examine how students have participated and progressed over time. They are also most helpful to instructors to assess their own teaching and to review what worked and what did not work in a class. Increasingly, learning analytics are seen as the mechanisms for mining this trove of data to improve learning and teaching. In sum, online technology allows for a more seamless sharing of evaluation and assessment activities, and provides a permanent, accessible record for students and teachers.

The six components of the model described above form an integrated community of learning in which rich interaction, whether online or face-to-face, can be provided and blended across all modules. Furthermore, not every course must incorporate all of the activities and approaches of the model. The pedagogical objectives of a course should drive the activities and, hence, the approaches. For example, not every course needs to require collaborative learning or dialectic questioning. In addition to individual courses, faculty and instructional designers might consider examining an entire academic program to determine which components of the model best fit with overall programmatic goals and objectives. Here, the concept of learning extends beyond the course to the larger academic program where activities might integrate across courses. For example, some MBA programs enroll a cohort of students into three courses in the same semester but require that one or more assignments or projects be common to all three courses.

The critical question for our discussion, however, is whether this Blending with Pedagogical Purpose model can be modified or enlarged to be considered a model for online education in general. By incorporating several of the components from other theories and models discussed earlier in this article, this is a possibility. Figure 5.8 presents a Multimodal Model for Online Education that expands on the Blending with Purpose approach and adds several new components from Anderson and others, namely, community, interaction, and self-paced, independent instruction.

First, the concept of a learning community as promoted by Garrison, Anderson, and Archer (2000) and Wenger and Lave (1991) is emphasized. A course

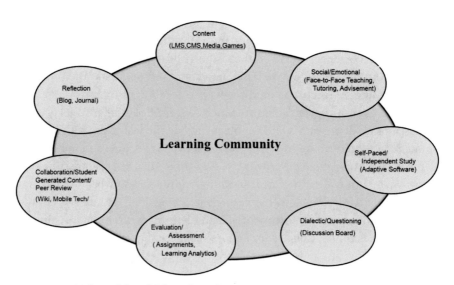

FIGURE 5.8   Multimodal model for online education

is conceived of as a learning community. This community can be extended to a larger academic program. Second, it is understood that interaction is a basic characteristic of the community and permeates the model to the extent needed. Third, and perhaps the most important revision, is the addition of the self-study/independent learning module that Anderson emphasized as incompatible with any of the community-based models. In this model, self-study/independent learning can be integrated with other modules as needed or as the primary mode of instructional delivery. Adaptive learning software, an increasingly popular form of self-study, can stand alone or be integrated into other components of the model. The latter is commonly done at the secondary school level where adaptive software programs are used primarily in stand-alone mode with teachers available to act as tutors when needed. Adaptive software is also integrated into traditional, face-to-face classes, such as science, where it is possible to have the instructor assign a lab activity that uses adaptive learning simulation software.

This Multimodal Model of Online Education attempts to address the issues that others, particularly Terry Anderson, have raised regarding elements that might be needed for an integrated or unified theory or model for online education. Whether or not this model finds acceptance is not yet clear. It is hoped that this article might serve as a vehicle for a critical examination of the model.

10   Applying the Integrated Model

To provide a clearer understanding of the integrated model, several examples of its application follow. Figure 5.9 provides an example of the model as a representation of a self-paced, fully online course. The three major components [in green] for this course are: content as provided on an LMS/CMS, a self-paced study module, and assessment/evaluation. Other components of the model, such as a blog or discussion board to allow interaction among students, could be included but are not necessarily needed. This example is most appropriate for online programs that have rolling admissions and students are not limited by a semester schedule. Students proceed at their own pace to complete the course as is typical in some distance education programs. This example is scalable and can be used for large numbers of students.

Figure 5.10 provides an example of another course that is primarily a self-paced, online course similar to that described in Figure 5.9 but is designed to have a teacher or tutor available as needed. A discussion board is also included to allow for ongoing interaction among students and teacher. This course would follow a semester schedule and would have a standard class size although most of the instruction would be provided by the self-paced study

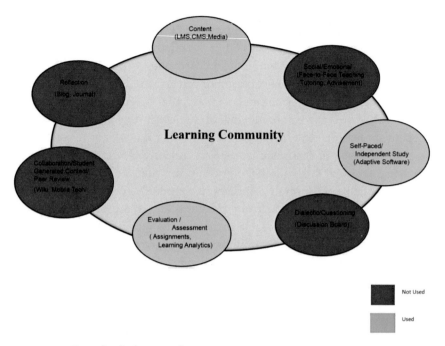

FIGURE 5.9   Example of a distance education course

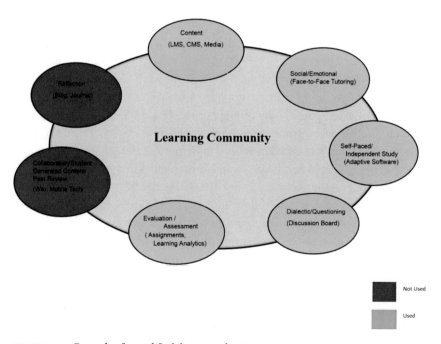

FIGURE 5.10   Example of a modified distance education course

module. A standard course organization would be used, with a teacher or tutor assigned to guide and assist with instruction. The teacher or tutor could help students struggling with any of the self-paced material. This type of course is increasingly common in secondary schools, such as in credit-recovery courses.

Figure 5.11 provides an example of a teacher-led, fully online course. Presentation of the course content is provided by a LMS or CMS along with other media and is used as needed by the teacher. The discussion board, blog, and wiki provide facilities for interaction among teachers and students, students and students, and students and content. In this course, the teacher could direct students to watch a fifteen-minute lecture available in the LMS database and then ask students to respond to a series of questions on the discussion board. Student responses can then be used as the basis for an interactive discussion board activity among students, guided by the teacher. The model also provides for reflection and collaborative activities.

Figure 5.12 provides an example of a blended course with instruction provided primarily by a teacher. The other modules are used to extend and enrich instruction. The teacher is the major guide for instruction and would be supplemented by content as needed by a LMS/CMS. The course would meet in a face-to-face classroom although some instructional activity would also be

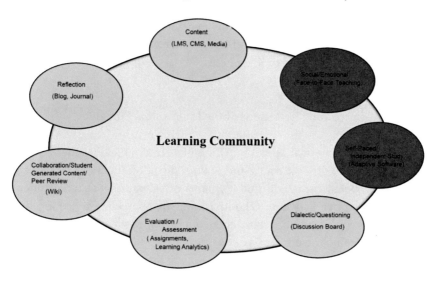

FIGURE 5.11   Example of a teacher-led fully online course

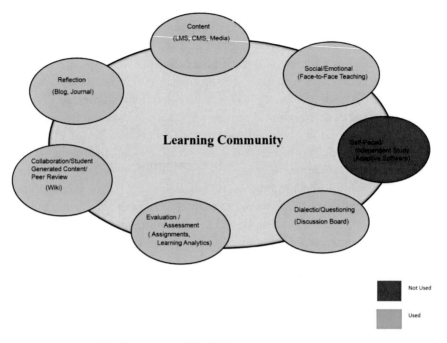

FIGURE 5.12   Example of a mainstream blended course

conducted online, either on a discussion board, a blog, or a collaborative wiki. The teacher would establish beforehand portions of the course that would meet in the face-to-face and online modes.

11   Attributes and Limitations of the Multimodal Model

The proposed Multimodal Model for Online Education includes many of the major attributes of other learning and online education theories and models. For example, behaviorists will find elements of self-study and independent learning in adaptive software. Cognitivists might appreciate reflection and dialectic questioning as important elements of the model. Social constructivists will welcome the emphasis on community and interaction throughout the model. Connectivists might value the collaboration and the possibility of student-generated content. Perhaps the most significant element of the model is its flexibility and ability to expand as new learning approaches, perhaps spurred by advances in technology, evolve.

The model is not without limitations. Learning theories can be approached through a number of perspectives and disciplines. Behavioral psychologists, cognitive psychologists, sociologists, and teacher educators might emphasize the need for deeper considerations of their perspectives for an online learning theory. The multimodal model here represents an integrated composite of several such perspectives but is essentially a pedagogical model and, therefore, may have greater appeal to instructional designers, faculty, and others who focus on learning objectives.

12   Conclusion

In this article, a number of major theories related to technology were presented, beginning with a review of major theories associated with learning. One critical question concerned whether an integrated or unified theory of online education could be developed. The work of Terry Anderson was highlighted. The article proposed an integrated model that described the phenomenon of pedagogically driven online education. Key to this model is the assumption that online education has evolved as a subset of learning in general rather than a subset of distance learning. As blended learning, which combines face-to-face and online instruction, evolves into the dominant form of instruction throughout all levels of education, it serves as the basis for an integrated model. It is likely that, in the not-too-distant future, all courses and programs will have some online learning components, as suggested in this integrated model.

– This chapter does not address change theory, an important, practical theory for any leader of Distance Learning. Go online to explore how to facilitate change. Identify at least three strategies that you would apply as a distance learning leader.
– Given Siemen's eight Principles of Connectivism and Harasim's three phases of Online Collaborative Learning, describe an activity incorporating these ideas through which you could lead faculty members toward using the Internet constructively in their learning.
– Using Picciano's Multimodel Model for Online Education, analyze one or more courses that you have taken or that you have taught by identifying the components that apply to that course or courses.

Acknowledgment

This chapter was previously published and is used here with permission from the author and publisher: Picciano, A. G. (2017). Theories and frameworks for online education: Seeking an integrated model. *Online Learning, 21*(3), 166–190. doi: 10.24059/olj.v21i3.1225

References

Anderson, T. (2011). *The theory and practice of online learning* (2nd ed.). AU Press.

Anderson, T., Rourke, L., Garrison, D. R., & Archer, W. (2001). Assessing social presence in asynchronous text-based computer conferencing. *Journal of Asynchronous Learning Networks, 5*(2). http://immagic.com/eLibrary/ARCHIVES/GENERAL/ATHAB_CA/Anderson.pdf

Atkinson, R. C., & Shiffrin, R. M. (1968). Human memory: A proposed system and its control processes. In K. W. Spence & J. T. Spence (Eds.), *The psychology of learning and motivation* (Vol. 2, pp. 89–195). Academic Press.

Barabasi, A. L. (2002). *Linked: The new science of networks*. Perseus Publishing.

Bloom, B. S. (1956). *Taxonomy of educational objectives handbook: Cognitive domains.* David McKay.

Bosch, C. (2016). *Promoting self-directed learning through the implementation of cooperative learning in a higher education blended learning environment* [Doctoral dissertation]. North-West University, Johannesburg, SA.

Bransford, J., Brown, A., & Cocking, R. (1999). *How people learn: Brain, mind experience and school.* National Academy Press/National Research Council.
    http://www.colorado.edu/MCDB/LearningBiology/readings/How-people-learn.pdf

Chomsky, N. (1959). A review of B. F. Skinner's verbal behavior. *Language, 35*(1), 26–58.

Dewey, J. (1916). *Democracy and education.* The Free Press.

Fredericksen, E. (2015, February 4). Is online education good or bad? And is this really the right question? *The Conversation.* https://theconversation.com/is-online-education-good-or-bad-and-is-this-really-the-right-question-35949

Gagné, R. M. (1977). *The conditions of learning.* Holt, Rinehart & Winston.

Gardner, H. (1983). *Frames of mind: The theory of multiple intelligences.* Basic Books.

Garrison, D. R., Anderson, T., & Archer, W. (2000). Critical inquiry in a text-based environment: Computer conferencing in higher education model. *The Internet and Higher Education, 2*(2–3), 87–105.

Garrison, D. R., & Shale, D. (1990). *Education at a distance: From issues to practice.* Robert E. Krieger.

Gibbons, A. S., & Bunderson, C. V. (2005). Explore, explain, design. In K. K. Leondard (Ed.), *Encyclopedia of social measurement* (pp. 927–938). Elsevier.

Graham, C. R., Henrie, C. R., & Gibbons, A. S. (2013). Developing models and theory for blended learning research. In A. G. Picciano, C. D. Dziuban, & C. R. Graham (Eds.), *Blended learning: Research perspectives* (Vol. 2). Routledge.

Harasim, L. (2012). *Learning theory and online technologies.* Routledge/Taylor & Francis.

Holmberg, B. (1989). *Theory and practice of distance education.* Routledge.

Jonassen, D. (1992). Designing hypertext for learning. In E. Scanlon & T. O'Shea (Eds.), *New directions in educational technology* (pp. 123–130). Springer-Verlag.

Jung, C. (1921). *Psychological types*. Rascher Verlag. [in German]

Knowles, M. S., Holton, E. F., & Swanson, R. A. (1998). *The adult learner* (5th ed.). Butterworth-Heinemann Publishers.

Lin, L., Cranton, P., & Bridglall, B. (2005). Psychological type and asynchronous written dialogue in adult learning. *Teachers College Record, 107*(8), 1788–1813.

Mayer, R. E. (2009). *Multimedia learning* (2nd ed.). Cambridge University Press.

McLuhan, M. (1964). *Understanding media*. Routledge.

Moore, M. (1989). Three types of interaction. *American Journal of Distance Education, 3*(2), 1–6.

Moore, M., & Kearsley, G. (1996). *Distance education: A systems view*. Wadsworth Publishing Company.

Picciano, A. G. (2009). Blending with purpose: The multimodal model. *Journal of Asynchronous Learning Networks, 13*(1), 7–18.

Schon, D. (1983). *Reflective practitioner: How professionals think in action*. Basic Books.

Shank, G. (1993). Abductive multiloguing: The semiotic dynamics of navigating the Net. *The Arachnet Electronic Journal of Virtual Culture, 1*(1).
http://serials.infomotions.com/aejvc/aejvc-v1n01-shank-abductive.txt

Siemens, G. (2004). *Connectivism: A learning theory for the digital age*.
http://www.elearnspace.org/Articles/connectivism.htm

Stephenson, K. (1998). *What knowledge tears apart, networks make whole*. Internal communication, No. 36. http://www.netform.com/html/icf.pdf

Wenger, E. (1998). *Communities of practice: Learning, meaning, and identity*. Cambridge University Press.

Wenger, E., & Lave, J. (1991). *Situated learning: Legitimate peripheral participation (Learning in doing: Social, cognitive and computational perspectives)*. Cambridge University Press.

Willingham, D. (2008). What is developmentally appropriate? *American Educator, 32*(2), 34–39.

CHAPTER 6

Analyzing Your Context to Administer and Improve Distance Learning

Atsusi "2c" Hirumi, Meredith Ratliff and Efrén de la Mora Velasco

Abstract

At the conclusion of this chapter, you will be able to better administer online courses and distance learning (DL) programs by:
– Viewing DL as a system to analyze key components and align vital DL functions;
– Distinguishing five levels of organizational effort to analyze gaps and achieve desired results;
– Analyzing evolving needs of faculty to facilitate improvement and innovation.

Keywords

systemic change – distance learning – distance learning systems – systems approach – needs assessment tools and techniques – innovation – competency-based education – big data analysis – artificial intelligence

1 Introduction

Every institution differs in terms of its human, physical, and capital resources, and how those resources are used. To effectively administer a DL program requires the ability to analyze its unique context. Assuming that institutions will offer an array of learning opportunities, it is also imperative to understand the differing needs of key system stakeholders, and how the resources used to facilitate DL are administered relative to the larger educational system. In addition, how one delimits the context and determines the relevancy of contextual factors depends in part on the individual. Relevance, in each case, is contingent on the experience of both the authors and readers, as demonstrated by the chapters in this book.

For this chapter, we define the relevant contextual factors as: (a) the functional components of a DL system; (b) the products, outputs, and outcomes of the DL system; and (c) the immediate, intermediate, and long-term needs of DL faculty. Accordingly, we've divided the chapter into three major sections to help you achieve the chapter objectives, including:

– Section 2: Analyzing Essential DL System Functions to Ensure Alignment;
– Section 3: Analyzing Organizational Efforts to Achieve Desired Results; and
– Section 4: Analyzing Evolving Faculty Needs to Improve and Innovate DL.

To gain further insights into key topics, we also integrated references to other related chapters in this book, and posed questions and self-assessments to encourage reflection and transfer.

2 Analyzing Essential DL System Components to Align Functions

Education is filled with examples of well-meaning interventions that have failed to reach their potential. The introduction of computers in education in the 1980s and 1990s is a classic example. When personal computers became affordable, we put thousands of them into classrooms and in computer labs across the country. The addition of computers in education has not reached its potential and education remains basically the same since the industrial revolution. Why? We continue to fail to view education as a system, a set of interrelated components that must be aligned to sustain change and facilitate student learning.

The concept of homeostasis, the tendency toward a stable equilibrium between interdependent elements, explains why education continues to mimic industrial age models of teaching and learning. We continue efforts to innovate education without aligning related system components, so once funding and interest in the innovation wanes, so does the change, and the system returns to its stable state. To make significant and lasting improvements, we must align system components and establish the infrastructure necessary to facilitate DL.

2.1 Form vs. Function

To establish new or improve existing DL programs, it's important to first view key components from a functional, rather than a structural perspective. A structural view delineates how an institution is organized by departments, jobs, and roles as typically illustrated by an organizational chart. Structural analysis of a system that centers on form versus function may limit vision, and inhibit substantive improvements. For example, if you view a car as having four wheels, a steering wheel and an engine, you may be able to envision a car with exotic parts, but it will still have four wheels, a steering wheel and an engine. If you begin by defining components from a functional perceptive, you may formulate new ways to achieve its purpose (e.g., transport 1–6 people over various terrain to specific destinations in a safe and comfortable manner); then you can restructure the organization, and align human, capital, and physical resources necessary to facilitate each function.

2.2   *Systems Approach*

Application of a systems approach to education is not new. Experts from varied disciplines made system concepts popular during the 1960s and 1970s. Alternative system models include, but are not limited to those posited by Moore and Kearsley (1996), Reigeluth and Garfinkle (1994), Banathy (1991), and Senge (1990) among others. While each model differs based on context and each author's interpretation of systems theory, there is one fundamental concept that is common across approaches: a system is a set of interrelated components that work together to achieve a common purpose. Figure 6.1 depicts ten interrelated functional components of a DL system, followed by a description of key factors to analyze when administering each function.

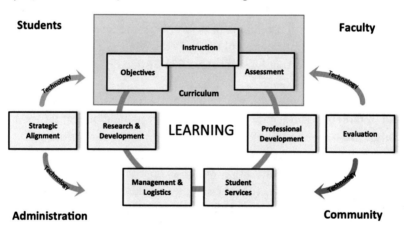

FIGURE 6.1   Functional system components and stakeholders

2.2.1   Strategic Alignment

The functions of strategic alignment are to (a) define the mission of the DL system, and the goals and objectives of vital DL system components; (b) ensure the DL mission, goals, and objectives are consistent with the values, beliefs, and attitudes of key system stakeholders; and (c) ensure alignment of the DL mission with the vision of the larger institutional (supra)system as depicted in Figure 6.2. Key system stakeholders provide input to generate strategic and tactical plans. The outputs of strategic alignment, in turn, should be used by management to formulate budgets.

Analyzing Key Factors. Figure 6.2 illustrates the relationships among vision, mission, goals, and objectives statements. We agree with Kaufman and Stakenas' (1981) proposition that we must create a common vision of an ideal society in order to achieve it. The mission should then describe the DL system's unique contribution to the vision. Each component of the system will then have its own goals and objectives that facilitate the achievement of the mission. A careful linkage between the vision, mission, goals, and objectives is crucial to success (Kaufman, 2006b).

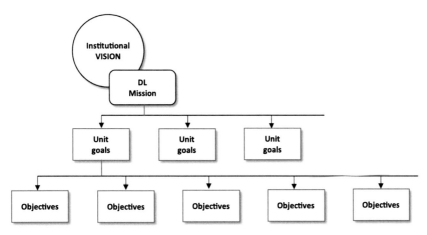

FIGURE 6.2   Alignment of system-wide vision and mission statements, and departmental (unit) goals, and objective

In addition to forming and aligning the vision, mission, goals and objectives of DL, the shared values, beliefs and attitudes (also referred to together as dispositions) of key system stakeholders' must be aligned to facilitate relevant behaviors as depicted in Figure 6.3.

The alignment of DL values, beliefs, and attitudes with the mission, goals, and objectives of DL demonstrates best practice in strategic alignment. Strategic plans are made to direct behavior, and organizational culture (the shared values and beliefs of the community) mediates such behavior. Thus, to achieve the mission, goals, and objectives of DL, it's essential for stakeholders to have a positive disposition toward implementing strategic and tactical plans.

JetBlue and Disney offer two examples of "best practice" in strategic alignment. It's exciting to hear the vast majority of JetBlue employees talk about

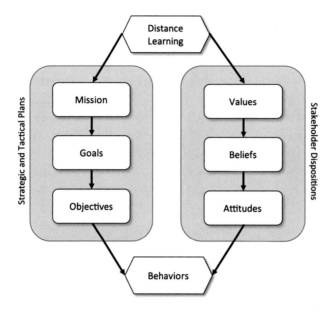

FIGURE 6.3
Alignment between
strategic planning and
institutional culture

the "Blue Juice," and it is even more impressive to see how much effort they put into using their core values to determine the direction of the company; from the most senior level down, they are one crew (Humphries, 2017). Disney uses Walt Disney's concept of creating magic to facilitate strategic alignment: Employees are cast members who are all invested in their role to create a magical experience for visitors. The entire theme park is a stage where the audience, the guests, experience the magic (Mapes, 2017). Both JetBlue and Disney emphasize all employees being a team, crew, and cast respectively, that work together to foster a quality experience for their customers. From the unique language used throughout the company to their community outreach programs, their image is well defined and unified; the customer experience is seamless and optimized by strategic alignment.

Similarly, DL needs to be a unified and integral part of your educational system. Integration requires top down and bottom up planning and implementation where administration, faculty, and student services all "buy in" to the same vision (Barak, 2012). With increased competition and demands to increase profits, retention, and diversity, branding strategies not only affect the perceptions of all stakeholders but also help recruit students in a global market and contribute to their identification with the institution (Hemsley-Brown, Melewar, Nguyen, & Wilson, 2016).

Related Book Chapters. Chapter 2 on Leadership provides further insights into strategic alignment, along with additional factors to consider when defining and aligning the vision, mission, goals and objectives of a DL system.

Reflections and self-assessments
- Have you or others in your institution aligned the vision, mission, and goals for DL?
- Do you know your faculty, staff, administration, and students' dispositions toward DL? Are they consistent with the vision, mission, and goals of DL?
- What (sub)system do you have for gathering data on key stakeholder dispositions, the achievement of strategic DL goals and objectives, and the use of these data to improve DL?

2.2.2 Research and Development

In comparison with successful industries, education invests relatively few resources for producing future improvements (Bowsher, 1989). There are certainly exceptions, particularly in higher education where millions are spent on research and development (R&D), but even those resources are relatively limited for innovating DL compared to other fields of study. The functions of R&D are to (a) acquire new knowledge related to teaching and learning, and the use of emerging DL technologies; (b) assure that this new knowledge is made readily accessible to relevant stakeholders; and (c) disseminate new knowledge generated by stakeholders to others both internal and external to the system.

Analyzing Key Factors. Information about DL and emerging technology serves as the primary inputs for R&D. Active R&D must stay abreast of advances in related fields and help stakeholders determine which advances can improve the curriculum as well as other system components to reduce cost and optimize learning. The primary function of R&D is to ensure that the DL system remains up-to-date, and that knowledge gained by stakeholders is made available to others external to the system to benefit the community and related professions.

Information about teaching, learning, and the use of technology generated by those within the system serve as primary outputs of R&D. The accessibility of such research remains as a fundamental issue for distance educators. However, the pressure to "publish or perish" creates a divide between educators and researchers. Researchers need to publish to be hired, retained, and promoted, but due to pressure for their publications to have impact, their work is largely published in academic journals with expensive subscriptions. Many are reluctant to publish in open access journals as they perceive them to be lower quality and lacking in peer review (Moksness & Olsen, 2017). Some funders and high-level publishers are encouraging the sharing of raw data sets (Piwowar & Chapman, 2010), but much of the information is still not readily usable by educators.

Technology is also rapidly changing the field of DL. R&D needs to be accessible for educators to stay abreast of such changes. Institutions may remedy these issues by: (a) incentivizing published research in high quality, open access journals (Rowley et al., 2017); and (b) fostering communities of practice between researchers and educators in which problems, solutions and data are readily and directly shared (Marques, Loureiro, & Marques, 2016). Both methods would require active participation by institutions to foster relationships between educators and researchers, and would benefit DL by reducing costs and providing for shared information in a timely manner.

Reflections and self-assessments
- What is currently done at your institution to disseminate research on learning and the use of emerging technologies to facilitate DL?
- Does your institution value research on teaching and learning? What do you do directly to stimulate, reward, or otherwise facilitate research and development?

2.2.3   Curriculum

Curriculum consists of three fundamental elements, including learning objectives, instructional strategies, and learner assessments. The elements are grouped to facilitate discussion of best practices that center on alignment.

Objectives. We define objectives as stated, measurable expectations for learning that may be referred to in many ways, such as, but not limited to terminal and enabling objectives, learning and performance objectives, competencies, outcomes, and goals. The primary functions of objectives are to identify and communicate the skills, knowledge, and dispositions (SKDs) that students should acquire upon completing relevant DL coursework and demonstrate when completing relevant learner assessments.

Reflections and self-assessments
- How are objectives and the curriculum defined at your current institution? Does your institution define and distinguish outcomes, goals and objectives? How about learning versus performance, or terminal versus enabling objectives?
- Can you readily distinguish measurable versus fuzzy objectives? How about learning and performance outcomes, goals, and objectives, and terminal and enabling objectives?

Instruction. Instruction is viewed as the deliberate arrangement of experiences that are intentionally designed to facilitate student learning (Driscoll, 2000). The functions of instruction are to formulate and facilitate the implementation

of an instructional strategy, including the design and sequencing of meaningful interactions, and the chunking and presentation of content information.
Instructional strategies present students with a comprehensive set of events
and activities within a lesson or module to facilitate learning that may range
from traditional teacher-directed methods, such as Gagne's (1977) Nine Events
of Instruction, to more modern student-centered, active strategies, such as the
5E Instructional Model (BSCS, 2005) (see supplemental handout on Grounded
Instructional Strategies for examples). To facilitate communications, we distinguish such comprehensive strategies from instructional tactics, that present
learners with a specific instructional event or activity, such as a demonstration,
assessment, or feedback.

Reflections and self-assessments
- Do you base the design and sequencing of instructional events and activities on an explicit instructional strategy?
- Why is it particularly important to base the design and sequencing of DL
  events and activities on an explicit instructional strategy?

Assessment. The function of assessment is to collect data on student performance, including conventional criterion-referenced multiple-choice, true-
false, and fill-in-the-blank type questions, which tend to evaluate learners'
capacity to memorize and recall facts, and performance-based checklists and
rubrics that assess students' ability to apply the knowledge and skills defined
by the curriculum in valid contexts. Both conventional and performance-based
assessments may also be used as entry-tests (to determine if students have
essential pre-requisite SKDs that are not covered in the instruction), pre-tests
(that assess students' SKDs to be covered in the instruction), practice-tests
(to monitor and assess students acquisition and development of SKDs during
instruction), and post-tests (to evaluate student achievement after instruction).

Reflections and self-assessments
- What type(s) of assessment are best used to assess students acquisition
  of knowledge? What type(s) of assessment are best used to assess students' application of knowledge?
- How do you ensure that your assessment methods and criteria are aligned
  to specified learning outcomes?
- How can you assess critical thinking and higher-order reasoning skills
  with a class of 100+ students?

Analyzing Key Factors. If we had to pick one best practice for improving training and education in general, and DL specifically, we would ensure alignment between (a) fundamental curriculum elements (i.e., objectives, assessments, and instruction), and (b) theory, research, and practice. Here, we note key factors to consider when analyzing the alignment of curricular elements within and across courses. Later, in Section 4 of this chapter, we discuss the alignment of theory, research, and practice (aka. evidence-based education) to guide the transformation of novice to expert distance educators.

In conventional classrooms, good instructors facilitate many interactions spontaneously, based on intuition and experience. By reading both verbal and non-verbal cues, they may clarify expectations, tell stories, describe how group activities are to be conducted, and explain what is going to be tested or how assignments will be assessed. In online learning environments, spontaneous asynchronous interactions are limited, and flaws in design, caused by a misalignment between objectives, assessments, and instruction, cannot be readily addressed and become amplified (Hirumi, 2002, 2013, 2014a). The alignment of fundamental instructional elements, as depicted in Figure 6.4, is one of the hallmarks of high-quality training and education that is particularly important for facilitating DL (Hirumi, 2005).

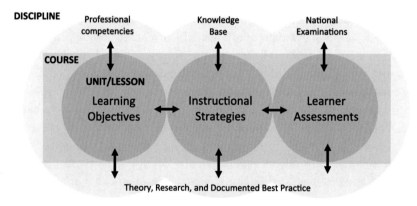

FIGURE 6.4   Alignment of curriculum elements

If a learning objective states that students will *list* 10 elements, the corresponding assessment should ask students to *list* 10 elements, and the instruction should present students with instructional events and activities, including content information, that facilitate the students' ability to *list* 10 elements. Furthermore, the goals and objectives, instructional strategy, and assessment of one course should foster the development of SKDs of concurrent or proceeding courses to formulate a cogent program of study. The elements should also be consistent with theory, research and documented best practices, as well as with professional competencies, knowledge-base, and national credentialing examinations (if any). Such alignment is a fairly straightforward concept that should be pervasive across all levels and sectors of training and education. However, in practice, such alignment is challenging and can be particularly problematic for distance learners.

At a distance, an instructor may not always be readily available to clarify requirements and decipher what is "need-to-know" versus "nice-to-know." Students, in turn, may find it difficult to discern what is expected of them, particularly if the objectives or assessment criteria are neither clear nor explicit, or if the relationship among objectives, or between objectives, assessments and instruction (including the content) is not always evident. In addition, if the essential instructional elements are neither clear, nor aligned, the instructor may be inundated by logistical questions online, leaving less time to facilitate critical thinking and provide meaningful feedback (Hirumi, 2003). When administering DL, faculty must be given the time and support necessary to align fundamental instructional elements.

Related Book Chapters. Chapter 7 Managing Course Designs and Chapter 8 Course Designs also refer to objectives and their alignment with strategies and assessments as well as details other aspects of design that are beyond the scope of this chapter.

Reflections and self-assessments
- Are the objectives, assessments, and instruction within courses and modules aligned? If so, how do you know?
- What explicit steps are completed to ensure alignment of objectives across courses to establish a cogent program of study where the development of vital skills, knowledge, and dispositions are intentionally fostered across courses?
- How can you assess critical thinking and higher-order reasoning skills with a class of 100+ students?

2.2.4   Management and Logistics

Management defines policy and procedures, allocates resources and tasks, and coordinates efforts among system stakeholders. In an online setting, management functions to ensure faculty have adequate time and assistance to design and deliver online coursework, and students have the technical assistance necessary to register for and complete the coursework. Management may also have to deal with the delicate political issues that sometimes arise when one institution is offering distance courses on what another institution regards as its "turf."

The function of logistics is twofold. The first is to acquire, install, maintain, and repair the mechanisms used to facilitate online learning. With a wide variety of learning and content management systems available, and rapid innovation in hardware and software, simply ensuring compatibility between on- and off-campus sites is sometimes difficult. With broadcast distance technologies, scheduling time in studios and on satellites can be complicated. With narrowcast distance technologies (e.g., Internet-based videoconferencing), providing adequate high-speed access for individuals with widely varying technologies is often a full-time job. The second function of logistics includes such things as registering students, arranging for off-campus sites, and shipping any materials, such as textbooks, that cannot be sent electronically. Because of the potential for online courses to enroll hundreds if not thousands of students, these tasks cannot be taken lightly.

Analyzing Key Factors. The notion of mission-based funding is not new (Watson & Romrell, 1999). Funds should directly support the mission of DL. Subsequently, DL budgets must be allocated to directly facilitate DL goals and objectives. Management and logistics, including the allocation of resources are particularly critical for sustaining and improving DL because of the typically large initial investment required to establish online courses and programs, and because of the difficulty in changing instruction and related functions once it is underway. Without mission-based funding, vision and mission statements may adorn the walls of educational institutions in a feeble attempt to inspire appropriate actions.

Related Book Chapters. Chapter 2 Leadership, Chapter 7 Managing Course Development Process, Chapter 11 Recruitment and Marketing, Chapter 4 Legalities, Policies, Ethics, and Accreditation.

Reflections and self-assessments
- What changes in management and logistics must be made to support DL at your school or institution?
- What must you do to ensure all other system components are aligned to support changes made to management and logistics to facilitate DL?

2.2.5   Student Services
Universities often have a division of student affairs that provide a wide range of services that support the educational mission of the institution. Student services may include, but are not necessarily limited to academic advising,

admissions, alcohol and drug education programs, career services, campus ministries, community service and service learning, counseling, financial aid, food services, fraternities and sororities, health centers, housing and residence life, multicultural programs, orientation, recreational sports, student activities, student discipline, and wellness programs.

Analyzing Key Factors. DL has amplified changes in student demographics by increasing accessibility for a diverse range of students, including those (a) with full time jobs and family responsibilities, (b) from different cultures, (c) with disabilities, (d) living in rural areas, and (e) who may not speak English as their primary language. Research, in turn, has shown that addressing the needs of diverse DL learners may benefit all students (Shimoni et al., 2013). Student services should be redesigned to be coordinated, holistic, and tailored to the institution's demographics and goals, not merely "web-ified" to offer existing solutions in a piecemeal manner (McCracken, 2005). Students need both synchronous and asynchronous (educational, library, and technical) support outside of regular business hours as well as universal design features to facilitate access, and a variety of modes for delivery of information and content. Additionally, students are not always aware of the resources available to them. An easily accessed portal with institutional resources and links to community resources is necessary to help those who may have issues with access (Shimoni et al., 2013). Broad support for library and research resources is also necessary for DL students, including general help and learning modules for tools and resources accessible on the library's site as well as targeted information embedded within courses (Brooke et al., 2013).

Related Book Chapters. Chapter 12 Student Support Services and Chapter 13 Student Success explore the role of student affairs and student support services in distance learning environments, including financial aid, tutoring, career and library services, on-boarding and co-curricular programming.

Reflections and self-assessments
- Considering the range of services needed by all students, what specific changes in student services must be made to support DL?
- What changes in management and logistics must be made to support the changes in student services?

2.2.6   Professional Development

Within a DL system, the primary functions of professional development (PD) are to ensure faculty, staff, and administrators' have the SKDs necessary to facilitate online learning. It defines what each stakeholder should know and be able to do, based on the functional goals and objectives delineated through strategic alignment. It also helps stakeholders assess their competency and provides opportunities for professional growth. Targeted proficiencies may include: (a) developing, implementing, and evaluating technology-based, student-centered learning environments; (b) enhancing students' basic, interpersonal, and critical thinking skills through the use of telecommunication technologies; (c) developing students' ability to process information, use resources, apply technologies, and understand complex systems; (d) accessing, retrieving, and transferring information through these technologies; and (e) making ethical and moral decisions associated with the use of computer technology and information.

In addition, PD provides incentives for faculty and administrators to use emerging technologies to facilitate learning. The intrinsic desire to better serve students provides the strongest motivation for teachers and administrators to use electronic networks, but improved telecommunications, and access to a variety of network resources also provides inducements for use. For educators who have yet to realize the benefits of telecommunications and DL, demonstration and training should be scheduled. Possible incentives could include compensatory time for receiving training outside regular school hours, travel support for attending local and state conferences on innovative applications of technology, and giving special provisions for obtaining additional computer hardware and software to instructors demonstrating exceptional proficiency.

Analyzing Key Factors. Over the past 20 years, we've learned that DL can be done well, or it can be done poorly. DL is a professional activity with evidence-based practices (e.g., Steinert et al., 2016; Cook et al., 2008). DL faculty, staff, and administrators need to be aware of such practices if you want students to succeed (e.g., Bates, 2019). For example,

- An appropriate mix of online and face-to-face learning must be chosen dependent on the context in which you are working.
- Many different synchronous and asynchronous approaches that can be used to facilitate online learning. The best choices will depend on your specific learning context. You need to be aware of the choices.
- Moving to online learning opens the opportunity to rethink teaching and learning; you may need to change from a lecture-type approach to a more interactive learning approach if you are to succeed online.[1]

Best practice also indicates that it is important for faculty to work with professional instructional designers and media producers if you want a high quality online course or program (Bates, 2019). However, conventional PD methods that pair faculty with educational specialists over several months may not meet current and future demands (Jones & Dexter, 2014). New developments in technology, world events, and most recently, emergency remote teaching due to COVID-19, create situations in which educators need faster results that are more targeted to their immediate needs rather than quality coursework (Hodges et al., 2020).

To address immediate needs, educators may initiate informal learning activities, such as forming personal learning networks, reading blogs and wikis, or participating in social media (Greenhalgh & Koehler, 2017; Jones & Dexter, 2014). Such activities enable educators to get targeted just-in-time (JIT) support to keep up with rapidly changing events and technologies. To support educators, institutions should recognize the time spent in formal and informal learning activities and allow both for PD. Formal activities provide valuable resources for educators, but networks, peer support, and embedded guides should also be employed for JIT support. Additionally, navigating resources and networking can be time consuming and cause information overload. PD should recognize the need for ongoing support and encourage faculty to familiarize themselves in one mode and slowly build their network as their comfort level increases (Trust, 2012).

Related Book Chapter. Chapter 9 Engaging Faculty in Online Education.

Reflections and self-assessments
– What do you currently do to assess the skills, knowledge, and dispositions of faculty and staff who are responsible for facilitating DL?
– What changes in professional development must be made to support DL in the future? What changes must be made to management and logistics to provide adequate professional development for all system stakeholders?

2.2.7   Program Evaluation

Evaluation provides meaningful feedback to system stakeholders about patterns of use and their impact on student learning and educator performance. It enables comparisons of performance with both standards and data-based judgments on how students and faculty are benefiting from access to technologies and the curriculum. It also assists faculty, staff, and administrators to take collective responsibility for the curriculum, helping them to continuously reflect and improve on educational practices. Note that evaluation is concerned with the operation of the entire system, whereas assessment is concerned with evaluating student achievement.

Analyzing Key Factors. DL program evaluation should be a continual process, not only analyzed during the creation of the program. No one rubric for determining effectiveness fits all DL programs because institutions differ in demographics and goals. However, programs such as Quality Matters can provide useful guidelines by providing rubrics for evaluating best practices in key areas such as communication, navigation, support, technology, and alignment of objectives and assessments within courses (Baldwin et al., 2018).

Such frameworks offer an excellent foundation for evaluating DL courses, but a quality program must also align with the goals of the institution, produce learning outcomes that are aligned with the goals, and allow flexibility for innovative teaching and integration of the affective aspects of learning (Bates, 2019). For example, the Online Learning Consortium's Quality Scorecard provides a suite for evaluating (a) the administration of online programs, (b) blended learning programs, (c) quality course teaching and instructional practice, (d) digital courseware practice, and (e) online student support.[2]

Related Chapter. Chapter 10 Quality Assurance.

> *Reflections and self-assessments*
> – What data do you currently gather to evaluate the effectiveness, efficiency, and quality of DL programs?
> – Do those data meet the needs and interests of key stakeholders?
> – What changes in program evaluation are necessary to continuously improve DL?

2.2.8   Technology

Emerging technology may be used to facilitate the design and delivery of the curriculum as well as facilitate key management and logistical functions by redefining communications within educational institutions. Electronic networks may be used to facilitate (a) communications among all system stakeholders; (b) the transfer of student and program data; and (c) articulation between on-campus and off-campus sites.

As discussed by Ninoriya et al. (2011), a content management system (CMS) is one that stores, displays, and shares data and digital content in a user-friendly way that does not require knowledge of programming or database management. In comparison, a learning management system (LMS) automates administration by tracking grades, attendance, and progress, and generating reports. The combination of these two systems into one robust, seamless design forms a learning content management system (LCMS). Despite the differences, LCMS is often referred to as LMS now that the systems have universally taken on a more integrated role. Platforms such as Canvas, Blackboard, Desire2Learn (D2L), and Moodle are the present-day interface for nearly all students with a combined 89.3% share of the LMS market, serving over 33 million students worldwide (Edutechnica, 2020).

Analyzing Key Factors. Despite the positive aspects of LMS functionality, learning systems have fallen under criticism for not producing better student outcomes (Alhazmi & Rahman, 2012). When used to facilitate teacher-centered learning, the passive presentation of content with little interactivity, can constrain student learning. Failure to align objectives, content, and assessments may also lead to inefficiencies, dissatisfaction, and suboptimal learning outcomes. Understaffed teams of educational specialist may also leave faculty without the support and data needed to improve programs during times of crises (Hodges et al., 2020).

Best practice in the use of technology and LMSs requires alignment across DL system components as discussed earlier in the chapter. A top-down approach begins with strategic alignment, professional development grounded in research-based evidence and sound pedagogy, along with on-going evaluations to inform continuous improvement. The evaluation techniques discussed in Quality Matters and formative evaluations can help prevent design flaws that result in courses misusing or underutilizing technology and LMS features. Conversely, technology and LMS can be used as tools in aiding the ongoing evaluation of courses and programs. As we discuss later under Section 4, Stage 3 – Future Needs to Innovate Teaching and Learning, big data analytics naturally embedded in the LMS can be used to inform faculty, departments, and institutions about key components of the system (Reigeluth et al., 2008).

Still, there are limitations to LMSs that cannot be overcome with the best planning and implementation, such as cost, and the inability to quickly adapt or integrate technologies. As such, the next generation of virtual learning environments is envisioned to be the learning ecosystem. Much like a living ecosystem, the learning ecosystem is comprised of the community, the technology, and the resources that are interrelated with open source software to enable it to adapt (García-Peñalvo et al., 2015). The basis of learning ecosystem in cloud computing creates an alternative framework to advance toward learning environments that are flexible and sustainable over time (Dong et al., 2009).

In a learning ecosystem, the flow of data among stakeholders becomes crucial as it informs policies, pedagogies, management, and technical services. Thus, for a learning ecosystem to be sustainable, planning must consider internal and external impacts, including: (a) educational policies and government regulations; (b) key stakeholders such as students, teachers, instructional designers; and (c) key learning and structural components including the LMS, tools, contents, and IT infrastructure (Redmond & Macfadyen, 2020).

Data infrastructure, storage, transmission, and security also become foundational and must be carefully planned (Redmond & Macfadyen, 2020). There is a plethora of conceptual and theoretical literature on learning ecosystems. However, literature regarding documented practices, successful case studies, implementation strategies per each component of the system, or evaluations of the system as a whole are still scarce. More research is needed to advance theory and practice regarding learning ecosystems.

Related Chapter. Chapter 14 Support Technologies.

Reflections and self-assessments
- What changes, if any, are necessary to the research and development and the professional development functions of the system to facilitate the proper acquisition, application, and evaluation of technology?
- What data, if any, are gathered to monitor and improve the application of technology across functions to facilitate DL?
- If you are charged with developing a learning ecosystem for a specific degree program, what components would you include to support learning ecosystem functionality?

3   Analyzing Organizational Efforts to Achieve Desired Results

To effectively administer DL, it is imperative to understand the relationship between the functional components of the DL system, and relevant system inputs and results. Figure 6.5 distinguishes five levels of organizational efforts, as posited by Kaufman's (2006a, 2006b) Organizational Elements Model (OEM), and applies the model to identify key elements of a DL system. As the figure suggest, the inputs of a DL system consist of the human, physical, and capital resources, including the SKDs of individual stakeholders, existing policies and procedures, required facilities, and budgets. The processes are defined

INPUTS	PROCESSES	RESULTS		
		Products	Outputs	Outcomes
¥ Human Resources ¥ Physical Resources ¥ Capital Resources	Students ... Faculty ... LEARNING ... Administration ... Community	¥ Discrete SKDs ¥ Completed courses ¥ Instructional materials	¥ Articulation ¥ Graduate ¥ Job placement ¥ Job retention	¥ Self-sufficiency ¥ Self-reliance ¥ Quality of life
	Internal to Organization		External to Organization	

FIGURE 6.5   Kaufman's OEM applied to DL

according to vital system functions that utilize the inputs to achieve results, as delineated in Section 2 on Analyzing Essential DL System Functions. Three levels of results distinguish internal DL products, and external system outputs and outcomes. Combined, the products lead to outputs, and the outputs result in outcomes that are measured in terms of impact on individual stakeholders, the community, and society.

Often, training and technology are prescribed to improve human performance without properly analyzing the context. However, such "shot gun" approaches to improvement, that start with solutions rather than well-defined problems, frequently do not achieve desired results. When stakeholders conduct needs assessments to solve problems or otherwise analyze the context to formulate tactical or strategic plans, they typically start by identifying input or process-oriented problems because that is what they face every day. How often have you heard people start the planning process by making statements such as, "we do not have sufficient funds, or computers, or personnel for improvement" or "we need more or better training" or "we need to improve the quality of instruction, the validity of assessments, or the management of resources?" As you administer DL systems, it is important to keep in mind that reducing or eliminating gaps in inputs and processes does not ensure achievement of desired results. To optimize your use of available resources when conducting a needs assessment or formulating strategic plans, it's imperative to start with measurable results-oriented problems or opportunities to achieve results. Then, after you identify a results-oriented performance problem, we recommend using a number of tools and techniques to determine how to best reduce or otherwise eliminate the problem.

3.1   Needs Assessment Tools and Techniques

Detailing needs assessment tools and techniques goes beyond the scope of this chapter. For more information on needs assessment (NA) tools and techniques as well as alternative process improvement methods, such as Lean Six-Sigma and root cause analysis, we refer you to the works of Rossett (1987, 2002, 2009), Kaufman (2006a, 2006b, 2011), Watkins, Meiers, and Visser (2012), and Andersen and Fagerhaug (2006). Here, to facilitate further inquiry and practice, we distinguish four fundamental types of NA data, and illustrate how you may identify a results oriented problem and formulate a plan for gathering NA data.

While many posit alternative approaches to NA and process improvement, we like to use Kaufman's OEM to identify a results-oriented problem (as discussed earlier in Section 3), and then use Rossett's (1987) fundamental types of NA data to analyze the problem and identify solutions, including feelings and facts about (a) optimal performance results, (b) actual performance results, (c) causes for performance discrepancies, and (d) potential solutions for resolving the specified problem.

To illustrate how you may identify a results-oriented problem and plan a NA, let's say a significant number of key stakeholders at your school are calling for you and other administrators to set aside time and money to train faculty on the design of DL coursework. Many are now online, but they argue that faculty need further training to go beyond emergency remote teaching to facilitate learning. While you may agree, you remember the importance of using the OEM to first identify a results-oriented problem, realize that time and money are inputs, and realize that faculty training and professional development are processes. So, to identify and achieve results, you ask yourself, what happens if faculty do not have resources and are not adequately trained? You reason that without resources and training, faculty may not generate high quality DL coursework, and without quality coursework, students may not acquire important SKDs. Moving up the results chain on the OEM, you further reason that without essential SKDs, students may not pass credentialing exams or obtain jobs, and may leave your institution unsatisfied with their education. Considering their importance, you decide to start the NA process by identifying job placement as the key output oriented performance problem.

The next step is to generate a plan for gathering the data necessary to analyze your context. Specifically, how will you (a) define optimal job placement rates, (b) determine actual job placement rates, (c) identify and rank causes for discrepancies found between optimal and actual placement rates, and (d) formulate appropriate solutions? Table 6.1 presents a template for planning NA data collection, including examples of data sources (e.g., institutional records, national reports, students), the number (#) or nature of each data sources (e.g., records kept over the last 5 years, 2 focus groups of 4 faculty members in each group, a survey of all staff), types of NA data (i.e., optimal and actual performance data, causes of performance gaps, and potential solutions), and related data gathering tools and analysis techniques (e.g., extant data analysis, interviews, focus groups).

Table 6.2 summarizes NA data gathering tools and techniques to help you generate a plan for gathering essential NA data. As a general guideline, each technique should be repeated until no new data is obtained. For example, interviews of students should be repeated until the same or similar responses are obtained from proceeding interviews.

After you implement your plan, the final steps are to compile and analyze the data, rank the causes, and formulate a solution system. Typically, substantive problems, such as job placement, are caused by a variety of factors that, in turn, warrant different solutions. For instance, to enhance students'

TABLE 6.1 Data sources, types, and tools for gathering NA data

Data sources	#	Type of NA data				Tools and techniques
		Optimals	Actuals	Causes	Solutions	
Institutional records	Last 5 years	X	X			Extant data
Strategic plans	Current recent	X			X	Extant data
National reports	Last 3 years	X	X	X	X	Extant data
Administrators	5	X		X	X	Interviews
Faculty	5 2 × 4 50	X		X	X	Interviews focus group survey
Students	5 3 × 3 500			X	X	Interviews focus group survey
Staff	2 × 3 all			X	X	Focus group survey

job placement, you may need to revisit strategic goals and reallocate finances to provide additional students with support services, supplement coursework with instruction on applying and retaining jobs, revise existing coursework to address essential 21st century skills, and provide training so teachers can effectively deliver new and revised coursework. Realizing you may not have sufficient resources to implement all of the recommendations, you may have to rank the causes based on relative impact, and then seek to implement a blend of solutions depending on available time and resources.

4   Analyzing Evolving Faculty Needs to Improve and Innovate DL

The progression from a novice to experienced distance educator is an evolutionary process that often goes through several distinct stages. To administer DL, it is important to analyze where your faculty are in the process to effectively address their differing needs. During the first stage, faculty, staff, and administrators work together to address the technical aspects of existing instructional

TABLE 6.2   NA data gathering tools and techniques

Extant data analysis	Job task/Critical incident analyses	Interviewing
Analyze existing data to: (a) examine results of perceived behavior, (b) seek truths through trends, (c) match corporate or agencies goals, (d) save money, and (e) verify other data.	Technique for finding and representing bodies of knowledge and skill to (a) establish what expert performers know and are able to do in useful detail, and (b) provide details of optimal performance	An interactive, real time communication to: (a) determine optimals, actuals, causes, & solutions, (b) make personal contact (establish dialogue), and (c) share ideas & engage in problem solving.
Steps	*Steps*	*Steps*
1. Examine the job and its outcomes	1. Find sources of expertise	1. Prepare for interview
2. Identify quantitative results of the job	2. Elaborate content	2. Begin interview, noting purpose
3. identify qualitative results of the job	3. Find structures or kinds of subject matter/job/task	3. Conduct interview
4. Determine how to get extant data and eradicate obstacles	4. Represent subject matter/job/task	4. Conclude interview
5. Examine data		

(cont.)

TABLE 6.2   NA data gathering tools and techniques (*cont.*)

Observations	Focus groups	Questionnaires/Surveys
Use senses to perceive what is going on at work at the time of performance, including (a) What does exemplary performance look like? (b) What does average performance look like? (c) What does below average performance look like? And (d) What might be causing the problem?	Purposeful gathering of three or more people (e.g., face to face, teleconferencing) to: (a) Solicit opinions on optimals, actuals, causes, and solutions; (b) Discuss options, determine alternatives; (c) Prioritize and decide; (d) Inform people about what's going on, and (e) Solicit support for effort and time.	Written and disseminated effort to acquire information from sources and find out what a lot of people think or feel about a problem, opportunity or new technology.
Steps	*Steps*	*Steps*
1. Prepare for observations	1. Prepare for group	1. Figure out what you need to know and from whom
2. Introduce yourself to environment	2. Launch the group	2. Write effective items
3. Conduct two stages (a) Holistic view, and (b) Structured observation guide	3. Facilitate meeting	3. Write good directions
4. Follow-up	4. Close the session	4. Write good cover letters
	5. Follow up	5. Pilot instruments

methods and materials and moving them online. The second major stage typically begins as educators realize that traditional, teacher-directed methods and materials are not suitable, or at least are not efficient, for facilitating learning online. The third prominent stage begins as educators begin to think outside-the-box to consider new and innovative ways of making significant and lasting improvements to DL.

As you consider each stage, it is important to keep in mind that all instructors will not be in the same stage at the same time. Some of your faculty may already be student-centered and facilitate active learning in conventional or blended learning environments while others primarily lecture and may have never used the LMS. Faculty may also require varying amounts of time and resources to go through each stage. Differing needs and interests serve to highlight the importance of analyzing your context to administer and improve DL.

4.1   *Stage 1: Immediate Needs to Move Online*

COVID-19 forced many schools to cancel conventional classes, including labs, internships, and other face-to-face (f2f) experiences, and mandated faculty to move online to continue teaching while keeping students, faculty, and staff safe from the virus. Administrators around the world mobilized campus support staff to help faculty digitize conventional classroom teaching materials, learn the basic functions of a learning management system, and utilize online discussion forums and web conferencing to facilitate synchronously and asynchronously individual, small group, and large class interactions. The acquisition of basic technical skills necessary to transform conventional classroom teaching methods and materials into accessible online learning resources, facilitated by the help of educational technologists, characterize the initial stage of an online DL educator.

The speed to which faculty move online, however, differs by context. Hodges et al. (2020) remind us that emergency remote teaching (ERT) is not the same as well planned online learning experiences that often take six to nine months to formulate, considering up to nine different dimensions of online learning (Means, Bakia, & Murphy, 2014) in a systematic fashion (Branch & Dousay, 2015).

The move to ERT serves as a microcosm of what most novice distance educators go through as they begin to transform their coursework for online delivery. When faculty first move online, they typically need help from campus support staff to learn to use web authoring tools and learning management systems to codify their teaching materials in readily accessible electronic format, and put their learning resources online to facilitate various computer-mediated interactions.

When web-based instruction first became popular, we learned that the use of interactive technology does not mean that meaningful interactions will occur (Hirumi, 2002). The use of email, online discussion forums, and web conferencing to facilitate online learning is pervasive, yet the return on investment in terms of learning is questionable. Learning management systems increase access to curriculum materials and the productivity of training and educational programs (e.g., number of online courses and the number of students completing coursework per unit of time) but they do not necessarily enhance the quality of the educational experience (Hirumi, 2005). For most, the move from conventional classroom teaching to highly effective, efficient, and engaging online learning takes time and requires educators to first learn the technical aspects of moving online before they have the time, capacity, and inclination to rethink their teaching methods and materials.

Reflections and self-assessments
– Does your current system have the capacity and resources to support faculty who are going online for the first time?
– What components of your current systems do you need to align to support faculty who are moving online for the first time?

4.2   Stage 2: Ensuing Needs to Transform Teaching and Learning

Soon after going online, educators often discover that traditional, teaching methods, that center on the transmission of information, may not be an effective approach for facilitating higher-order thinking, particularly in DL environments (Bates, 2019). As noted earlier, good instructors facilitate many different spontaneous interactions in conventional classrooms that help overcome challenges inherent in relatively passive, teacher-directed methods. However, the opportunity to facilitate spontaneous, real-time interactions based on verbal and non-verbal cues becomes constrained online. But without interactivity, instruction may simply become, "passing on content as if it were dogmatic truth, and the cycle of knowledge acquisition, critical evaluation, and knowledge validation, that is important for the development of higher-order thinking skills, is nonexistent" (Garrison & Shale, 1990, p. 29). Meaningful synchronous and asynchronous interactions must be carefully planned and sequenced to realize the potential of telecommunication technologies for facilitating learning (Hirumi, 2013).

We postulate student-centered instructional strategies as ideal complements for facilitating DL, providing faculty with a sound pedagogical foundation for designing and sequencing meaningful online interactions (Hirumi, 2014a,

2014b, 2014c). Advocates of student-centered learning believe that the more students actively manipulate information through the interleaving of assignments and the elaboration of new materials, the more likely they will retain and transfer the information (Brown, Roediger, & McDaniel, 2014). Figure 6.6 compares the configuration of stakeholders, basic resources, and flow of information in a teacher-directed versus a student-centered learning environment (Hirumi, 2002). Under the traditional teacher-directed approach, teachers serve as the center for epistemological authority, controlling students' access to and interpretation of information. Teacher-directed learning evolved to increase the number of students receiving instruction from an expert – a necessary function during the agricultural and industrial age. Teacher-directed methods involve an additive process where all students within a class or grade level learn the same information at the same time at the same rate.

Yet we know that students have different learning needs and interests, and learn at different rates using different resources in different places. Students continually revise their perceptual frameworks by reading, discussing, writing, and reflecting on material (Meyers & Jones, 1993). Their frameworks also continue to accumulate at an exponential rate in forms never before encountered. The information explosion has revolutionized the way we receive data and transformed information into knowledge. Far from being the center of authority, teachers must now struggle to keep up with what their students are finding online through the Web and social media. It is clear that we must foster students' "ability to know when there is a need for information, to be able to identify, locate, evaluate, and effectively use that information for the issue or problem at hand" (Association of College & Research Libraries, 2016, p. 8), and

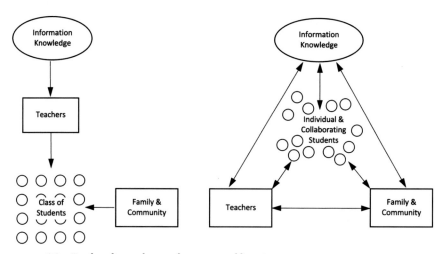

FIGURE 6.6   Teacher-directed vs. student-centered learning

devise new ways of teaching and learning to prepare students to succeed in modem society.

Active, student-centered learning has not been easy to implement in the past, because it is a laborious and time-intensive approach that was not practical within the constraints of traditional classrooms. Fortunately, technological advances are making student-centered learning more viable. Improvements in storage and networking are making rapid access to vast stores of knowledge possible. Students can work both synchronously and asynchronously in groups and individually to explore problems and formulate solutions, and become active knowledge workers rather than passive knowledge recipients. Teachers must also become facilitators and mentors, rather than lecturers and graders. Their role is to help students access, interpret, organize, apply, and transfer information to solve practical, authentic problems, while gaining expertise not only in the content area, but also in self-regulation (Zimmerman, 2000), meta-cognition (Veernman, Hout-Wolters, & Afflerbach, 2006), and information literacy (Elmborg, 2006; Koltay, 2011). Students gain the ability to improve their performance by applying technology to frame and resolve ill-defined problems.

To facilitate the transformation from teacher-directed to student-centered (and hypothetically, other approaches to teaching and learning), we also posit that educators and designers follow a systematic design process that is grounded in research and theory. The use of outputs from one design task as inputs to proceeding tasks helps to ensure the alignment of course objectives, assessments, and instruction, as well as to ensure the alignment of research, theory, and practice. The notion of grounding the design of instruction on research and theory, however, is not new. To optimize learning and achieve results that are generalizable beyond the unique conditions for which they are prepared, Hannafin, Hannafin, Land, and Oliver (1997) suggest that the design of instruction must be rooted in a defensible theoretical and empirical framework. In other words, key design decisions should be traceable to and based on evidence derived from research, theory, and/or documented best practices.

Without the systematic application of evidence, educational activities, whatever their intent, represent "craft-based" approaches to education and training; that is, instructional solutions that are crafted by one person for one specific environment based on their experience. Such activities are not necessarily ineffective. However, they may not be applicable to circumstances beyond those in which they are employed. Best practice involves the integration of professional judgement and experience with the knowledge that comes from the critical appraisal and application of research and theory.

A DL administrator may need to align research and development to facilitate evidence-based practice and guide substantive changes to the curriculum.

With that said, in promoting the use of grounded practices for advancing DL, it is important to remember that evidence-based education is not a panacea; it does not provide ready-made solutions to the challenges and complexities of modern DL. Instructional design, grounded in evidence, is a set of principles and practices that may transform the way faculty view DL and enable them to make professional judgements and deploy their expertise in a systematic manner.

Related Chapter. Chapter 8 Design and Teaching.

Reflections and self-assessments
- Do the majority of educators at your institution facilitate active, student-centered learning?
- To what extent do the educators at your institution follow a systematic approach to the design of instruction that demonstrates evidence-based educational practices?

4.3 *Stage 3: Future Needs to Innovate Teaching and Learning*

Education is mired in an industrial age model of education. Conventional degree and certificate programs hold time constant and allow achievement to vary (Reigeluth & Garfinkle, 1994). While people learn at different rates and have different learning needs, students are required to start and complete a pre-defined set of courses, and learn basically the same content, the same way, at the same time, and in the same amount of time. Students who may have already mastered some skills and knowledge are not allowed to advance at their own rates, and those who need more time and support are often left behind. The industrial age model of education advanced learning beyond the preceding agricultural-age, one classroom schoolhouse, but has long reached its asymptotic upper limit in terms of productivity (Branson & Hirumi, 1994).

To realize significant increases in productivity, we must allow time to vary and ensure high-standards of achievement (Banathy, 1991). We should neither group students into courses, nor should we give them static content to be completed in fixed amounts of time. Rather, we should establish competency-based programs that set high standards for achievement and allow students to advance to those standards at their own rates (Jones & Olswang, 2017).

4.3.1 Competency-Based Education

Competency-based education (CBE) seeks to afford learners more adaptive and personalized learning experiences (Colson & Hirumi, 2017) while addressing a number of socio-economic factors, such as declining completion rates, and increasing access to diverse learners (Burnette, 2016; Klein-Collins, 2013). CBE reduces time and cost by awarding academic credentials for demonstrating mastery of skills associated with an individualized set of modules rather than a predefined program of coursework, and further increases accessibility by allowing students to start and complete the modules based on their needs and schedules (within reason).

The notion of holding achievement constant and allowing time to vary to increase the productivity and accessibility is not new. Building on advances in teaching and learning catalyzed by the transformation of teacher-directed to student-centered learning, CBE chunks skills, knowledge, and content information into small units of instruction. CBE also uses smaller units along with authentic assessments to prescribe individualized programs of study that enable students to demonstrate mastery, and earn degrees and certificates at their own rate. A shift in higher education to competency-based models began in the early 1970s with the publication of McClelland's (1973) article on, "Testing for Competence Rather than for Intelligence." Now, nearly 600 public and private universities across the United States are offering educational programs that focus on the development of core job related competencies using flexible delivery methods that address individual learning needs (Corcoran, 2014).

CBE in Action. For examples that illustrate the current state of CBE, we recommend that you examine the Handbook of Research on Competency-Based Education in University Settings (Rasmussen, Northrup, & Colson, 2017) that includes chapters on: the systematic review of CBE efforts in the health professions (Wu, Martin, & Ni, 2019); the Western Governors University, a non-profit, online, competency-based university (Mendenhall, 2017); FlexPath, a competency-based option for pursing a degree at Capella University (Pearce & Worden, 2017); and two associate's degrees, one for Child Development (Washington & King, 2017) and the other on Engineering Technology (Boyer et al., 2017).

Based on recent case studies, it's clear that CBE has yet to reach its potential. Constrained by the time and resources necessary to facilitate individual mastery, further advances in infrastructure are necessary to realize the potential of CBE. As we mentioned before, learning ecosystems can provide for the adaptive learning needed to support CBE but are still in their infancy. Additionally, advances will need to be made in how we gather and analyze big data, and how we automate the processing of these data.

Related Chapter. Chapter 8 Design and Teaching.

4.3.2   Big Data Analytics in Education

The proliferation of mobile technologies allows technology providers and educational institutions to gather massive amounts of data about students and faculty behaviors. The term "Big Data" refers to data "so large or so complex that conventional applications are not adequate to process them" (Sin & Muthu, 2015, p. 1035). The advantage of big data lies in having real-time, direct and contextualized information to base evaluations and decision-making, rather than self-reports that can suffer from biases and inaccuracies (Macfadyen et al., 2014).

In the current educational context, the following platforms may be used to gather big data, including:

– Massive Open Online Courses (MOOC) that capture data on the location of registrants, number of clicks, pages visited, comments, answers to open-ended questions, and reactions or ratings (Clow, 2013).
– Learning Management Systems that capture data on time spent on the platform or on specific pages, pages views, number of clicks, submissions, grades, and discussion topics and submissions (Siemens & Long, 2011).
– Learning applications such as RealizeIt, H5P, Materia, and NearPod that can be readily integrated with an LMS or can function independently to collect data on individual time spent on activities and resources within pages, number of individual attempts and scores per attempt per learning activity, and individual answers to open-ended or close-ended learning activities.
– Social media where web crawlers and application programming interfaces (API) can be used to gather information on posts, comments, photographs, likes, and ratings from vast data sources.

Technology makes it relatively easy for educators to obtain these data. The main challenge is to process and give meaning to the unstructured data so educators can inform their policies, pedagogies, and services. Data analytics focus on gathering, analyzing, and reporting big data from students' online actions, and finding context that can be used to evaluate different dimensions of the educational system (e.g., curriculum, student services, and technology). Data analytics use varying techniques to give meaning to big data by identifying patterns that can turn into predictive models (Sin & Muthu, 2015). Such analyses can be applied to complex visual graphics or textual data (Bienkowski, Feng, & Means, 2014). Predictive models, in turn, can be used to identify factors that explain students learning behaviors, learning outcomes, motivation, and risk of attrition (Sin & Muthu, 2015).

4.3.3   Artificial Intelligence (AI)

There is no single definition of AI but commonalities are apparent among different definitions. Popenici and Kerr (2017) define AI as "computing systems that are able to engage in human-like processes such as learning, adapting, synthesizing, self-correction and use of data for complex processing tasks"

(p. 2). AI is also known as automation technologies that can support management and logistics via intelligent business applications, such as chatbots, to provide guidance. AI can also be used to analyze qualitative information by automating tools that dig into and analyze qualitative data available in learning ecosystems.

Current uses of AI in education include applications in case-based reasoning and social robots (Voskoglou, 2019). Case-based reasoning presents students with scenarios in which they use given factors to formulate and test solutions to authentic challenges. AI builds ever-increasing libraries of cases with both correct and incorrect answers. Social robots can understand speech and facial expressions and are used to interact with humans. Social robots can be used in the classroom to increase motivation and to assist autistic children in learning social cues and behavior (Kim et al., 2013). AI is also being used increasingly in adaptive learning to make the system more reactive and predictive to student needs, not just based on student responses, but also by analyzing their affective states, levels of knowledge, skills, and personality traits (Almohammadi et al., 2017).

There are also challenges to data security and ethics. With vast stores of data, student privacy and security of that data must be considered. Additionally, since algorithms are created by humans, there is a potential for biased inputs. Another challenge is that AI and big data have led to a tension between data-driven and theory-driven research approaches, which put at risk the generation of new knowledge. Both approaches should work together to advance the educational ecosystem and not act as rivals (Maass et al., 2018). The emergent penetration of AI is in a maturing process and more research is needed to take advantage of the potential and minimize related risks.

Reflections and self-assessments
- Do you believe competency-based education, coupled with big data, [big] data analytics, and artificial intelligence will revolutionize education? If so, how? If not, why?
- What other innovations may significantly increase the quality and productivity of education, and students learning experiences?

5   Conclusion

The complex nature of CBE and related use of emerging technologies to innovate education brings us back to the initial premise of this chapter: To realize and sustain significant improvements, we must view DL as a system, a set of interrelated components that must work together to facilitate DL. In this chapter, we posited ten functional components of a DL system and suggested that the alignment of the ten components is vital to sustain and improve the system over time. During our discussion, we also analyzed key factors to consider when administering and improving each function, paying particular attention to the internal and external alignment of fundamental curricular elements (i.e., the learning objectives, instructional strategy, and learner assessments) as the hallmarks of high-quality education. We then distinguished five levels of organizational effort to illustrate the importance of initiating needs assessments and strategic planning by identifying opportunities or problems with DL products, outputs, or outcomes to achieve desired DL results. Finally, we characterized three stages of DL and noted how the needs of DL educators evolve as they go through the stages to improve and innovate DL. By viewing DL as a system, distinguishing levels of organizational effort, and examining the evolving needs of faculty, we hope you are better able to analyze the unique context of your institution to administer and improve DL.

Notes

1   https://www.tonybates.ca/2016/08/21/online-learning-for-beginners-10-ready-to-go/
2   https://onlinelearningconsortium.org/consult/olc-quality-scorecard-suite/
    ?gclid=CjoKCQjwk8b7BRCaARIsAARRTL4fVU-Y2yJZ2RhIr6SoFcrQE1p9Z_wBqthi9Z32_
    lTjzBnFDfReilwaAuoKEALw_wcB

References

Alhazmi, A. K., & Rahman, A. A. (2012). Why LMS failed to support student learning in higher education institutions. In *2012 IEEE Symposium on E-Learning, E-Management and E-Services*. IEEE.

Almohammadi, K., Hagras, H., Alghazzawi, D., & Aldabbagh, G. (2017). A survey of artificial intelligence techniques employed for adaptive educational systems within e-learning platforms. *Journal of Artificial Intelligence and Soft Computing Research, 7*(1), 47–64. https://doi.org/10.1515/jaiscr-2017-0004

Andersen, B., & Fagerhaug, T. (2006). *Root cause analysis: Simplified tools and techniques* (2nd ed.). ASQ Quality Press.

Association of College & Research Libraries. (2016). *Framework for information literacy.* http://www.ala.org/acrl/sites/ala.org.acrl/files/content/issues/infolit/framework1.pdf

Baldwin, S., Ching, Y.-H., & Hsu, Y.-C. (2018). Online course design in higher educa-
    tion: A review of national and statewide evaluation instruments. *TechTrends, 62*(1),
    46–57. https://doi.org/10.1007/s11528-017-0215-z

Banathy, B. H. (1991). *Systems design of education: A journey to create the future.* Educa-
    tional Technology Publications.

Barak, M. (2012). Distance education: Towards an organizational and cultural change
    in higher education. *Journal of Enterprising Communities: People and Places in the
    Global Economy, 6*(2), 124–137. https://doi.org/10.1108/17506201211228930

Bates, A. W. (2019). Ensuring quality teaching in a digital age. *Teaching in a Digital Age.
    BC Campus.* https://opentextbc.ca/teachinginadigitalage/chapter/11-1-what-do-we-
    mean-by-quality-when-teaching-in-a-digital-age/

Bienkowski, M., Feng, M., & Means, B. (2014). *Enhancing teaching and learning through
    educational data mining and learning analytics: An issue brief.* http://www.ed.gov/
    technology.

Bowsher, J. (1989). *Educating America: Lessons learned in the nation's corporations.* John
    Wiley & Sons, Inc.

Boyer, N., Roe, E. A., Ross, K., Jones, P., Bucklew, K., & Conliffe, M. (2017). Polk State
    College's Engineering Technology OEEE associate's degree. In K. Rasmussen, P.
    Northrup, & R. Colson (Eds.), *Handbook of research on competency-based education
    in university settings* (pp. 308–339). IGI Global.

Branch, R. M., & Dousay, T. A. (2015). *Survey of instructional design models.* Association
    for Educational Communications and Technology (AECT).

Branson, R. K., & Hirumi, A. (1994). Designing the future: The Florida schoolyear 2000
    initiative. In G. Kearsley & W. Lynch (Eds.), *Educational technology: Leadership per-
    spectives* (pp. 91–112). Educational Technology Publications.

Brooke, C., McKinney, P., & Donoghue, A. (2013). Provision of distance learner support
    services at U.K. universities: Identification of best practice and institutional case
    study. *Library Trends, 61*(3), 613–635. https://doi.org/10.1353/lib.2013.0003

Brown, P. C., Roediger, H. L., III, & McDaniel, M. A. (2014). *Make it stick: The science of
    successful learning.* Belknap Press of Harvard University Press.

BSCS Center for Professional Development. (2005). *Learning theory and the BSCS 5E
    instructional model.* Retrieved November 15, 2005, from http://www.bscs.org/
    library/handoutlearningtheory5E.pdf

Burnette, D. M. (2016). The renewal of competency-based education: A review of the
    literature. *The Journal of Continuing Higher Education, 64*(2), 84–93.

Clow, D. (2013). MOOCs and the funnel of participation. In *Proceedings of the third
    international conference on learning analytics and knowledge (LAK '13)* (pp. 185–189).
    Association for Computing Machinery. https://doi.org/10.1145/2460296.2460332

Colson, R., & Hirumi, A. (2017). A Framework for the design of online competency-
    based education to promote student engagement. In K. Ramsussen, P. Northrup, &
    R. Colson (Eds.), *Handbook of research on competency-based education in university
    settings* (pp. 168–185). IGI Global.

Cook, D. A., Levinson, A. J., Dupras, D. M., Erwin, P. J., & Montori, V. M. (2008). Internet-based learning in the health professions: A meta-analysis. *JAMA, The Journal of the American Medical Association, 10*, 1181.

Corcoran, T. (2014). *Psychology in education: Critical theory ~ practice.* Springer.

Dong, B., Zheng, Q., Yang, J., Li, H., & Qiao, M. (2009). An e-learning ecosystem based on cloud computing infrastructure. In *Proceedings 2009 ninth IEEE international conference on advanced learning technologies* (pp. 125–127). doi: 10.1109/ICALT.2009.21

Driscoll, M. P. (2000). *Psychology of learning for instruction* (2nd ed.). Allyn and Bacon.

Edutechnica. (2020). *LMS data – Spring 2020 updates.* Edutechnica. https://edutechnica.com/tag/lms/

Elmborg, J. (2006). Critical information literacy: Implications for instructional practice. *The Journal of Academic Librarianship, 32*(2), 192–199.

Gagne, R. M. (1977). *The conditions of learning* (3rd ed.). Holt, Rinehart, and Winston.

García-Peñalvo, F. J., Hernández-García, Á., Conde, M. Á., Fidalgo-Blanco, Á., Sein-Echaluce, M. L., Alier, M., Llorens-Largo, F., & Iglesias-Pradas, S. (2015). Learning services-based technological ecosystems. In *Proceedings of the 3rd international conference on technological ecosystems for enhancing multiculturality* (TEEM '15) (pp. 467–472). Association for Computing Machinery.

Garrison, D. R., & Shale, D. (1990). *Education at a distance: From issues to practice.* Krieger.

Greenhalgh, S. P., & Koehler, M. J. (2017). 28 days later: Twitter hashtags as "just in time" teacher professional development. *TechTrends, 61*(3), 273–281. https://doi.org/10.1007/s11528-016-0142-4

Hannafin, M. J., Hannafin, K. M., Land, S., & Oliver, K. (1997). Grounded practice in the design of learning systems. *Educational Technology Research and Development, 45*(3), 101–117.

Hemsley-Brown, J., Melewar, T., Nguyen, B., & Wilson, E. J. (2016). Exploring Brand Identity, Meaning, Image, and Reputation (BIMIR) in higher education: A special section. *Journal of Business Research, 69*(8), 3019–3022. https://doi.org/10.1016/j.jbusres.2016.01.016

Hirumi, A. (2002). The design and sequencing of e-learning interactions: A grounded approach. *International Journal on E-Learning, 1*(1), 19–27.

Hirumi, A. (2003). Get a life: Six tactics for reducing time spent online. *Computers in Schools, 20*(3), 73–101.

Hirumi, A. (2005). In search for quality: A review of distance education guidelines and industry standards. *Quarterly Review of Distance Education, 6*(4), 309–330.

Hirumi, A. (2013). Three levels of planned e-learning interactions: A framework for grounding research and the design of e-learning programs. *Quarterly Review of Distance Education, 14*(1), 1–16.

Hirumi, A. (Ed.). (2014a). *Grounded designs for online and hybrid learning: Practical guidelines for educators and instructional designers. Book I – design fundamentals.* International Society for Technology in Education.

Hirumi, A. (Ed.). (2014b). *Grounded designs for online and hybrid learning: Practical guidelines for educators and instructional designers. Book II – Designs in action.* International Society for Technology in Education.

Hirumi, A. (Ed.). (2014c). *Grounded designs for online and hybrid learning: Practical guidelines for educators and instructional designers. Book III – Trends and technology.* International Society for Technology in Education.

Hodges, C., Moore, S., Lockee, B., Trust, T., & Bond, A. (2020). The difference between emergency remote teaching and online learning. *EDUCAUSE Review, 27.* https://er.educause.edu

Humphries, D. (2017). *Culture is the DNA of the company: An interview with JetBlue's SVP of talent, Rachel McCarthy.* Indeed. https://www.indeed.com/lead/culture-is-dna-company-interview-jetblue

Jones, K. A., & Olswang, S. G. (2017). Building competence: A historical perspective of competency-based education. In K. Rasmussen, P. Northrup, & R. Colson (Eds.), *Handbook of research on competency-based education in university settings* (pp. 28–40). IGI Global.

Jones, W. M., & Dexter, S. (2014). How teachers learn: The roles of formal, informal, and independent learning. *Educational Technology Research and Development, 62*(3), 367–384. https://doi.org/10.1007/s11423-014-9337-6

Kaufman, R. (2006a). *Change, choices, and consequences: A guide to mega thinking and planning.* HRD Press Inc.

Kaufman, R. (2006b). *Mega planning: Practical tools for organizational success.* Sage Publications.

Kaufman, R. (2011) *A manager's pocket guide to strategic thinking and planning.* HRD Press, Inc.

Kaufman, R., & Stakenas, R. G. (1981). Needs assessment and holistic planning. *Educational Leadership, 38*(8), 612–616.

Kim, E., Berkovits, L., Bernier, E., Leyzberg, D., Shic, F., Paul, R., & Scassellati, B. (2013). Social robots as embedded reinforcers of social behavior in children with autism. *Journal of Autism & Developmental Disorders, 43*(5), 1038–1049. https://doi.org/10.1007/s10803-012-1645-2

Klein-Collins, R. (2013). *Sharpening our focus on learning: The rise of competency-based approaches to degree completion.* Occasional Paper #20. www.learningoutcomesassessment.org

Koltay, T. (2011). The media and the literacies: Medica literacy, information literacy, digital literacy. *Media, Culture & Society, 33*(2), 211–221.

Maass, W., Parsons, J., Purao, S., Storey, V. C., & Woo, C. (2018). Data-driven meets the-ory-driven research in the era of big data: Opportunities and challenges for infor-mation systems research. *Journal of the Association for Information Systems, 19*(12), 1. https://doi.org/10.17705/1jais.00526

Macfadyen, L. P., Dawson, S., Pardo, A., & Gaševic, D. (2014). Embracing big data in complex educational systems: The learning analytics imperative and the policy challenge. *Research & Practice in Assessment, 9,* 17–28. https://doi.org/10.1177/0002764213479363

Mapes, T. (2017). *Walt Disney's dream culture.* https://www.linkedin.com/pulse/walt-disneys-dream-culture-tara-mapes

Marques, M. M., Loureiro, M. J., & Marques, L. (2016). The dynamics of an online com-munity of practice involving teachers and researchers. *Professional Development in Education, 42*(2), 235–257. https://doi.org/10.1080/19415257.2014.997396

McClelland, D. C. (1973). *Testing for competence rather than for intelligence.* Retrieved September 11, 2020, from https://search.ebscohost.com/login.aspx?direct=true&db=edsbas&AN=edsbas.EC63C664&site=eds-live&scope=site

Means, B., Bakia, M., & Murphy, R. (2014). *Learning online: What research tells us about whether, when and how.* Routledge.

Mendenhall, R. (2017). Western governors university: CBE innovator and national model. In K. Ramsussen, P. Northrup, & R. Colson (Eds.), *Handbook of research on competency-based education in university settings* (pp. 379–400). IGI Global.

Meyers, C., & Jones, T. B. (1993). *Promoting active learning: Strategies for the college classroom* (1st ed.). Jossey-Bass.

McCracken, H. (2005). Web-based academic support services: Guidelines for extensi-bility. *Online Journal of Distance Learning Administration, 8*(3). http://www.westga.edu/~distance/ojdla/fall83/mccracken83.htm

Moksness, L., & Olsen, S. O. (2017). Understanding researchers' intention to publish in open access journals. *Journal of Documentation.* https://doi.org/10.1108/JD-02-2017-0019

Moore, M., & Kearsley, G. (1996). *Distance education: A systems view.* Wadsworth.

Ninoriya, S., Chawan, P., & Meshram, B. (2011). CMS, LMS and LCMS for elearning. *International Journal of Computer Science Issues (IJCSI), 8*(2), 644.

Pearce, K., & Worden, B. (2017). FLEX path: Capella University's innovative pathway to a degree. In K. Ramsussen, P. Northrup, & R. Colson (Eds.), *Handbook of research on competency-based education in university settings* (pp. 340–351). IGI Global.

Piwowar, H. A., & Chapman, W. W. (2010). Public sharing of research datasets: A pilot study of associations. *Journal of Informetrics, 4*(2), 148–156. https://doi.org/10.1016/j.joi.2009.11.010

Popenici, S. A. D., & Kerr, S. (2017). Exploring the impact of artificial intelligence on teaching and learning in higher education. *Research and Practice in Technology Enhanced Learning, 12*(1), 22. https://doi.org/10.1186/s41039-017-0062-8

Rasmussen, K., Northrup, P. T., & Colson, R. (2017). *Handbook of research on competency-based education in university settings*. IGI Global.

Redmond, W. D., & Macfadyen, L. P. (2020). A framework to leverage and mature learning ecosystems. *International Journal of Emerging Technologies in Learning (iJET)*, *15*(5), 75–99. https://doi.org/10.3991/ijet.v15i05.11898

Reigeluth, C. M., & Garfinkle, R. J. (1994). Envisioning a new system of education. In C. M. Reigeluth & R. J. Garfinkle (Eds.), *Systemic change in education*. Educational Technology Publications.

Reigeluth, C. M., Watson, W. R., Watson, S. L., Dutta, P., Chen, Z., & Powell, N. D. (2008). Roles for technology in the information-age paradigm of education: Learning management systems. *Educational Technology*, 32–39.

Rossett, A. (1987). *Training needs assessment*. Educational Technology Publications.

Rossett, A. (2002). *The ASTD e-learning handbook*. McGraw-Hill.

Rossett, A. (2009). *First things fast: A handbook for performance analysis* (2nd ed.). Jossey-Bass.

Rowley, J., Johnson, F., Sbaffi, L., Frass, W., & Devine, E. (2017). Academics' behaviors and attitudes towards open access publishing in scholarly journals. *Journal of the Association for Information Science and Technology, 68*(5), 1201–1211. https://doi.org/10.1002/asi.23710

Senge, P. (1990). *The fifth discipline: The art and practice of the learning organization*. Doubleday/Currency.

Shimoni, R., Barrington, G., Wilde, R., & Henwood, S. (2013). Addressing the needs of diverse distributed students. *The International Review of Research in Open and Distributed Learning, 14*(3), 134–157. https://doi.org/10.19173/irrodl.v14i3.1413

Siemens, G., & Long, P. (2011). Penetrating the fog: Analytics in learning and education. *EDUCAUSE Review, 46*(5), 30. https://doi.org/10.17471/2499-4324/195.

Sin, K., & Muthu, L. (2015). Application of big data in education data mining and learning analytics-a literature review. *ICTACT Journal on Soft Computing, 5*(4).

Steinert, Y., Mann, K., Anderson, B., Maureen Barnett, B., Centeno, A., Naismith, L., Prideaux, D., Spencer, J., Tullo, E., Viggiano, T., Ward, H., & Dolmans, D. (2016). *A systematic review of faculty development initiatives designed to enhance teaching effectiveness: A 10-year update: BEME guide No. 40*. https://doi.org/10.6084/m9.figshare.3487268.v2

Trust, T. (2012). Professional learning networks designed for teacher learning. *Journal of Digital Learning in Teacher Education, 28*(4), 133–138. https://doi.org/10.1080/21532974.2012.10784693

Veernman, M. V. J., Van Hout-Wolters, B. H. A. M., & Afflerbach, P. (2006). Metacognition and learning: Conceptual and methodological consideration. *Metacognition and Learning, 1*, 3–14.

Voskoglou, M. G. (2019). Artificial intelligence as a tool in the modern education. *International Journal of Applications of Fuzzy Sets and Artificial Intelligence, 9*, 125–138. http://eclass.pat.teiwest.gr

Washington, V., & King, B. N. (2017). Child Development Associate (CDA) credential: A competency-based framework for workforce development. In K. Ramsussen, P. Northrup, & R. Colson (Eds.), *Handbook of research on competency-based education in university settings* (pp. 284–307). IGI Global.

Watkins, R., Meiers, M. W., & Visser, Y. L. (2012). *A guide to assessing needs: Tools for collecting information, making decisions, and achieving development results.* World Bank.

Watson, R. T., & Romrell, L. J. (1999). Mission-based budgeting: Removing a graveyard. *Academic Medicine, 74*, 627–640.

Wu, W., Martin, B. C., & Ni, C. (2019). A systematic review of competency-based education effort in the health professions: Seeking order out of chaos. In K. Ramsussen, P. Northrup, & R. Colson (Eds.), *Healthcare policy and reform: Concepts, methodologies, tools, and applications* (pp. 1410–1436). IGI Global.

Zimmerman, B. J. (2000). Attaining self-regulation: A social cognitive perspective. In M. Boekaerts, P. R. Pintrich, & M. Zeidner (Eds.), *The handbook of self-regulation* (pp. 13–39). Academic Press.

CHAPTER 7

Managing the Course Development Process

Anthony A. Piña

Abstract

In this chapter, online/distance learning administrators are provided with the major components of the administrative process for developing online courses: Environment, Standards and Evaluation, Roles and Responsibilities, and Operations. Within each of these components are specific decision items with examples to allow online/distance administrators to create and manage a course development process that is appropriate for their institution.

Keywords

course development – distance education – online courses – distance learning administration – strategic management – project management – instructional development

1   Introduction

The genesis of online education at many colleges and universities occurs when individual faculty members determine to "put their face-to-face course online." As more faculty become involved, individual online courses begin to be grouped into fully online concentrations, minors, certificates and degrees. At some point in their evolution, online courses and programs begin appearing on the radar of academic and administrative leadership. To varying degrees, leaders start to formulate policies, procedures and processes to regulate and guide the development of online education at their institutions, in order to address the issues that tend to manifest when courses are created independently from one another (Piña et al., 2018).

Managing the process of online course development allows institutions to scale the development of online courses, better align individual courses to program-level learning outcomes, contain development costs, eliminate redundancies in the curriculum, and create a more consistent experience for online learners (Cini & Pineas, 2018). The purpose for this chapter is to assist online/

© KONINKLIJKE BRILL NV, LEIDEN, 2021 | DOI: 10.1163/9789004471382_007

distance learning administrators to formulate a process to manage the development of online courses.

Each institution has its own unique culture. What works well for one school, college, university, organization, or company may be less effective for another. Given that there is no "one size fits all" model for managing online course development, this chapter will provide the online/distance learning administrator with different aspects, ideas and examples to consider in determining what to adopt and what to adapt. Some of these models will involve changing existing culture and will need to be implemented strategically and incrementally.

It is important to differentiate between managing an online course design process and designing and developing an individual online course. Individual course development is an essential component of the course design process and is the focus of the chapter on "Course Designs for Distance Online Teaching and Learning" in this book (Cifuentes, 2021, Chapter 8, this volume). This chapter will explore the context and controls within which course design and development occurs.

Introduction Questions
- How did online learning begin at your institution?
- Where is your institution in its adoption and implementation of online learning? 1) Few or no fully online courses; 2) several online courses but no fully online program or degree; 3) few online programs or degrees; 4) many online programs or degrees.
- How is online course development managed at your institution? 1) Not Managed: Individual faculty operate autonomously and independently; 2) Distributed: Each academic unit (department/school/college) operates separately and distinctly from the institution's other academic units; 3) Coordinated: There is a set of institutional policies and procedures adhered to by all academic units of the institution.

2   Course Modality

Courses are also increasingly classified by "modality" (i.e. the mode in which instruction is delivered). On-campus courses – in which all class sessions are held in a physical location where students must be present at the same place and time – are often referred to as face-to-face, classroom-based or traditional courses. Other common modality classifications include (Sener, 2015):
- *Web-enhanced*: On-campus courses with required in-class or outside-of-class activities that are done online.

- *Synchronous* (*or Remote*): Courses in which students and instructors meet at the same time (synchronously) but are separated geographically. Students and instructors can see and communicate with each other in real time, often via room-based videoconference systems or on users' devices using web conferencing applications.
- *Hybrid* (*or blended*) *courses*: Courses in which some of the class sessions are held in a physical location and others are offered online.
- *Online*: This usually designates courses in which all class sessions are offered online – though some institutions classify courses as online if 80% or more of the course is delivered online (Allen et al., 2016).
- *HyFlex* (*Hybrid-Flexible*): Courses which combine on-campus and online students into a single course (Beatty, 2020).

This chapter focuses primarily upon managing the process of online course development. However, the concepts and principles may be applied to courses regardless of environment or modality.

Course Modality Questions
- Does your institution have policies that require on-campus and online versions of a course to have the same student learning outcomes and – where possible – the same or similar ways to assess those outcomes?
- Does your institution have requirements from state licensing agencies or accrediting bodies that influence what and how instruction may be offered online?

3 Establishing the Course Development Process

As an institution grows its online program and course offerings to include multiple disciplines within the institution, the process of managing course development can become multifaceted and complex. An Online/Distance Learning Administrator must think of the process both *systemically* and *systematically*. These two things are not the same. Both educational institutions and the course development process are examples of systems, which can be thought of as a "whole" with parts that operate within the whole (like the different part of the human body). System thinking implies that one understands interrelationships and interconnectedness of these parts of the whole (Carr, 1996). When someone happens to one of the parts, it can affect another part of the system.

The process of developing online courses is a system in which manipulation of one of its parts (e.g. whether the process is centralized or decentralized) may have a major effect on other parts of the process/system, including the roles of faculty and instructional designers, quality and consistency of courses, development timelines, etc. (Carr, 1996). When online course development is not done systemically, then different areas or persons within the institution may become victims of unintended consequences, such as double-booked personnel or resources.

Additionally, the course development process should be systematic in that it is established, planned, and carried out in a deliberate way that considers the different decisions that must be made and the tasks that must be done. Leaving out parts of the process can result in having to address problems later in an ad-hoc manner.

3.1   Components and Decision Items

Table 7.1 lists the different components and decision items to be considered when systematically formulating and managing an institutional online course development process. It is important to remember that although each of these components needs to be considered and addressed, it does not mean that they must be addressed in only one way. Different institutions have different cultures and different needs that will dictate how certain items on this list will be addressed. Systematic also does not mean that the components and decision

TABLE 7.1   Decision items related to components

Component	Decision item
Environment	– Internal or external development
	– Centralized or decentralized development
Roles and responsibilities	– Faculty roles
	– Scope of work, compensation, and intellectual property
	– Instructional designer roles
Standards and evaluation	– Minimum standards
	– Evaluation and approval of online courses
Operations	– Classification of course development types
	– Curriculum mapping
	– Independent or guided design
	– Accessibility
	– Timelines
	– Tracking and managing development projects
	– Assessing and improving the course development process

items must be addressed in the order in which they are listed below. While it is true that the Environment component will influence everything that follows, the rest of the list may need to be considered in a different order, depending on the needs and circumstances within the institution.

4   Environment

4.1   *Internal or External Development*

Prior to and in the early years of the new millennium, the idea that a college or university's online courses and programs would be created and/or managed outside of its own academic departments and faculty would hardly have been entertained. Online learning was still considered by many to be at the fringe of U.S. higher education, dominated primarily by larger publicly-traded for-profit institutions, such as the University of Phoenix, and a limited number of specialized public and private non-profit institutions, such as University of Maryland University College (now University of Maryland Global Campus).

However, during the past two decades, online enrollments have consistently been the most steadily growing sector of higher education (Seaman et al., 2018). This growth, coupled with overall college and university enrollment declines since 2011 (National Center for Education Statistics, 2019; National Student Clearinghouse, 2020), has influenced many institutions to adopt online learning as a strategy to grow the institution, increase student access or – in some cases – to save the institution from demise (Ubell, 2017).

The Online Program Management (OPM) market was established to provide two basic types of services to institutions wishing to offer fully online programs: (1) A full-service model, where the OPM agreement includes all of the services for developing, supporting and promoting the online program or (2) an a la carte model, where the institution contracts only for specific services (e.g. instructional design, marketing, promotion, analytics, support) provided by the OPM (Pelletier, 2018). Major players in the OPM arena include Pearson Embanet, 2U, Academic Partnerships, Bisk Education, Pearson Learning and Wiley Education Services.

Using an OPM can have inherent advantages, such as being able to deliver courses and programs at scale more rapidly than internally-created courses and programs, provide up-front funding, marketing and analytics services and expertise that may be unavailable at the institution (Busta, 2019). Disadvantages of using an OPM may include lack of faculty input into course and program development, "cookie cutter" courses and programs that are essentially the same as those provided to the OPM's other clients, high percentages of tuition revenue going to the OPM to recoup the company's initial investment, and the dependency upon the OPM, which may make it difficult for an institution to establish its own online programs (Springer, 2018).

An in-depth analysis of the OPM arena is beyond the scope of this chapter and the decision whether or not to utilize an OPM is often made at the highest levels of institutional leadership. The purpose for discussion OPM here is to point out that if the institution has a full-service OPM agreement, the role of the online/distance learning administrator may be limited to merely functioning as an account manager or liaison. There may be little authority to influence the remaining aspects of the course development process outlined in this chapter. However, if the agreement with the OPM is "a la carte," then the online/distance learning administrator should intervene and advocate – to the greatest extent possible – for the ability to establish and manage the course development process.

4.2   *Centralized or Decentralized Development*

The other foundational item in the establishment of the course management process is whether course management is centralized or decentralized at the institution. This tends to be highly influenced by institutional culture – particularly the strength or weakness of leadership to enact institution-wide policy and operations, compared to that of academic units and faculty to resist centralization.

At one end of the spectrum is the institution where resources and personnel for online course development are centralized in a department or group that is available to each of the institution's academic units. In this situation, the online/distance learning administrator has the greatest ability to manage the course development process throughout the institution and to implement the ideas presented in this chapter (Bergeron & Fornero, 2018).

At a completely decentralized institution – one in which academic departments, schools or colleges are run autonomously from each other – the online/distance learning administrator may be facing the prospect of having to work with multiple distance learning programs, each operating differently from each other. In that case, the online/distance learning administrator may not be in a position to manage the course development process and the best that can be done it to establish positive working relationships with the various units in order to serve as a consultant to influence the adoption of best practices for online course development (Bergeron & Fornero, 2018).

In the case where an individual academic department, school or college has a sufficiently large online program to have its own online/distance learning administrator or coordinator, or in cases where institutions lie somewhere between fully centralized and fully decentralized, the operational aspects and the decisions made about them will still apply.

Environment Questions
- Does your institution partner with an online program management (OPM) provider for services? Which services? Does the OPM agreement with your institution affect the course development process?
- Does your institution have 1) a centralized center, department, office or team that is responsible for online course development or 2) is it decentralized, with individual academic units operating their own online programs independently of each other or 3) something in between?
- Does the online/distance learning administrator have the authority to make decisions regarding the process of online course development?

5 Roles and Responsibilities

5.1 *Faculty Roles*

One of the pivotal factors influencing how the course development process is managed is the role that the faculty member plays within that process. Institutional culture, employment and bargaining agreements, interpretations of accreditation guidelines, and the ability or willingness or an institution to provide personnel and resources to the online course development process, will largely determine the role of faculty play in course development. Three common course development models based on roles played by faculty are autonomous, partnership and team.

In an *autonomous* model, the responsibility for developing the online course rests completely upon an individual faculty member, who is usually not obligated to work with anyone else at the institution (Hawkes & Coldeway, 2002). The level of autonomy given to faculty for course development varies among institutions – and may vary within an institution. Under a *full autonomy* model, the faculty member is given complete control over the development and dictates the design, layout, navigation, use of tools and course content. Training in how to develop online courses, use of course templates and access to instructional design support – if available – tends to be optional. The faculty member assumes the roles of subject matter expert, instructional designer and course developer in the learning management system (LMS). In a *limited autonomy* model, training and other items or resources may be required, but the faculty member is still solely responsible for the development of the course.

When most colleges and universities first start offering online courses, faculty tend to operate autonomously. As online learning becomes more established at these institutions, many continue to rely on the autonomy model – either in its full or limited variety. The advantages of doing so include not having to invest in a full team of instructional designers and other professional and avoiding faculty pushback and accusations of violating academic freedom. Also, some may interpret language from accreditation agencies as support for a faculty autonomy model, such as Standard 10.4.c from the Southern Association of Colleges and Schools Commission on Colleges: "The institution … places primary responsibility for the content, quality, and effectiveness of the curriculum with its faculty" (SACSCOC, 2018, p. 95).

Challenges for online/distance learning administrators at institutions that rely upon the full autonomy model include: the inability to establish minimum standards of course quality across the institution; lack of consistency between courses (or even between different sections of the same course); and the inability to establish equivalency between online courses and their analogous on-campus (face-to-face) courses (Garrett et al., 2020). While it is commonly understood that teaching online versus face-to-face requires different skills, it is just as true that teaching online and developing online courses require different skills.

In a *partnership* development model, the faculty member partners with an additional person – most often an instructional designer – to develop the online course (Xu & Morris, 2007). Instructional designers receive training in their disciplines to include adulty learning theory, instructional design, instructional strategies, assessment of learning outcomes, online learning and delivery, program evaluation and other topics that tend not to be included in the academic training of most college and university faculty. While the faculty member serves as the subject matter expert, the instructional designer can provide faculty with ideas for structure, format and strategies to make their courses more successful (Xu & Morris, 2007). The instructional designer can help assure that student learning outcomes are well aligned with the assignments, activities, test, etc. that assess those outcomes.

At some institutions, the faculty member is responsible primarily for developing and vetting raw course content, while the instructional designer builds the course in the LMS, thus freeing the faculty member from the tasks of formatting course content, creating grade books, building and configuring tests, assignment drop boxes and discussion forums, and making certain that the course follows accessibility guidelines. The success of the partnership model is highly dependent upon whether the faculty member accepts the instructional designer as a true partner versus a mere subordinate.

In a *team-based* development model, the faculty member works as part of a design and development team of three or more individuals (Hawkes & Coldeway, 2002). The faculty member serves as the subject matter expert, while technical development tasks may be done by instructional designers, content editors, multimedia developers, graphic designers, psychometricians, copyright specialists or instructional or information technologists (Hixon, 2008). This model is found in institutions with well-established online programs that are seen as central to the institution's mission and function and at institutions that develop large numbers of online courses.

While the training of faculty is often not considered to be part of the course development process per se, the role that faculty play in the course development process dictates the training that they should receive prior to beginning development on an online course (Slaughter & Murtaugh, 2018). In an autonomous model, the faculty need far more extensive training, as they will be assuming the roles of all members in the partnership and team-based model (see the section on Instructional Designer Roles).

5.2   *Scope of Work, Compensation and Intellectual Property*
Determining the role of faculty is also related to three other decision items: The *scope of work*, the method and conditions for compensation and the rights to the intellectual property of the course. The scope of work (i.e. what needs to be done for the work to be deemed complete) should be explicit and written down, so that there is a common understanding between the Online/Distance Learning Administrator and the faculty member.

Another decision regarding the role of faculty is how the faculty member will be *compensated* or incentivized for online course development. At institutions in which course development is decentralized, the decision for compensation is often made by the leader of the academic department, school or college. Three common models for compensation are:
-   Online course development is seen as an expected part of the faculty member's basic responsibilities with no extra remuneration
-   The faculty member receives a release from teaching in exchange for developing an online course
-   The faculty member receives a stipend payment or another form of compensation for developing an online course

Related to the faculty member's compensation is the "ownership" of the course. Faculty who teach on-campus courses or who "put their courses online" often assume ownership of the course (e.g. "I put MY course online"). When a faculty member is being paid to develop an online course or is given a release from teaching, this institution must male clear whether the compensation is a "work-for-hire," where the institution owns the result of the work or if there is some kind of shared ownership. Typically, the institution's existing intellectual property policy applies to paid development on online courses, but it needs to be written down and agreed to by the faculty member before development starts.

At institutions where online course development is centralized, the Online/ Distance Learning Administrator will often have the ability to contract with and pay faculty/subject matter experts. The advantage of this situation is that the Online/Distance Learning Administrator is able to enter into a written contractual agreement with a specified scope of work, standards and benchmarks and conditions for payment. The Online/Distance Learning Administrator can withhold payment until the terms of the agreement are met. This is rarely the case when the faculty member is granted release time or a stipend by the academic unit. An example faculty/SME agreement is included in Appendix A.

5.3   *Instructional Designer Roles*

As online learning has increased at colleges and universities, the recognition and need for instructional designers has become more pronounced (Decherney & Levander, 2020). Instructional designers (IDs) are academic professional who are trained in adult learning, instructional strategies and interventions, assessment of learning outcomes and effective strategies for course development and teaching online that the majority of faculty do not receive in their discipline-based masters or doctoral programs.

Many academic leaders and faculty members understand the value-add that IDs bring to their institutions generally and to the online course development process in particular. However far too many do not. This often results in institutions with only one ID to work with all faculty (Garrett et al., 2020) or designating persons with the title "instructional designer" who do not have the academic preparation in instructional design and are expected to learn on-the-job. M. David Merrill has called these "designers-by-assignment"-rather than designers by training (Merrill, 2007, 2014).

A recent survey of 2,360 faculty and 102 online/distance learning administrators found that only 25% of faculty had worked with an instructional designer to create or revise an online course, while 23% had worked with an instructional designer to create or revise an on-campus course (Jaschick & Lederman, 2017).

The role of the ID in the course development process is determined largely by the role given to or assumed by the faculty member. In an *autonomous* model, IDs are often viewed as optional or expendable. Faculty may view the instructional designer as a non-peer who is "trying to tell me what and how to teach," not knowing or recognizing the distinct expertise and experience that the ID brings to the course development process (Dimeo, 2017). In an autonomous faculty model, the ID is often relegated to a subordinate or assistant role, rather than a collaborative one. The 2020 CHLOE 5 report from Eduventures found that "when faculty members design their own courses without instructional design input, the resulting courses are paradoxically light in direct faculty-student and student-student interaction, and, instead, are heavily weighted toward student engagement with course materials" (Garrett et al., 2020, p. 18).

In a *partnership* or a *teams-based* model, the instructional designer is assigned either voluntarily or by mandate. The success of this model is also determined largely by the relationship between the faculty member and the instructional designer (i.e. whether the faculty member considers the instructional designer as a mere subordinate or assistant who is expected to upload the faculty member's content into the LMS without critique or whether the faculty member accepts the instructional designer as a true partner and collaborator for the course (Xu & Morris, 2007). Partnership and team-based development has the potential to increase the quality of the online course and lighten the load of the faculty member – if the faculty member will embrace working alongside other professionals (Hawkes & Coldeway, 2002).

> *Roles and Responsibilities Questions*
> – When an online course is created, who "owns" the course – the faculty member or the institution? Does your institution have an intellectual property policy in place?
> – What is the compensation structure for faculty engaged in online course development? Is there a consequence if faculty do not complete the course development?
> – How much control and power does your institution grant to its faculty regarding online course development? If the faculty member is being compensated, are there any requirements to utilize instructional designers and/or to receive training?
> – Is there a common understanding about what is expected from those involved in course development? Is that expectation written?

6   Standards and Evaluation

6.1   *Minimum Standards*

One of the common expectations for Online/Distance Learning Administrators is to promote online course quality. "Quality" can be a nebulous term, as there is no common understanding of what constitutes a quality college or university course. It is widely known among online/distance learning professionals that online courses are generally held to an expectation of quality that on-campus courses are not. It is also common for programmatic accrediting and licensing agencies to expect that the institution demonstrate that online courses are equivalent to their on-campus counterparts.

Over the past two decades, organizations, vendors and professional associations have distilled research and best practices in order to formulate standards and rubrics to guide the development and assessment of online course (Martin & Kumar, 2018). These include Quality Matters (Maryland Online, 2017); the iNACOL Standards for Quality Online Courses (iNACOL, 2011); Blackboard's Exemplary Course (Blackboard, 2017); Open SUNY Course Quality Review (OSCQR) (Online Learning Consortium, 2018; Open SUNY, 2018); the OLC Quality Scorecard for Online Programs (Shelton, 2010), and the Association for Educational Communications and Technology (AECT) Instructional Design Standards for Online Courses (Piña, 2017). These standards "provide people and organizations with a basis for mutual understanding, and are used as tools to facilitate communication, measurement, commerce and manufacturing" (CEN-CENELEC, 2018, p. 1).

Quality Matters, Open SUNY/OLC OSCQR, iNACOL and Blackboard Exemplary Course take the form of rubrics or checklists that are often used as formative evaluation tools to identify areas of weakness in the design of an online course and to guide design improvements. Since they are all based on sound instructional design principles, there is a good deal of redundancy among these tools. Both Quality Matters and the Online Learning Consortium offer consultation and evaluator certification services to institutions wanting to utilize these tools. The AECT Standards are different, as they are research-based principles that are designed to be used from the beginning of the course development process in order to guide the development of the online course (Piña & Harris, 2019). The OLC Quality Scorecard is much broader in nature and is intended to be used to evaluate institution-wide online programs and operations – rather than individual online courses or degrees (Shelton, 2010).

Some colleges and universities prefer a "best of all worlds" situation by creating their own institutional standards based on one or more of the standards and rubrics listed previously. An example of an institution-based standards document for online master courses is provided in Appendix B.

6.2   *Evaluation and Approval of Online Courses*
Once standards and guidelines have been adopted for online course development, a mechanism needs to be put in place for quality assurance, evaluation

and approval for newly developed or re-developed online courses. Whether an institution adopts one or more of the standards and rubrics mentioned above or creates its own, a decision needs to be made regarding how to use the standards, rubrics, etc. to evaluate/certify/approve online courses.

Some institutions will assign course evaluation to individual faculty members, who may or may not receive formal training in how to use the tool. Other institutions may leave the evaluation of courses up to the program or department chair or to the associate dean or the dean. An institution may also employ ad hoc or standing evaluation committees to evaluate online courses. The committee may include faculty, instructional designers and/or other instructional support personnel. Some or all of these may become certified as Quality Matters or OSCQR evaluators. Regardless of the configuration, quality assurance is best achieved when there are other eyes – besides those of the course developer – looking at the course.

Standards and Evaluation Questions
- Does your institution have minimum expectations for online course quality? Are these based on an "outside' set of standards (e.g. QM, OSCQR, AECT)?
- If so, how important are quality standards to the institution? Are all faculty expected to adhere to quality standards in online course development?
- How does your institution assure that quality standards are met? Is there a formal process? If so, is that process institution-based or discipline/academic unit-based?

7 Operations

7.1 *Classification of Course Development Types*
Not all online course development projects are the same. Developing a new online course from the ground-up requires a significantly different amount of time and resources than a course for which a textbook revision merely necessitates relatively minor alterations of content within a few lessons. To manage staffing, timelines and payment, online/distance learning administrators can create a classification of courses, such as the one below:
- New Course Development (development of a course that did not exist previously
- Course Redevelopment (significant moderation or rebuilding of an existing course)

- Partial Course Redevelopment (relatively minor modifications of an existing course)
- Blended/Hybrid Development (development of a course combining online
  and on-campus content and activities)

An example of a course classification matrix can be found in Appendix C.

7.2   *Course/Curriculum Mapping*

One of the biggest challenges of the autonomous course development model
mentioned earlier is that it can facilitate a condition where online courses are
created "in a vacuum," separate and distinct from other courses and from program-level outcomes. This can lead to redundancy in the curriculum, where
different courses are teaching the same thing. Even worse, this can facilitate
curriculum holes or gaps, where certain program-level outcomes may not be
addressed by any of the program's courses. A highly useful tool for online/dis-
tance learning administrators is the course map. A course map is a course architecture document that lists the course's learning outcomes, the lesson-level
outcomes (objectives), how each outcome will be assessed, instruction and
resources to help learners achieve the outcomes and how the course-level
outcomes align to the program-level outcomes assigned to the course (Ibrahim
et al., 2015).

Couse maps can be utilized for many different functions, including facilitation
of periodic curriculum review, documentation for accreditation and licensing
visits and evidence for the equivalence of online and on-campus courses.[1]

7.3   *Independent or Guided Design*

One of the key decisions that will inform the online course development process is whether or not the design, navigation and formatting of the course will
be done: (1) independently (i.e. left up to the discretion of individual faculty
members); (2) guided by standardized or adopted templates or (3) a course
master.

Independent: In a traditional setting, it is assumed that the faculty member
who develops a course is the same one who will always teach the course (Piña
& Bohn, 2016). The course reflects the personal style and preferences of the
individual faculty member. The differences between the courses of different
instructors could introduce variety, interest and highlight the personality of
each instructor. The differences could also introduce difficulty and confusion
in students due to inconsistent interfaces, navigation, layout and use of course
tools and procedures (Slaughter & Murtaugh, 2018, p. 261). In addition, an
online course developed to be used exclusively by a specific faculty member
may be challenging for a different faculty member assigned to teach the course.

Template: Institutions with larger online programs and those with many students who may be new to the online learning experience are increasingly utilizing templates to provide a common and predictable look and feel to their online courses. "Providing a template for instructional designers and subject matter experts to compile the necessary content for the online courses they are developing allows for consistency across the design and development cycle. Using a design template also allows for the organization of the course information in a streamlined manner" (Slaughter & Murtaugh, p. 261). Templates can vary widely in their design, but tend to be organized so that students can find their instructional content, assignments, grades, communication tools and other items with the least amount of guesswork necessary. Courses featuring templates tend to be easier for adjunct faculty to adapt to, compared to courses in which each one looks and acts differently. Some faculty dislike course templates, as they feel their ability to be creative with the design of their courses could be stifled.

Master Course: Institutions using master online courses take the concept of a course template to the next level. An online master course can take different forms, but a common one is for all sections of a given course (e.g. English Composition) to have the same structure and course content (introduction, learning outcomes, instructional material, readings and assignments/assessments). A master course contains all of the necessary content to be taught by any qualified faculty member, so they tend to be advantageous for adjunct faculty and for new faculty. For institutions that provide stipends for course development, master courses are more economical and easier to show consistency across course sections.

Some faculty are opposed to master courses – whether they are developed in-house or by publishers or OPMs – and may refer to them as "canned courses." They may express concern that master courses inhibit academic freedom. However, this may be addressed by providing faculty with editor access in the learning management system, allowing them to add their own content and personalize the course.

7.4   *Accessibility*

Online/distance learning administrators need to be aware of institutional policies and federal guidelines regarding accessibility of online materials – including online courses. As the student body becomes more diverse – including students with differing physical and cognitive abilities – what is done within the design of online courses can impose or remove barriers to learning (Rao et al., 2015). Advocacy groups for sight- and hearing impaired students have vigorously pursued legal action against higher education institutions – from K-12 schools to the most prestigious universities in the U.S. – due to their online websites, courses or other materials not being accessible to students with disabilities.[2]

Accessibilityguidelinesforonlinecoursesshouldincludespecificitemsrelated to formatting, use of alt-text for images, captioning for videos (Moorefield-Lang, 2019). The DO-IT Center at the University of Washington provides accessibility resources for both educators and students at https://www.d.umn.edu/~lcarlson/atteam/lawsuits.html. The World Wide Web Consortium (W3C) has partnered with edX to make an online introductory course on web accessibility available for free.[3]

Universal Design for Learning (UDL) is the next generation of accessibility for education. It is based on the principle that removing barriers and adding choices will benefit not only students with physical disabilities, but also many students who are not considered disabled or students who do not wish to be labelled as disabled (Tobin, 2013; Tobin & Behling, 2018). UDL was is based upon three major principles developed by the Center for Applied Special Technology (Tobin, 2013):
– Provide multiple means of engagement
– Provide multiple means of representation
– Provide multiple means of action and expression

These principles are further defined on the CAST website.[4] Applying UDL across all of an institution's online courses can be a daunting task. Tobin and Behling (2018) provide ideas for how to implement UDL incrementally.

7.5   Timelines for Course Development

How long does it take to develop an online course? The length of time that should be allotted for a single course development project depends largely on who is developing the course, the conditions of that person's employment or compensation, and when the course is expected to be deployed (Slaughter & Murtaugh, 2018). If a full-time or adjunct faculty member is receiving a course release to develop a course, then it is usually expected that they will complete their tasks within an academic term (i.e. semester or quarter). If the faculty member is receiving a stipend for the project and the course is not expected to be deployed in the near future, the deadline for completion might not be for several months.

Faculty frequently underestimate the amount of time required to develop an online course and frequently overestimate the time that they have available to work on course development. Therefore, a timeline should be established with set deliverables required at regular intervals (e.g. the same time each week). The timeline needs to be written and signed as part of the SME

Agreement. Appendix D provides a sample course development timeline based upon a 15-week semester.

7.6 Tracking and Managing Development Projects

While a timeline and an SME agreement might be sufficient to manage a single course development project, the online/distance learning administrator will likely have several course developments happening at the same time. Managing multiple course developments requires an organized way to keep track of the progress of current development projects, prioritize projects, reference past projects, schedule future projects and allocate resources and staffing (Piña & Sanford, 2017).

Some have found success using Gantt charts to track individual development projects (Li & Shearer, 2005), while others have made use of the more robust features of MS Project for management and documentation (Abdous & He, 2008). Benson et al. (2004) utilized a training performance management system based upon the ADDIE framework (Analysis, Design, Development, Implementation and Evaluation) to support both instructional designers and project managers of training.

Another approach is to incorporate a customized relational database to manage the course development process. This includes tracking each course and listing the assigned SME and instructional designer, when the course is due, the status of the course development (i.e. whether it is on schedule), the quality assurance cycle, and whether the course has been evaluated and approved by the academic college who requested the course. The course development database – created using Microsoft Access – also sends messages to key personnel when certain milestones have been met. A detailed description of the database and its functionality can be found in Piña and Sanford (2017).

7.7 Assessment and Improvement of the Course Development Process

Higher education accrediting agencies, such as the Southern Association of Colleges and Schools Commission on Colleges, require that academic units and support units perform regular quality assurance by formulating expected outcomes, assessing those outcomes, and making improvements based upon the outcomes assessments (SACSCOC, 2018). Martin and Kumer (2018) state that "Quality assurance is a systematic approach to check whether online learning meets specific requirements based on a set of standards and frameworks" (p. 272).

This is true whether the development of an individual online course or the institution-wide course development process is being assessed. However, there is a much larger literature and research base for designing, developing, teaching and assessing individual online courses than there is for leading managing and assessing online learning at the program or institution level (Piña et al., 2018). A recent EBSCO literature search failed to find any publications on how to assess the effectiveness of instructional design or online development departments or teams. There is a clear need for more work to be done in this area.

The OLC Quality Scorecard for Online Programs (Shelton, 2010) is one of the few tools to target the various areas of online education for the entire institution. While it is a highly useful tool for this purpose, it provides little guidance to online/distance learning administrators for how to assess the online course development process.

For assessment to be useful and meaningful (and not merely a box to be checked), it must (1) generate data that can be used to drive improvements and (2) be based upon the actions of the unit being assessed – rather than being dependent upon actions undertaken outside of the unit. For example, certain data – such as the quantity of new and redeveloped courses created annually – is relatively easy to gather and report. However, if the number of courses created is completely dependent upon requests coming from the academic departments, there may be little that online/distance learning administrators or their teams can do to significantly affect those numbers. So quantity of course developed might not be a very useful assessment metric to inform improvement.

One promising assessment strategy for assessing support units is measuring the satisfaction of constituents, which can include faculty subject matter experts who develop courses, faculty who teach newly developed or redeveloped online courses and students who enroll in newly developed or redeveloped online courses. Slaughter and Murtaugh (2018) recommend a survey for subject matter experts to identify strengths and weaknesses in the course development process. A list of survey items for subject matter experts, teaching faculty and students is provided in Appendix E.

Operations Questions
- When each online course is developed, will that course be taught exclusively by the person who created the course, or will different sections of the same course be taught by different faculty members?
- Will adjunct faculty be teaching any of these courses? Are adjunct faculty allowed to be used as faculty subject matter experts for course development?

– How do you assure that courses are aligned to program-level outcomes?
– Does your institution wish to scale/increase the efficiency of online course development?
– Is having a consistent course look, feel and navigation for students important to your institution?
– Should all course developments be treated and compensated the same, regardless of their size and scope?
– How long should be allotted for course development
– What steps are taken to make sure that online courses are accessible to learners with disabilities?
– How do you keep track of the past, current and future status of online course development projects?
– How do you know whether your institution's online course development is going successfully? How do you know where improvements need to be made and whether the improvements work?

8   Summary and Conclusions

The purpose for this chapter is to provide online/distance learning administrators with the various components and decision items to allow for the formulation of a process for course development. These components and decision items will have to be addressed at some point, so it is best to address them sooner, rather than later. No two colleges or universities are alike. By providing various alternatives for each decision item, online/distance learning administrators will be able to craft a process that will be comprehensive and well-aligned to the unique needs, characteristics and culture of their institutions.

Notes

1   An online tool for constructing a course map is available at
    https://www.coursemapguide.com/
2   A list of accessibility lawsuits, complaints and settlements involving more than 40 schools, colleges and universities is available at https://www.d.umn.edu/~lcarlson/atteam/lawsuits.html
3   See https://www.edx.org/course/web-accessibility-introduction
4   See http://udlguidelines.cast.org/

References

Abdous, M., & He, W. (2008). Streamlining the online course development process by using project management tools. *Quarterly Review of Distance Education, 9*(2), 181–188.

Allen, I. E., Seaman, J., Poulin, R., & Straut, T. (2016). *Online report card: Tracking online education in the United States.* Babson Survey Research Group. https://onlinelearningsurvey.com/reports/onlinereportcard.pdf

Ashbaugh, M. L. & Piña, A. A. (2014). Improving instructional design processes through leadership-thinking and modeling. In B. Hokanson & A. Gibbons (Eds.), *Design in educational technology: Design thinking, design process and the design studio* (pp. 223–248). Springer.

Beatty, B. J. (2020) *Hybrid-flexible course design: Implementing student-centered hybrid classes.* EdTech Books. https://edtechbooks.org/hyflex

Benson, A. D., Bothra, J., & Sharma, P. (2004). TPMS: A performance support tool for Cisco training program managers. *Tech Trends, 48*(2), 54–79.

Bergeron, M. Z., & Fornero, S. C. (2018). Centralized and decentralized approaches to managing online programs. In A. A. Piña, V. L. Lowell, & B. R. Harris (Eds.) *Leading and managing e-learning: What the e-learning leader needs to know* (pp. 29–44). Springer.

Blackboard. (2017). *Exemplary course program rubric.* http://www.blackboard.com/resources/catalyst-awards/bb_exemplary_course

Busta, H. (2019). As traditional colleges grow online, OPM relationships shift. *Education Dive.* https://www.educationdive.com/news/as-traditional-colleges-grow-online-opm-relationships-shift/549414/

Carr, A. A. (1996). Distinguishing systemic from systematic. *Tech Trends, 41*(1), 21–30.

CEN-CENELEC. (2018). *The importance of standards.* The European Committees for Standardization and Electrotechnical Standardization. https://www.cencenelec.eu/research/tools/ImportanceENs/Pages/default.aspx

Cifuentes, L. D. (2021). Course designs for distance teaching and learning. In L. D. Cifuentes (Ed.), *A guide to administering distance learning.* Brill.

Cini, M. A., & Prineas, M. (2018). Scaling online learning: Critical decisions for e-learning leaders. In A. A. Piña, V. L. Lowell, & B. R. Harris (Eds.), *Leading and managing e-learning: What the e-learning leader needs to know* (pp. 305–320). Springer.

Decherney, P., & Levander, C. (2020). The hottest job in higher education: Instructional designer. *Inside Higher Ed.* https://www.insidehighered.com/digital-learning/blogs/education-time-corona/hottest-job-higher-education-instructional-designer

Dimeo, J. (2017). Why instructional designers are underutilized. *Inside Higher Ed.* https://www.insidehighered.com/digital-learning/article/2017/11/01/reasons-why-faculty-members-dont-collaborate-instructional

Garrett, R., Legon, R., Fredericksen, E. E., & Simunich, B. (2020). *CHLOE 5: The pivot to remote teaching in spring 2020 and its impact, the changing landscape of online education, 2020.* Quality Matters. qualitymatters.org/qa-resources/resource-center/articles-resources/CHLOE-project

Hawkes, M., & Coldeway, D. O. (2002). An analysis of team vs. faculty-based online course development. *Quarterly Review of Distance Education, 3*(4), 431–442.

Hixon, (2008). Team-based online *course* development: A case study of collaboration models. *Online Journal of Distance Learning Administration, 11*(4).

Ibrahim, W., Atif, Y., Shuaib, K., & Sampson, D. (2015). A web-based course assessment tool with direct mapping to student outcomes. *Journal of Educational Technology and Society, 18*(2), 46–59.

iNACOL. (2011). *Version 2: National standards for quality online courses.* International Association for K-12 Online Learning.

Jaschick, S., & Lederman, D. (2017). 2017 survey of faculty attitudes on technology. *Inside Higher Ed Report.* https://www.insidehighered.com/booklet/2017-survey-faculty-attitudes-technology

Li, D., & Shearer, R. (2005). Project management for online course development. *Distance Learning, 2*(4), 19–23.

Martin, F., & Kumar, S. (2018). Frameworks for assessing and evaluating e-learning courses and programs. In A. A. Piña, V. L. Lowell, & B. R. Harris (Eds.), *Leading and managing e-learning: What the e-learning leader needs to know* (pp. 271–280). Springer.

Maryland Online. (2017). *Non-annotated standards from the QM higher education rubric* (5th ed.). https://www.qualitymatters.org/sites/default/files/PDFs/StandardsfromtheQMHigherEducationRubric.pdf

Merrill, M. D. (2007). The future of instructional design: The proper study of instructional design. In R. A. Reiser & J. V. Dempsey (Eds.), *Trends and issues in instructional design and technology* (2nd ed., pp. 336–341). Pearson.

Merrill, M. D. (2014). My hopes for the future of instructional technology. *Educational Technology, 54*(4), 22–26.

Moorefield-Lang, H. (2019). Accessibility in online course design. *Library Technology Reports, 55*(4), 14–16.

National Center for Education Statistics. (2019). *College navigator.* Institute of Education Sciences. http://nces.ed.gov/collegenavigator/

National Student Clearinghouse. (2020). *Current term enrollment estimates.* https://nscresearchcenter.org/tag/enrollment-trends/

Online Learning Consortium. (2018). *OLC OSCQR course design review scorecard.* https://onlinelearningconsortium.org/consult/oscqr-course-design-review/

Open SUNY. (2018). *OSCQR – The open SUNY course quality review rubric.* https://oscqr.org/

Pelletier, S. (2018). The evolution of online program management. *Unbound: Reinventing higher education.* https://unbound.upcea.edu/leadership-strategy/continuing-education/the-evolution-of-online-program-management/

Piña, A. A., & Bohn, L. (2016). Assessing online faculty. In A. A. Piña & J. B. Huett (Eds.), *Beyond the online course: Leadership perspectives on e-learning* (pp. 317–330). Information Age Publishing.

Piña, A. A., & Harris, P. (2019). Utilizing the AECT instructional design standards for distance learning. *Online Journal of Distance Learning Administration, 22*(2).

Piña, A. A., Lowell, V. L., & Harris, B. R. (2018). *Leading and managing e-learning: What the e-learning leader needs to know.* Springer.

Piña, A. A., & Sanford, B. K. (2017). The ID database: Managing the instructional development process. *Tech Trends, 61*(4), 331–340.

Rao, K., Edelen-Smith, P., & Wailehua, C. (2015). Universal design for online courses: Applying principles to pedagogy. *Open Learning, 30*(1), 35–52.

SACSCOC. (2018). *Resource manual for the principles of accreditation: Foundations for quality enhancement.* Southern Association for Colleges and Schools Commission on Colleges. https://sacscoc.org/pdf/2018%20POA%20Resource%20Manual.pdf

Seaman, J. E., Allen, I. E., & Seaman, J. (2018). *Grade increase: Tracking distance education in the United States.* Babson Survey Research Group. https://onlinelearningsurvey.com/reports/gradeincrease.pdf

Sener, J. (2015). Updated e-learning definitions. *Online Learning Consortium OLC Insights.* https://onlinelearningconsortium.org/updated-e-learning-definitions-2/

Shelton, K. (2010). A quality scorecard for the administration of online education programs: A delphi study. *Journal of Asynchronous Learning Networks, 14*(4), 36–62.

Slaughter, D. S., & Murtaugh, M. C. (2018). Collaborative management of the e-learning design and development process. In A. A. Piña, V. L. Lowell, & B. R. Harris (Eds.), *Leading and managing e-learning: What the e-learning leader needs to know* (pp. 253–270). Springer.

Springer, S. (2018). One university's experience partnering with an Online Program Management (OPM) provider: A case study. *Online Journal of Distance Learning Administration, 21*(1).

Tobin, T. J. (2013). Universal design in online courses: Beyond disabilities. *Online Classroom, 13*(12), 1–3.

Tobin, T. J., & Behling, K. T. (2018). *Reach everyone, teach everyone: Universal design for learning in higher education.* West Virginia University Press.

Ubell, R. (2017). How online can save small, private colleges from going under. *EdSurge Digital Learning in Higher Ed.* https://www.edsurge.com/news/2017-11-21-how-online-can-save-small-private-colleges-from-going-under

Xu, H., & Morris, L. V. (2007). Collaborative course development for online courses. *Innovative Higher Education, 32*(1), 35–47.

Appendix A: Sample Course Development SME Agreement

To: <Name>

We are pleased to extend to you this offer to work as a Subject Matter Expert (SME). This role will be separate and distinct from any other employment or assignment with the SU and you will report directly to the Associate Provost or designee for the duration of this project.

Roles

The SME, Instructional Designer (ID), Academic/Discipline Dean and Associate Provost and VPAA/Provost and have distinct roles as defined below.

- SME: Creates and/or selects content, learning activities, and assessment measures that enable students to meet the approved learning objectives; follows SU Standards for Online Master Courses and university policies.
- ID: Assesses whether content meets SU standards; develops content provided by the SME into an educationally sound online course; manages project deadlines; initiates SME payment process for completed and approved work.
- *Academic Dean* or designee: Requests course development; recommends SME; approves course maps and evaluates final course for discipline approval/deployment.
- *Associate Provost/Chief Online Learning Officer*: Oversees online course development and policy; supervises SMEs and IDs; works with SMEs and IDs to resolve any disagreements relating to course development; authorizes SME payment.
- *Vice President of Academic Affairs/Provost*: Authorizes or denies requests for release time for course development.

Scope of Work

You will serve as a SME for development of <Course Code and Title>. It is anticipated that you will complete this assignment during the <Term> term 20<XX>. Your responsibilities will be to:

- If not completed previously, successfully complete all parts of the "Subject Matter Expert Training" course in the learning management system *prior* to the initial (week 1) meeting with the ID.
- Adhere to the course maps, the University Standards for Online Courses and revise all material identified by the ID as not meeting the Standards or policy requirements.
- Adhere to the development timeline for delivering course content.

- Submit materials electronically (Course Map, Weekly Content Templates, etc.) to the ID.
- If not already specified in the course map, compose weekly lesson objectives (written as measurable student learning outcomes) based upon the course objectives.
- Provide an introduction to each week's lesson that gains the students' attention, provides context for the lesson, lists the lesson objectives, and explains the importance and relevance of the topics to be covered.
- Compose and/or select content (e.g. readings, articles, websites, audio and video resources, etc.) and learning activities that support all lesson objectives; synthesize content into a coherent unit of instruction. Free/open education resources should be preferred over paid resources, unless there is a compelling reason for the latter.
- Assure that video content includes the ability to display closed captioning.
- Create and/or select assignments and assessments that measure all course learning outcomes and each weekly lesson objective.
- Provide estimates of the amount of time required for students to complete the weekly instruction, activities, assignments and assessments.
- Supplement vendor or web-based content with original content as needed.
- Cite and reference all non-original material per current American Psychological Association (APA) style guidelines. Link to non-original materials on the Internet. Do not submit copyrighted content without permission.
- Work collaboratively with the ID – maintaining at least weekly communications.

Weekly Time Commitment

Course teaching and course development are considered to be equivalent loads. Federal guidelines for adjunct faculty work hours stipulate 2.25 hours of weekly work for each credit-hour of the course. Therefore, in order to adhere to the course development timeline, you should be prepared to devote an average of approximately 6.5–7 hours per week (for a 3 credit-hour course) to your online course development tasks, for the duration of this agreement. If your other obligations do not permit you to allot sufficient time to complete the course development on schedule, you should not sign this Agreement.

If you have been assigned as a SME to develop a course and will be released from a teaching load, you will be receiving the same payment as if you were teaching the course. It is expected that you will dedicate no less time and effort to this course development project than if you were assigned to teach a regular class and will complete all tasks in the Scope of Work (see "Compensation for full-time faculty (course development in place of teaching load" below).

Term of Assignment

This Agreement is not intended to modify or replace any existing agreement, contract, policy, or terms governing your existing employment with the institution. The length of the assignment is the course development timeline. *If you are working on a 15-week course, you should not assume that you can deliver all 15 weeks of content during the last week of this agreement, as this will delay the approval of the content and will delay your payment.*

This Agreement may be terminated by either party at any time for any reason, with at least ten (10) days written notice. In accordance with Section XX of the Faculty/ Staff Manual, failure of the SME to maintain weekly communication with the ID or a delay of delivery of course content by more than 2 weeks (unless prior arrangements have been made with the ID) will be considered as having voluntarily terminated this Agreement.

Compensation for Full-Time (Overload) and Part-Time Employees

This is a <Scope> course development. You will be compensated $<Amount>, subject to normal withholdings, for the completion of all tasks listed in the Scope of Work of this Agreement. Note that full course development, and partial course development have different expectations and levels of payment. Payment will be authorized upon the determination by the ID that all submitted materials have met the University Standards for Online Courses, policies and regulations. Content not meeting the Standards and regulations must be brought into compliance before payment is authorized.

Compensation for Full-Time Employees (Teaching Release for Course Development)

NOTE: All releases from teaching for course development must be requested by the Dean and have prior approval from the VP of Academic Affairs/Provost. If you have been assigned as a SME to develop a course and will be released from a teaching load, you will be receiving your normal payments as if you were teaching the course. You will be held responsible for the completion of all tasks listed in the Scope of Work and for adhering to all requirements, timelines and stipulations contained within this Agreement. Your assignment will be considered complete upon the determination by the ID that all submitted materials have met the University Standards for Online Master Courses policies and regulations. Content not meeting the Standards and regulations must be brought into compliance before your assignment is considered complete.

Intellectual Property

This agreement establishes a work-for-hire relationship between you and the university. The institution retains the intellectual property rights for the course and its contents (excluding those items in which the copyright is owned by another entity and the university is using the content by permission). Permission to use the course and its contents outside of normal duties with the university may only be granted with written permission of the VPAA/Provost.

Original Content and Attribution

It is expected that you will create original content and may select some non-original content for this course. By signing this Agreement, you acknowledge that you will not represent content created by others as your original work and that all non-original content submitted by you will be properly attributed according to copyright law and APA guidelines and that material submitted by you will have proper permissions for use and not cause the University to be in violation of copyright or other applicable laws. Material available on the Internet will include links to the original source.

Nondisclosure

SME shall not, at any time during or after the term of this Agreement, in any manner, either directly or indirectly, divulge, disclose, or communicate to any person or entity, or use for SME's own benefit or for the benefit of any other person or entity, and not for the benefit of SUS, any information or data of a confidential or proprietary nature acquired from SUS or its affiliates, or SME's work product, without the express prior written consent of an authorized executive officer of SUS. The provisions of this article shall survive the termination or expiration of this Agreement and any amendments to it.

Appendix B: Sample Standards for Online Master Courses

Course Structure

a. University templates and structure for navigation, syllabi, course schedule, course materials and content delivery are followed.
b. Where available, the course syllabus resides on the master syllabus repository and is linked from within the course.
c. Meet the Instructor section and contact information for the academic program leader is provided.
d. Links or contact information are provided for student resources, including: I.T. helpdesk, LMS after-hours support, academic services, tutorial services and library support.
e. Unique hardware and software technology requirements for the course are stated.

f. Instructions, tutorials and technical support information for setup, configuration, access and use of software and technologies required for the course are provided for instructors and students.

g. Course Schedule includes major weekly topics, required readings, assignments, due days, grading criteria and descriptions of graded assignments.

h. Course Materials/Course Outline includes instructor information, course policies and other materials required for the course and instructions for accessing and using the materials.

i. Information in the Syllabus, Course Schedule, Weekly Assignments and Grade Book are aligned.

j. Weekly lessons are organized by weeks, modules or topics, not by textbook chapters.

k. References to specific textbook pages are to be found only on the Course Schedule and Assignments pages.

Lesson Structure

a. Introduction
    i.   Includes stories, scenarios, images and/or other items to gain learner's attention and introduce the topic.
    ii. Draws upon the learner's prior knowledge and experience to connect with the topic.
    iii. Provides context for the lesson (i.e. where it fits within the course).
    iv. Lists learner objectives for the lesson.

b. Instruction (lesson) includes:
    i.   Instructional content to present the topics (e.g. written, audio, video).
    ii. Instructional activities to facilitate active learning and achievement of the objectives, such as role play; case study; debate; discussion; virtual field trips; web quests; group/team collaborations; procedural/step-by-step tasks; audio/video/written interviews; practice-feedback activities; self-assessments; blogs; wikis; or individual or group research.

c. Assignments includes:
    1.   Readings, including textbooks, journal articles, newspaper articles, magazine articles, websites, blogs or publisher-supplied materials.
    ii. Assessments aligned with each lesson objective, such as written projects, papers, journals, reflections, discussion forums, tests/quizzes/exams, etc.

Learning Objectives

a. Course objectives are stated in terms of measurable student learning outcomes
b. Course objectives are appropriate to the academic level of the course.

c.   Course objectives are aligned with program-level learning outcomes.

d.   All weekly lesson objectives are aligned with course objectives.

Assessments/Assignments

a.   Each weekly assessment/assignment is aligned to and measures one or more weekly objectives.

b.   Assessments/Assignments are appropriate to the academic level of the course.

Regular and Substantive Interaction

a.   Course provides opportunities for instructor to initiate interaction and interact regularly and substantively with students (e.g. course announcements, discussion forums, virtual meetings, assignment annotations/feedback).

b.   Expectations for instructor and student interaction are stated clearly (e.g. will provide feedback on assignments, will participate in discussion forums, will provide timely answers to question, etc.)

c.   Student-student interaction (e.g. discussion forums, chat, teams) and student-content interaction (e.g. tutorials, games) is provided where appropriate to the learning objectives.

d.   The Discussion Forum tool can be used for different purposes: however, online discussions should require interaction and do not have a single correct answer.

e.   Online discussion assignments specify the requirements for both the initial posts and the responses. Response requirements should be specific and based on the lesson (not just "respond to two classmates").

f.   Online discussion assignments facilitate or require instructor interaction as appropriate.

g.   Use of synchronous sessions in asynchronous courses are designed to either be optional or to be recorded for viewing by students who cannot attend the live session.

Instructional Materials

a.   Whenever appropriate and feasible, courses should utilize free/open educational resources.

b.   As appropriate, multiple forms of media (text, images, audio, video, animation) should be used to facilitate multimodal learning. Media should be representative of the diversity of the population.

c.   Videos should be less than 15 minutes in length whenever possible.

d.   Materials from 3rd party vendors and publishers will have completed the formal technical adoption procedure prior to the development or revision of the master course.

Formatting of Content

a. Course follows university online course style policies.3
b. Use of first-person and instructor-specific language in course is avoided.

Copyright

a. Course materials follow federal copyright rules, guidelines and licensing agreements.
b. All non-original material is properly cited and attributed according to APA style guidelines.
c. Materials originating on outside websites are linked – rather than copied – into the LMS.

Accessibility

a. Course follows University policies and Online Course Accessibility Guidelines, including captioning of videos used in master courses and avoiding table-based formatting.

Federal Requirements

a. Course adheres to federal credit hour definition (approximately 9 hours of average total weekly student work for a 3 semester-credit-hour course).
b. To meet federal requirements for online student engagement, each week has a minimum of one assignment to be submitted by students.
c. The LMS grade book includes all graded course assignments, including assignments generated from outside the LMS.

References

– AECT (2017). Instructional Design Standards for Distance Learning. Retrieved from http://aect.org
– Blackboard Inc. (2012). Blackboard exemplary course program rubric. Retrieved from http://blackboard.com/catalyst
– Maryland Online, Inc. (2017). Quality Matters: Non-annotated standards from the QM higher education rubric. Retrieved from https://www.qualitymatters.org/qa-resources/rubric-standards/higher-ed-rubric
– Online Learning Consortium (2018). OSCQR course design review scorecard. https://onlinelearningconsortium.org/consult/oscqr-course-design-review/

Appendix C: Sample Course Development Matrix

Item	Course update	Partial course development	Full course development
SME primary role	Identifies changes from new/updated textbook and sends to Online Instruction Technologist (OIT)	Develops new content and finds/implements content from multiple sources	Develops new content and finds/implements content from multiple sources
Instruction (readings, lecture, videos, tutorials, links to resources, etc.)	New/updated textbook edition OIT updates links and references to assigned readings and resources OIT updates text information OIT corrects typos, grammar and other minor errors	Addition of new instruction in 20% to 50% of course Addition of new multimedia content in up to 50% of course	Addition of new instruction in more than 50% of course Addition of new multimedia content in more than 50% of course Replacement of paid content with free/OER materials*
Assignments/ assessments (exams, discussions, drop boxes, etc.)	OIT corrects settings OIT updates text information OIT corrects typos, grammar and other minor errors	Addition of new assignments/ assessments in 20% to 50% of course	Addition of new assignments/ assessments in more than 50% of course Replacement of paid content with free/OER materials*
New hybrid course w/no online version	N/A	Up to 50% of class sessions meet online	More than 50% of class sessions meet online
SME agreement	NO	YES	YES
Course load equivalent	N/A	½ of a course load	1 course load
Payment (overload)	Stipend	½ payment	Full payment

Appendix D: Sample SME Course Development Timeline

Course number:
Course name:
Subject Matter Expert (SME):
Instructional Designer (ID):
Start date:
Scheduled term for delivery:
Scheduled completion date:

Due date	Deliverable
Kickoff Week 1	*Course development team meeting: SME, ID, Discipline Leader, other team members as needed.*
	– SME begin development of Course Map – a plan listing course objectives, weekly objectives, topics/lectures that address each objective, assessment measures for each objective
Monday Week 2	– Course Map
Monday Week 3	– Week 1 Content – Lecture/learning activities/assignments w/titles and directions/assessment items using the Weekly Content Template
	ID reviews and returns Week 1 content with comments and suggestions as necessary.
Monday Week 4	– Week 2 Content
Monday Week 5	– Week 3 Content
Monday Week 6	– Week 4 Content
Monday Week 7	– Week 5 Content
Monday Week 8	– Week 6 Content
Monday Week 9	– Week 7 Content
	– Midterm Assessment using required assessment format(s)
Monday Week 10	– Week 8 Content
Monday Week 11	– Week 9 Content
Monday Week 12	– Week 10 Content
Monday Week 13	– Week 11 and Week 12 Content
Monday Week 14	– Week 13 and Week 14 Content

(cont.)

Due date	Deliverable
Monday Week 15	– Week 15 Content – Final Exam using required assessment formats – Summary/Evaluation/Closing Comments using Weekly Content Template
After delivery of all content	*SME and ID verify Syllabus, Course Map, assessment and assignment titles, descriptions, and directions. When all requirements for SME Agreement have been met, payment to SME will be authorized.*

Appendix E: Sample Survey Questions

Survey Items for Subject Matter Experts (Slaughter & Murtaugh, 2018, p. 263)
– What did you like about the course development process?
– Were there any requirements that hindered your development progress?
– How would you improve the course development process?
– Had you ever developed this course before?
– How many hours per week did you spend on course development?
– Did you develop new and original content for this course?
– Are you interested in developing more courses for us?
– Please provide suggestions for future subject matter experts based on your experiences with the design and development process.

Survey Items for Students Enrolled in Newly Developed/Redeveloped Course
– The course was easy for me to navigate.
– This course used enough resources like videos, websites or activities to enhance my learning experience.
– The lesson's instructional materials (readings, videos, links, activities, etc.) prepared me for my assignments.
– The assignments (papers, projects, labs, etc.) were appropriate for the lesson topics.
– The quizzes/tests/exams were appropriate for the lesson topics.
– The online discussions helped me to understand the lesson topics.
– Instructions provided for assignments were clear and easy to understand.
– Links to outside materials worked as they should.
– The course was free of typos and grammatical errors.
– Please explain any "disagree" or "strongly disagree" answers.

*Survey Items for Instructors Enrolled in Newly Developed/Redeveloped
Course*

– The course followed a logical sequence.
– The individual lesson objectives were adequately taught and assessed.
– Content in this course was relevant to the topic of the course.
– This course used adequate resources like videos, websites, or games to enhance the educational experience.
– The assignments stimulated critical thinking appropriate to the course's level.
– Instructions provided for assignments were clear.
– Links to outside materials/multimedia were functional.
– The course was free of typos and grammatical errors.
– Please explain any "disagree" or "strongly disagree" answers.

CHAPTER 8

Course Designs for Distance Teaching and Learning

Lauren Cifuentes

Abstract

This chapter provides guidance for administering strategies for overcoming two persistent barriers to instructors' willingness to develop and teach online courses. In addition to addressing barriers, as a distance learning administrator you need to arrange for professional development that prepares instructors to (a) use distance learning technologies, (b) design accessible courses that are free of copyright infringements, (c) follow a systemic & systematic design process, (d) create a course-map, and (e) modularize course content. You also need to address instructors' readiness to teach engaging online courses and programs by facilitating persistence with high levels of presence, interaction, engagement, support, feedback, community, and cultural responsiveness. Beyond fundamentals of online course design, instructors benefit from professional development in constructivist, student-centered course design, motivational learning design; and integrating open educational resources and social media in courses to support active inquiry and multimodal learning. Instructors also need preparation in the basics of how to flip and blend face-face courses, build competency-based instruction, and use learning analytics to understand the impacts of inputs on student outcomes.

Keywords

online course design – design for online learning – online teaching – instructional design for online courses – course mapping – modularizing content – professional development for online learning – professional development for online teaching

1   Introduction

A distance-learning (DL) administrator's responsibilities include supporting online course and program design, development, and delivery. Success requires that you build relationships with academic leaders to determine their wishes and needs, set benchmarks, and devise strategies for meeting goals. In

addition, coordinating efforts and aligning aspirations with centers for teaching excellence, funded projects, Faculty Senate, and librarians also helps DL
administrators meet your institution's academic mission. Most importantly,
you must establish relationships with instructors who teach online or are
learning to teach online.

Online instructors need to be able to apply different instructional strategies
than they would in the face-face classroom. Knowing fundamental pedagogical
principles described in this chapter regarding how to design and deliver online
courses in response to what we know about how people learn will help instructors offer effective and efficient courses and programs. Of course, in addition
to promoting pedagogical principles, professional development opportunities
must include training in how to use technologies that allow for online course
delivery (see Chapters 9 and 14).

2   Overcoming Barriers

Two persistent barriers that you must address are (1) course ownership, and
(2) instructors' time constraints and academic goals. A distance learning (DL)
administrator must either be able to make their institution's guidelines for
course ownership known or develop them in collaboration with upper administration and faculty. Course ownership is a significant issue related not only
to your institution's business model, but also to faculty incentive and quality
assurance. On the topic of ownership, Madeleine Albright quotes Larry Sum-
mers, once the head of Harvard, as offering that, "no one washes a rented car"
(Albright, 2020, p. 100). When instructors own a course, they take care of it by
designing it well, inserting their experience and special level of expertise into
it, and revising it in response to student input.

In the 1990's when the Educational Technology Masters' program was
funded by Texas A&M University to go fully online, I made an appointment
with the Dean of Faculty to discuss the issue of course ownership. I had heard
other faculty members complain that online courses are owned by the institution where they are created, and they were adamant that they did not want to
go online because it would mean giving their intellectual property away. Much
to my surprise, when I arrived at the meeting, the vice provost of that enormous R1 university was at the table wanting to hear and discuss my thoughts.
I realized then what an important issue it was. We concluded that, when the
university paid for course development, the university owned all rights to an
online course until that amount of funding had been earned by the university,
at which point the course met the conditions for joint ownership between the

institution and the instructor. If the instructor were to leave the institution, they could take their course with them, but they would also leave their course with the university. This became the guideline for the Texas A&M University System's twelve campuses.

Later as a distance learning administrator, I saw how important it was to convey solid guidelines regarding course ownership. Many instructors were unwilling to go online because they did not want to put in the hard work of designing and developing a course and sharing their expertise knowing that the university could give that course to another faculty member or adjunct to teach. They were not thrilled with the idea of putting their hearts and souls into something that would be passed along to others. I found that even when we provided financial incentives, instructors chose to develop courses that focused only on the basics. They left out engaging elements and their professional experiences that they felt were trademarks of their personal quality-teaching. To ensure quality, ownership as well as incentives, are substantial factors that must be addressed with individuals or teams that design, develop, and teach online courses.

> Learn about the ownership guidelines at your institution. Do they satisfy both instructors and the institutional mission?

A second barrier to instructors' willingness to develop and teach online courses is their perception that they would waste time in the face of their academic goals and responsibilities to conduct research and publish new knowledge. Until the Covid-19 crisis, many if not most instructors resisted teaching online. However, I found that the ability to teach from a field location where faculty members conducted research or from a conference where they presented their research findings incentivized some faculty to build an online course environment. In addition, many realized that they could conduct research and publish insights regarding online teaching in their fields.

Instructors can test theories to learn more about how people learn in their fields of study, thereby informing course design and online teaching practice. Research evidence is needed across and within disciplines regarding methods for understanding the relative importance of instructional features of online courses and programs that induce student effort and learning. In addition, interactions among instructional features and factors in the learning context, learner characteristics, and specific types of learning tasks (e.g. Blooms taxonomy) need to be more deeply understood. For instance, instruction could be better personalized if we knew whether or not students with certain characteristics benefit more from a particular feature than do others and if certain strategies are most effective in specific disciplines.

With technological advances come changes in the ways that people learn and the ways that instructional opportunities can be provided. Crowd-sourcing, data analytics, social media, gaming, machine learning, artificial intelligence, mobile-learning, virtual and augmented reality, and 3-D printing all open exciting possibilities for conducting research. Experts across disciplines can raise questions and provide evidence regarding how to design and develop courses and programs, best analyze learners for personalization, implement instruction, and evaluate success. For more on barriers and how to overcome them see Chapter 3 and Cifuentes et al. (2018).

Write and share a research question the answer to which would inform online learning administration.

3   Designing Accessibility and Copyright Compliant Courses Laws

As I was working in my DL office, a staff member came to me in a rush of concern that a professor had told a student that, although the student was deaf, the professor would not close-caption the videos uploaded to his online course and the student would have to drop the course. Knowing his rights, the student came to our office to report the offense prior to his next step. If the professor continued to insist, then he would report the violation at the state level to initiate a lawsuit (see Chapter 4). In order to comply with moral and ethical principles, best practices, and laws, within two days our offices had scrambled to close-caption the videos. The professor was required to take our professional development workshop on accessibility.

A DL administrator must systemically and systematically address accessibility for online learning. It is the law that online courses be accessible whether or not students who need accommodations and modifications are enrolled. Accessible courses benefit all students (Balaji & Chakrabarti, 2010). For instance, conscientious students appreciate being able to view course content several times and some find that multiple modes of content delivery facilitate their deep understandings. Application of universal design principles during course design and development enhances "a product's usability for the broadest audience without diminishing its function" (Burgstahler & Cory, 2008, p. 214) and assures that course designs meet accessibility standards (see Chapters 4 and 7).

DL administrators need to advance the mission of accessibility compliance in online courses by building an inclusive campus support infrastructure. To facilitate frequent collaboration across campus, regularly scheduled meetings should include the office of disability services, information technology, marketing and communications, the library, the Title IV and Section 508 coordinator, faculty members, students with disabilities, and leaders in other relevant departments that serve to support students.

The major roles that DL offices play in assuring accessibility are to provide professional development to instructors and review courses for accessibility. The hope is that through professional development, compliance will follow. Professional development needs to prepare instructors to:
- know and abide by accessibility laws,
- apply universal design principles in courses,
- address needs of students with different disabilities,
- make course files accessible,
- request publishers to provide accessible digital resources, and
- access and use existing free software to transcribe and close-caption media.

Ideally you offer such professional development both face-face and online so that instructors can choose their preferred mode of learning. You also need to provide instructors with the criteria that will be used to review their courses for accessibility. And you need to allocate human resources to support accessibility compliance for development and delivery of professional development, support materials, course-reviews, and evaluating and documenting outcomes (Cifuentes et al., 2016).

> Locate an online tutorial for closed captioning a YouTube video. Use the tutorial to closed caption an instructional video (perhaps one that you have shot).

In addition to safeguarding instructors and your institution from lawsuits for being inaccessible, you must provide instructors with interventions for helping them follow copyright and fair use law. Both individual professors and institutions can be sued and can lose copyright cases. In May, 2011 the trial phase began in a lawsuit against Georgia State University for copyright infringement: Cambridge University Press et al. v. Patton et al. It was the first time a university had been sued for such a violation. The Atlanta district court endorsed fair use. However, publishers (Cambridge, Oxford, and Sage) appealed. In October 2014, the Eleventh Circuit Court remanded the case to the lower court. They determined that fair use must be determined on a case-by-case or work-by-work basis.

Instructors commonly copy articles off the Internet and drop them in their courses. This is a breach of copyright law. In order to legally upload copyrighted, full text of articles or book chapters to your online course, copyright clearance must be obtained. A legal alternative is for articles or book chapters to be placed on electronic reserve by school libraries upon request by the instructor. Once copyright approval is granted, schools pay for each item that they put on reserve. Then items are available online through the school library electronic reserves and can be downloaded and printed or saved to each student's computer in .pdf format. However, the student should not share the document with others. If a publisher has allowed copyright approval to be purchased in the past, there is no guarantee they will continue to do so. Publishers often do not grant permission to place large works such as book chapters or textbooks on reserve.

Go to Wikipedia.org to read the definition and details of Fair Use. Given an online course, determine if copyright laws have been broken by inclusion of content copied and pasted from the Internet. Discuss the four factors judges use to determine whether the use made of a work in any particular case is a fair use.

4   Systemic and Systematic Online Course and Program Design Processes

As a distance learning administrator, you should develop professional development in systemic and systematic online course design processes. Foundational to instructional and learning design theories is that effective instruction is designed both systemically and systematically. Systemically in that quality learning design addresses the complex learning system, including the learning context; learner's traits, characteristics, needs, motivators, and interests; and conditions necessary for developing specific types of knowledge and skills.

For a deep understanding of how to analyze your learning context see Chapter 6. Analyzing learners at an institution is complicated and requires exploration of existing data about the student body. With Covid-19, most higher education students became online learners. Individuals in the diverse population of learners in higher-education vary across entry skills, digital literacy, information literacy, reading and writing literacy, time management, and online communication skills (Rovai, 2003). Students also vary in their finances, hours of employment, family responsibilities, outside encouragement, opportunity for transfer, and life crises (Bean & Metzner, 1985). In spite of varied traits and characteristics, the vast majority of learners hope to persist in their studies and earn degrees. DL administrators need to facilitate delivery of professional development that facilitates student persistence by personalizing the learners' experience. Attending to learners' wide-ranging traits and characteristics increases their engagement and satisfaction.

Analyzing types of learning involved in courses, most commonly known as cognitive task analysis (see Chapter 13 for evidence of its usefulness), and designing courses accordingly is a powerful means to student competence. Identifying to-be-learned psychomotor skills, attitudes, information, procedures, concepts, problem-solving strategies, and metacognitive strategies is an essential act when designing effective learning environments because the process leads to identification of course and program objectives (Hattie, 2008). Objectives are often based on external standards and materials such as text-books, the instructor's expertise, state or national standards, workforce demands, or the unique learning context. Analyzing course goals in order to identify course objectives and the conditions under which they can be learned involves instructors asking and answering the questions, "what tasks do students need to be able to do as a result of taking this course? And, "what do students need to be able to succeed in those tasks?" Answers to these questions provide the basis for performance objectives. Bloom's hierarchical taxonomy is a framework for identifying performances described in course objectives (Anderson & Krathwohl, 2001).

In addition to addressing elements of the instructional system, effective learning designers use a systematic process commonly known as backward design wherein designers develop assessments before identifying the strategies that lead to student success (Wiggins & McTighe, 2005). Course designers keep the end in mind by asking what evidence students need to produce in order to demonstrate their having met course learning goals and objectives. Most models used for systematically developing learning experiences, have the following in common: Design and development begins with goal setting and analyzing goals to establish performance-based objectives. Then, in an iterative process and not necessarily in this sequence, course designers develop assessments aligned to those objectives or to a set of chunked objectives; determine what materials, activities, strategies, and assignments will scaffold success on assessments; and, formatively evaluate learners' success and satisfaction to inform revision (Dick et al., 2016; Morrison et al., 2011). When assessments align with objectives, they often involve review or observation of authentic performances or portfolios. These are known as authentic assessments.

Most instructors require professional development in how to analyze and account for the learning system (Paloff & Pratt, 2011; Stavredes, 2014). To provide such professional development, support, and community building, your office needs to develop a rich array of workshops and web resources for teachers and students or select existing, copyright free resources to share with instructors and students.

4.1   Course-Mapping and Modularizing

Preplanning when designing courses by mapping and modularizing facilitates development of courses that are organized and easy to navigate. Alignment of course elements can be facilitated by using a planning matrix, also known as a course map, to illustrate the scope and sequence of a course. In a course-map, objectives, assessments, activities, materials, strategies, and assignments are described for each major course topic and each topic represents what will become a course module. This preplanning saves time, helps instructors create an organized course, and facilitates alignment among course elements. In a well-planned, aligned course, students are informed of expectations, receive the scaffolding necessary to meet expectations, and are assessed to determine the extent that they were able to meet expectations. The Online Course-Map Guide[1] provides details and a template to follow.

A consistent organizational structure within modules helps students easily navigate their course. For instance, each module might contain sections with the headings: (a) Attention; (b) Objectives; (c) Learning Materials; (d) Activities; (e) Assignments; (f); Discussion; and (g) Assessments. Content for each section is based upon decisions made during construction of the course-map. Typically, each module includes objectives, assessments on chunks of objectives, readings, activities, assignments, and learning objects that provide for multi-modal learning, interaction among students in group-work and/or discussions, and rubrics describing the criteria for assessment.

Additionally, when a class is designed to include interaction among students, students' commitment to the course is enhanced. Describing a course's modular structure in the syllabus helps students know what to expect in terms of navigation. To stick with a course, students need confidence that they can succeed. Therefore, expectations need to be clearly and regularly stated in objectives sections that frame the course.

> As a DL administrator, write a sentence describing something you would like instructors to be able to do when designing or delivering an online course. Explain the relevance of the capability. List materials they will need to succeed. List activities they should conduct to be successful. How would you determine the extent to which instructors were successful?

5   Instructors' Readiness to Teach Online

Online instructors' roles and competencies differ from those of face-to-face teachers (see Chapters 7 and 9). They need institutional support in online course design, development, and teaching to transition from face-face teaching to online teaching and often need to work closely with an instructional designer or team who facilitates the process.

Administrators must be knowledgeable about the differences between face-to-face course designs and online course designs. They must be familiar with the criteria used to judge quality as they oversee compliance with quality standards and help to ensure that instructors offer courses that are accessible, outcomes-focused, rigorous, engaging, easy to navigate, collaborative, and copyright compliant. See Chapter 10 for a discussion of quality criteria and measures. In addition, below is a discussion of principles of quality course design that might be included in professional development for those who design and develop online courses.

One of the main jobs of a distance learning administrator is to oversee delivery of professional development in online course design, delivery, and teaching. Kumar et al. (2019) interviewed eight award-winning online faculty members from across the United States to explore their insights on elements of their course designs. The five main areas that emerged from the data analysis were (a) authentic and relevant course materials that connect to practice, (b) the use of multimedia resources, (c) student creation of digital content individually and collaboratively, (d) students' reflection on learning, and (e) the instructor's explanation of the purpose of activities, technologies, and assessments in the online course. A DL administrator's job is to support instructors as they include each of these elements in their courses.

5.1   *Presence*
Perhaps other DL administrators have experienced what I found when I first arrived in my administrative position. Several instructors treated their online courses as correspondence courses. Their courses were distributed online at the beginning of the term, they entered grades for midterm and final exams, and they rarely entered the course until it was time to submit grades. I want to think that this no longer happens anywhere, but I fear that, particularly in courses developed without the appointed instructor's input, some online courses are delivered with low levels of teaching presence or interaction.

Students' regular and frequent presence in a course is critical and must be modeled and emphasized by instructors. Both should log in regularly and contribute. Instructors should make frequent announcements, contribute to discussions, and scaffold assignments as well as encourage students to communicate with them for help or clarification through email, discussion boards, chat rooms, texts, or video-conferencing. To assure that time does not get away from them, at the beginning of each term, instructors need to block time on their calendars for such communications as well as for providing feedback on assignments.

Cognitive, social, and teaching presence are each important in online courses as described by the community of inquiry (CoI) model for online instruction discussed in Chapters 5 and 13 (Garrison & Anderson, 2003). Cognitive presence involves the instructor providing suggestions, resources, examples, prompts, hints, constructive feedback, and other types of guidance to trigger students' participation in exploration and integration of ideas, problem solutions, and/or resolution. The instructor continuously directs students' both collectively and individually toward goal attainment, supports discourse around to-be-learned concepts, and helps students regulate their own learning. Instructors can encourage critical thinking and creativity by facilitating debate, identifying assumptions, challenging the importance of context, and encouraging reflective skepticism (Brookfield, 1987; Stavredes & Herder, 2014).

Building social presence involves promoting instructors and learners' interactions around their personal and professional interests and getting to know each other as people who function beyond schooling, support each other, and strive to be critical thinkers. Social presence can be encouraged in online discussion, group work, and peer reviews of assignments. Instructors set the climate, engage with learners, and support discourse. When instructors promote social presence, technology becomes transparent and learners feel a sense of being together rather than separated by time and location (Lehman & Conceicao, 2010). Social presence reduces learners' feelings of isolation and provides them with a learning community that may extend beyond their course.

Teaching presence refers to the instructors' actions that support learners' cognitive and social processes that help them realize meaningful and educationally worthwhile learning outcomes. To teach effectively online, instructors keep abreast of and apply emerging technologies and pedagogy/andragogy and provide students with guidance for how to use those technologies. Instructors establish teaching presence by interacting regularly and frequently with learners.

> Share the idea that you think is most important concerning the value of presence and ask others to do the same. Discuss why you chose the ideas that you each chose.

5.2   *Interaction*

The U.S. Department of Education's regulation states that in courses in higher education instructors must interact regularly and substantively with students as described in Chapter 4. The four criteria for meeting the expectation are that the interactions are:

- initiated by the instructor,
- regular and frequent,
- substantive and of an academic nature, and
- initiated by an instructor who meets accrediting agency standards.

This regulation is based on what we know about how people learn: interaction leads to learning, feedback leads to revision of mental models, discussion leads to reflection, and reflection leads to transformation (Clark & Mayer, 2011; Bransford et al., 1999).

Seven types of interaction are important to consider in online learning environments. For a course to be effective each should be addressed in course design, development, and delivery. First, learner-interface interaction depends on clean course structure that eases navigation and renders the technology as transparent as possible so that students do not have to spend much time wondering where to go next. Second, learner-support should be made easy for students to access on a just-in-time basis. Third, learner-context interaction involves the way course activities fit into the context of the degree program, department, college, campus, and community. Fourth, fifth, and sixth are learner-instructor, learner-expert, and learner-learner interactions. Seventh is the learner-content interaction that should be the focus and be facilitated by the other six types of interaction.

LMSs provide online tools to create engaging strategies and frequent instructor-to-student interactions as well as student-student interactions about content. Which tool to use depends on the outcomes you and students want to achieve and affordances of the tool. For instance, if you want students to collaboratively develop a single product, a collaborative wiki-type environment would be the appropriate tool. If you want students to socially reflect on an issue, social media and discussion forums are appropriate when the instructor or peers provide quality prompts. Often, instructors need to model interactive processes, demonstrate that they are present, and evaluate interactive processes for learners to engage in interactions. To ensure instructor or expert-to-student interaction, instructors can hold office hours; send regular emails, messages, and announcements requiring action; respond to students' private reflections; provide feedback regarding student work; encourage students' self-directedness; assign activities that require interaction; and schedule regular interactions on their personal calendars.

Student-student interaction expands students' worldviews providing them with opportunities to question previously held beliefs and explore new ones. Learning in a social context makes learning pleasurable and engaging for most learners and helps them establish a professional learning community. Instructors need to use online tools to create engaging strategies that require frequent student-to-student interactions about content. They might require students to express, discuss, and comment on each other's ideas; review and revise each other's work; or work on projects, solve problems, or address cases in small groups.

> Create a rigorous assignment requiring instructors to interact with each other for learning about online teaching. Decide how many points the assignment should count toward a certificate in online course design, development, and delivery.

5.3   *Engagement*

Over the years I have heard many instructors lament that online courses cannot be as engaging as face-to-face courses. However, students' engagement in any course depends on the way a course is designed and delivered, the activities, and the assignments. Becker's (2015) Venn diagram (see Figure 8.1) illustrating that student engagement is the intersection between their motivation and active learning, shows us where the focus lies when teaching an engaging course; it lies with students' interests and performances, not with instructors' performances such as lectures. Most importantly, engaging courses are learner-centered rather than teacher-centered. Learners' motivations are considered so that they stay focused on activities that keep them on the road to success.

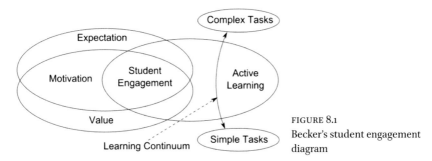

FIGURE 8.1
Becker's student engagement diagram

Authentic learning experiences often involve students stepping away from the LMS and performing tasks in real-world contexts (Herrington et al., 2010). Models describing engaged, authentic learning typically include apprenticeships, collaboration, reflection, coaching, multiple practices, and articulation about practices. Students perceive tasks to be real and, therefore, worth doing. Students can engage online in activities that keep them busy exploring and discussing ideas, asking questions and finding answers, making or constructing things, and expressing themselves. The online environment has the advantage over face-face classrooms in that students can post their work for all to see. I have found that this practice raises the bar for students as they share perspectives, comment, and reflect on others' contributions.

> What three compelling points would you share with instructors as to why posting a collection of recorded one-hour long lectures three times a week is not the most effective way to present content in an online course.

5.2   *Support and Feedback*

Students need to feel supported as they progress through an online course, and when they do, they stick with their program (Tinto, 2012). Although ensuring presence and interaction, and offering engaging learning experiences increase the likelihood that students will know that instructors are available to support them, the most impactful supports instructors can provide learners are frequent procedural, cognitive, and metacognitive scaffolds and feedback that supports their achievement of learning objectives, whether those objectives are supplied by the instructor or generated by students. Therefore, distance learning administrators should help instructors know how to scaffold learning and provide constructive feedback.

Procedural scaffolds include orientations at the beginning of terms to clarify course goals, expectations, and processes such as due dates and discussion protocols. In addition, instructors should provide optional tutorials guiding students through technologies they may or may not know how to use, as well as step-wise explanations of assignments.

Cognitive scaffolds help students organize their thoughts and lead to understanding of concepts. In addition to well organized course content, instructors might include advance organizers such as summaries, concept maps, or checklists of main ideas in modules and alternate pathways to follow and resources from which to choose.

One major task of online students is to manage their own learning. As a DL administrator, your job is to share with instructors ways to help students self-regulate. Metacognitive scaffolds support students as they make their way through online studies. McGuire (2015) identifies methods for teaching students how to learn in the context of their college studies regardless of their

discipline. McGuire's research indicates that when instructors encourage these activities, students' performances dramatically improve:
  – review past exams and class notes,
  – study course content as early as possible and repeat those studies,
  – begin work on assignments as soon they know of the assignment,
  – repeatedly read textbook content,
  – aim for 100% understanding,
  – use intense study sessions, and
  – study in groups.

Historically, college courses typically included one or two midterm exams and one final exam. Grades on those events provided students with the only feedback they might receive. Now, learning scientists have determined that frequent scaffolding of assignments and feedback that is clearly aligned to learning objectives or outcome statements are most facilitative of student learning because they allow students to be engaged and grow in their competence (Bransford et al., 1999). In short, multiple criterion-referenced feedback loops provide students with information focused on their performance that confirms or counters their understanding and provides insight. Feedback loops help students progress through objectives toward a goal.

Watch the video, *Teaching Without Walls: 10 Tips for Online Teaching*, created by Michael Wesch and posted on YouTube.[2] Make note of his 10 tips and place them in order of importance from your perspective. Share with others to see the extent of shared agreement.

5.3   *Online Community and Cultural Responsiveness*
Distance learning administrators need to support instructors as they strive to be inclusive and culturally responsive to their students. In addition to delivering engaging course content, instructors need to engage students on a personal level by responding to their specific learning needs. Such responsiveness increases student persistence and satisfaction in online courses (Hebert, 2006). As expressed earlier, learners vary across multiple traits and characteristics. In addition to what was mentioned earlier in this chapter, students vary in their expectations regarding the teacher's role, levels and origin of motivation, desire for control of their own learning, wish to customize their own learning experiences, value of errors, approach to addressing course activities, focus on theoretical understanding versus real-world application, and appreciation of collaborative opportunities (Edmundson, 2007). Courses and programs must

adapt to this diversity (Gunawardena et al., 2019). In today's globalized world, teachers can assume that diverse students will arrive to their courses and will vary across the above attributes as well as many others not listed here.

To best address diverse learners, online courses need to incorporate cultural inclusivity and universal design principles that draw those learners into learning experiences by inviting them to follow authentic learning paths that resonate with their past experiences and learning goals (Herrington et al., 2010). Authentic, experiential learning engages diverse students in working together to solve real problems; address real cases; research, create, and publish original products; or participate in real-world projects. Such coursework empowers students to make their own choices, apply their own experiences, and set their own paths for learning, particularly important for adult learners. Meaningful learning experiences resonate with students when they are embedded in the diverse social and physical contexts within which they will be used or when such contexts are simulated. And most higher education students expect learning experiences with the flavor of the unique context of their institution (Gunawardena et al., 2019).

The Association of American Colleges and Universities identified establishing, building, and maintaining learning communities as a high-impact practice that leads to student success (Brownell & Swaner, 2010). As Jody Donovan (2015) claims in her blog, "taking an online course should be more than sitting in front of a computer – real engagement involves becoming a part of the community of learners." Learning communities provide diverse college students with a sense of belonging to a group that shares their goals and interests. Often individuals in that shared community interact through social media beyond their courses and become colleagues as they build their careers. Community rarely happens in the context of a single course. Rather, community can be formed at the program level by intentionally coordinating and linking the content of courses, materials, assignments, grading rubrics, and course resources within programs. Instructors and program coordinators should be prepared to orient students to expectations across a program; use instructional-teams; and use engaging pedagogies (Brownell & Swaner, 2010).

Palloff and Pratt (2011) created a framework for distance learning that generates growth of learning community in online programs. Their framework advises that:

- Online courses should include focused outcomes with buy-in from everyone in a program and time spent sharing goals.
- Content knowledge should be achieved actively through and with interaction and feedback.
- Classes should include facilitated collaboration.

– Faculty guidance toward teamwork with mutually negotiated guidelines should be in place to help students be part of a learning community.

The hope of online learning communities is that they increase comfort, communication, and collaboration among students and with instructors. Online collaboration tools and social media promote learners' senses of community and increase the knowledge flow between students (Bliss & Lawrence, 2009; Dawson, 2006; Kumi-Yeboah, 2018). Knowledge flow facilitates social negotiation of meaning as learners construct their own understandings.

Gunawardena, Frechette, and Layne (2019) developed an innovative approach to creating what they call Wisdom Communities, or WisComs, to guide the development of culturally inclusive learning environments. The stated goal of participants in a WisCom is to cultivate wisdom through transformative learning.

Sociocultural learning theories frame the design, development, implementation, and evaluation of WisComs that support inclusion of learners from diverse cultures. The theories provide a rational for building an online learning community that facilitates discovering content knowledge, problem-solving, thinking critically, and forming identity. The sociocultural perspective on learning emphasizes that learners develop and learn by transforming their understandings through socially shared activities. Each learner has unique knowledge, needs, experiences, culture, and expectations that, when shared, can broaden others' perspectives and knowledge bases while they themselves benefit from those others. Learners with diverse levels of competence learn from one another and their instructors.

In a WisCom, students use technologies to communicate with one another online. Social interaction, dialog, discourse, collaborative problem-solving, and construction of new knowledge with instructors and peer guidance are the fundamental activities of WisComs. Gunawardena calls this transactional approach "distributed co-mentoring." Although socio-cultural learning theories have been proposed for many years, developing learning environments that facilitate sociocultural learning has been difficult if not impossible until the advent of online learning technologies. Such technologies can bring experts and learners together in distributed learning communities to contribute to each other's learning synchronously and asynchronously. In addition, advanced technologies can help identify students' needs and digital agents can differentially scaffold learning to personalize the learning process according the needs of each learner.

Along with distributed co-mentoring, learner support plays a critical role in WisComs. As thoroughly discussed in Chapter 12, student retention, motivation, professional identity formation, academic achievement, satisfaction, engagement, and success all hinge on students knowing that they are supported (Mehran et al., 2010). Therefore, a WisCom includes access to interactive activities and services intended to support and facilitate the learning process of each student. Students in a WisCom collaboratively follow an inquiry cycle of learning challenges, exploring possibilities and resources, continuous reflection, negotiation among fellow participants, and preservation of their new-found knowledge in artifacts. "The [WisCom] framework incorporates several core elements: wisdom, community, communication, technology, co-mentoring, learner support, collaborative problem solving, and transformative learning" (Gunawardena, 2020, p. 21). Figure 8.2 illustrates the WisCom framework.

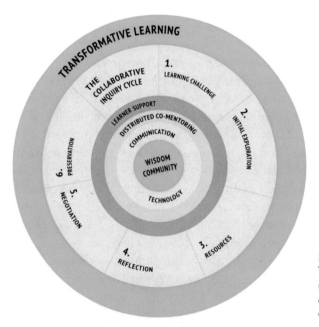

FIGURE 8.2
WisCom framework
(from Gunawardena
et al., 2019, created by
Casey Frechette)

Use the WisCom Framework to brainstorm specific ways to personalize and build community in an online degree program prior to term start dates, at the start, pre-midterm, post-midterm, close of term, and post-close.

Gamrat (2020) generated a graphic representation of strategies to use while developing and teaching a course where students feel welcome and connected to the instructor, the course, and each other. The author shared specific actions for creating a caring, inclusive environment. These are categorized as (1) set clear expectations with students, (2) communicate and collaborate regularly, and most importantly, (3) iteratively improve the design of student experiences. Figure 8.3 reiterates points made throughout this chapter and provides specific and useful suggestions for instructors to improve their teaching practices.

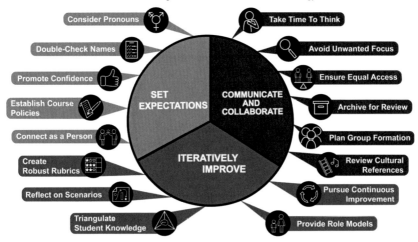

FIGURE 8.3   PennState's model of factors in inclusive teaching and course design

5.4   *Constructivist, Student-Centered Courses*

To captivate hearts and minds, instructors need to provide meaningful experiences for students that address their interests. Dewey (1938) identified our four human interests to be tapped in educational environments: Conversation or communication, inquiry or finding things out, making or constructing things, and artistic self-expression. E-learning that is scenario or case-based, problem-based, inquiry-based, service-based, or project-based provides contexts for fulfilling these interest (Herrington et al., 2010). Constructivist learning theory tells us that learning facts, procedures, concepts, principles, problem-solving, metacognitive skills, and theories takes place in the context of meaningful experiences. Knowledge is individually and socially co-constructed by learners based on their interpretations of their experiences in the world. Knowledge cannot be transmitted from one expert to many learners. Rather, educational and social experiences facilitate knowledge construction differently for each individual.

Given meaningful experiences that involve collaborative activity, most learners feel pleasure from their effort and are most willing to spend the time necessary to learn. In addition, when students work with other learners, they negotiate meaning and broaden their perspectives. Therefore, authentic learning in courses occurs in teams just as activity in the workplace is typically conducted in teams.

Authentic learning also occurs in student-centered courses in which students focus on their own performances and progress toward competence rather than on instructor's performances, such as lectures. In student-centered courses, instructors establish fundamental objectives or students may determine their own objectives. Instructors assist and mentor learners in goal-setting, designing or selecting learning tasks, task performance, and evaluating performance and learning (Reigeluth et al., 2017). Instructors provide access to resources so that students can choose their own paths to achieving objectives. Student-centeredness means that students determine how they accomplish objectives, which content best supports their progress, what support and resources they will use to meet the objectives, and what they will do in what order to succeed. Instructors assess students based upon their attainment of objectives. Shared rubrics allow students to participate in evaluation of their own learning. In constructivist, student-centered online courses, learners' tasks should be authentic or realistic, be of interest to learners, and involve active learning through projects, problem-solving, inquiry, service, or case analysis.

Think of a span of time when you learned a great deal about a specific topic. Share your experience with others and learn of theirs. What was the topic of study? What were some of the activities? If an instructor was involved, what role(s) did they play in your learning? Did you learn in isolation or with others? What made the experience work for you? What and how did you learn? Did you learn anything unexpected? How does your experience compare and contrast with the experience of the people with whom you shared? What strategies from your learning experience can you encourage instructors to incorporate in their courses?

5.5   *Motivate Students to Engage*

McGuire (2015) proclaims that "an unsupportive environment is the number one obstacle to student motivation that faculty have enormous power to change" (p. 76). Distance education administrators need a deep understanding of how to motivate two audiences: students and instructors. Expectancy-value theory (Eccles & Wigfield, 2002) and the ARCS Model of motivation for learning and performance (Keller, 2010) frame motivational design for online learning and provide motivating strategies. Expectancy-value theory links individuals' expectations and task values and beliefs to performance, persistence, and task choice. The ARCS model identifies attention, relevance, confidence, and satisfaction as keys to motivation. Cifuentes et al. (2018) explored the application of these two theories when designing tactics for lifting barriers to adoption of learning technologies.

Expectancy-value theory purports learners are motivated by clearly stated expectations because they clarify for students' what it takes to be successful so that they can perform accordingly toward achievement (Eccles & Wigfield, 2002; Tinto, 2012). DL administrators can facilitate a campus culture of clarity regarding expectations by providing a syllabus template with the following components: goal and performance objectives statements, details for how and when students contact instructors, IT help, LMS support, and accessibility support, a course schedule with a comprehensive list of assignments, their point distributions, and due dates.

The A in ARCS theory stands for generating and sustaining students' attentions. To capture interest, Keller (2010) recommends using novel approaches and injecting personal and/or emotional material. To stimulate an attitude of inquiry, he recommends asking probing questions, creating paradoxes, generating inquiry, and nurturing thinking challenges. To maintain attention, he recommends variations in presentation of content, concrete analogies, human interest, examples, and unexpected events.

When students perceive the relevance (R), they value course content and opt to engage, are satisfied with instruction, persist in their efforts, and choose to work on those tasks (Eccles & Wigfield, 2002; Shernoff et al., 2003). A belief that course content is relevant and valuable in their lives is a necessary ingredient for engagement. To meet learners' needs, Keller recommends providing explicit statements or examples of the utility of the instruction. Through introductions, surveys, and discussions, instructors should ascertain and be responsive to students' motives by providing personal achievement opportunities, cooperative activities, leadership responsibilities, and positive, enthusiastic role models. Also, Keller recommends using familiar materials and concepts by providing concrete examples and analogies related to the learners' work and background.

Students' confidence (C) refers to their perception of being able to have coursework under control and the expectation for success in a course (Keller, 2010). Infusing learners with confidence requires clear expectations, providing brief, challenging experiences that lead to success, allowing students to have personal control, and providing feedback that attributes success to personal effort (Dweck, 2006).

As for instructors, they want and need for their students to experience satisfaction (S) in their courses. Both pride in work, as well as promotion and
tenure depend on positive student evaluations. Keller proposes the following
strategies for supporting student satisfaction:
- Provide links to tutorials so that learners do not have to spend time frustrated by the technology. Applications that might be used by instructors to
  enrich students' experiences should be identified and provided by the DL
  administrator.
- Provide feedback that reinforces positive feelings for personal effort and
  accomplishment.
- Use verbal praise, real or symbolic rewards, and incentives, or let learners
  present the results of their efforts.
- Make performance requirements consistent with stated expectations, and
  use consistent measurement standards for all learners' tasks and accomplishments (Keller, 2010).

A course environment can be intentionally designed to support students'
expectations, attentions, perceptions of the value and relevance of course content, confidence, and satisfaction. For instance, the typical module I develop
begins with an attention getter that provides an example of the utility of the
module's content or an inspiring representative case. Each module in my
course, Critical Digital Literacy, begins with Why Is This So Important. Module 1 begins with links to two YouTube sites, one that defines digital literacy
and the other that emphasizes the importance of being digitally literate. After
the attention getter, I present the objectives that clarify expectations for that
module. The module's structure is clearly aligned to objectives so that learners
are not daunted by navigation and can focus on course content and activities.

Kochtanek and Hein (2000) describe the online instructor's role as one who
"rather than merely putting information into the head of the student, creates
an environment where students themselves can arrange existing knowledge
and create their own learning constructs" (p. 281). Beyond design, delivery also
involves attending to motivating strategies. The motivating instructor clarifies
expectations, directs students' attention, shares the value and relevance of
what students are spending time doing, and helps learners feel confident and
satisfied with their efforts.

Courses taught from a constructivist, student-centered perspective motivate students because the focus of both instructors and students is on personal
growth applicable in the real-world. Similarly, competency-based courses prepare students for success in the workplace. Culturally responsive instruction
and multimodal materials tend to motivate students with personally relevant content provided to individuals and groups. Administering professional

development that prepares instructors to create learning environments where students desire to learn and commit to do so will enhance the culture of your institution from both students' and instructors' perspectives. For more on motivation see Chapter 13.

- Describe two or three strategies to include in instructors' professional development that would help motivate them to adopt learning technologies.
- Describe two or three strategies to include in online courses to help motivate students to learn content in a course.

5.6   *Online Educational Resources and Social Media*

Online instructors enhance course content and facilitate students' construction of their own learning paths by providing online resources in the form of text-based supplemental resources, images, audio and video recordings, voices and perspectives in podcasts, field experiences, games, collaborative tools, simulations, and virtual or augmented reality. There are millions of powerful online educational resources (OERs) and social media tools in any field that can support teaching and students' learning. These resources make it possible for students to set their own paths and follow their own interests.

Because it so easy to access OERs, it is critical that, instructors and learners are prepared to evaluate materials before they trust that the source is credible, upload them, or link to them. Also, they must know how to attribute copyright to materials lifted from the web. With such easy availability, one can clutter up a course with too many or tangential OERs. The selection criterion of most consequence is the extent to which the OER supports student attainment of course goals and objectives. A guiding rule is, if it doesn't help students meet objectives, do not use it. To determine the usefulness of a specific OER, ask: to what extent is the object directly relevant to course objectives? Does it enhance the content? Beware! Might it contribute to cognitive overload? And, will students know how to learn from it? Online educational resource evaluation criteria include:

- Accuracy: Does the source list the author(s) and institution that published the content and provide a way of contacting them?
- Authority: Does the source list author credentials and is its domain preferred? Preferred domains include .edu, .gov, .org, and .net?
- Objectivity: Does the source provide accurate, balanced information with limited advertising?

- Currency: Is the source current and updated regularly and are links (if any) live and up-to-date?
- Coverage. Can students view the information --not limited to fees, browser technology, or software requirements?
- Interactivity: Can students have meaningful interactions with the OER?
- Usability: Is navigation of content clear?

Once instructors and learners locate and evaluate resources they can insert them in appropriate locations in the course design or, if they are a student, refer to them in their course products.

Most importantly, OERs and social media empower learners to choose their own study materials that facilitate their achievement. Instructors should encourage students to seek learning materials that fill their needs and help them know how to apply evaluation criteria. In any course, students should be encouraged to use online materials, collaboration tools, and social media to facilitate their goal attainment.

Go online to locate 3 graphics and/or tables that illustrate a topic related to online course delivery. Craft prompts that, when coupled with the artifacts, would guide instructors through an online discussion.

6   Flipping and Blending Face-Face Courses

Our university was on an island with limited space. The president expressed the need for faculty to blend courses, meeting face-face just one or two days a week and offering online activity to fulfill course requirements. This would free up space for others who also blend their courses. Therefore, one of the six objectives in my office's collaboratively developed strategic plan was to "Provide instructor development and support for blended and online course delivery to relieve space constraints and transform teaching methods, thereby encouraging retention of students." We never met that goal of relieving space-constraints. However, in attempting to I learned that to do so would require a shared commitment and coordination among the provost, deans, department chairs, faculty, the facilities officer, the office of institutional research, and the registrar's office. As a result of Covid-19, however, the complex task of arranging course offerings and space to depend more on online delivery has taken on a sense of urgency.

A DL administrator strives to grow online course and program offerings by increasing instructors' use of online tools in face-face courses (Gautreau, 2011; Roblyer & Doering, 2012), blended and flipped courses (Abeysekera & Dawson, 2014; P. McGee, 2014; Picciano et al., 2014), as well as fully online courses. The centers for teaching excellence at the three campuses where I have worked help to facilitate this mission in collaboration with the DL office. Teaching centers provide professional development in the andragogical aspects (methods and principles used in adult education) of blending and flipping, while DL offices provide workshops in how to apply technologies to andragogical methods.

Sometimes a specific incident, such as Covid-19 can catalyze progress toward a mission. Such was the case on my campus long before Covid-19 when our office conducted a student needs analysis and we learned that many of our students were confused about how they were doing in their classes due to inconsistent use of the LMS grade book. Some students thought they were failing when they were doing well, while others thought they are doing well when they were not. A caring Faculty Senate took up the cause with us and we launched a promotional campaign for instructors with the goal of a high percentage of instructors adopting LMS features that address students' confusion and a high percentage of students able to accurately interpret their standing in their courses and programs of study. With the entire campus on board, we were able to widely promote use of our LMS tools such as rubrics and gradebooks for providing students with timely, accurate, and constructive feedback. This, in turn, facilitated adoption of tools that helped instructors feel more able to hybridize or flip their courses, or even to develop their courses fully online.

> Describe a professional development activity for faculty who currently teach fully-face-to-face that would compel them to consider blending their courses.

6.1   *Competency-Based Courses and Programs*

Competency-base education (CBE) is characterized by two elements: credit for attainment of competence rather than seat time (as with credit hours) and technology-enabled personalization (COE Forum, 2015). Learners progress at their own paces through course or program content based on achievement of specified objectives or competencies. This ensures that they are not forced to move on to the next topic without mastering the current one and no one has to spend time focusing on what they already know. Developers of online CBE align assessments with competencies and enter these in the LMS.

In 2015, our team received a College for All Texans Foundation grant to help build a CBE undergraduate degree program in Mechanical Engineering Technology. Although competencies in the program had already been identified for accreditation purposes, we worked with faculty and sought employer input to refine them. Each competency had to be stated in terms of learner performance with active unambiguous language in terms of what students had to be able to demonstrate. We modularized courses and developed criterion-referenced assessments of mastery of each competency. After mapping each program-competency to assessments, these were entered in the Blackboard "Goal-Performance" tool. As students took assessments, the technology kept records of each students' progress toward competence, allowing them to place-out of instruction based on performance on assessments, and generating reports of their progress. In addition, other instructional programs adopted the Goal-Performance tool which assessed how well the programs facilitated each students' learning of each competency. Therefore, programs with national standards, such as Counseling Psychology and Nursing, benefitted from the ability to determine student mastery of standards by tying competencies to assessments in the LMS.

CBE programs are complex to administer because they disrupt many standard processes of higher education such as course terms, program delivery models, student advising, faculty roles, the credit hour, transcripts, financial models, accreditation, and curriculum design and development. Often, students require individualized and intensive support to succeed in CBE programs. Therefore, some CBE programs hire success coaches and subject matter tutors to provide personalized attention, as well as data analysts to manage programs.

> Identify the tools in an LMS that automate links between assessments and competencies. Explore the tool's capabilities.

7   Learning Analytics

As a DL administrator you will need to take advantage of analytics software to summarize and report on your institution's academic online presence and instructors' and students' use of online course tools. In addition, Google analytics provides free data about use of your office website so that you can determine how much interest it draws from what sectors and what features are most effective.

Your learning management system (LMS) typically includes the option to purchase data analytics regarding instructor and student activity in online courses. Analytics software provides data on individual components of courses and student performance within a course, across courses in a program, and across programs within an institution. While access to the programmatic and institutional analytics provided by an LMS requires having administrative privileges, some course analytics are available to instructors as they teach their courses. Analytics show by student the number of page views and participations in a course; submissions; and on-time, late, and missing work. Empowering instructors to know how often each student enters their course-site and uses various course tools, and enabling them to closely monitor achievement in their courses can improve their responsiveness to student needs.

In addition to providing data about student performance, an administrator can gather estimates of LMS tool use across your campus. Learning analytics provide system reports regarding how the LMS is being used, learning outcomes in courses and programs, student retention, and course completions for your entire institution. Data regarding use of tools in courses, across a program, or across the entire institution provide insight into trends and allow for validation of strategies to be shared campus-wide. For instance, although our LMS's analytics could not describe the quality of online discussions on our campus, we could learn the number of courses where online discussions were used each semester and the percentage of students participating regularly in online discussions. We could also learn the extent that instructors used the "Comments" option to give students feedback when they entered grades in the gradebook. Most importantly, we could track students' achievement of specific competencies within a program as well as collect data for determining long-term achievement results. This was an effective and efficient way of creating a substantial report for accreditation, and our findings informed the professional development we provided to instructors.

What are some questions you might find answers to by using learning analytics when reporting to your institution's president, instructors, and students regarding the status of online learning?

8   Conclusions

In summary, a significant responsibility of a DL administrator is to build supports for online course and program design, development, and delivery. To be successful, one must establish relationships with administrators, staff, instructors, and students and devise tactics for lifting barriers as well as addressing instructors' concerns regarding course ownership and time away from research. Data analytics will help you, instructors, and administrators understand the impacts of efforts.

I am aware that some may be disgruntled that while suggesting that constructivist course designs best support learning, I am promoting an objectivist course structure. However, I would argue that reconciliation between objectivism and constructivism can transpire when carefully composed course and module objectives and activities initiate constructivist learning (Jonassen et al., 2003). For instance, objectives that would encourage constructivist learning might read: You will be able to locate resources that help you reach your professional goals; you will be able to access others who agree and/or disagree with your perspective; you will generate a solution to the problem of ...; you will be able to set and attain a learning goal; or you will be able to apply [a tool] to address [a problem]. A course that is designed to provide choice in content with activities that support problem, project, service, inquiry, and/or case-based learning allows for personalized, constructivist learning.

Most instructors benefit from professional development in online course design, development, and delivery. In addition to how to use the LMS and other technologies that facilitate distance learning, those who teach online should be versed in the following topics:
– Policies regarding accessibility, copyright, and interaction.
– Alignment among objectives, assessments, strategies, and content.
– Modularizing course content.
– Social, cognitive, and teaching presence.
– How to develop and deliver an interactive learning environment.
– Student support for engagement.
– Cultural responsiveness and learning community.
– Authentic, constructivist, student-centered learning.
– Motivational strategies for design and delivery.
– How instructors and students can use OERs and social media for learning.
– How to flip and blend face-to-face courses.
– Fundamentals of building competency-based courses and programs.

Gunawardena et al.'s (2019) Wisdom Communities (WisCom) model includes guides for designing culturally responsive, transformative learning experiences in a collaborative learning cycle to frame effective online teaching; Keller's (2010) motivational design model includes addressing attention, relevance, confidence, and satisfaction; and Tinto's (2012) retention model includes clear expectations, support, feedback, and engagement. When instructors apply the principles and strategies proposed in these three theoretical models, they deliver engaging courses that encourage students' retention and lifelong learning.

All activities in the office should center around promoting adoption of learning technologies and pedagogies that support students' learning. Distance learning administrators need to help instructors set clear expectations, scaffold learning, engage students in authentic activities, create community, and attend to students' motivations. In my experience, professional development in each of these topics helps faculty members be better teachers whether they teach face-to-face, flipped, blended, or fully online.

9   Recommended Support Materials

- Accessibility checklist
  (https://depts.washington.edu/uwdrs/faculty/online-course-accessibility-checklist/)
- Universal design (http://udlguidelines.cast.org/)
- Stanford University Libraries (https://fairuse.stanford.edu/overview/fair-use/four-factors/)
- Teaching Effectively during Times of Disruption
  (https://bit.ly/stanfordteachingdisruption)
- From Florence Martin, University of North Carolina Charlotte
  (https://bit.ly/2vTtklX)
- OER repositories:
  - Khan Academy (https://www.khanacademy.org/)
  - EdTechBooks.org (https://edtechbooks.org/)
  - Repository of repositories at Texas A&M University–Corpus Christi
    (https://iol.tamucc.edu/repositories.html)
  - MERLOT (https://www.merlot.org/merlot/)
  - OER Commons (http://www.oercommons.org/)
  - EngageNY (https://www.engageny.org)
  - National Geographic (https://www.nationalgeographic.com/)
  - The National Science Foundation
    (https://www.nsf.gov/news/classroom/education.jsp)
  - Google Art Project
    (https://artsandculture.google.com/partner/moma-the-museum-of-modern-art)
  - WISE (http://wise.ssl.berkeley.edu/)

- Flickr: The Commons and flickr/Creative Commons provide access to publicly-held collections of photographs.
- Online Learning Consortium Quality Scorecard Suite: https://onlinelearningconsortium.org/consult/olc-quality-scorecard-suite/
- Competency-Based Education Network (CBEN). A national consortium for designing, developing, and scaling new models for student learning. http://www.cbenetwork.org/
- Educause library of competency-based education articles and resources. http://www.educause.edu/library/competency-based-education-cbe

Notes

1   See https://www.coursemapguide.com/
2   See https://www.youtube.com/watch?v=D7vooDcxUaA

References

Abeysekera, L., & Dawson, P. (2014). Motivation and cognitive load in the flipped classroom: Definition, rational and a call for research. *Higher Education Research & Development, 34*, 1–14.

Albright, M. (2020). *Hell and other destinations.* Harper Collins.

Anderson, L. W., & Krathwohl, D. R. (Eds.). (2001). *A taxonomy for learning, teaching and assessing: A revision of Bloom's taxonomy of educational objectives* (Complete ed.). Longman.

Balaji, M. S., & Chakrabarti, D. (2010). Student interactions in online discussion forum: Empirical research from 'media richness theory' perspective. *Journal of Interactive Online Learning, 9*(1), 1–22.

Bean, J. R., & Metzner, B. (1985). A conceptual model of nontraditional undergraduate student attrition. *Review of Educational Research, 55*, 485–650.

Becker B. A. (2015). *A new meta-model of student engagement: The roles of student motivation and active learning.* Paper presented at International Conference on Education. https://www.brettbecker.com/wp-content/uploads/2015/05/IICE-13-_Becker_-419_Camera-Ready.pdf

Bliss, C. A., & Lawrence, B. (2009). From posts to patterns: A metric to characterize discussion board activity in online classes. *Journal of Asynchronous Learning Networks, 12*(2), 15–32.

Bransford, J., Brown, A. L., Cocking, R. R., & National Research Council (U.S.). (1999). *How people learn: Brain, mind, experience, and school.* National Academy Press.

Brookfield, S. D. (1987). *Developing critical thinkers: Challenging adults to explore alter-native ways of thinking and acting.* Jossey-Bass.

Brownell, J. E., & Swaner, L. E. (2010). *Five high-impact practices: Research on learning outcomes, completion, and quality.* Association of American Colleges and Universities.

Burgstahler, S. E., & Cory, R. C. (2008). *Universal design in higher education: From principles to practice.* Harvard Education Press.

Cifuentes, L., Janney, A., Guerra, L., & Weir, J. (2016). A working model for complying with accessibility guidelines for online learning in a regional university with limited resources. *TechTrends, 60*(6), 557–564. doi:10.1007/s11528-016-0086-8

Cifuentes, L., Suryavanshi, R., & Janney, A. (2018). *Motivating instructors and administrators to adopt e-learning.* In A. A. Piña, V. L. Lowell, & B. R. Harris (Eds.), *Leading and managing e-learning: What the e-learning leader needs to know.* Springer.

Clark, R. C., & Mayer, R. E. (2011). *E-learning and the science of instruction: Proven guidelines for consumers and designers of multimedia learning* (3rd ed.). Pfeiffer.

COE Forum. (2015). *The CBE and PLA playbook.* The Advisory Board Company.

Dawson, S. (2006). A study of the relationship between student communication interaction and sense of community. *The Internet and Higher Education, 9*(3), 153–162.

Dewey, J. (1938). *Experience and education.* Kappa Delta Pi.

Dick, W., Carey, L., & Carey, J. O. (2016). *The systematic design of instruction* (8th ed.). Pearson.

Donovan, J. (2015). The importance of building online learning communities [Blog post]. http://blog.online.colostate.edu/blog/online-education/the-importance-of-building-online-learning-communities/

Dweck, C. S. (2006). *Mindset.* Random House.

Eccles, J. S., & Wigfield, A. (2002). Motivational beliefs, values, and goals. *Annual Review of Psychology, 53*, 109–132.

Edmundson, A. (2007). The Cultural Adaptation Process (CAP) model: Designing e-learning for another culture. In A. Edmundson (Ed.), *Globalized e-learning cultural challenges* (pp. 267–290). Information Science Publishing.

Gamrat, C. (2020). Inclusive teaching and course design. *EDUCAUSE Review: Transforming Higher Education.* https://er.educause.edu/blogs/2020/2/inclusive-teaching-and-course-design

Garrison, D. R., & Anderson, T. (2003). *E-learning in the 21st century: A framework for research and practice.* Routledge/Falmer.

Garrison, D. R., Anderson, T., & Archer, W. (2010). The first decade of the community of inquiry framework: A retrospective. *The Internet and Higher Education, 13*(1–2), 5–9.

Gautreau, C. (2011). Motivational factors affecting the integration of a learning management system by faculty. *Journal of Educators Online, 8*(1), 1–25.

Gunawardena, C. N. (2020). Culturally inclusive online learning for capacity development projects in international contexts. *Journal of Learning for Development, 7*(1),
5–30. https://jl4d.org/index.php/ejl4d/article/view/403

Gunawardena, C. N., Frechette, C., & Layne, L. (2019). *Culturally inclusive instructional
design: A framework and guide for building online wisdom communities.* Routledge.

Hattie, J. (2008). *Visible learning: A synthesis of over 800 meta-analyses relating to
achievement.* Routledge.

Hebert, M. (2006). Staying the course: A study in online student satisfaction and retention. *Online Journal of Distance Learning Administration, 9*(4), Winter.

Herrington, J., Reeves, T. C., & Oliver, R. (2010). *A guide to authentic e-learning.* Routledge.

Jonassen, D. H., Howland, J., Moore, J., & Marra, R. M. (2002). *Learning to solve problems
with technology: A constructivist perspective* (2nd ed.). Prentice Hall.

Keller, J. M. (2010). *Motivational design for learning and performance: ARCS model
approach.* Springer.

Kochtanek, T. R., & Hein, K. K. (2000). Creating and nurturing distributed asynchronous
learning environments. *Online Information Review, 24*(4), 280–294. https://doi.org/
10.1108/14684520010350632

Kumar, S., Martin, F., Budhrani, K., & Ritzhaupt, A. (2019). Award-winning faculty
online teaching practices: Elements of award-winning courses. *Online Learning,
23*(4), 160–180. doi:10.24059/olj.v23i4.2077

Kumi-Yeboah, A. (2018). Designing a cross-cultural collaborative online learning framework for online instructors. *Online Learning, 22*(4), 181–201. doi:10.24059/
olj.v22i4.1520

Lehman, R. M., & Conceicao, C. O. (2010). The role of presence in the online environment. In R. M. Lehman & C. O. Conceicao (Eds.), *Creating a sense of presence in
online teaching: How to "be there" for distance learners.* Jossey-Bass.

McGee, P. (2014). Blended course design: Where's the pedagogy? *International Journal
of Mobile and Blended Learning, 6*(1), 33–55.

McGuire, S. Y. (2015). *Teach students how to learn.* Stylus.

Morrison, G. R., Ross, S. M., Kalman, H. K., & Kemp, J. E. (2011). *Designing effective
instruction* (6th ed.). Wiley.

Palloff, R. M., & Pratt, K. (2011). *The excellent online instructor: Strategies for professional
development.* Jossey-Bass.

Picciano, A. G., Dziuban, C. D., & Graham, C. R. (Ed.). (2014). *Blended learning: Research
perspectives, Volume 2.* Routledge.

Reigeluth, C. M., Myers, R. D., & Lee, D. (2017). The learner-centered paradigm of education. In C. M. Reigeluth, B. J. Beatty, & R. D. Myers (Eds.), *Instructional-design theories and models, Volume IV* (pp. 5–31). Routledge.

Roblyer, M. D., & Doering, A. H. (2012). *Integrating educational technology into teaching* (6th ed.). Allyn and Bacon.

Rovai, A. P. (2003). In search of higher persistence rates in distance education on line programs. *The Internet and Higher Education, 6*(1), 1–16.

Shernoff, D. J., Csikszentmihalyi, M., Schneider, B., & Shrnoff, E. S. (2003). Student engagement in high school classrooms from the perspective of flow theory. *School Psychology Quarterly, 18*(2), 158–176.

Stavredes, T. (2014). *Effective online teaching.* Jossey-Bass.

Stavredes, T., & Herder, T. (2014). *A guide to online course design: Strategies for student success.* Jossey-Bass.

Tinto, V. (2012). *Completing college: Rethinking institutional action.* University of Chicago Press.

Wiggins, G., & McTighe, J. (2005). *Understanding by design* (2nd ed.). Merrill Prentice Hall.

CHAPTER 9

Engaging Faculty through Professional Development and the Course Development Process

Josh Strigle and Jennifer Veloff

Abstract

At the conclusion of this chapter, a new e-learning administrator will be able to:

- Develop comprehensive faculty support and course development strategies on their campus;
- Identify faculty readiness standards and key indicators of excellent online teaching;
- Distinguish between elements of professional development strategies and plans;
- Compare different models of faculty professional development for online teaching and learning; and
- Make observations about the differences between ownership, incentives, and compensation models.

Keywords

engagement – faculty development – design – faculty support – compensation – incentives – intellectual property

1 Introduction

Just as institutions see student engagement as essential to successful course and program completion, engagement between the faculty and e-learning administration is essential to a successful online program. The e-learning administrator and their team often play an active role in developing faculty members' skills in teaching with technology as well as in conducting research about implementation and impacts of technology adoption.

A comprehensive strategy for faculty engagement goes beyond the need to select appropriate technologies or administer compliance with accreditation guidelines. Given that faculty are generally hired based on their subject matter expertise, they have a variety of needs when preparing to teach online. From new technologies to new methods as well as tasks and competencies, faculty always have more to learn.

To support faculty in online learning spaces, administrators should consider building out a comprehensive professional development plan for every online faculty member that includes many different elements. An administrator must take into account the individual needs of each faculty member, whether or not they have had exposure to the online modality, their attitude toward and motivation to teach online, their technical readiness, and the administrative vision for the program they teach in. There are many different models to assist with delivering these plans.

An administrator must get to know their institution's mission, history, and culture before successful implementation will be possible. Administrators must know how to navigate institutional culture by becoming familiar with policies and practices surrounding compensation, incentives, and intellectual property. This is an area where many distance learning administrators may feel powerless in the face of college policy but there are a variety of strategies available to help one engage with faculty and departments in this area. There are, no doubt, many other things to consider in this area but this chapter is designed to help you begin to address this key element of a successful online program and administrative career.

2   Administering Faculty Support and Development

Thinking Ahead: As an aspiring e-learning administrator, what is your vision for faculty engagement? What would be your first step toward implementing this vision?

As you, the e-learning administrator, seek to promote engagement between your department and the faculty, your first priority will be to make sure adequate faculty support measures are in place. This support, as we will discuss later in the chapter, goes far beyond professional development and technology support but those are likely the cornerstones of your implementation. In order to be successful, you will need to build a team for this implementation. You and your team will work with faculty from a variety of disciplines, with varying experiences and skill sets. Your job will be to put interventions in place that will engage faculty, some unwillingly, and prepare them to convey knowledge in an environment that many of them are not familiar with. It will be through this lens that your office builds and maintains an effective relationship with the institution's faculty and helps them stay equipped to serve in an instructional environment that evolves much more quickly than the traditional classroom.

As an online administrator, one of the reasons you exist is to ensure the success of your e-learning program. As with any program, administration's support of faculty is foundational to that success (Barefield, 2013). A recurring theme throughout this chapter will be that, as much as possible, your engagement with faculty should be supportive. Depending on your institutional structure, you may have to engage them through evaluation and, hopefully very rarely, disciplinary action. Although there are multiple types of support to be discussed in this chapter, the cornerstone is likely development, which we will look at from a variety of perspectives.

Whichever administrative model your institution uses, it is imperative that you have the right team to design the professional development experiences. The role of instructional designers is critical in this process and they should be involved from the early planning stages, all the way through analysis of results and revision of the content (Seepersaud, 2018). Designers are trained to help in these processes, generally through an advanced degree, heavy on instructional design theory or through a combination of education and teaching experience. They are able to help faculty to optimize their instructional interventions and allow them to concentrate on the subject matter itself. Some institutions also delineate another role, the instructional technologist. A critical component of this design is the effective use of the available technology which is why institutions have the role of instructional technologist to assist in this area. A common scenario that might play out in supporting a faculty member might be as follows:

- *Faculty member:* I need to deliver a particular concept online and measure student learning.
- *Designer:* That can be accomplished through presenting your information in the following structure. We will need to identify a technology solution to allow students to provide evidence of their learning.
- *Technologist:* I have researched the functions you requested and have identified technologies X and Y. Please review them and select the one that best meets your instructional goals.

This three-member team allows each member to focus on their specialty, allowing for full support of the faculty member. At some of the smallest institutions, the e-learning administrator may be required to serve as both designer and technologist. Another undesirable scenario occurs when no support team is in place at all. In this scenario, the faculty member may be required to serve all of these functions, which should be avoided, if at all possible (Barefield, 2013).

To extend the theme of the team approach, most effective support programs facilitate peer support among faculty. Heasley and Terosky (2015) point to the need for these learning communities as a missing element in many institutions' faculty support and development programs. Coswatte Mohr and Shelton (2017) also noted the need for faculty to feel connected, to avoid feelings of isolation. As you develop your support program, you must intentionally build professional learning community from the beginning. This could be accomplished in a number of ways and will vary according to institution. In a large university, each college probably has specific goals for the e-learning implementation and enough faculty to create their own learning community. A development and support initiative designed specifically for their college may be in order. Your engagement team may assign members specifically to that community so they can have go-to individuals to rely on when they need support.

For community colleges and smaller universities, disciplines may not have the sheer numbers to support this model. In that case, creating communities of practice among disciplines with similarities may be the answer. Faculty from the math department might be put in a cohort with those from the science department. Fine arts might be paired with communications. Just as with other models, including designers and technologists from your team will keep your department engaged with faculty. Without that intentional involvement, you run the risk of the faculty community becoming isolated from your team. This isolation may eventually lead to an antagonistic relationship with faculty. It is important that faculty know they can rely on your department for expert advice, while they build the skills they need to be self-sufficient.

Another aspect of the community building process is the selection of specific technologies required to facilitate online instruction, such as online course evaluation systems or test-proctoring software. Processes used can create strife among faculty, other instructional offices, and the Information/Institutional Technology (IT) department. It might be easy for you, especially if you have a background in technology, to be inclined to unilaterally select technologies for faculty to use. This isn't always the best situation. Mandernach (2020) pointed out that the role of technology is to support the faculty member's educational needs and Barefield (2013) asserted that the role of technology support is to remove barriers to success and create a supportive environment. These conditions cannot be satisfied if administration selects technology in a vacuum. This brings us back to including your administrative team in the community of practice and the hypothetical conversation above. When your team is embedded in faculty discussions, in a supportive way, they can act as ambassadors between faculty and administration and help communicate the technology needs of each group. This is further complicated when IT divisions have a third set of technology priorities that differ from e-learning administration and faculty. Most institutions have an IT committee to attempt to balance the competing priorities, ensure adoptions are compatible with each groups' needs and prioritize finite resources.

This type of community approach is a best practice and strategy available to institutions to help them overcome a variety of barriers to engagement. Throughout this chapter we discuss ways in which e-learning changes the complex dynamics of higher education institutions. As barriers are discovered, a supportive community is essential to maintaining progress. Sometimes simply allowing each group to participate in the administrative process will be enough to foster the culture of support that you seek to promote.

> *Looking Back*: After reading this section, has your vision changed? What specific skills might you need to work on to be able to administer faculty development in the ways described here?

3   Faculty Readiness and Developing Excellence in Online Teaching

> *Thinking Ahead*: As an aspiring e-learning administrator, what online teaching competencies are important to you? How would you know if faculty are meeting and exceeding these competencies?

If support is the foundation for success, ensuring faculty are ready for their role is the most basic form of support. As you begin to identify how to engage your faculty and shape what professional development plans will look like, it is important to begin mapping out competencies and markers of excellence for faculty at your institution (Martin et al., 2019). These items can be as simple as how faculty members will use the learning management system (LMS), to more advanced indicators including what it might look like when faculty transfer knowledge to students. In order to know if your professional development plans are successful, you will need to know what effective teaching looks like in an online environment and what competencies are important for faculty to have before beginning to teach online.

Before diving into competencies, it is important to start with determining why faculty are pursuing professional development for online teaching and learning. Are they doing this for recognition, promotion, or personal growth, or were they told by their department that this is something they need to do? Determining their motivation up front will help you (the administrator), and the instructional design team, to discover the mindset of the faculty member you may be working with in the design and development of an online course. We recommend offering a survey for faculty up front to determine their reasons for professional development and their pedagogical, technical, and administrative skills. Penn State provides an excellent online readiness survey in the public domain (Williams, 2020). This type of survey will help you determine the driving factors and/or motivations of faculty developing online courses. It can be implemented before faculty go through training, when they begin building a new course, or at any point in their planning process for putting their course online.

Neibuhr et al. (2015) were able to identify several reasons why faculty pursue professional development including lack of familiarity with online education, technology, and best practices for putting their course materials (lectures, assignments, etc.) online. They recommend ten best practices: (1) build on what they know, (2) identify resources, (3) model best practices, (4) attend to instructional design, (5) emphasize copyright, (6) encourage content development before learning the software, (7) provide support, (8) provide feedback, (9) recognize and reward success, and (10) expect changing technologies. Following these practices can help faculty recognize the rewards of professional development for online teaching and learning.

When you begin looking at competencies for teaching online, you will need to determine the critical skills every faculty member should have at your institution, in order to support student success online. Most of these competencies are going to be similar across institutions but there may be some that are very specific to your institution. Martin et al. (2019) were able to identify six general competencies: (1) designing activities and assignments, (2) organizing materials and assessments, (3) feedback and grading, (4) timely communication, (5) time management, and (6) technical knowledge.

We'll dive into each of these competencies briefly to get a better understanding of why these have been identified as important for faculty teaching online. During the design and development phase of building an online course, faculty should be proficient in designing activities and assignments that support the course level learning outcomes and assessing what knowledge the students should have before they leave the course. Faculty should also know how to organize their course materials in a logical way to ensure the student's experience is not confusing or frustrating. Providing a structure that's easy to navigate and one that allows the students easy access to support is critical to their success.

When faculty move into facilitating an online course, feedback and grading become essential. Engagement with students through feedback and grading helps to keep students motivated in the course. Students depend on feedback from the instructor so they are prepared for more advanced assignments and are able to increase their understanding of how to apply the concepts being covered in the course. Communication between the faculty member, the class, and individual students should be timely and supportive. Since students and faculty are separated by space and time, it is important for faculty to let students know up-front when the student can expect to receive a response. This helps to develop trust from the students and provides a reliable mechanism for support. Faculty should also have good time management skills to ensure they're able to give feedback, grade, and communicate with their students effectively. And lastly, knowledge of technology and how to use it efficiently will help to support the work that's being done in the course. Faculty proficiency with the LMS, web conferencing software, or other technical tools adopted by the institution provides a seamless user experience.

Competencies and best practices for supporting and training faculty are also outlined by many accrediting bodies, non-profit organizations, and regional compacts. For example, the Higher Learning Commission (HLC) and the National Council for State Authorization Reciprocity Agreements (NC-SARA) have agreed on using the Council of Regional Accrediting Commissions (C-RAC) Guidelines for the Evaluation of Distance Education (2009). Section six of the guidelines outline one of the hallmarks concerning faculty professional development and support (Council of Regional Accrediting Commissions, 2009):
- Faculty responsible for delivering the online learning curricula and evaluating the students' success in achieving the on-line learning goals are appropriately qualified and effectively supported.

Examples of evidence:
- On-line learning faculty are carefully selected, appropriately trained, frequently evaluated, and are marked by an acceptable level of turnover.
- The institution's training program for on-line learning faculty is periodic, incorporates tested good practices in on-line learning pedagogy, and ensures competency with the range of software products used by the institution.
- Faculty are proficient and effectively supported in using the course management system.
- Faculty members engaged in on-line learning share in the mission and goals of the institution and its programs and are provided the opportunities to contribute to the broader activities of the institution.

- Students express satisfaction with the quality of the instruction provided by on-line learning faculty members.

One final example comes out of the Online Learning Consortium (OLC) and their Quality Scorecard for the Administration of Online Programs (2018). OLC's model outlines several best practices and competencies related to training and supporting faculty in regards to course development and teaching online. The scorecard provides several strategies directly aligned to professional development including (OLC, 2018):

- The institution ensures faculty receive training, assistance, and support to prepare faculty for course development.
- Faculty have access to training, online resources, and support related to Fair Use, plagiarism, and other relevant legal and ethical concepts.
- The institution ensures faculty receive training, assistance, and support to prepare faculty for teaching online.
- Faculty are provided on-going professional development related to online teaching and learning.
- Faculty are informed about institutionally supported education technologies and the selection and use of new tools.

Now that you have the resources to identify competencies and markers of excellence for faculty at your institution (Martin et al., 2019), you can begin to plan how to address them at your institution. It will be important to think about what effective teaching looks like in an online environment and what competencies are important for faculty to have before beginning to teach. We will now explore elements and models for professional development in our next section.

Looking Back: After reading this section, have you added to or removed some of the competencies you identified? How would you measure effective teaching online? What does that look like?

4 Elements of Professional Development

Thinking Ahead: What do you believe is the most important element of a successful professional development program? Is that true for all types of higher education institutions?

As you are planning a professional development program that will both engage faculty and make them ready for teaching online, there are a number of elements you will need to consider. In addition to the skills you are trying to teach, what aspects of the faculty member are you trying to develop? What is your administrative vision for this development program? Are you focused solely on the technical aspects of teaching online? Does your team have the background to provide training in a variety of areas? You will need to know your institution to know the appropriate areas that your office is responsible for providing development. You and your team will need to be fully engaged with both the faculty and administration to develop a comprehensive process.

It is helpful to consider the field of professional development in academia before focusing on the narrower topic of developing online faculty. Previous studies of the subject of faculty development seem to suggest it is centered around "activities and programs designed to improve instruction" (Amundsen, 2005). Improving instruction certainly should still be the goal of an online faculty development program. One of those studies broke the topic down to a more granular level. Centra (1989) identified four main elements: personal, professional, instructional, and organizational development. Some of the specific skills mentioned in the article, interpersonal, career development, life planning, course design and development, instructional technology, and others, are definitely within the realm of what the e-learning administrator needs to address (Amundsen, 2005). In fact, we have already covered a number of them in this chapter. Reflect on the topics of development from 1989, long before the advent of e-learning as we know it. All of them are directly relatable to e-learning today.

Interpersonal skills relate to the ability of the faculty member to communicate and empathize with students at a distance. Life planning and, by extension, time management and goal setting are keys for both online faculty and students. Both groups have regular tasks, such as completing assignments, grading assignments and participating in communication, that are mutually critical to the success of the course. If either party fails to complete their tasks, the course will not be successful. Course design is under much more scrutiny in e-learning than in the traditional classroom. And instructional technology has moved far beyond the basic role it played in 1989. Now course design is at the forefront of academia.

It is time for you to explore your administrative vision for the professional development program you will implement. How well do you know your institution? Which of the areas of development described above fit into the mission of your department? The answers to those questions will vary greatly from institution to institution, largely based on the type of institution you work for and your placement within the organizational structure. You might head a large, centralized campus unit that functions as its own virtual college, within a major university. In this case, every aspect of faculty development is likely within your purview. Alternately, you might be in the technology support department of a small community college. In this case, the only area of development that you are able to conduct may pertain to the technology and how to implement it. Regardless of where you are, institutional administrators must coalesce around a vision for developing instruction at your institution and avoid a haphazard program that leans more heavily on one aspect of development than another (Coswatte Mohr & Shelton, 2017).

These factors create a need for you to decide on a style of professional development. Again, thinking more broadly about development, Amundsen (2005) identifies four styles that can be used: skills, method, process, and discipline. The first style focuses on improving a teaching behavior or problem. The second style focuses on a preferred teaching method or approach. The third style focuses on the process of learning to teach oneself. The last style groups faculty by discipline (Amundsen, 2005). An example of the method-based approach for e-learning might be a workshop series with each session focusing on a different aspect of e-learning, such as communication, presence, interaction, alignment, and evaluation. A popular methods-based approach that might be taught, as the central element of a development plan, is adaptive learning. There are many process-based programs, to teach faculty how to teach online. As previously discussed, grouping faculty into learning communities, by discipline, is still a popular and effective way to get them to engage with a development program. We will provide examples of this in the models of professional development section. You can see how, as e-learning administrators, we can pull elements from these styles and apply them to our implementations.

All truly successful professional development programs likely foster three key elements, according to Chen et al. (2002); flexibility, connectedness, and collegiality. Faculty have a variety of demands on their time, which they cannot always predict. Having the ability to participate in professional development in a way that works for them is critical. Maintaining a sense of connectedness is important for the faculty member, in the same way it is for students in a class. This is because the faculty member, in many ways, becomes the student. If they feel disconnected with the facilitators or their colleagues, they will not persist. Collegiality is important in any interaction with faculty. Creating an adversarial relationship with faculty will doom your initiative. Likewise, a few faculty allies can go a long way toward your success.

In planning development content, a balance needs to be struck among content, pedagogy, and technology (Chen et al., 2012). As mentioned previously, not all of these aspects may be addressed by your team but they should be part of a comprehensive professional development plan at your institution. At many community colleges, including one that will be discussed in the models section, it is common to have technology training located under the e-learning team, pedagogy concerns located under an office of teaching and learning, or something similar, and content concerns addressed within the academic department. Without excellent coordination among these different offices, this decentralization can lead to a lack of effectiveness. Small institutions often lack the funds to set up a full e-learning administrative unit to address all of these issues. A centralized e-learning unit, such as is often found at larger institutions, often simplifies the coordination of such initiatives.

There are an almost endless number of topics that might be covered in a development program. Coswatte Mohr and Shelton (2017) grouped them into themes around faculty roles, classroom design, learning processes, and understanding legal issues. These themes agree with our commentary in previous sections around faculty readiness and the competencies that are required to meet that threshold. Exactly what topics you focus on within these themes may depend on your institution, the needs of your students and what specific e-learning modalities you offer.

Looking Back: Considering your own skill set, are there things you will need to learn before you are prepared to put together a successful professional development program?

5   Models of Professional Development

Thinking Ahead: What are some models of professional development that you feel might be suited to online faculty? What factors might make those models better suited than others?

There are a number of factors at play when selecting a model of professional development to use. As in the previous section, you must know your institution before you will select the most effective model. Various factors, such as the location of your faculty and their workload will influence your decision as well as administrative priorities. You will also have different delivery modalities from which to choose. You must choose a model that meets the needs of the faculty so they can consume it in a way that is appealing and engaging to them and still achieves your goals for development.

Faculty development has historically been a face-to-face endeavor, not too different from a traditional classroom. A trainer fills the role of the faculty member and faculty become students. This model was prevalent in the early days of online education, since online educators were almost exclusively local classroom faculty who were simply retooling to teach an online class or two. As online courses became a more established modality, this model needed to change for a variety of reasons. The two most prevalent reasons were that faculty members were becoming increasingly dispersed geographically and both they and the administration were beginning to see the need for them to experience learning in an online environment.

A model that has become quite common in higher education is the online moderated development program. Institutions set up an online course, designed to model the design elements they wish faculty to implement and instructional designers act as faculty to moderate the course. As mentioned earlier, a common barrier to faculty readiness to teach online is that they have never taken an online course. This method of delivering faculty development seeks to, at least partially, overcome that barrier. In fact, in many universities, this type of development program may be delivered as a graduate course for academic credit. We will discuss such a program later in the chapter. In this section, we will discuss two similar, non-credit bearing programs from two small, but very different, institutions.

One small college, serving a primarily rural district, saw a tri-fold need to formalize its on-going and well established training program for online and hybrid faculty. The first need was to better serve faculty with development that would benefit them in the ways just mentioned. The second was that a statewide quality course designation system was being implemented and they needed a vehicle to train faculty in those design standards and systematically review courses accordingly. The third was the on-going need to document compliance with principles such as accessibility and copyright.

At this institution all faculty who teach in a reduced seat-time distance format (online or hybrid) are required to participate in a three-semester process. During their first semester, they take a six to eight-week online course experience, moderated by an instructional designer.

Below is the course outline:
– Course development, including online pedagogy and required design elements
– Compliance concerns, including ADA and copyright.
– Effective online assignments
– Assessment
– Further course design considerations
– Accessibility considerations
– Introduction to the quality review

The last part of the course leads into their work for the second semester of the process. Faculty are given an entire semester, with the help of an instructional designer, to redesign their courses to prepare for the quality review process based on a nationally recognized rubric to which the institution subscribes. During the third term, the faculty member's courses are reviewed and they are given time to fix any remaining issues. This process is designed to repeat every three years.

With the onset of the Covid-19 pandemic, this institution modified its professional development incrementally. The first phase was to create an online resource course in the LMS (Canvas). The goal was not for faculty to properly design online courses; rather, it was to help faculty present enough materials online to their students so that they could complete the period from spring break to the end of the term. E-Learning staff conducted live remote workshops and offered face-to-face consultations during a one-week period between spring break and the implementation of a work-from-home policy. During the summer term, workshops in the form of a boot camp continued, specifically on effective use of synchronous delivery tools and accessibility concerns. The course was designed as a two-week intensive process to cover the basics of online pedagogy and statutory compliance. The goal was to move all college faculty through the process in ten weeks, rather than spreading them over a three-year period. This boot camp is not a substitute for the full process and, once the pandemic has passed, courses not previously approved for online delivery, will have to complete the application and development process, or return to traditional lecture format.

In another example at a smaller research university, the distance learning team developed their faculty development program to meet the needs of their faculty and students for a specific discipline. This smaller engineering university designed their faculty e-learning program around the university's teaching and learning center's course development process that addressed designing curriculum for STEM students. This process was designed to be very linear and focused on course level learning outcomes, aligning assessments to outcomes, designing learning activities, and using strategies to infuse educational technology into the online learning experience.

The program was developed as a fully immersive, five-week (50-hour), asynchronous online course with all materials and assignments in the LMS (Canvas). It was designed to cover and simulate three types of learning interaction: student-to-student, instructor-to-student, and student-to-content. The course engages faculty in the online environment so they can experience the course as a student does with assignments and discussions centered on the LMS, online education, course level learning outcomes, assessments, and learning activities. The course then shifts to course facilitation to prepare faculty for using the LMS for grading, building community, and instructor presence.

The course level outcomes include constructing general observations about teaching and learning in the classroom and online and creating a course map using a teaching and learning framework to structure an online course with Specific, Measurable, Achievable, Relevant, and Timely (S.M.A.R.T.) learning outcomes. Faculty also design assessments (both formative and summative) and/or learning activities that measure student achievement of the course learning outcomes. Faculty learn how to apply online standards and best practices in designing and facilitating a high-quality online course to a predetermined course that they will build in the LMS. Since STEM courses are very software focused, they also evaluate available educational technology resources used in online courses.

The faculty development course encourages interaction among faculty in several ways throughout the five weeks together. At the beginning of the course, faculty are required to post a video introduction and respond to each other in the Let's Get to Know Each Other discussion. As the course progresses, faculty members peer review each other's course maps to provide feedback on their course level learning outcomes, assessments, and modular structure. The peer review provides an opportunity for faculty to not only get feedback on their maps but to also see what other faculty are doing in their courses. The training course provides several discussion opportunities on topics such as online learning, assessments, and a reflection on their experiences in the course. Faculty are encouraged to attend office hours together and post to a general Q&A discussion with any questions or observations about the course. Feedback from the course has consistently shown that faculty value their interactions with other faculty.

Large institutions, with robust e-Learning teams, are well positioned to design world class faculty development programs. There are many such programs, but we will discuss one in particular. It was developed in the infancy of online learning as we know it. Starting in 1998 a large public research university saw the need to develop excellent online courses from the outset and developed an 8-week hybrid model of professional development (Chen et al., 2012). This model took advantage of the fact that university faculty were largely local to the institution, and that there was a team of instructional designers available to help faculty. This program included online components, so that faculty could learn in the modality in which they would teach. Over an eight-week period, faculty attended face-to-face workshops, worked in a lab setting, participated in online components, and had scheduled meetings with their assigned instructional designer (Chen et al., 2012).

Over the next 12 years, the course incrementally evolved until, in 2010, both faculty and institutional needs were no longer being met by the process. Chen et al. (2012) noted, among other things the faculty wished the course to include less teaching theory, recognize their prior experience, and allow hands on opportunities earlier in the process. All of these reflect the time that had elapsed and the collective experience and comfort that was being gained with the modality. Chen et al. (2012) also noted the administrative need to accommodate more faculty in the process and to do so without proportionally increasing demands on instructional designers and other resources. The process was redesigned, still maintaining a hybrid delivery model, but requiring less scheduled face-to-face interaction, therefore meeting the needs of all stakeholders.

This institution also modified their development approach during the pandemic. Cavanaugh (2020) noted that the university was seeking to make their development program "better all the time" as the pandemic wore on and evolved. He elaborated that the focus was not on truly developing courses to the institutions standards but on improving them, through better development each semester. Knowing that their flagship development course was not scalable during such an event, they created an accelerated model, similar to other institutions. During the abrupt transition to online delivery, during spring of 2020, they used ad-hoc consultations with faculty to move the remainder of the term online. To prepare for summer, they focused on training faculty to use the technology to teach synchronously online and, for fall, developed an abbreviated version of their full development program. The "Essentials of Online Teaching" course would be designed to be a stackable credential, a step closer to their full certification (Cavanaugh, 2020).

All of these models retain some reliance on a trainer or facilitator and some restrictions as to time and or place. For many institutions, these are appropriate models because they mimic the modalities in which the faculty will be teaching. In other scenarios, or for other types of content delivery, faculty may need to interact with training that is not bound by these restrictions. Faculty, just as students, may need to be provided with a development timeline that they can participate in on their schedule, in their location, or one they can jump into and out of when they want. "Any Day Any Place Teaching" is a model that seeks to deliver quality training content that can be consumed online in small chunks and is not dependent on a facilitator (Neibuhr et al., 2015). Much, if not all, of the subject matter discussed in these models can be addressed in this model, and it's important to note that it removes many of the other models' restrictions. However, It is not without its challenges. Feedback is still a critical part of the learning process so it is difficult to completely remove the human factor from the content delivery. Neibuhr et al. (2015) note that it might not matter as much who gives the feedback (i.e. it doesn't have to be the content developer) as long as someone does.

As you seek to plan a particular development model for your institution, you will need to keep many institutional-specific variables in mind. Whether you choose an online moderated, hybrid or any day, any place model, you will not be successful if it is not a good fit for your institution. It will not be a good fit if it doesn't support the faculty, help them attain their instructional goals, and help them to be more effective educators.

Looking Back: If you were in an administrative role, what features of the models we discussed would you adopt for faculty development?

6   Ownership, Incentives, and Compensation

Thinking Ahead: How does your institution determine who will own an online course? Is this determined at an administrative (President/Provost/Dean) or faculty level (Faculty Senate/Union)? What compensation/incentive models do you have, if any, at your institution?

Now that you've had an opportunity to dive into planning for professional development, defining faculty competencies, and identifying important elements and models for professional development, we will wrap this chapter up with a section on ownership, incentives, and compensation. Beyond development, an institution must support the motivations; financial, professional and intellectual, of the faculty member. Addressing how content will be owned by the institution and/or faculty member as well as providing incentives or compensation for training and development will go a long way towards supporting these motivations.

Maslow created his hierarchy of needs model in 1954 and it still provides us with some clues as to how we can best motivate people. His five-level hierarchy can be viewed as a continuum of motivators which begins with basic physiological needs, continues through social motivators, and then peaks with one's self-actualization (Aanstoos, 2019). As addressed in Maslow's Hierarchy of Need, if a person's basic human needs are met then they can move toward achieving self-actualization and in this case become a highly trained and effective online instructor (Kenrick et al., 2010). As you plan your compensation and incentives model, it helps to determine to which types of motivations your faculty might best respond.

Before diving into incentive and compensation models, as well as barriers, we need to explore the basics of the complex topic of ownership and copyright of intellectual property (IP). All instructional materials such as multimedia (video, animations, simulations, etc.), assessments, and scholarly publications fall into the category of IP. When produced by the faculty member with the support of the institution for an online course, there must be a clear policy defining who retains ownership and rights to these materials. The American Association of University Professors defines copyright as the "bundle of rights that protect original works of authorship fixed in any tangible medium of expression, now known or later developed, from which they can be perceived, reproduced, or otherwise communicated, either directly or with the aid of a machine or device" (aaup, n.d.).

As we've seen, ownership of materials can be dependent on a number of factors at an academic institution:

1. Existing institutional policy surrounding intellectual property and own-ership.
2. The creation and use of instructional materials and multimedia by the faculty member prior to developing the online course.
3. Investment of resources in the creation of instructional materials by the institution in the form of instructional design support and multimedia creation.
4. Copyright of any outside materials used by the developer of the online course or when the faculty member considers "taking [the] course to other institutions" (Kranch, 2008).
5. Work release or monetary compensation provided to the faculty member for the development of the fully online course.

Below you will find language used by a small research university to address intellectual property, ownership, and copyright as it relates to online courses and materials. Some items of note about this institution: the faculty senate shares governance with the administration, online education is fairly new to the institution, and online education is developed through the teaching and learning center. This statement is a part of their online courses and programs procedure documentation:

In general, ownership of academic instruction materials by [institution] fac-ulty members is treated the same regardless of delivery modality (see Faculty Handbook) for the course (e.g., traditional face-to-face, hybrid, online, etc.). The critical distinction in ownership between online courses and all of these other course modalities is that [institution] will own the online course as a whole, including any videos contained therein and associated technical infra-structure by which the course is delivered (collectively, the "Online Course"). What this means is that while faculty members retain ownership rights in the academic instructional materials they have included within an online course, and as a result may use, modify, and disseminate these as they see appropriate; faculty members may not export, upload, distribute, transfer, sell, license, or otherwise disseminate the Online Course in its entirety. Decisions on the re-use of developed content (e-media and other recorded content) will be made by the academic department (department head or program coordinator/lead) in consultation with the original content developer (when reasonable) and new instructor. [Institution] will encourage new instructors to re-record any media containing an original instructor's voice or image.

The American Association of University Professors (aaup, n.d.) provides sample contract language to identify conditions where the university would retain copyright:

The university shall own copyright only in the following 3 circumstances:

1.   I. The college or university expressly directs a faculty member to cre-ate a specified work, or the work is created as a specific requirement of employment or as an assigned institutional duty that may, for example, be included in a written job description or an employment agreement.

2.   II. The faculty author has voluntarily transferred the copyright, in whole or in part to the institution. Such transfer shall be in the form of a written document signed by the faculty author.

3.   III. The college or university has contributed to a "joint work" under the Copyright Act. The institution can exercise joint ownership under this clause when it has contributed specialized services and facilities to the production of the work that goes beyond what is traditionally provided to faculty members generally in the preparation of their course materials. Such arrangement is to be agreed to in writing, in advance, and in full conformance with other provisions of this agreement.

Johnson (2006) provides additional resources for intellectual property and copyright and has encouraged faculty to become more familiar with the Acts and Case Law: Digital Millennium Act 1998 and Technology, Education, and Copyright Harmonization Act 2002.

When determining which incentives and compensation model would work best for your institution, it's important to have a good understanding of all the different models available to you as a distance education administrator. There are five models that rise to the top in the literature;

1. direct compensation for developing online,
2. royalty payments,
3. recognition,
4. professional development opportunities, and
5. workload release.

Although this is not a comprehensive list of what every institution provides to faculty, these are strategies that should be considered by your institution.

Compensation paid directly to faculty in the form of a stipend or overpay can be an effective strategy for motivating faculty to participate in professional development (Berg, 2000). While some institutions pay based on the amount of hours a faculty member spends in the training, others provide "release time" or pay faculty based on the rate they would receive to teach a course at their institution. Royalty payments could be an effective motivator for faculty to take professional development for developing online courses. Faculty are motivated to complete training and develop the online course for any future compensation that would come from the course being offered to students at their institution (Berg, 2000).

Recognition can also be a powerful motivator for faculty to participate in professional development. Receiving a certificate of completion or a special recognition from the President or Provost of an institution can be all that's needed to inspire faculty to complete training and begin development of an online course (Clay, 1999). In some cases, faculty are only interested in the professional development opportunity associated with learning about online/ distance education. They are driven to learn as much as they can about online education so they can become an effective online educator (Shea, 2019). Faculty can also be inspired to participate by being offered a workload release for their time. Relieving faculty from their teaching responsibilities enables them to be immersed in the professional development opportunity (Clay, 1999).

Without compensation, recognition, release time for training or designing/ building the online course, or royalty payments, faculty will be less likely to participate and build online courses. Institutions need to be willing to invest in one or more of these incentives to support and inspire faculty to participate, actively engage, and complete professional development training opportunities.

Looking Back: What barriers/obstacles to online course and program development do you see at your institution? Using some of the strategies in this chapter, how can you work towards overcoming these barriers?

7   **Conclusion**

We have seen that administrative engagement with faculty is one of the key components of successful online learning implementation. There are many ways to engage with faculty but we have focused only on those which are supportive and will foster a collaborative relationship, rather than an adversarial one between you and your faculty. An effective way to foster this supportive relationship is through a community of practice. If you are allowed to build the proper team, with instructional designers and technologists, you can use a variety of strategies to collaborate with faculty, as well as other functional areas of your institution. These collaborations will help faculty members feel supported and included, rather than imposed upon and isolated.

Building your faculty development program requires careful planning and deliberate execution. Faculty have a variety of motivations for participating in these programs and they arrive at them with a variety of different skill levels. It is important to teach competencies and, at the same time, model teaching behaviors. Establishing faculty competencies provides a framework for faculty to follow to allow them to effectively facilitate a course. The teaching behaviors they learn through professional development experiences move them toward true online teaching excellence.

Development includes more than instruction in how to use the tools of the online teacher; it addresses all aspects of the faculty member's professional life and often offers them personal development opportunities as well. Many aspects of your program will be determined by the type of institution you are a part of and your placement therein. The elements of an effective development program for online faculty are well rooted in classical professional development theory, with the primary evolution being that it is very commonly delivered online.

This wasn't always the case. In the early days of preparing faculty to teach online, both trainers and faculty were used to the face-to-face training methods. Over time, programs gradually changed to include supplemental content online, then to a moderated format with a structured pace and to where we are now, with learn on demand online development. At the time this text was written, development programs were changing rapidly in response to the CoVid-19 crisis and the immediate demands placed on all stakeholders in online higher education.

In order to fully support engagement between administration and faculty, we discussed incentives and compensation. Understanding how best to approach this topic requires an understanding of human motivation and your institution's faculty in particular. An effective compensation model will likely be some mix of compensation, intellectual property considerations, and recognition.

We have examined a number of different aspects of engaging faculty in professional development for e-learning. While mastering all of them will be difficult, it is important to begin thinking strategically about how to address these responsibilities at your institution. As you may have noted, some tasks described may not fall within your administrative responsibility, but will be addressed by others. However, by having knowledge of these responsibilities, you will help to ensure a successful e-learning implementation.

8 Resources

1. Penn State Faculty Self-Assessment https://behrend-elearn.psu.edu/weblearning/FacultySelfAssessment
2. Council of Regional Accrediting Commissions (c-rac) https://nc-sara.org/resources/council-regional-accrediting-commissions-c-rac-guidelines
3. Quality Scorecard for the Administration of Online Programs https://onlinelearningconsortium.org/consult/olc-quality-scorecard-administration-online-programs/
4. Acts and Case Law: Digital Millennium Act 1998 https://www.copyright.gov/legislation/dmca.pdf
5. Technology, Education, and Copyright Harmonization Act 2002 https://www.copyright.gov/docs/regstat031301.html

References

Aanstoos, C. M. (2019). *Maslow's hierarchy of needs*. Salem Press Encyclopedia of Health.

American Association of University Professors [aaup]. (n.d.). *Sample intellectual property policy & contract language*. Retrieved June 9, 2020, from https://www.aaup.org/issues/copyright-distance-education-intellectual-property/sample-ip-policy-language

Amundsen, C., Abrami, P., McAlpine, L., Mundy, A., Wilson, M., Weston, C., & Krbavac, M. (2005). *The what and why of faculty development in higher education: An in-depth review of the literature*. AERA.

Barefield, A. C. (2013). Leadership's role in support of online academic programs: Implementing an administrative support matrix. *Perspectives in Health Information Management*.

Berg, G. A. (2019). Early patterns of faculty compensation for developing and teaching distance learning courses. *Online Learning, 4*(1). https://doi.org/10.24059/olj.v4i1.1912

Cavanagh, T. (2020, May). *Constraints for fall 2020 in the context of COVID-19.* Florida Virtual Campus Meeting, Distance Learning Support Services.

Centra, J. A. (1989). Faculty evaluation and faculty development in higher education. In J. C. Smart (Ed.), *Higher education: Handbook of theory and research* (pp. 155–179). Agathon Press.

Chen, B., Sugar, A., & Bauer, S. (2012, September 4). Effective faculty development through strategies for engagement and satisfaction. *EDUCAUSE Review.* https://er.educause.edu/articles/2012/9/effective-faculty-development-through-strategies-for-engagement-and-satisfaction

Clay, M. (1999). Development of training and support programs for distance education instructors. *Online Journal of Distance Learning Administration, 2*(3).

Coswatte Mohr, S., & Shelton, K. (2017). Best practices framework for online faculty professional development: A Delphi study. *Online Learning, 21*(4). https://doi.org/10.24059/olj.v21i4.1273

Council of Regional Accrediting Commissions. (2009). *Guidelines for the evaluation of distance education (On-line learning).* http://download.hlcommission.org/C-RAC_Distance_Ed_Guidelines_7_31_2009.pdf

Johnson, L. (2006). Managing intellectual property for distance learning. *Educause Quarterly.*

Kenrick, D. T., Griskevicius, V., Neuberg, S. L., & Schaller, M. (2010). Renovating the pyramid of needs: Contemporary extensions built upon ancient foundations. *Perspectives on Psychological Science: A Journal of the Association for Psychological Science, 5*(3), 292–314. https://doi.org/10.1177/1745691610369469

Kranch, D. A. (2008). Who owns online intellectual property? *The Quarterly Review of Distance Education, 9*(4), 349–356.

Martin, F., Budhrani, K., Kumar, S., & Ritzhaupt, A. (2019). Award-winning faculty online teaching practices: Roles and competencies. *Online Learning, 23*(1). https://doi.org/10.24059/olj.v23i1.1329

Niebuhr, V., Niebuhr, B., Trumble, J., & Urbani, M. (2014). Online faculty development for creating e-learning materials. *Education for Health, 27*(3), 255. https://doi.org/10.4103/1357-6283.152186

Online Learning Consortium [OLC]. (2018). *Quality scorecard for the administration of online programs.* https://onlinelearningconsortium.org/consult/olc-quality-scorecard-administration-online-programs/

Seepersaud, D. (2018). Faculty development: The critical element. *Distance Learning, 15*(1), 37–39.

Shea, P. (2019). Bridges and barriers to teaching online college courses: A study of experienced online faculty in thirty-six colleges. *Online Learning, 11*(2). https://doi.org/10.24059/olj.v11i2.1728

Terosky, A. L., & Heasley, C. (2015). Supporting online faculty through a sense of community and collegiality. *Online Learning, 19*(3). https://doi.org/10.24059/olj.v19i3.673

Williams, V. (2020, June 8). *Readiness for online learning* [Education]. Penn State, The Pennsylvania State University. https://pennstate.qualtrics.com/jfe/form/SV_7QCNUPsyH9fo12B

CHAPTER 10

Quality Assurance in Online Education

Karen Swan

Abstract

This chapter is about quality assurance in online education. Specifically, it is about assuring that the quality of education offered online is at least equal to the quality of education offered to traditional students. After completing this chapter, you should have a general understanding of the issues surrounding quality assurance in five areas – access, learning effectiveness, faculty satisfaction, student satisfaction, and cost effectiveness – as well as some notion of ways of ensuring quality in those spheres.

The chapter begins with a little bit about the history of online learning in the US and introduces the Sloan Consortium and its five pillars of quality in online education. It then discusses each of the pillars in turn – access, learning effectiveness, faculty satisfaction, student satisfaction, and cost effectiveness. Key issues in each pillar area and potential measures for assessing them are discussed. More time will be spent exploring learning effectiveness because, in my opinion, learning is, or should be, at the center of everything we do in education. To that ends, two instruments for assessing learning effectiveness are presented – the Quality Matters rubric and the Community of Inquiry survey. The chapter concludes with a discussion of the interrelationships among the quality pillars and the importance of all in upholding the quality of online education.

Keywords

quality pillars of online education – access – learning effectiveness – faculty satisfaction – student satisfaction – cost effectiveness/scale – Quality Matters (QM) rubric – Community of Inquiry (CoI) survey

1   Sloan-C and the Five Quality Pillars of Online Education

> *quality assurance* (*noun*) – the maintenance of a desired level of quality in a service or product, especially by means of attention to every stage of the process of delivery or production. (www.lexico.com)

Quality assurance has been an important part of online learning for almost as long as it has been practiced, at least in the United States. In the United States in the early 1990s, before there was a commercial internet and the digital networks that did exist were only accessible to academics and defense contractors, Ralph Gomory, then President of the Alfred P. Sloan Foundation, established the Learning Anytime, Anyplace grant program. The program's goal was to explore the educational opportunities provided by digital networking technologies for people who could not easily attend regularly scheduled post-secondary classes.

Under the direction of Frank Mayadas, who became the founding president of the Sloan Consortium (Sloan-C; which evolved into the Online Learning Consortium or OLC), more than $72,000,000 was provided to seed online learning programs at over 346 institutions of higher education, the consortium members, who built and shared knowledge about the rapidly evolving practice of online learning (Picciano, 2013). In 2000, it was estimated that nearly two-thirds of all the credit courses offered online in the US were offered by Sloan-C member institutions (Mayadas, 2001). Imagine that.

In many ways, online learning in the United States owes its unique evolution to Drs. Gomory and Mayadas and Sloan-C. The early courses and programs funded through Sloan-C would have been incredibly important in themselves as proofs-of-concept. However, perhaps more important was the consortium's insistence that any learner who engaged in online education should have, at a minimum, an education equal in quality to the education traditionally provided face-to-face students at the institution offering it. Distance education has been around since the introduction of correspondence schools in the nineteenth century. This was the first time, however, anyone suggested distance learning could, moreover should, be equal in quality to traditional, campus-based education, and Sloan-C put considerable money behind this concept.

Why is that important? I believe it is important because it took online learning in a different direction as Sloan-C member institutions tried to replicate the class-based, inquiry-oriented education enjoyed by traditional students for their online cousins. Thus, while distance education at the time was materials and teacher-centered, online learning took a student-centered approach; where distance education relied on independent study and tutors, online learning focused on collaboration and discussion and instructors, and in the case of Sloan-C members, the same instructors who taught the on-campus versions of the same courses.

Sloan-C's insistence on quality is also important because it clearly established the need for metrics to ensure quality. Indeed, Dr. Mayadas maintained that the quality of online education needed to match the quality of traditional education in five inter-related areas, namely, access, learning effectiveness, faculty satisfaction, student satisfaction, and cost-effectiveness, and outlined metrics for institutions to consider to make sure they were meeting quality standards in each area (Online Learning Consortium, 2020). He likened these spheres of quality to pillars holding up a roof, arguing that all five were necessary to support quality online learning, that the collapse of any one pillar endangered the overall quality of an institution's online programs. Each of the five pillars and the metrics associated with them are explored in the remainder of this chapter.

2   Access

Access for traditionally under-represented populations is in many ways Sloan-C's cornerstone pillar. It is the reason Dr. Gomory began the "Learning Anytime, Anyplace" program to begin with, and notions of equal quality are central to it. Access is concerned with ensuring that people who might otherwise be unable to attend classes can participate in higher education and acquire the college degrees and certificates that are increasingly so critical to full participation in the larger society.

Janet Moore (2005) maintained that the goal of access was that "all learners who wish to learn online have the opportunity and can achieve success." Examples of practices that support access include but are not limited to: the provision of diverse learning activities for learners of varying abilities including at-risk students and students with disabilities; the availability of courses when students want and/or need them; connectivity to support services including tutors, financial services, library services, the registrar, and so on; and reliable and functional technology and technology support.

According to the Online Learning Consortium (2020), access includes three areas of concern: academic (e.g., tutoring, advising, library services); administrative (e.g., financial aid, disability support); and technical (e.g., hardware reliability, help desk). One way to evaluate access, then, is in terms of how well an institution is providing academic, administrative and technical services to online students. Traditional tools for measuring access have also included student and provider surveys, narrative and case study descriptions, focus groups, and help desk and support services logs. These days, however, perhaps the most useful measures employ learning analytics.

Learning analytics can provide descriptive statistics that tell how many under-represented students have enrolled in specific programs of interest, what services they avail themselves of, and their success rates, and these can be broken out by student characteristics. The application of more advanced statistics allows for the investigation of really interesting questions concerning access, such as how different support mechanisms influence the success of varying student populations, whether financial aid impacts student success, especially among traditionally disenfranchised populations, and if gender, age, and/or socio-economic status affect student progression. What distinguishes analytic studies, and makes them so useful, is that they use very large data sets that can include the entire student populations of particular institutions or across institutions, and so explore specific questions of interest, including questions concerned with access.

For example, a series of analytic studies utilizing large data sets and exploring the effects of online delivery on undergraduate student retention and progression (Jaggers et al., 2013; James et al., 2016; Johnson et al., 2015; Shea & Bidjerano, 2018; Swan & James, 2017) has shined a light on the efficacy of online courses at the community college level. Findings are mixed across the studies but seem to suggest that online courses do provide access to higher education for underserved populations (Swan & James, 2017). However, some researchers have found that, at the community college level, students were more likely to withdraw or fail online courses than face-to-face courses, that online course completers had lower grades in comparison to students completing face-to-face courses, and that these negative effects were more pronounced for males, African-Americans, younger students, and students with lower GPAs, (Hart et al., 2016; Jaggers & Xu, 2010; Johnson et al., 2015).

However, there have been other findings that confound these results. For example, Wladis, Conway, and Hachey (2016) found that, while students enrolled in online courses were more likely to drop them, taking online courses had no direct effect on college persistence. Researchers in both California (Johnson et al., 2015) and New York State (Shea & Bidjerano, 2014, 2016) took that one step farther and found that community college students who took at least some courses online were more likely to earn an associate's degree or transfer to a four-year institution than those who did not. Indeed, our own research (James et al., 2016) suggests that students, including community college students, who take some of their courses online and some face-to-face are retained at rates equal to or better than similar students taking only online or only face-to-face classes.

In my opinion, what these big data studies reveal about access is that online learning does increase non-traditional students' access to higher education, but that it also does have some negative effects. In my opinion, we should be working to mitigate these by ensuring that online students have access to support services at least comparable to those available to on campus students, and that we should encourage local students to take some face-to-face classes.

What do you think?

Another aspect of access that has become increasingly important is ensuring access to online learning for students with disabilities. As of January 18, 2018, new requirements to Section 508 of the Rehabilitation Act of 1973 require information and communications technology (hence all online courses and programs) at all institutions receiving federal funds be accessible to the widest range of people with disabilities. Information and communication technology is considered accessible if it can be used as effectively by people with disabilities as it can by those without, so the accessibility requirements are absolutely congruent with the thinking in which the quality pillars are grounded. True accessibility provides for not just the sightless and the hearing impaired but also the color blind, those prone to seizures, and people with physical limitations that require keyboard navigation rather than the use of a mouse. The considerations for accessibility are proactive, they must be built into all materials regardless of whether or not disabled students are enrolled. Thus, they are not to be confused with the mandate to provide accommodations for students with disabilities, which are provided on demand (Lagrow, 2017).

Except as regards full access for disabled students, the access pillar is unlike the other quality pillars in that it sets the context for the rest. Access is the condition which demands equal quality for online students in the areas of learning effectiveness, faculty satisfaction, student satisfaction, and cost.

3   Learning Effectiveness

Although we sometimes seem to lose sight of it, the goal, the raison d'etre, the stuff of education is learning. This is at least as true of online education as it is of traditional education. The learning effectiveness pillar is concerned that online students' learning be at least as robust as that of students in similar traditional classes (Online Learning Consortium, 2020). This does not mean that online learning experiences should try to duplicate those in traditional classrooms. Differing delivery modes have different characteristics that matter or that can be made to matter in teaching and learning (Salomon, 1981; Twigg, 2001). Rather it means that instructors and course developers should take advantage of the unique characteristics of online environments to provide learning experiences that represent the distinctive quality of the institutions offering them.

Robert Kozma (1991), for example, extolled the capacity of online environments to individualize instruction. Garrison and colleagues (2001) explored the ability of online environments to support both reflection and collaboration and related these to John Dewey's notion of inquiry. The point is that, just as there are effective pedagogies in classroom-based teaching and learning, so there are instructional practices that are particularly effective online.

Another way to look at learning effectiveness is in terms of interactivity. No matter what theories of learning we hold, interaction in some form is integral to our understanding of how people learn (Bransford et al., 2000). Michael Moore (1989) identified three types of interactions that support learning in traditional classrooms that need to be transformed to support distance learning: interaction with content, interaction with instructors, and interaction with peers. Interaction with content refers both to learners' interactions with the course materials and to their interaction with the concepts and ideas they present. Interaction with instructors includes the myriad ways in which instructors teach, guide, correct, and support their students. Interaction among peers also can take many forms – collaboration, discussion, debate, peer review – as well as informal and incidental interactions among classmates. Each of these modes of interaction support learning and each can be uniquely enacted in online learning environments.

In 1994, Hillman and colleagues identified a fourth type of interaction, learner-interface interaction, which they defined as the interaction that takes place between a student and the technology used to implement online learning. They contended that such interactions were critical simply because failure to interact successfully could dramatically inhibit learning. Perhaps you have stories about student misconceptions concerning how a particular technology works. When mice were just becoming popular as input devices I remember a woman in one of my classes picking her mouse up and talking into it. I believe issues of interface are equally important in online learning today. Indeed, in a study of online courses in the State of New York system, I found that clarity and consistency in interfaces was a significant predictor of student satisfaction and perceived learning (Swan, 2001).

One way to evaluate learning effectiveness, then, is in terms of how well individual courses and/or programs are providing for interactions with content, instructors, peers, and interfaces. Another way is to compare learning outcomes in similar courses offered online and face-to-face. Of course, an enormous number of research studies of this sort have been done. Some of the most recent syntheses of these have been conducted by Bernard and his colleagues (2014). These authors reviewed 16 meta-analyses which in turn looked at literally thousands of primary studies comparing online and classroom instruction. They concluded there is consensus that online learning can be at least as effective as classroom instruction, with small effect sizes indicating that online learning may be somewhat more effective. However, Bernard and colleagues also found wide variability among studies, thus raising questions about the contexts in which online learning is most effective, and bringing us back to issues of interactivity.

The most commonly used measures of learning effectiveness, however, are not measures of learning effectiveness at all, but rather measures of the quality of online course designs and learning processes in online courses: the Quality Matters (QM) rubric and the Community of Inquiry (CoI) survey respectively.

3.1   *Quality Matters (QM) Rubric*

Quality Matters (QM) is the leading quality assurance organization for online and blended course design. An educational nonprofit, QM began with a small group of faculty in the MarylandOnline (MOL), Inc. consortium who were trying to solve the common problem of how to measure and guarantee the quality of online and blended courses across the University of Maryland system.

In 2006, Quality Matters (QM) was incorporated as an educational nonprofit, and now offers a complete framework for institutional online quality assurance, including a course design rubric, a process for both informal/internal and formal/external quality reviews, and professional development on online learning topics (Shattuck et al., 2014). QM is a provider of online learning professional development and has trained over 90,000 faculty and staff. Nearly 1,300 member-institutions in all 50 states and 20 countries participate in some level of adoption and adaptation of the QM Standards, professional development, and course review processes to assist with their own quality assurance for online learning.

The Quality Matters (QM) rubric is a faculty-oriented, process centered, peer review instrument based on instructional design principles designed to assure quality design in online and blended courses. It is based on an input model of learning in online education. The QM rubric is grounded in an instructional design approach which assumes that effective learning flows from well-specified outcomes, objectives and assessments.

QM is currently using the Sixth edition of the QM Higher Education Rubric, which includes 42 specific review standards, each with a complete annotation that provides examples and detailed guidance. These are organized under eight general standards: Course Overview & Introduction, Learning Objectives, Assessment & Measurement, Instructional Materials, Learning Activities

& Learner Interaction, Course Technology, Learner Support, and Accessibility & Usability. The QM rubric reflects the latest in online learning research and effective practices and is regularly updated and revised by an external committee of faculty, researchers, instructional designers, and other online learning experts.

A formal Quality Matters review is carried out by three trained reviewers who work together to decide whether or not individual items are met and to provide suggestions for improvement. QM standards are either met or not, and many of them must be met for a course to be considered to have achieved quality. A QM redesign involves addressing the issues identified by the reviewers and resubmitting the course for approval. The Quality Matters rubric can also be used informally as a guide for designing online and blended classes or for redesigning existing courses.

The Quality Matters rubric, then, addresses course design, and, it should be noted, addresses it from an objectivist perspective. The QM rubric does not address course implementation and/or the processes of learning, nor does it purport to do so, taking a kind of "if you build it [right] they will come" approach. It is, however, thoroughly grounded in educational research, practitioner-based, and constantly updated to align with best practices in instructional design for online learning.

There are other course design instruments. The Open SUNY Course Quality Review (OSCQR) is another measure gaining popularity in the US. It was created and is used by the State University of New York's online learning network and distributed by the Online Learning Consortium as well. It has 50 items in six categories: Course Overview and Information, Course Technology and Tools, Design and Layout, Content and Activities, Interaction, and Assessment and Feedback. The items are assessed as being sufficiently present, or needing minor, moderate, or major revisions (or not applicable). The scale is thus seen as a tool to support continuing improvement as opposed to a kind of pass/fail certification. It is also more focused on design elements than objectives and pedagogy.

In addition, many institutions have adopted their own standards of course design. For example, the California State University, Chico (2009) developed their Rubric for Online Instruction. Like OSCQR, the Chico State Rubric supports three levels of continuing improvement – baseline, effective, and exemplary – and it covers six categories: Learner Support and Resources, Online Design and Organization, Instructional Design and Delivery, Assessment and Evaluation of Student Learning, Innovative Teaching with Technology, and Faculty Use of Student Feedback. Unlike OSCQR and QM, the Chico State Rubric includes some items that relate to course implementation.

Do you or your institution have a preferred measure of quality course design? If so, what is used? If not, what quality measure would you choose to implement as a DL administrator?

3.2 *Community of Inquiry (CoI) Survey*

The Community of Inquiry (CoI) Survey only looks at course implementation and does so in terms of learning processes. The CoI survey is based on the Community of Inquiry (CoI) framework (Garrison et al., 2000) which is a social constructivist, process model of learning in online environments. The CoI framework assumes that effective online learning requires the development of a community that supports meaningful inquiry and deep learning (Rovai, 2002; Shea, 2006). It has been quite widely used to inform both research and practice in the online learning community and an increasing body of research supports its efficacy for both (Arbaugh et al., 2008; Swan et al., 2009).

Similar to the way in which the Quality Matters rubric assumes that high quality course designs ensure high quality learning, the Community of Inquiry (CoI) framework assumes that high quality learning takes place when three "presences" – social, teaching, and cognitive presence – support its development (see Figure 10.1).

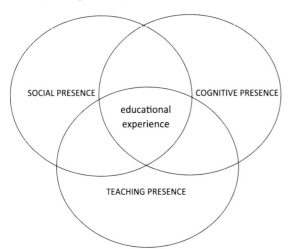

FIGURE 10.1
The CoI framework (adapted with permission from Garrison et al., 2000)

Social presence refers to the degree to which participants in online communities feel socially and emotionally connected with each other. A number of research studies have found that the perception of interpersonal connections with virtual others is an important factor in the success of online learning (Richardson & Swan, 2003; Smith-Jaggars & Xu, 2016; Richardson et al., 2017).

Teaching presence is defined as the design, facilitation, and direction of cognitive and social processes for the realization of personally meaningful and educationally worthwhile learning outcomes. Researchers have documented strong correlations between learners' perceived and actual interactions with instructors and their perceived learning (Richardson & Swan, 2003), and between teaching presence and student satisfaction, perceived learning, and development of a sense of community in online courses (Shea et al., 2005). In fact, the body of evidence attesting to the critical importance of teaching presence for successful online learning continues to grow (Garrison & Cleveland-Innes, 2005; Swan & Shih, 2005; Vaughn & Garrison, 2006; Kozan & Richardson, 2014), with the most recent research suggesting it is the key to developing online communities of inquiry (Kucuk & Richardson, 2019).

Cognitive presence describes the extent to which learners are able to construct and confirm meaning through course activities, sustained reflection, and discourse (Garrison et al., 2000). It is conceptualized in terms of practical inquiry progressing from a triggering event through exploration and integration and culminating in resolution. Although instantiating the full practical inquiry cycle in online discussion can be difficult, when students are tasked with solving a problem and explicit facilitation and direction are provided, students have been shown to progress to resolution (Shea & Bidjerano, 2009; De Leng, Dolmans, Jöbsis, Muijtjens, & van der Vleuten, 2009). Indeed, under the right conditions, cognitive presence has been linked to perceived and actual learning (Akyol & Garrison, 2011).

In 2008, researchers working with the CoI framework developed a survey designed to measure student perceptions of each of these presences (Arbaugh et al., 2008). The Community of Inquiry (CoI) survey consists of 34 items (13 teaching presence, 9 social presence, and 12 cognitive presence) that ask students to rate their agreement on a 5-point Likert scale (1 – strongly disagree; 5 – strongly agree) with statements related to the three presences. The survey has been validated through factor analysis (Arbaugh et al., 2008) and used to further explore the CoI framework and the interactive effects of all three presences (Garrison, Cleveland-Innes, & Fung, 2010). It should be noted, moreover, that while perceptions are a subjective matter and subjective measures may not be everywhere appropriate, in this case, in a constructivist frame, they are very appropriate. The CoI survey provides a measure of learning processes in online courses that is grounded in the perceptions of learners and that explores what happens within the courses themselves. It has been used internationally to inform both the research and the practice of online education.

There are many other ways of determining whether and what students are learning online, not the least of which involve learning analytics. The nature of online delivery makes it possible to keep track of student activities in learning management systems (e.g., what pages they visit, how much time they spend on each) and to link these to learning outcomes on many levels. It is important, however, not to confuse measures of learning with learning itself, or to eschew the learning of important things like ethics and aesthetics simply because they are not quantifiable. What is critical is that institutions decide what learning outcomes are important to them and their missions and agree upon ways of ensuring that these outcomes are achieved with high quality.

4   Faculty Satisfaction

The third pillar of quality online education is faculty satisfaction. Clearly, if faculty are not happy teaching online, the quality of online education will suffer. Faculty satisfaction centers on the idea that instructors find the online teaching experience personally rewarding and professionally beneficial. According to Janet Moore (2005), institutional factors related to faculty satisfaction can be placed in three categories: support, rewards, and institutional study/research. She further maintained that faculty satisfaction is enhanced when the institution supports faculty members with a robust and well-maintained technical infrastructure, training in online instructional skills, and ongoing technical and administrative assistance. Faculty members also expect to be included in the governance and quality assurance of online programs, especially as these relate to curricular decisions and development of policies of particular importance to the online environment.

Faculty satisfaction is also closely related to an institutional reward system that recognizes the rigor and value of online teaching. Satisfaction increases when workload assignments/assessments reflect the greater time commitment in developing and teaching online courses and when online teaching is valued on par with face-to-face teaching in promotion and tenure decisions. A final institutional factor impacting faculty satisfaction is commitment to the ongoing study and the consequent enhancement of the online faculty experience.

Faculty satisfaction is clearly ostensive; the only way to be sure to meet this quality standard is to engage the faculty in assessing and enhancing satisfaction. Thus, many institutions create their own faculty satisfaction surveys and periodically canvass online instructors. Often issues explored are purely local.

Does your institution survey online faculty? Has surveying faculty led to the identification of issues and/or increased faculty satisfaction?

In spring 1999, 105 faculty teaching courses in the State University of New York (SUNY) Learning Network (40%) completed a survey related to faculty satisfaction with teaching online (Fredericksen et al., 2000). The researchers conducting the study found that the factors that significantly contributed to faculty satisfaction included student performance, level of student interaction in the course, reason for choosing to teach online, satisfaction with the SUNY Learning Network, a positive perception of the technology, low levels of technical difficulties, and how well the faculty got to know their students.

In a follow-up study of 913 faculty, Shea and colleagues (2005) used a 34-item survey instrument to explore potential barriers to the adoption of online learning. They found that four factors were significantly associated with faculty satisfaction and their corresponding likelihood to adopt or continue online teaching including: levels of interaction in their online courses, technical support, a positive learning experience in developing and teaching their courses, and the discipline area in which they taught. Instructors in the math/science, humanities, and business/professional development disciplines tended to report higher levels of satisfaction with online teaching than instructors in other discipline areas.

Hiltz and colleagues (2007) used structured focus group interviews to explore factors that motivate and/or inhibit faculty teaching online. They found that leading motivators were the flexibility asynchronous online learning enables, more personal interactions with individual students and whole class community building, better course management, the ability to reach more and more diverse students, and the challenges, technical and creative, the online medium affords. Major sources of dissatisfaction were increased work, the limitations of the online medium, the lack of adequate support and supportive policies for teaching online, and the fact that online learning is not good for some students. Focus groups also might be a good way to identify issues that could be then included in a survey given to all faculty.

Although the variability of findings in faculty surveys points to the localness of the faculty satisfaction construct, it does make sense to develop and validate an instrument that could be used to measure perceived faculty satisfaction with online teaching across institutions. Doris Bolliger and Oksana Wasilik (2009) did just that. Their Online Faculty Satisfaction Survey (OFSS) consists of 28 items with which respondents indicate their agreement on a 4-point Likert scale, as well as six demographic and experiential questions. The researchers tested the survey with 102 faculty teaching online in the 2007/2008 school year. They used factor analysis to confirm that three factors affected the satisfaction of the faculty who completed the survey, which they categorized as student related factors, instructor related factors, and institution related factors. Mean scores on these subscales were considerably higher for student-related factors than for either instructor related or institution related factors. This suggests that interactions with students and the way they occur online were of primary importance to the faculty surveyed.

I am writing this in the midst of the COVID-19 pandemic when we are hearing about how teachers were really frustrated with what many are calling "remote learning," because no one had time to plan for carefully crafted online learning before we were told to shelter in place. It is clear that many of the issues identified in the studies we have reviewed are the source of teachers' frustrations with online instruction. Hopefully, if we need to teach remotely again, we will work to resolve some of these issues because faculty satisfaction is a critical part of successful online teaching and learning.

In addition, there are items on common checklists for assuring quality online learning that address issues uncovered in studies such as those we reviewed. However, I think it really makes sense to find a way to periodically check with faculty to assure they are happy teaching online. That might be as simple as cultivating good relations with faculty and having an open-door policy so that they bring issues to you before they become problems. Focus groups and faculty surveys are also good ways to explore faculty satisfaction. No matter how you investigate online faculty satisfaction, however, the really important thing is to follow through on your findings to ensure the strength of this critical quality pillar.

5   Student Satisfaction

Certain measures of the effectiveness of education and training, such as the Kirkpatrick scale (Kurt, 2018), place satisfaction at the lowest, most elemental level of evaluation. However, it is important to note that the most elemental level is also fundamental. Student satisfaction is a vital element in the overall quality of online learning. Indeed, student satisfaction is closely linked with retention: unless students are happy online, they will not stay, and unless students stay, there are no higher levels of learning. Indeed, early research into online learning often used student satisfaction and perceived learning as outcome measures (Hiltz et al., 2000; Swan, 2001; Shea et al., 2002); I believe rightly so.

Student satisfaction is another quality that can only be measured ostensively; only the students themselves know whether they are satisfied. The best way to explore it, therefore, is to ask the students. I think most of us have some sort of course evaluations at our institutions, but these do not often distinguish online courses from traditional face-to-face ones, or cover satisfaction beyond the course or issues that are unique to the online environment. Student surveys and focus groups specifically designed for online learners, as well as focused attention to student feedback might be the best way to ensure quality in student satisfaction.

According to Sener and Humbolt (2003), student satisfaction with online learning can be usefully divided into several areas: student satisfaction with courses, student satisfaction with programs, and student satisfaction with the overall learning experience.

At the most basic level, student satisfaction with individual courses involves determining whether students are generally satisfied with their online courses and their learning in them, or perhaps whether they would take another online course or recommend them to their friends. More in-depth evaluations focus on one or more specific issues related to courses, such as the capabilities of the instructor, course design, and/or the level of interactions with the instructor and other students. For example, an early study I completed (Swan, 2001) explored relationships between course design and student perceptions in 73 SUNY Learning Network courses in the spring 1999 semester. I found that three general factors – clarity of design, interaction with instructors, and active discussion significantly influenced students' satisfaction and perceived learning. Similarly, Shea and colleagues (2002) found that student-faculty and student-student interaction were among the variables most strongly correlated with student satisfaction and reported learning.

I would imagine that interactivity is as important today, as it was two decades ago. What do you think? Do you think that interactions with people – instructors and fellow students – are integral to student satisfaction? Why or why not?

For example, educators concerned with the Community of Inquiry (CoI) framework have linked student satisfaction and perceived learning to the development of social (Richardson & Swan, 2003; Swan & Shih, 2005), teaching (Anderson et al., 2001; Shea et al., 2002, 2005), and cognitive (Garrison & Clevelend-Innes, 2005; Richardson & Ice, 2010; Akyol & Garrison, 2011) presence in online courses. Other factors found to be related to student satisfaction include: clear goals and expectations for learners, multiple representations of course content, frequent opportunities for active learning, frequent and constructive feedback, flexibility and choice in satisfying course objectives, and instructor guidance and support (Swan, 2003).

Student satisfaction with online programs includes basic satisfaction with particular programs of study, as well as specific issues that directly impact student satisfaction with programs, including administrative support, such as registration and placement, and academic services, such as advising and tutoring. Student satisfaction with the overall learning experience may simply involve combining course and program satisfaction, but in the case of online learning it must also include the technology supporting courses and programs and support for it, as well as such things as the availability of courses and the length of semesters. Measures of these latter two satisfaction categories are most commonly found in general checklists such as the Online Learning Consortium's Quality Scorecard (Shelton, 2010; Online Learning Consoritum, 2020), or the University Professional and Continuing Education Association's (2020) Hallmarks of Excellence. The Online Learning Consortium (2020) also has a Quality Scorecard for Online Student Support specifically designed to address such issues as: admissions, financial aid, library services, and services for students with disabilities.

How is student satisfaction addressed at your institution?

6   Cost Effectiveness/Scale

The final pillar of quality in online education is cost effectiveness/scale. In the early days of the Learning Anytime, Anyplace program, this pillar was known simply as cost effectiveness (Picciano, 2013). Clearly, when online programs were just getting started it was very important to make sure they were cost-effective, both for the institution and for the students, lest they were unsustainable. As initial courses and programs gained footholds in their institutions, the importance of scale became clear. Initial courses were hand-crafted by pioneering faculty who did not require a lot of institutional support. To grow these into programs that could match traditional on-ground offerings required finding ways to spread technology, administrative, faculty development, and student support costs across multiple courses and programs; in a word, to scale them. Today, the success of for-profit and large public online programs (such as Southern New England and Arizona State Universities) is dependent on models of scale that make it possible for these institutions to add or cancel tens of sections of a single course in very short amounts of time.

According to Frank Mayadas (2001), cost effectiveness/scale is the mechanism that enables institutions to offer their best educational value to learners while achieving capacity enrollment. The combination of commitment to quality and finite resources require continuous improvement policies that include cost effectiveness measures and practices. The goal is to control costs so that tuition is affordable yet sufficient to meet development and maintenance costs – and to provide a return on investment in startup and infrastructure. General checklists such as the Online Learning Consortium's Quality Scorecard (Shelton, 2010; Online Learning Consoritum, 2020), or the University Professional and Continuing Education Association's (2020) Hallmarks of Excellence provide some items that address continuous improvement.

At the beginning of this chapter, I argued that in many ways online learning in the United States owes its unique character to its beginnings in Sloan-C's Learning Anytime, Anyplace program. In the early 1990s there were some colleges and universities who viewed online learning as a kind of cash cow, seeing it as a way to bring in money by building on the development of large computer assisted instruction systems to deliver individualized instruction to a large number of students at minimal cost (Twigg, 2000). Mayadas' (2001) insistence on quality operationalized as being at least as good as that offered to traditional students across all five quality pillars resulted in a focus on smaller, cohort-based classes and robust interaction among students and instructors that mirrored the inquiry-based model dear to higher education. Thus, the cost-effectiveness quality pillar is seen as one of five pillars that work together to support online learning. On the one hand, access, learning effectiveness, and faculty and student satisfaction cannot be sacrificed to bring in more money. On the other hand, these other quality areas must be cost-effective to be maintained.

One way to explore cost-effectiveness, then, is to compare the costs and benefits of delivery modes by discipline and educational level, faculty salary, workload and ongoing professional development, capital, physical plant and maintenance investment, equipment and communications technology costs, scalability options, and/or various learning processes and outcomes, such as satisfaction levels and retention rates (Bishop, 2003). Rumble (2001) suggests that cost-effectiveness be concerned with comparing inputs (e.g., the costs of course and program development, delivery and administration) with outputs (e.g., student progression and retention, student and faculty satisfaction, access to higher education for traditionally underserved populations). Although many, especially those in state legislatures, assume that online education should be less expensive to deliver, the truth is that it probably is not. Indeed, a recent study (Poulin & Straut, 2017) that surveyed 197 US campus leaders found that, in general, the cost of providing online courses was the same as or more than the cost of providing face-to-face education.

Of course, higher education has long been infamously bad at understanding costs (Rumble, 2001), but the situation is changing for several reasons. First, there has been a public outcry about college costs. Second, the rise of for-profit online institutions has shown that it is possible to develop quite accurate business models and cost-benefit analyses (although many would argue that costs and benefits at traditional institutions include those around such intangibles as the creation of knowledge, community service, and access to higher education for underserved populations). Third, the creation and evolution of MOOCs has hinted at ways higher education can be made available at significantly lower cost (Yuan, 2014). Finally, learning analytics make it much easier to explore the costs and benefits of online learning at both micro and macro levels.

7 The Five Pillars Redux

In my opinion, the five pillars of quality online education identified by Frank Mayadas (2001) – access, learning effectiveness, faculty satisfaction, student satisfaction, and cost-effectiveness – are as relevant today as they were when he first introduced them. I believe anyone involved in the administration of online programs should consider and reconsider them frequently. Major instruments designed as guides for online administrators, such as the OLC *Quality Scorecard for the Administration of Online Programs* (Online Learning Consortium, 2020) and the UPCEA *Hallmarks of Excellence in Online Leadership* (University Professional and Continuing Education Association, 2020), have more categories and many more detailed practical items to which administrators are encouraged to attend. Such checklists are very good and extremely useful, but I believe attention to access, learning effectiveness, faculty satisfaction, student satisfaction and-cost effectiveness is still the foundation on which quality online programs are built.

What do you think?

References

Akyol, Z., & Garrison, D. R. (2011). Understanding cognitive presence in an online and blended Community of Inquiry: Assessing outcomes and processes for deep approaches to learning. *British Journal of Educational Technology, 42*(2), 233–250.

Anderson, T., Rourke, L., Garrison, D. R., & Archer, W. (2001). Assessing teaching presence in a computer conferencing context. *Journal of Asynchronous Learning Networks, 5*(2), 1–17.

Arbaugh, J. B., Cleveland-Innes, M., Diaz, S., Garrison, D. R., Ice, P., Richardson, J. C., Shea, P., & Swan, K. (2008). Developing a community of inquiry instrument: Testing a measure of the Community of Inquiry framework using a multi-institutional sample. *The Internet and Higher Education, 11*(3–4), 133–136.

Bishop, T. (2003). Linking cost-effectiveness with institutional goals: Best practices in online education. In J. Bourne & J. C. Moore (Eds.), *Elements of quality online education, practice and direction* (pp. 75–86). Sloan Center for Online Education.

Bollinger, D. U., & Wasilik, O. (2009). Factors influencing faculty satisfaction with online teaching and learning in higher education. *Distance Education, 30*(1), 103–116.

Bransford, J. D., Brown, A. L., & Cocking, R. R. (2000). *How people learn: Brain, mind, experience, and school.* National Academy Press.

California State University, Chico. (2009). *Rubric for online instruction.* https://www.csuchico.edu/eoi/_assets/documents/rubric.pdf

De Leng, B. A., Dolmans, D. H. J. M., Jöbsis, B., Muijtjens, A. M. M., & van der Vleuten, C. P. M. (2009). Exploration of an e-learning model to foster critical thinking on basic science concepts during work placements. *Computers & Education, 53*(1), 1–13.

Fredericksen, E., Pickett, A., Shea, P., Pelz, W., & Swan, K. (2000). Factors influencing faculty satisfaction with asynchronous teaching and learning in the SUNY learning network. satisfaction with asynchronous teaching and learning in the SUNY learning network. *Journal of Asynchronous Learning Networks, 4*(3), 245–278.

Garrison, D. R., Anderson, T., & Archer, W. (2000). Critical inquiry in a text-based environment: Computer conferencing in higher education. *The Internet and Higher Education, 2,* 87–105.

Garrison, D. R., Anderson, T., & Archer, W. (2001). Critical thinking, cognitive presence, and computer conferencing in distance education. *The American Journal of Distance Education, 15*(1).

Garrison, D. R., & Cleveland-Innes, M. (2005). Facilitating cognitive presence in online learning: Interaction is not enough. *American Journal of Distance Education, 19*(3), 133–148.

Garrison, D. R., Cleveland-Innes, M., & Fung, T. (2010). Exploring causal relationships among cognitive, social and teaching presence: Student perceptions of the community of inquiry framework. *The Internet and Higher Education, 13*(1–2), 31–36.

Hillman, D. C., Willis, D. J., & Gunawardena, C. N. (1994). Learrner-interface interaction in distance education: An extension of contemporary models and strategies for practioners. *The American Journal of Distance Education, 8*(2), 30–42.

Hiltz, S. R., Coppola, N., Rotter, N., Turoff, M., & Benbunan-Fich, R. (2000). Measuring the importance of collaborative learning for the effectiveness of ALN: A multi-measure, multi-method approach. In J. Bourne (Ed.), *Online education: Learning effectiveness and faculty satisfaction* (Vol. 1, pp. 101–120). Sloan-C.

Hiltz, S. R., Kim, E., & Shea, P. (2007, February). *Faculty motivators and de-motivators for teaching online: Results of focus group interviews at one university.* Paper presented at the 40th Annual Hawaii International Conference on System Sciences (HICSS'07).

Jaggars, S. S., Edgecombe, N., & Stacey, G. W. (2013, April). *What we know about online course outcomes.* Community College Research Center, Teachers College, Columbia University.

James, S., Swan, K., & Daston, C. (2016). Retention, progression, and the taking of online courses. *Online Learning Journal, 20*(2), 75–96.

Johnson, H., Cuellar Mejia, M., & Cook, K. (2015). *Successful online courses in California's community colleges.* Public Policy Institute of California.

Kozan, K., & Richardson, J. C. (2014). Interrelationships between and among social, teaching and cognitive presence. *Internet and Higher Education, 21*, 68–73.

Kozma, R. B. (1991). Learning with media. *Review of Educational Research, 61*, 179–211.

Kucuk, S., & Richardson, J. C. (2019). A structural equation model of predictors of online learners' engagement and satisfaction. *Online Learning, 23*(2), 196–216.

Kurt, S. (2018). *Kirkpatrick model: Four levels of learning evaluation.* https://educationaltechnology.net/kirkpatrick-model-four-levels-learning-evaluation/

Lagrow, M. (2017). The section 508 refresh and what it means for higher education. *Educause Review.* https://er.educause.edu/articles/2017/12/the-section-508 refresh-and-what-it-means-for-higher-education

Mayadas, F. (2001). Testimony to the Kerrey Commission on web-based education. *Journal of Asynchronous Learning Networks, 5*(1), 134–138.

Moore, J. C. (2005). *The Sloan consortium quality framework and the five pillars.* SCOLE.

Moore, M. G. (1989). Three types of interaction. *American Journal of Distance Education, 3*(2), 1–6.

Online Learning Consoritum. (2019). *Our quality framework.* https://onlinelearningconsortium.org/learn/quality-framework-narrative-5-pillars/

Online Learning Consortium. (2020). *OLC quality scorecard suite.* https://onlinelearningconsortium.org/consult/olc-quality-scorecard-suite/

Picciano, A. G. (2013). *Pioneering higher education's digital future: An evaluation of the Sloan Foundation's anytime, anywhere learning program (1991–2012).* Graduate Center, City University of New York.

Poulin, R., & Straut, T. T. (2017). *Distance education price and cost report.* WICHE Cooperative for Educational Technologies (WCET).

Richardson, J. C., & Ice, P. (2010). Investigating students' level of critical thinking across instructional strategies in online discussion. *The Internet and Higher Education, 13*(1–2), 52–59.

Richardson, J. C., & Swan, K. (2003). Examining social presence in online courses in relation to students' perceived learning and satisfaction. *Journal of Asynchronous Learning Networks, 7*(1), 68–88.

Rovai, A. P. (2002). A preliminary look at structural differences in sense of classroom community between higher education traditional and ALN courses. *Journal of Asynchronous Learning Networks, 6*(1), 41–56.

Rumble, G. (2001). The costs and costing of networked learning. *Journal of Asynchronous Learning Networks, 5*(2), 75–96.

Salomon, G. (1981). *The interaction of media, cognition and learning.* Jossey-Bass.

Sener, J., & Humbert, J. (2003). Student satisfaction with online learning: An expanding universe. In J. Bourne & J. C. Moore (Eds.), *Elements of quality online education, practice and direction* (pp. 245–259). Sloan Center for Online Education.

Shattuck, K., Zimmerman, W., & Adair, D. (2014). Continuous improvement of the QM Rubric and review processes: Scholarship of integration and application. *Internet Learning, 3*(1), 25–34.

Shea, P. (2006). A study of students' sense of learning community in online environments. *Journal of Asynchronous Learning Networks, 10*(1), 35–44.

Shea, P., & Bidjerano, T. (2009). Community of inquiry as a theoretical framework to foster "epistemic engagement" and "cognitive presence" in online education. *Computers & Education, 52*(3), 543–553.

Shea, P., & Bidjerano, T. (2018). Online course enrollment in community college and degree completion: The tipping point. *International Review of Research in Open and Distributed Learning, 19*(2) 283–293.

Shea, P., Li, C., Swan, K., & Pickett, A. (2005). Developing learning community in online asynchronous college courses: The role of teaching presence. *Journal of Asynchronous Learning Networks, 9*(4).

Shea, P., Pickett, A., & Li, C. (2005). Increasing access to higher education: A study of the diffusion of online teaching among 913 college faculty. *International Review of Research in Open and Distance Learning, 6*(2). http://www.irrodl.org/index.php/irrodl/article/view/238

Shea, P. J., Pickett, A. M., & Pelz, W. E. (2003). A follow-up investigation of "teaching presence" in the SUNY learning network. *Journal of Asynchronous Learning Networks, 7*(2), 61–80.

Shea, P., Swan, K., Fredericksen, E., & Pickett, A. (2002). Student satisfaction and reported learning in the SUNY learning network: Interaction and beyond. In J. Bourne & J. Moore (Eds.), *Elements of quality online education* (pp. 145–156). Sloan-C.

Shelton, K. (2010). A quality scorecard for the administration of online education programs: A Delphi study. *Journal of Asynchronous Learning Networks, 14*(4), 36–62.

Swan, K. (2001). Virtual interactivity: Design factors affecting student satisfaction and perceived learning in asynchronous online courses. *Distance Education, 22*(2), 306–331.

Swan, K. (2003). Learning effectiveness: what the research tells us. In J. Bourne & J. C. Moore (Eds.), *Elements of quality online education, practice and direction* (pp. 13–45). Sloan Center for Online Education.

Swan, K., Day, S. L., Bogle, L. R., & Matthews, D. B. (2014). A collaborative, design-based approach to improving an online program. *Internet and Higher Education, 21,* 74–81.

Swan, K., Garrison, D. R., & Richardson, J. C. (2009). A constructivist approach to online learning: The Community of Inquiry framework. In C. R. Payne (Ed.), *Information technology and constructivism in higher education: Progressive learning frameworks* (pp. 43–57). IGI Global.

Swan, K., & James, S. (2017). Online learning gets a passing grade: How online course taking impacts retention for university students. In S. Whalen (Ed.), *Proceedings of the 13th National Symposium on student retention* (pp. 246–256). The University of Oklahoma.

Swan, K., & Shih, L.-F. (2005). On the nature and development of social presence in online course discussions. *Journal of Asynchronous Learning Networks, 9*(3), 115–136.

Twigg, C. (2000). *Innovations in online learning: Moving beyond no significant difference.* The Pew Learning and Technology Program, Rennselaer Polytechnic Institute.

University Professional and Continuing Education Association. (2020). *UPCEA hallmarks of excellence in online leadership.* https://upcea.edu/resources/hallmarks-online/

Vaughan, N., & Garrison, D. R. (2006). How blended learning can support a faculty development community of inquiry. *Journal of Asynchronous Learning Networks, 10*(4), 159–132.

Yuan, L., Powell, S., & Olivier, B. (2014). *Beyond MOOCs: Sustainable online learning in institutions.* Centre for Educational Technology, Interoperability and Standards University of Bolton.

CHAPTER 11

Marketing and Recruitment

Adam Schultz and Rachel Mork

Abstract

At the conclusion of this chapter, you will know how to:
– Get the support and funding you need to effectively market your program
– Identify your prospective student audience
– Establish your brand and archetype
– Engage with your target audience
– Plan and execute changes to your website and marketing strategy
– Test, measure, refine, and improve your marketing strategy to get results

Keywords

higher education marketing – college program marketing – how to market college programs – university program marketing – increase student enrollment – higher education recruitment – college program recruitment – university program recruitment

1 What Got You Here Isn't Going to Get You There

Unless your career path included business school, we're willing to bet the knowledge that got you to this position as Administrator for distance learning was not because of your expertise in marketing, IT, or creative work. Now, you might be expected to plan, direct, and/or execute marketing initiatives on a large scale, often with a limited budget. You may also have been tasked with student recruitment, yet you have no formal training in traditional marketing, internet marketing, or websites.

In order to achieve your goal – to effectively recruit students to your online program – you have to know how to operate and manage an integrated marketing campaign. You may think marketing challenges are too complicated for you to do well or you may think that launching a website and some marketing campaigns is easy. The answer lies somewhere in the middle. No, you do not have to get a degree in marketing to master this. You need specific knowledge and adequate resources to do this well. The key question is: What is the best way to get your program in front of your target students in an increasingly online world? You need your website to act as a sales funnel to engage prospective students in a way that will result in applications.

To make this practical, we have provided examples and samples. We encourage you to take the examples provided in this chapter to your team so they can use them as a springboard for solutions that work for your particular program, department, or institution. Practical examples are useful to help the people working with you know what "good enough" looks like.

Begin by building your team. The vast majority of deans, department heads, and program coordinators tasked with student recruitment need a team if they are to be successful. A successful team consists of a chairperson, a champion, and resource-specific team members. Everyone on the team needs to be informed of and unified in seeking accomplishments of the specific goals that will deliver the desired results. In this section, you will learn what you need to do to recruit, inspire, and operate a successful team.

1.1   *Chairperson*

Your chairperson is a decision-maker with access to resources. In many cases, this is who you are. In other cases, this is who you tap when you need money, resources, other team members, or approvals from the higher ups or the folks holding the purse-strings. Your chairperson may be a development officer, department head, or a provost, but whatever the title, your chairperson is the person who makes the final call when you need approvals or funding.

To figure out who your chairperson/s is/are, ask yourself: Who has the authority to approve my plans? In most cases, you will have a few people in power from which to choose. Of most importance is the character trait of good judgement. You want to work with a decision-maker that is an open-minded, good listener who prides themselves on making fact-based, data-driven decisions and allows for exploration as you propose and try new marketing strategies that will require trial and error. If possible, avoid any rigid, old school or stuck-in-the-past decisionmakers. You need an ally with access to resources who can make final calls.

1.2   *Champion*

Your champion has political skills. They know how to network; they are known for getting things done. They connect you with resources, partnerships, and the people who can accomplish your goals. In a nutshell, your champion is resourceful and responsive. They believe in your vision.

What connections do you need? You probably need access to a web developer who can build or improve your website. You need a Pay Per Click (PPC) marketing expert and the funding to support an online marketing campaign.

You need someone who will find funding for your project and give you the authority required to test marketing strategies. Your champion is a resourceful person who believes in your mission. They may never actually work for you, but they will get you people, allowances, and resources you need.

1.3   Resource-Specific Implementation Team Members

Next you need to ask yourself the following questions: Who else can join me in this effort? Who can do what? You may have to do several of these tasks your-selves, but you can probably find other people who will share the workload with you.

For starters, you need to know who manages the web presence you use to market your program. Do you have access to web development help? What about online marketing assistance? Do you have a social media channel, and if so, who is maintaining it? What about content writers for your website, social media, and advertising?

You can't do it all, and you probably only have the internal resources avail-able for a fraction of their time. You may need to look to the private market or interns who will serve your program, or you may need to partner with another department or program to share resources.

Some of the team members you will want to identify include people who have experience with one or more of the following:
– IT and supportive structure
– Website design and development
– Marketing copywriting
– Online advertising
– Social media
– Outreach and community engagement
– Partnership development
– Print, direct mail and traditional media outreach

Which of these roles can you fulfill? What do you want to invest your time doing? Even if you can do it all, you probably don't have *time* to do it all. Reach out to your internal service groups; you may discover you have more support than you realize. You just need to recruit them to your team.

2   Building Your Team

Once you've identified who your potential team members are, engage with them. Every university is structured differently, and the climate of your partic-ular institution or the size of your area of influence may dictate the depth and breadth of your team. As you initiate with each team member, you'll need to keep in mind that each of these people has needs and agendas of their own. Whenever possible, align yourself with their missions. Help them see how helping you will help the university at large. Remind them that the success of a handful of programs can elevate an entire university's reputation, and a successful marketing strategy, once tested and proven, can be applied to other segments of the institution.

2.1   *Team Goals*

It is important to evaluate how we think about and define goals. You need to set goals, but just as importantly, you need to be able to measure how success- ful or unsuccessful you have been in meeting goals. To this end, we suggest you use the SMART goal system. Smart goals are goals that are specific, measurable, actionable, reasonable, and timely. When we talk about goals in this chap- ter, we are encouraging you to apply those metrics to your goals. An cxample SMART goal is: We need to recruit x number of people that meet [this criteria] within [this timeframe].[1]

> *Your Turn*:
> – Which team members do you currently have? Which team members do you need to recruit?
> – What SMART goals can you identify right now? Test them against the five SMART metrics.

3   Understanding Prospective Students

Marketing strategies are vastly more effective when you know who your tar- get audience is and the strategy is tailored to that audience. Many universities assume all prospective students are alike; this assumption could not be more wrong. Take a look at your actual student body. You need to base your market- ing strategies on the needs and actions of real people. It's important to figure out the answers to the following questions:
– What drives these people?
– What do they want?
– What would incentivize them to enroll in my program?
– What obstacles are in their way?

To get the answers to these questions, you need to ask real questions of real people, and then use those answers to build your personae. Personae are abstract representations of real people. Before I get into the process you need to follow when building your personae, take a look at a few examples from a user target personae we crafted for a community college (see Figure 11.1).

Susie Beasely, High School Senior, Associate's Degree Program Applicant

Summary: Susie is a high school senior with below-average grades. She's never really taken school that seriously and now is starting to realize she should have. She has not applied to any four-year colleges, and she suspects that she wouldn't be accepted even if she did apply. She works at a pizza joint and is tempted to just keep working her minimum wage job, but her parents have made it clear that she won't be able to support herself if she doesn't choose a trade.

How she becomes a student: Susie needs help finding a clear path to a career she can believe in. She's unsure if it's worth it to actually spend money on an education, and the community college needs to convince her that she can get a useful certificate or degree in a short amount of time that will translate to a career she will enjoy.

What matters to Susie? Susie cares about Path, Program, Price, and Potential.

Dionne Simpson, Has a Degree but Needs Continuing Education

Summary: Dionne is a young single mother working in the healthcare industry. She loves her job, but her place of employment requires continuing education classes to keep her license current. She has limited time and resources. She doesn't own a car, so she prefers online coursework that empowers her to manage the many demands upon her.

How she becomes a student: To catch Dionne's eye, the community college needs to showcase convenience, affordability, and safety.

What matters to Dionne? Dionne cares about Programs, Price, and overcoming Problems such as convenience, timing, safety, and transportation.

FIGURE 11.1   Example personae

Now compare Susie Beasely and Dionne Simpson to a sample from a user-target personae below that we created for a prestigious business college (see Figure 11.2).

Erin Rosberg, MBA Applicant

Summary: Erin is a rising associate at Coca Cola with a dream of becoming a partner at a top consulting firm or starting her own product firm. 710 on the GMAT, 2 promotions in 5 years, already making over $75k annually and is looking to get her "card stamped" at a premier MBA program in order to move up the ranks and make over $100k after graduation.

Demographic Snapshot: 28, married, no children, lives in an apartment complex in "Buckhead", uptown Atlanta.

Education: Graduated Cum Laude from Dartmouth with a 3.7 GPA majoring in organic chemistry.

Employment: Manager at Coca Cola in Atlanta, Georgia.

Application Quality: Erin's academic background and work performance to date is exceptional in almost every way.

Desired Transition: To cement her rising star status with acceptance and training from a top 10 full-time MBA program and be "guaranteed" future success.

Likely Alternatives:
- UVA
- Emory
- University of Chicago

Priorities in Rank Order:
- Prestige
- Placement
- Programs

How She Becomes a Student:
While Erin is partially married to "making the top 10", this ranking is a proxy for the following:
1. Acknowledgement of her excellence.
2. A promise that she will receive a special development experience.
3. The knowledge that she will have access to premium job placement.

FIGURE 11.2   Example personae for a prestigious business college

When creating your personae, follow this process and ask the following questions:
- What students typically enroll in each program?
- What do those students want and why?
- What attracts those students? What presents as an obstacle to enrollment?
- What makes a bad student? Who have you been attracting that you'd rather not? Sometimes knowing what you don't want will help you determine what kind of student you do want.

– Who are you trying to reach that you don't normally attract? Is it reasonable to try a different tactic, or are you wasting marketing dollars if you market to that sort of student?

If you have the funding or time to interview actual students, do it. You can interview students in calls, questionnaires, or focus groups. Have a base set of questions, but be sure to follow up and dig deep when you get surprising answers.

3.1 *Using the Information Gathered Through the Personae Development*

Use the information you gathered through interviews, questionnaires, and focus groups to analyze the following assumptions about alumni, students, employers, and both undergraduate and graduate applicants:

1. What characterizes and differentiates the various types of people in each market? Who are they? What problems are they trying to solve? How can we help them?
2. For alternate solutions to their problems how do those competitor entities speak to the audience? What brands, messaging, and benefits/tradeoffs accompany these choices?
3. How does the direct competition succeed and fail in targeting the same groups of people?

While writing the personae, you will discover trends you should pay attention to. For example, does the typical student in one of your primary personae groups work full time and therefore need evening, online, or asynchronous classes?

One of the most profound revelations we have uncovered through the personae process is related to the issues that prevent students from enrolling – especially issues that have nothing to do with competition. These non-competitive barriers turned out to be much more powerful than we ever imagined. Here's one example that completely transformed a marketing campaign for a state university we've worked with for almost a decade.

One of the underperforming programs we were tasked to promote is particularly appealing to people who have been in the military and are looking to transition to civilian careers. The program's website did not make it clear that students could transfer military experience into college credit. Many of these people assumed that college was not an option for them at all because they could not afford four years of college or they felt they did not qualify for college off their high school record. Once we made it clear on the website that ex-military personnel could get college credit for their service and that this both qualified them for admission and cut their costs, enrollments to the program doubled in the next six months.

You'll use the information you gather from your personae as the foundation for your marketing strategy. At a minimum, you want a personae work-up of your current student, your ideal student, and a student that isn't a good fit. Sometimes, the write up of the "not a good fit" personae is the most instructive in identifying opportunities for transformation.

Your Turn (you'll want to uncover the following):
- What is your target student market? Don't aim to recruit students outside your school's realistic reach. In other words, if you are the dean of a prestigious law school you need to market a completely different set of factors than you will if you are the director of a community college.
- What factors have historically resulted in student enrollment and success? These factors should be front and center in your marketing strategy.
- What factors have historically acted as barriers to enrollment? These factors should be addressed and countered.
- What advantages do you have over the competition? How can you spotlight these advantages?

You'll want to revisit these discoveries as you create, deploy, test and redeploy marketing strategies. If something isn't working with your campaign, it probably comes back to your assumptions made here. After your first year of testing marketing strategies and comparing your actual students to your personae, you will probably need to make adjustments. If you do a good job of targeting these key personae, you should be successful. Your personae is the starting point for everything that follows, so you want to make this as accurate as possible.

4   A Clear & Actionable Strategy

Now that you know who your target personae is, you can set goals as part of a clear and actionable marketing strategy. Go to our adaptation of 20 Brand Archetypes[2] developed by Forty Agency (now Crowd Favorite), to determine who you are in relation to your target personae.

4.1   *Developing Your Strategy*
After you determine your brand archetype, you need to build a set of assumptions (which you will test through your marketing plan) that fills in the following blanks:

> In a world of _____, we are a _____ that helps
> _____ become _____.

To find the descriptors that belong in those blank spots, you will need to discover the following about your target personae:

- What is the world they believe they exist in?
- Who do they see themselves as?
- Who do they want to become?
- How are we to facilitate that transformation?

Then ask yourself:

- Who is our competition, both direct and indirect?
- Who are you, and who are you not?
- Who do you want to be seen as? How do you play a role in their story?

Use these questions to figure out the relationship between you, your audience, and the marketplace in general. It's important to always see yourself in your audience's eyes. You need to focus on how the prospective student sees you, and then, how you want to be seen. Brands can be authentic to who you are now, or aspirational to who you want to become. If you go aspirational, be ready to make the organizational changes necessary to fulfill that promise.

Then figure out which archetype you are. Are you a hero? A nurturer? A servant? A scholar? Not who you want to be, but who you are to your student population. Use this to cultivate a brand that your student population needs.

Here's an example to help you see what this looks like. We worked with a small religious private college. A higher-than-average percentage of their student population consisted of young adults who had been homeschooled, and the college was known for producing graduates who went on to work in servant-oriented professions such as the ministry or teaching. Many of the families that chose to send their freshman to this college were looking for a safe, personal experience more akin to a Christian summer camp than a large state university or an ivy league experience.

For this audience, it was more important for us to be a nurturer than a scholar or an explorer. Their student population needed to know that the school would hold their hand every step of the way to help them find success in a purpose-driven career. We emphasized this role on every page by showcasing their mentorship programs, the high level of professor-to-student engagement and the close-knit community the college was known for. We used language that was personal, comforting, and assuring (see Figure 11.3).

Your brand story impacts your copy, the images you use, how you tell your story, your messaging and ultimately, your advertising. Tapping into your

FIGURE 11.3   Example web copy for the nurturer archetype

archetype facilitates the emotional connection and excites students so they want to enroll in your program. If you find your messaging isn't connecting, you can re-examine it in the light of what your competitors have decided to do as they represent themselves to the same audience. Look to your competitors to see how they show themselves to be an explorer, a scholar, etc. Are they connecting with your prospective students better than you are? Then maybe you're missing something in messaging. Take a look at the images you've been using on your site and in social media. Do they represent your student population? What about the words you've used? Are you inspiring them to become who they want to be? Or do you need to change your messaging?

4.2   *Your Engagement Strategy*

After you've decided what you want to say and how you want to say it, you need to figure out how you can get in front of your prospective audience. Common engagement platforms are:

– Websites
– Online communities
– Professional organizations
– Schools
– Search engine results
– Digital advertising
– Social media posts

- Lists (email addresses, physical addresses)
- Print and traditional marketing ads
- Organizations
- Magazines and online zines

Run an inventory of all the ways you could get in front of these people, asking the following:
- Where are they looking?
- Which keywords would you like your website included for in search engine results?
- What story will you tell?
- What facts and data matter to them?
- How will you get that message to them and engage them?

Now ask yourself: Which of the following actions will they most likely be interested in taking? Do they want to:
- Visit campus?
- Tour on campus?
- Download courses?
- Review curriculum and courses?
- Learn about financial aid?
- Request information?
- Ask a question?
- Fill out a contact form?
- Explore financial aid options?
- Download information?
- Start the application process?

Your goal is to build a human relationship that convinces your audience to take the next step. How are you going to get them in the door, and once you do, what are you going to ask them to do? Write out your action goals and ask yourself: How and why are they going to do each step?

Your Turn:
- What are your goals?
- How will you measure success for each goal?

Apply the SMART goal metrics to those goals. Your evaluation doesn't need to be fancy, but it needs to be documented so you will definitely know if your efforts worked or did not work.

5   Your Website as the Keystone

Your website is the most powerful tool you have for reaching your target audience. Whenever possible, everything should come through your website. Why? Because your website has tremendously valuable measurement capabilities. Through Google Analytics, you can track almost anything a person does on your site, giving you exceptional insight into what your target audience wants and how to get them to apply to your program.

To get started, find out how much control you have over your website. Are you authorized to add content? Change images? Add features? Access and improve Google Analytics reporting about website traffic? The more you can control your website, the more you can control content, your story, your calls to action, your answers to questions, and your analytics.

Your program pages have to provide answers to essential questions so prospective students feel comfortable applying. Every program microsite, program pages section, or program page needs to be deep enough to sell enrollment in that program. It is challenging to make a single page provide all the information you need.

We've had the most success with program microsites. A microsite is a small website focused on delivering information about a program or set of related programs. Microsites are valuable because you can flesh out the answers to prospective students' questions. You can add and control content and test which pages are being successful and which are not garnering attention. The microsite below promotes several related programs (see Figure 11.4).

This program's microsite content clearly ties the programs to specific careers (see Figure 11.5).

The existence of career information on your program pages accomplishes four goals.

1.   It creates compelling justification for enrollment in your program. The correlation between your program and preparation for career advancement is clear.

2.   It gets prospective students to your page because your site shows up in searches for careers-related keywords. A student searching "how to become a GIS data analyst" may find your geospatial information and technology program.

3.   It helps the prospective student feel comfortable with your program. The longer the student spends on your website reading about your program and career options, the more likely they are to feel like your program is the right fit. You become the familiar option. The program that provided helpful information. You become the obvious best choice.

FIGURE 11.4   Microsite program overview page

FIGURE 11.5   Program microsite career content

4. It gives you the keywords on the page that you need in order to run effective Pay Per Click (PPC) ad campaigns. Google considers your ads to be relevant if the page content matches the keywords in your digital ads, and this is your chance to sync those.

We also include Apply pages. On a "How to Apply" page, students can get the answers they need, and applying is simple. You may think your application process is simple, but most of the time it isn't. Make sure the steps to applying are clearly delineated.

5.1 Another Excellent Option: A Program Section on Your Main Website

If you don't have the funding to create microsites to promote your programs, program sections (a collection of related pages) on a larger site is an excellent option.

As you can see, each program on this university website has a subsection consisting of several pages nested in one area, in this case, Master's Degrees. We split access to the most important information into two navigations: the main navigation and the sidebar (see Figure 11.6).

FIGURE 11.6   Example program section on a centralized website

5.2   *Main Navigation and Essential Pages*

Each tab in the main navigation opens to its own page while keeping the user in that subsection of the website. We have found that the following pages deliver the material prospective students need to engage and enroll:

– Program Overview (Program description, eligibility, cost)
– Careers
– Courses
– Faculty
– Tuition/Cost
– FAQS
– About Us
– How to Apply
– Blog or News

If you click on About Us, for example, you will learn about the program without leaving the other essential information. In addition to Apply and About Us pages, a good FAQS section is invaluable for answering questions, making students feel secure and adding valuable keywords to the page, which in turn improves your Search Engine Optimization (SEO) real estate.

5.3   *Bare Minimum: A Deep Page for Each Program*

If you absolutely have only one page per program to work with, you can still make improvements that will prove effective. It's less than ideal, but with creativity you can get the information onto the page. Look into options like accordioning the content, as showcased on this page. When this page first loads, much of the page content is hidden (see Figure 11.7).

When you click on an accordion menu link, the content from that section expands. In this case, the link clicked is Online Undergraduate Certificate in Horticultural Science (see Figure 11.8).

This page has an accordion nested inside the accordion. Each of the answers to these questions remains hidden until clicked (see Figure 11.9).

Check with your IT team or hire an outside developer to help you figure out how to make the information available in a clear, actionable way that is aesthetically pleasing.

5.4   *The Essentials: What Every Program Microsite, Section, or Page Needs*

How much information do you need to provide for each program? How deep is deep enough? This is what we've found to be essential. Each program page, set of pages or microsite needs to, at the very least, provide answers to the following questions:

FIGURE 11.7   Example web page with content utilizing accordion structure

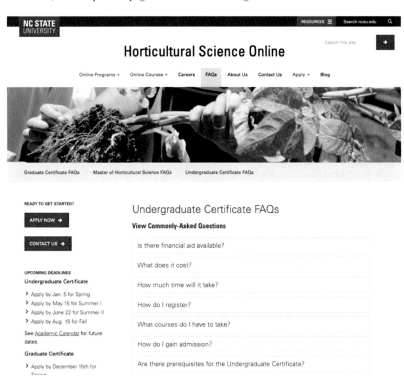

FIGURE 11.8   Example web page with accordion partially opened

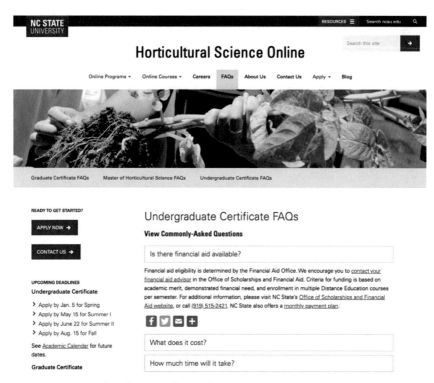

FIGURE 11.9   Example web page with accordion open

- What material, knowledge, and credentials does the program deliver? What degree, certification, or licensure will I have when I have completed the program?
- Am I eligible? What are the eligibility requirements?
- How much does the program cost, and what financial aid is available?
- What is the time and schedule commitment required to complete this program?
- What careers are supported by this program? If I complete this program, what careers will I be qualified to pursue?
- What does the curriculum look like? What courses are required and offered?
- Who is teaching the courses? Who is the program coordinator? What is their expertise?
- How do I apply?
- How can I request more information or contact the Program Coordinator?

The answers to these questions should be easily accessible within a click or two and without leaving the program page section of the site.

5.4.1 An Engaging Sidebar

The sidebar is a perfect spot to place your main Calls to Action (CTAs). A picture and contact information builds an electronic relationship, which is the beginning of a real relationship. Remember: choosing a program often boils down to: "Do I feel connected? Will I receive personal attention?"

5.4.2 More about Content

As you design your program microsite, section of a larger site, or page, you will want to re-evaluate your content with an eye on the factors you uncovered during the personae process. Your brand and archetype should dictate your headlines, CTAs, images, video, and tone and voice. Adjust your messaging and images to reflect your brand story archetype and color your language, images, and CTAs with your brand story. The following are examples:

Nurturer
– "We're here for you every step of the way! Apply now!"
– Pictures of professors and students working together hand-in-hand.

Achiever
– "Take your life to the next level!"
– Images of someone giving an exceptional presentation or getting a high five.

Servant
– "Make a difference with a degree in X!"
– Photos of students helping others with their craft

Once you've revised your content, you'll want to go in and search engine optimize (SEO) it in a way that preserves the voice and story but ensures that the program name is in the first paragraph of the main page (at the bare minimum, in the first paragraph), each page has a unique and highly searchable keyword that ties into any PPC ads you may be running, all images have keyword-rich alt text, and the page meta descriptions are keyword-rich and compelling.

5.4.3 Common Challenges

It's not unusual for program coordinators to approach me saying they are facing significant limitations. Perhaps the only online presence your program has is a single page on a larger site, or perhaps they do not have access to the analytics metrics about site traffic on a site they do not own. The best solution to this problem is to devote some of your budget to the creation of a microsite that you own and on which you can manage the analytics.

If you are not allowed to create a microsite, then we encourage you to push back hard for influence on the content on the site and access to analytics so you can see what's happening. If you can't control your site content and don't have access to analytics, you're flying blind. Insist upon control of these two factors. At the very least, maintain a spreadsheet that tracks your engagements and results.

Note: You may need to win over a new champion who can influence a chair-person so you get what you need. Don't be afraid to be the squeaky wheel. Play the politics to get what you need to know what your successes are so that you can repeat them.

One labor-intensive but worthy workaround is to run marketing to the Program page. When people do contact you, ask how they found you; keep a log of which outreach, ad, or marketing effort resulted in the contact. Then, at the bare minimum, you have an idea of what is working and what is not.

5.4.4 Analytics: Measure So You Can Manage

Whether you have microsites, program sections, or program pages, you need to use analytics to measure impacts. This means you need to make sure Google Analytics has been set up on your site, and that you can gain access to your analytics dashboard. Talk to someone who knows how to set conversion goals and interpret your analytics. There are other options for analytics, but at Verified Studios, we use Google Analytics because it is robust, flexible, and free.

5.4.5 A Starting Point

On a baseline level, you need to use Google Analytics to measure how many visitors you have to each program (unique and repeat visitors), and which pages visitors spend the most time on and visit the most often. In addition, you need to know how many people perform the following actions:
- Click on your Apply button
- Fill out your Contact form
- Request information or otherwise take action that indicates interest (downloads a PDF)
- Visit the Cost or Financial Aid page
- Visit the How to Apply page

Google Analytics reports come in many shapes and sizes (see Figure 11.10).

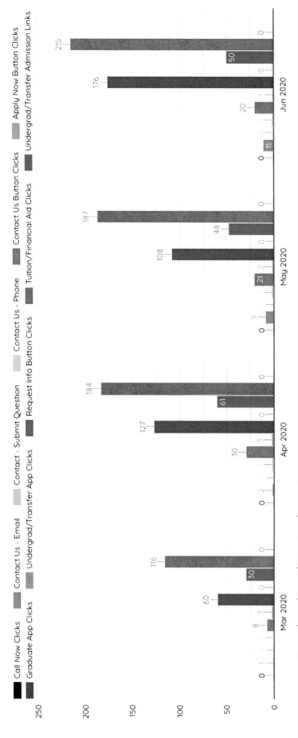

FIGURE 11.10 Example goal completion trends report

6 Digital Relationship Management

It's important to think about the digital relationship you have begun with
the prospective student as a vital part of your marketing strategy. This is your
chance to pique their interest and invite them to engage with you or take next
steps. You will probably never meet this student in person even if they enroll
in your program, but you can influence their likelihood of applying from the
get-go if you understand how digital relationships work.

6.1 *Email*

One of the most powerful digital relationship tools you have access to is email.
You can leverage this tool through one of three ways: send out cold emails to
lists of email addresses you can purchase, set up a responsive email campaign
that responds to form fills (contact us and request information buttons on your
site), or email newsletters to those who sign up to receive your publication.

6.1.1 Cold Email Campaigns

If you purchase a list of email addresses, you can send cold emails out to what
you hope to be your target audience. For low cost, you can purchase email tools
you can plug into your gmail and that lets you send out 20 emails at a time
and will let you track how many people open your email, click on the links, or
respond to you. This is similar to cold call sales.

6.1.2 Responsive Email Campaigns

When a prospective student finally reaches out through filling out a *contact
us* or *request information* form, you need to be ready. Any initiative taken by a
prospective student is incredibly valuable, and many programs leave this up to
whoever is set up to receive the contact forms. This person is often a very busy
professor or an administrator who is not emotionally invested in replying to
the lead. If you don't have staff available to respond to the inquiry with a phone

call, you will want to assign someone to respond with emails. In advance, you will want to write out email templates for each appropriate response so the person responding can quickly and easily provide answers and personal service. One of the most effective ways to turn warm leads into applications is to set up a Customer Relationship Management (CRM) email campaign using an autoresponder. An effective CRM email campaign is set up to send an automatic response about 30 minutes after any form fills come in so the prospective student gets immediate personal attention.

Emails in such a campaign should be written in a casual, personal, and friendly tone, signed by the Program Coordinator, sent from the Program Coordinator's email address, and tailored to the type of request made. For example, if the student clicked on your "Request Info" button, you should have an email set up that responds, welcomes the prospective student, shares basic information about the program, invites the student to ask more questions, and says that the professor will get back to them with more details soon. That professor should then be notified and added to the email thread so the professor can respond with more details, as if they just didn't have time at the very moment the first email came in.

These emails are very effective tools to help get you to take the next step. Ask yourself: if they emailed you in week one, what will you send them in week two? Anticipate the needs of prospective students and tailor the emails to those needs. From our experience, they want to hear about program details (example: this program is tailored to working professionals and therefore is flexible), financial aid options (and links to the financial aid office), alumni stories of how the program resulted in career opportunities, and deadline reminders. Test your email campaign's effectiveness by tracking email opens and clicks and tracking applications initiated through the email campaign.[3]

6.2   *Newsletters*

If you feel you have truly interesting, helpful, or exciting news to share on a regular basis, a newsletter is a great way to stay in touch with interested students. Just make sure the information is truly of value, and mail it consistently. Once a month is a pretty good interval; you don't want to burn out a prospect. Don't start a newsletter if you aren't prepared to keep up with it. Put your efforts into a short email drip campaign instead.

Some newsletter topics to consider are financial aid options, alumni success stories that spotlight people who match your personae, research opportunities, faculty accomplishments that might entice a prospective student to want to study with that professor, student accomplishments, helpful tips for applying, and upcoming events.

6.3   *Zoom Calls or Webinars*

Another way to connect is by providing online sessions through which prospective students can meet faculty and ask questions. Zoom calls and webinars make it possible for students to feel connected and part of the team before they've even applied, and that emotional connection is what you're trying to build. Your possible topics can be the same as the ones listed for newsletters.

Your Turn:
- Your goal in all of this is to show prospective students the level of support they can expect from your program. *Telling* them they will be supported and engaged is one thing; *showing* them is more powerful and will make your program stand out.
- Ask yourself: Which areas of your digital strategy need improvement?
- List ideas for improvement and prioritize them.

7   Effective Marketing Campaigns

How do you know if your marketing campaign is effective? Check for the following:
- Who is your audience?
- Where does your audience search for programs like yours?
- What is the hook?
- How will you present that hook to your audience once you get in front of them?
- What do you think their response will be? (What action do you hope they will take?)
- How can you measure your effectiveness? (Clicks, site visits, form fills, attendance to webinars, applications, enrollments?)

On any given campaign, you need to have a hypothesis to test. Every effort you spend time or money on needs to earn its right to be done again. The goal here is to figure out what works for you and your prospective student but there is no silver bullet here, especially since what works for one group may not work for another. What you need to do is put forth hypotheses, test the effectiveness, and track what works and what does not. Then you need to see if you can repeat success. If your hypothesis doesn't work, you need to drop it and try something new.

8 Digital Advertising & Search Engine Optimization (SEO)

Looking for the easiest way to get traffic to your site (and hopefully applications to your program)? The easiest way is paid search advertising. That's Google ads and Bing ads – online keyword-search ads in general.

8.1 *How Does Paid Search Advertising Work?*

Paid search marketing is advertising within the sponsored listings of a search engine or a partner site by paying either each time an ad is clicked (pay per click – PPC) or when an ad is displayed.

To understand how this works, it's important to grasp what a search engine results page (SERP) is. When you search keywords on a search engine (i.e., Google), the search engine delivers a list of website listings (site title, links and meta description) in response to your search. This is a SERP. Most of the listings are organic search results – web pages that the search engine algorithm decided were good matches to your keyword query.

Paid search ads are the ads you see when you search for a keyword term and you see a listing marked "Ad." They are deliberately styled like the organic search result listings so they will blend in with the organic search results (see Figure 11.11).

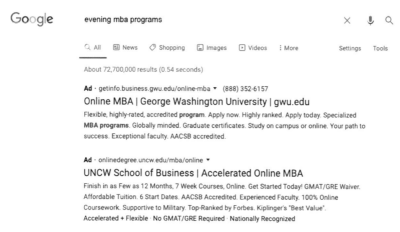

FIGURE 11.11   Example Google ads in search results

8.1.1 Display Ads

One form of PPC ad is the display ad. Display ads show up on websites you visit, usually looking like a box or a banner with a call to action.

The example ads shown below pull dynamically from a database of information about careers, salaries, and related academic programs. These ads clearly establish a career-to-program path, making a compelling case for prospective students interested in career advancement (see Figure 11.12).

8.1.2   Why Paid Search?

Paid search ads are incredibly helpful for several reasons: they quickly and effectively get traffic to your website, they can increase your website visibility on search engines, improving your organic search traffic (traffic you did not pay for), especially if the content on your site is strategically written to work with PPC ads. Also, paid ads get results much more quickly than changes to your site will deliver. This is because good SEO doesn't happen overnight. You will have to invest in years of site copy improvements for you to get somewhat similar SEO results as you can get with the combination of SEO optimized web content plus paid ads.

Paid search ads deliver the following advantages: you can get on the first page of Google results immediately, you can reach your target audience quickly and easily, and people who click on paid search ads are likely to be ready to act (comparatively), and you will have access to paid search analytics, which gives you valuable, measurable information.

A lot of people are intimidated by paid search ads, especially if they've never used them before. Yes, learning how to use the Google ads console is hard. We understand that you probably don't have time to teach yourself how to use this tool. However, you probably have access to internal resources who do know how to run PPC ads or you can hire outside contractors to handle this piece of the puzzle for you.

8.2   *What Exactly Is SEO and How Does It Work?*

How you write your website content matters. It's not enough to provide a generally good description of your program. You need to think about what

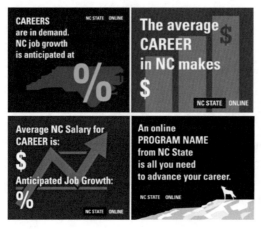

FIGURE 11.12
Example display ads

keywords your target audience will type into a search engine when looking for your program and then make sure those keywords appear in your web copy. However, you can sound like a robot or destroy your brand voice and tone by dumping a bunch of keywords into your web copy. Instead, you need to write content that is both keyword rich and natural.

This is one of the reasons your program pages must be deep. You need a significant amount of room to provide truly good, compelling content that covers the keywords associated with your program in a professional and readable way. You need good SEO real estate so that you can show Google that you are an authority and deserve to rank high in searches.

Here's the problem: you are competing with all the other programs just like yours. How many programs like yours exist? 50? 100? 500? Let's say you are marketing a biology program, and there are 300 other biology programs also vying for that top search engine result page. What have you done on your website to prove to Google that you deserve to be featured in the top dozen search results?

8.2.1 Optimizing Your Program Site or Pages

This is another area where tapping an internal resource or an outside contractor can save you a lot of time and energy. A person with experience in this can quickly put together a list of recommendations that include:
– Keywords
– A SEO site map
– Examples of SEO optimized copy
– Meta descriptions and alt text

With a set of SEO recommendations, you can quickly and easily update your site copy and metadata on the back end of each page (see Figure 11.13).

Page Name/Image	Page URL	Primary Keyword	Alt text
Home	https://ncstate-delta-geospatial-information-technology.mystagingwebsite.com/	master of GIST	master's degree in GIS
Carousel Slide #1		online masters in GIST	graduate degree in geospatial information technology
Carousel Slide #2		online GIST Program	online degree in GIS
Carousel Slide #3		masters of GIST programs	master's of GIST online
Carousel Slide #4		master of GIST online	Get an online master of GIS degree
Online Master of GIST	https://ncstate-delta-geospatial-information-technology.mystagingwebsite.com/online-master-geospatial-information-technology/	GIST degree	
Online Courses	https://ncstate-delta-geospatial-information-technology.mystagingwebsite.com/online-courses/	master's in GIST online degree	master of science in GIS
Faculty & Staff	https://ncstate-delta-geospatial-information-technology.mystagingwebsite.com/faculty-staff/	GIST	how do I become a GIS data analyst
Student Experience	https://ncstate-delta-geospatial-information-technology.mystagingwebsite.com/student-experience/	master's degree in GIST	Requirements to work in GIS
FAQs	https://ncstate-delta-geospatial-information-technology.mystagingwebsite.com/faqs/	GIST master's degree online	GIS careers
About Us	https://ncstate-delta-geospatial-information-technology.mystagingwebsite.com/about-us/	GIST graduate program	what do you need to get a job in GIS

FIGURE 11.13   Example SEO map

An SEO optimized page features the keywords in the text in a prominent yet natural way. It is augmented by SEO metadata, which is entered on the back end of the site. Search engines use the metadata to understand what the page is about and how this page relates to other pages on the site and on the internet as a whole (see Figure 11.14).

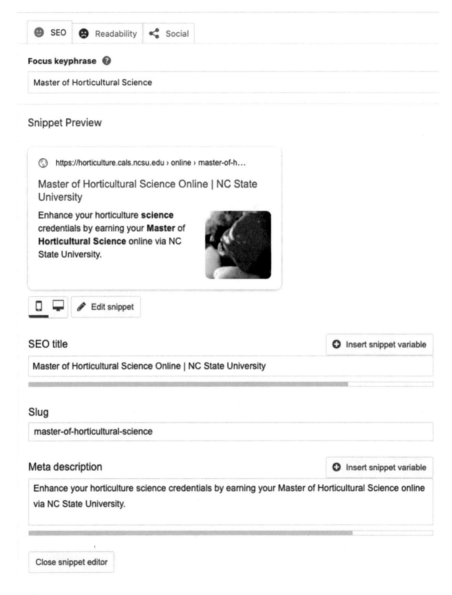

FIGURE 11.14   Example wordpress page back end (SEO optimization)

Metadata analysis is provided by SEO tools (see Figure 11.15).

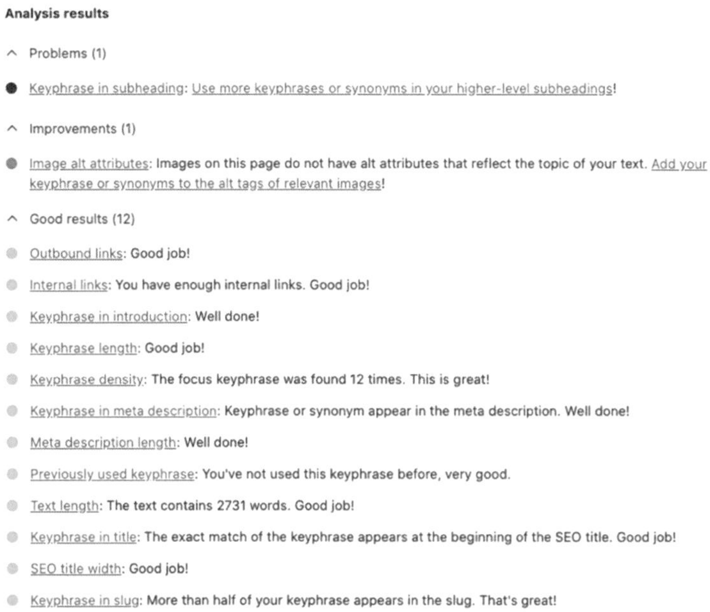

Analysis results

∧ Problems (1)

● Keyphrase in subheading: Use more keyphrases or synonyms in your higher-level subheadings!

∧ Improvements (1)

◉ Image alt attributes: Images on this page do not have alt attributes that reflect the topic of your text. Add your keyphrase or synonyms to the alt tags of relevant images!

∧ Good results (12)

◉ Outbound links: Good job!

◉ Internal links: You have enough internal links. Good job!

◉ Keyphrase in introduction: Well done!

◉ Keyphrase length: Good job!

◉ Keyphrase density: The focus keyphrase was found 12 times. This is great!

◉ Keyphrase in meta description: Keyphrase or synonym appear in the meta description. Well done!

◉ Meta description length: Well done!

◉ Previously used keyphrase: You've not used this keyphrase before, very good.

◉ Text length: The text contains 2731 words. Good job!

◉ Keyphrase in title: The exact match of the keyphrase appears at the beginning of the SEO title. Good job!

◉ SEO title width: Good job!

◉ Keyphrase in slug: More than half of your keyphrase appears in the slug. That's great!

FIGURE 11.15   Example metadata analysis

8.2.2   An Important Aspect of SEO: Links

One of the most important pieces of SEO that is often neglected is link building. Links from other sites to your pages send a signal to Google that your site is enough of an authority that other people want to link to your site.

Links that end in .edu are especially respected by Google, so you will definitely want to ask your department and related sites to link to your site. Reach out to your partners and ask for links from the following:

– Your school and department
– Peer departments and programs
– Professional organizations and industry partners

The more high-quality links you can get, the better. Show search engines that your content is valued.

8.3   *PPC and SEO Together: A Winning Combination*

When you optimize your pages to match your paid search ads, you unleash a powerful marketing tool. All of these efforts, when combined, are going to help you get more traffic to your website.

As you explore your options in paid advertising, you'll discover that keywords vary in value. This is because some keywords are highly searched and some are not; some keywords are easy to rank for (meaning your website will show up on the first page or two of search results), and some are very difficult to rank for. These values are related to how many people are searching for these keywords and how many websites are optimized for those keywords. It's a competition.

You will discover that some keywords are cheaper but cheaper is not always better. If you can get high quality traffic from a keyword (meaning you attract the attention of your target audience and they take action), you may not need a lot of traffic.

Using analytics, you will be able to calculate your cost per conversion, which is how much site traffic or how many actions (i.e., click on the Apply button) you were able to capture per dollar you spent on paid advertising. This is where your putting forth of hypotheses and testing those ideas is very valuable. With a smart paid search, accompanied by excellent SEO, you can get results and get them quickly.

Your Turn:
- Evaluate your PPC and SEO plan.
- Is your website or program page optimized for SEO?
- Are you still relying on traditional advertising methods instead of digital ads?
- Do you have a digital marketing expert on your team that you can tap for advice and direction? If not, how much budget can you put towards hiring a digital marketing consultant?

9   Social Media & PR

Social media has been all the rage for a while now, but here's some advice you might not have heard: don't do it if you aren't going to keep up with it. A social media presence is a relationship, and you don't want to initiate a conversation and then disappear, nor do you want to leave a prospective student cold because you aren't investing time into it.

Our advice is to either get an effective strategy set up and someone (good and responsible) to man it, or don't post at all. This is the same with public relations efforts in general. If you can find partners that are willing to post about your program on their websites, social media channels, and newsletters, that's great. Just make sure you are ready to reciprocate so you don't burn any bridges.

Some topics to post about are announcements; awards; celebration of the achievements of your current students, faculty and alumni; research projects; grants; and department level news. Whoever you put in charge of your social media and public relations efforts should be aware of your brand story, messaging, and goals. Make sure they know how to handle tricky current events issues and the university brand. Protect your reputation while networking.

Having trouble figuring out what to write and post about? You can always simply share success stories of your students. After all, their success is your success.

Every semester, follow up with current students and graduates and record their stories. Share these stories on the website, as blog posts and through your newsletter or email campaigns. Alumni success stories give a personal face to your program. If possible, collect pictures and videos of current students and alumni (get permission to share) for this purpose. You'll want to do this both while they are in your program and immediately after they graduate.

9.1   Print & Outdoor Advertising

While this may be what you are comfortable with, this is the last thing you should do for several reasons. One, both of these advertising methods are pricey, and two, it's very hard to measure their effectiveness. Before you invest a significant chunk of your budget in print or outdoor advertising (billboards and such), you need to ask yourself if you have evidence this is bringing in new students. Does this match the educational environment? For example, if you are marketing an online program, it only makes sense that your ads are also online. Can you prove a reasonable return on investment?

If you insist on doing direct mail, invest money in good, high quality lists. In general, we recommend you move away from print advertising and invest in digital.

9.2   In Person & Digital Events

In person and digital events (such as webinars) are great ways to build the personal relationship we've been talking about, but to make this happen, you've got to show up. Put somebody on your team on research duty to identify the following types of events:
- High school or college events
- Recruiting fairs

- Local employer's activities
- Conferences
- Large employer or professional organization events
- Lunch and learns

Build an events calendar for the year, assign attendees to represent your program, and track the success rate of participation. Was it worth the effort? Stop attending or hosting the events that don't deliver. As with everything in this plan, you need to test, adjust efforts, and retest until you know what gets the attention of your target audience.

10   Analytics & Forecasting

Analytics might be our favorite piece of the marketing puzzle, perhaps because this is where you get to test the strategies you've been working so hard to form as you build your marketing plan. Analytics can be applied to measure a lot of factors, but some are far more important for your causes than others. The following are what we consider to be the most important factors to evaluate every month.

You will want to examine reports on the following categories of data:
- What's bringing people to your website?
- What's happening once they get there?
- How successful are your paid ad campaigns?
- How successful are your content, social media, and SEO efforts?
- How successful are your Calls to Action (CTAs)?
- How to use your website to track and see impact from in person events and out-reach based marketing campaigns

As you read the reports, look for clues as to why the numbers are up, down, or stagnant.

10.1   *What's Bringing People to Your Website?*
A Sessions by Source report tells you how much of your site traffic is organic (meaning it came from someone typing a keyword into a search engine like Google), paid (CPC, which is your paid search ads), referral (from someone clicking on a link on a different site), or other (such as typing the URL into the browser) (see Figure 11.16).

A Top Keywords report tells you which keywords performed best. These are the top ten keywords that brought people to this program page (see Figure 11.17).

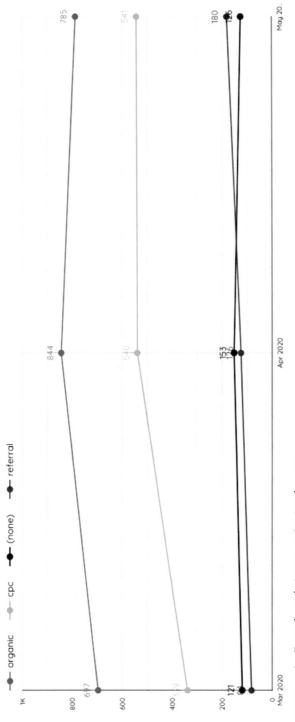

FIGURE 11.16 Example analytics report: Sessions by source

Top Keywords by month

	Search keyword	Conversions ▾	Clicks	Impressions	Avg. CPC
1.	gis certificate	3	230	5,128	$10
2.	+GIS +degree	2	49	1,956	$14.86
3.	+online +gis +program	2	19	557	$13.53
4.	+NC +state +geospatial	1	21	147	$4.1
5.	+geospatial +certificate	1	12	187	$10.28
6.	+geospatial +masters +online	1	12	281	$17.12

FIGURE 11.17   Example top keywords report

10.2   *What's Happening Once They Get to Your Site?*

It's one thing to know that people are visiting your website. You also need to know what people do once they get there. How does that behavior change over time?

10.2.1   Program Page Traffic Summary

This report tells you how many users visited the site, how many times they visited (sessions), how many pages they went to when on the site (pageviews), and how long they spent on the site (on average) (see Figure 11.18).

Program Page Traffic Summary by month

Month of Year ▾	Users	Sessions	Pageviews	Avg. Time on Page
May 2020	1,486	1,632	2,532	00:01:50
Apr 2020	1,478	1,663	2,635	00:01:58
Mar 2020	1,129	1,241	1,994	00:01:45
Feb 2020	243	203	362	00:01:25
Jan 2020	181	97	222	00:01:51
Dec 2019	130	59	173	00:01:23
Nov 2019	143	61	176	00:01:29

FIGURE 11.18   Example traffic report

The Most Visited Pages report tells you exactly which pages were visited by how many people (users), how many times (sessions), and how long they stayed on the page (on average). This information helps you know which pages have the most valuable content on them. You can use a report like this to see what a successful page looks like. Compare your successful pages with your unsuccessful pages to learn how to make all your pages perform well (see Figure 11.19).

Most Visited Pages for selected date range

	Page	Users ▾	Sessions	Avg. Time on Page
1.	/program/master-of-geospatial-information-science-and-technology/	5,800	6,342	00:02:30
2.	/program/graduate-certificate-in-geographic-information-science/	3,529	4,020	00:02:22
3.	/program/graduate-certificate-in-geographic-information-science/courses/	1,038	379	00:03:14
4.	/program/master-of-geospatial-information-science-and-technology/courses/	868	345	00:03:30
5.	/program/master-of-geospatial-information-science-and-technology/how-to-apply/	373	304	00:03:42

FIGURE 11.19   Example most visited pages report

Since return on investment is always a concern, you will want to look at conversion rates and cost per conversions (see Figure 11.20).

PPC Careers Campaign Summary by month

Month ▾	Campaign	Impressions	Clicks	CTR	Conversions	Avg. CPC	Conv. rate	Cost / conv.	Cost
Jun 2020	GIST_Search_Careers	26,840	331	1.23%	2	$14.89	0.6%	$2,463...	$4,927
May 2020	GIST_Search_Careers	29,557	375	1.27%	0	$8.27	0%	$0	$3,101.33

FIGURE 11.20   Example PPC careers campaign summary

Social media impact can also be measured (see Figure 11.21).

Social Network		Sessions ⌄ ↓	Pageviews
1.	Twitter	6 (66.67%)	6 (60.00%)
2.	Facebook	1 (11.11%)	1 (10.00%)
3.	LinkedIn	1 (11.11%)	2 (20.00%)
4.	reddit	1 (11.11%)	1 (10.00%)

FIGURE 11.21   Example social media report

10.2.2   Social Traffic

Are people clicking on your Apply button? What about your Contact Us or your Request Info buttons? Sometimes design, placement, or size is an issue. You may want to play around with how and where call-to-action (CTA) buttons appear (see Figure 11.22).

This report helps you determine what users are interested in. Did they fill out a contact form? Research financial aid? Download a PDF? This report also shows you where the traffic came from. For example, in May, five people who found the page through organic search (typing a keyword into a search engine

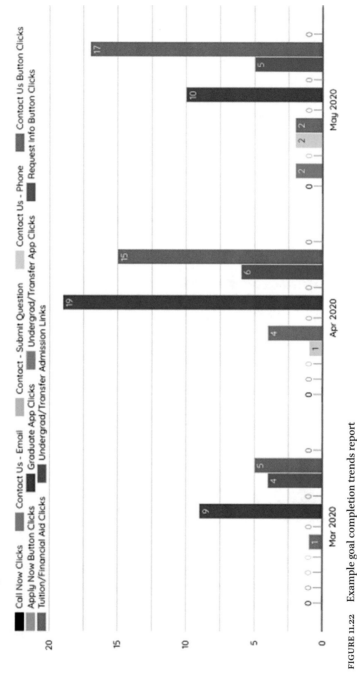

FIGURE 11.22   Example goal completion trends report

like Google and clicking on your page listing) decided to fill out a contact form (see Figure 11.23).

Event Breakdown by Month, Source

| | | | | | Medium / Total Events | |
Month of Year	Event Category	organic	(none)	cpc	referral	Grand total
May 2020	contact form	5	8	3	2	18
	Financial Aid	3	5	1	-	10
	Total	8	13	4	2	28
Apr 2020	Financial Aid	6	2	4	-	14
	contact form	2	8	-	-	10
	downloads	1	2	-	-	3
	Total	9	12	4	-	27

FIGURE 11.23   Example event breakdown report

10.3   *Tracking the Impact of In-Person Events*
You can also use Google Analytics to track the impact of in-person events and outreach-based marketing campaigns. Google Analytics tracks details of users such as geographic location and IP names. By comparing user activity spikes and user location information, you can deduct the impact of events and outreach.

10.4   *Using Analytics to Improve Your Marketing Strategy*
The reports we've featured in this chapter only scratch the surface of what data you can pull from Google Analytics. Work with someone experienced and have them set up a Data Studio dashboard for you, and you'll have more than enough material to pull from.

This is how you test the hypotheses you've formed and executed. For example, you may find the answers to the following:
- Did the addition of careers content drive more traffic to your program pages? Once there, did they ask for information or apply?
- Did posting application deadlines create a spike in applications? We've often seen applications rise just before, on and right after the application deadline, which is why we encourage you to post them on the site in a prominent location. If your program is on rolling admissions, set a "priority" deadline and you'll get similar results.
- What have you learned about the timeline of a marketing strategy? Did you start marketing soon enough, or will you need to start sooner to get results in the next application cycle?

If you get really good with this, you can even forecast matriculation down to approximate cost and timing.

> *Your Turn*:
> – Do you have access to site analytics?
> – Do you have someone on your team who can set up a dashboard for you?
> – Can they also interpret analytics in a meaningful way?
> – What metrics will you track? List them now.

11   Conclusion: Optimizing Your Marketing Efforts

Naturally, this chapter only provides a brief overview of the many aspects of higher education recruitment and marketing strategies. However, we hope you now have a good feel for where to begin as you:
– Find the support and funding you need to effectively market your program
– Identify your prospective student audience
– Establish your brand and archetype
– Engage with your target audience
– Plan and execute changes to your website and marketing strategy
– Test, measure, refine, and improve your marketing strategy to get results

You won't get it all right immediately; no one does. However, by taking the steps outlined in this chapter you can get the ball rolling in the right direction. Act with intention, test your theories, and document successes and failures. Evaluate and adjust your plan accordingly. In time you'll find success.

Notes

1   If you aren't familiar with SMART goals and how to use a SMART goal system, visit the Corporate Finance Institute (https://corporatefinanceinstitute.com/resources/knowledge/other/smart-goal/).
2   https://www.verifiedstudios.com/marketing-strategy-archetypes/
3   Not sure how email campaigns work? Check out an example of an email campaign we designed to further your understanding of this strategy (https://docs.google.com/document/d/1XUahxrQ6dSHbQPihN2aGieXgDbnpoLC2WrD_zvIFYek/edit?usp=sharing).

CHAPTER 12

Student Affairs and Support in Distance Learning Environments

Renay M. Scott

Abstract

– Explore the role of student affairs and support services in distance learning environments.
– Understand students' support needs in distance learning environments.
– Understand the importance of on-boarding students in distance learning environments.
– Identify the role of the library and librarians in distance learning environments.
– Explain the role of financial aid, tutoring, career services and co-curricular programming in distance learning environments.

Keywords

college admissions – tutoring – advising – student support services – library services

1 Introduction

University A, a brick and mortar, residential research university serving first generation, underrepresented minorities needs to find new markets to grow enrollment. The institution commits to developing an on-line service college reaching a similar student population in the remote parts of the state and perhaps globally. University B, a regional, selective admission institution facing two weeks to move all courses from face to face delivery to remote delivery because of a pandemic, mobilizes academic units with faculty already delivering their courses on-line to work with faculty who never have taught in any other than face to face modality.

At each institution the Vice President of Enrollment Management and the Vice President of Student Life talk about what student support services, if any, need delivery modifications. University A undertaking to develop a distance learning college within the university establishes a steering committee with several subcommittees. One subcommittee explores how to deliver student affairs and support programs to distance learners. Because of a pandemic, University B, faces limited time to adjust and adopts a reactionary stance never considering what, if any, support services need to be converted to remote delivery. University B begins the process by bringing together all the vice presidents.

University B immediately identifies the need to ensure technology support for students, tutoring services, and advising as the first three priorities supporting faculty converting their courses to distance delivery. Recognizing that they will continue remote delivery in the subsequent semester, University B starts planning how financial aid, disability services and the library will be converted to remote delivery. The Student Affairs subcommittee at University A determines to begin working by identifying the student journey from onboarding through commencement. In addition to traditional services, University A identifies their desire to provide clubs and organizations, affinity groups, career services, and student government experiences within the distance learning program.

Both universities facing real situations within the higher education sector over the past year, find they intuitively know student support services need to be part of the program yet are ill equipped for planning. Student affairs professionals should embrace the new frontier and recognize their role as distance learning increases in prevalence. While distance learning programs have been around over twenty years, student support services evolve within those programs as institutions discover that student retention and completion depend upon more than well-designed courses. Knowing what support services are needed and designing them to meet the learners' needs depends upon researching best practices and understanding student development theory within the context of distance learning environments. Mehran et al. (2010) found a positive correlation between support services and academic achievement in online programs. However, researchers seeking information about what works in remote environments are finding a dearth of evidence examining support service infrastructures (Wheelan, 2016, p. 38). NASPA recognizing the need for student affairs professionals to engage within distance learning programs acknowledges that "while student services is seen more as an administrative necessity by some mainstream academics, the online distance education leaders recognize that effective student services, and a focus on students generally, are critical to the long-term viability of distance education (Benke & Miller, 2013, p. 220).

2   Who are the Learners in Distance Learning Programs?

Some higher educational professionals imagine students in a distance learning environment to be independent, place-bound, motivated, goal oriented and self-starters who bring a wealth of worldly experience into the classroom (Clinefelter, Aslanian, & Magda, 2019, p. 219). Even as early as 1998, Thompson (1998) reported that such homogeneity doesn't exist in distance learning programs (p. 10). Dabbagh (2007) described on-line learners as heterogenous, bringing multiple learning styles and generational differences into distance learning environments (p. 217).

Many individuals entering distance learning programs bring with them responsibilities and multiple concerns. Capranos and Dyers (2020) identifies 63% of distance learners as concerned about time management and finances while 60% are concerned about managing their learning and work commitments (p. 27). Forty-one percent of distance learners are also concerned about managing their family commitments (Capranos & Dyers, 2020, p. 27). Factoring these concerns along with understanding varied learning styles and generational differences must guide designing student support structures within a distance learning program.

3   Admissions

Beginning the discussion of student affairs in distance learning environments with the admissions process seems natural. Five percent of prospective undergraduate students never enrolled in college prior to seeking admission to a distance education program while 48% previously attended college within five or more years (Magda, Capranos, & Aslanian, 2020, p. 14). Of those transferring with credits, 12% of undergraduates and 16% of graduate students worry about obtaining previous transcripts (Clinefelter, Aslanian, & Magda, 2019, p. 14). In addition to obtaining transcripts, 10% of undergraduates and 12% of graduate students worry about articulating previous credits into a new distance learning program (Clinefelter, Aslanian, & Magda, 2019, p. 29).

Clinefetter, Aslanian, and Magda (2019) report that 87% of individuals enrolling in distance learning programs have transfer credit (p. 13). Articulating previously earned credit remains an important factor in timely completion of college for students seeking programs that fit with their responsibilities and need for career advancement. Fifty-six percent of all prospective students previously earned credit with 13% earning ninety or more credit hours (Clinefelter, Aslanian, & Magda, 2019, p. 14).

Developing timely, effective transcript evaluation is vital for attracting students to a program. How institutions approach this process is important for the timing of when a student can begin coursework. Prospective learners eagerly anticipate starting on their program of study. Some institutions choose to wait for official transcripts while allowing students to begin their program. They provide guidance on how many courses students can take before official transcripts arrive and they can continue with the remainder of their program. Other institutions may accept unofficial transcripts and communicate tentative admission and credit acceptance. The decision to allow students to start on their program of study must be carefully considered.

> *Discussion*:
> University A has the luxury of exploring what, if any admission criteria are needed. University B does not. If you were the student affairs leader at University A, how would you work with academic leadership to identify the admission criteria and how might you market the program to prospective students?

4   Orientation

Student affairs professionals considering how to on-board students through an orientation process must have a good understanding of the characteristics these students possess and the skills they will need at the beginning of their program to experience success. Accepting that learners bring a variety of needs to the distance learning environment and that immediate success will enhance their retention, becomes the starting place for designing an orientation. Organizing student characteristics into three constructs; academic, social, and motivational, aids designers in constructing on-boarding activities ensuring initial support that helps learners begin with early success. Attending to the social needs of the learner means helping them build relationships with fellow students, faculty, and most importantly their advisor. Creating opportunities to interact with their advisor within the orientation and reinforcing the all-encompassing nature of advising ensures that students have at least one person they can reach out to throughout their program.

Learners tend to be highly motivated at the beginning of their distance learning programming. Despite the necessary motivation, often these learners have attended college previously and are questioning their preparation. Each learner may have previously experienced some success, but they also experienced challenges that caused them to stop-out. Usually they lack the necessary academic support structure to support them through their academic journey. The orientation process can build on the learner's motivation and give them confidence that, this time, they will succeed by helping them engage with the technology used in the distance learning delivery model that they will experience once they begin their coursework. While these distance delivery models can include both asynchronous and synchronous delivery, the orientation process should mirror the course delivery model so as to begin to familiarize the learner with the learning environment they are about to experience.

Using the orientation as a way to test the technology each student has along with the technology skills they bring, can quickly help the student affairs professional identify which students need more support than the others. The orientation should be set up to include the minimum skills that each student will need to perform in order to be successful in the distance delivery model. For example, if students need to take and submit assessments in the LMS, the orientation should require students to perform this skill. If students need to upload a video of a speech, then the orientation should require students to create and upload a video. Orientation designers need to work closely with academic programs to ensure they have identified all of the basic, frequently applied skills necessary to participate in class and submit assignments.

The assignments within the orientation process should familiarize the learners with the course organization that will comprise the majority of their courses delivered through the LMS. Those assignments can be designed to familiarize students with the support structures available to them. For example, if the distance delivery model includes a writing center or writing tutors, the learners should be asked to visit the writing center virtually and work with a professional on a written assignment as part of their orientation. Other assignments can reinforce the netiquette expectations of the institution.

5   Student Technology Support Services

Making sure students know how to use the necessary technology embedded within the program starts in orientation. Making sure that students know what technology they need and ensuring they can obtain it is equally important. The admission and orientation processes should include clear and repetitive communication about the basic technology that students will need throughout their program of study and how they may obtain it for themselves. Some distance learning courses may require special technology that must be communicated as part of the course registration process, in the course syllabi, and in the course LMS. Software bundles should be made available to students through institutional site licenses and remain active while the student is enrolled in the distance learning program. Bookstores may make available software bundles to students that remain with the student even after they have graduated or leave the distance learning program.

In addition to ensuring students know what technology they need and have access to obtaining it, distance learning programs need to provide a 24-7 help desk to answer student's technology questions and troubleshoot technology problems that will inevitably arise. Some of these questions may be answerable through a chat bot on the distance learning program's web site. Universities may also consider contracting with technology support companies to provide this support should the institution not have the expertise available or be able to provide 24-7 technology support. It is vital to have a technology support structure available to students no matter what type of technology support structure fits with the distance learning business model.

6   Advising

The importance of advising can't be stressed enough with respect to distance learning programs. Advisors serve as the main point of contact between the institution and the learner (Benke & Miller, 2013, p. 204). Determining what advising will mean in a distance learning program demands forethought and design. Advising structures take many forms in a brick and mortar University. Advising can represent academic program planning, career exploration, financial aid planning, course scheduling, and admission guidance. Advising can be centrally staffed by professional advisers, decentralized with professional advisors, decentralized with faculty advisors, or a mix model that can include many different combinations. The advising model that works for a brick and motar institution may not be adequate for distance delivery (Benke & Miller, 2013, p. 204). In face-to-face delivery programs students have many different people they can reach out to for support and guidance. However, advising in distance learning programs is more comprehensive than simply providing support for course registration. Advisors may provide support linked to career exploration, completing program requirements, or applying for commencement. Advisors may be the bridge between the student and the other existing support structures discussed below. Within distance delivery programs, the professional advisor, sometimes called the distance learning coach, becomes the main person for students to contact.

Learners in distance delivery programs often feel isolated and this isolation can impact their retention and success. Consequently, the learner's advisor tends to be the constant person available to the learner whenever they need assistance during their coursework. Studies demonstrate that students prefer one-on-one, or real-time advising (Benke & Miller, 2013, p. 210). Meeting students' expectations requires establishing a stable advising team with clear expectations about timelines for responding to learners who reach out to them.

Deciding about the structure of advising is dependent upon the design of the curriculum. If the program of study is narrowly defined with few choices or electives, the registration process may not need significant levels of advising. Thus, advisors time is freed up for connecting with the learner by building a relationship that helps the learner feel free to reach out to the advisor whenever they need. If the curriculum includes many choices, advising support will be more complex and may not afford the advisor as much opportunity to build a relationship with their advisee or provide other supports the learner may need.

In addition to the structure of advising, professional development for advisors will determine their ability to provide support beyond course registration. Training should include information about the programs, the structure, academic policies, program milestones, and important deadlines. Broadly defined, professional development for the advisor may include information about financial aid, financial planning, career exploration, and the availability of and access to the range of support structures.

Building a stable, professional advising team is foundational to student support and success in distance learning environments. National Academic Advising Association (NACADA) represents themselves as the global community for academic advising and is comprised of members from professional advisors, counselors, faculty, administrator, and students working to enhance the student experience. Ensuring advisors have access to their professional association and participate in on-going training about student development theory, research, and best practices ensures that advisors will deliver the support distance learners need.

Discussion:
Returning to the two universities, student affairs professionals must work with advising staff to ensure they are prepared for the launch of distance delivery programs and courses. How would you work with advising staff and academic units to begin outlining the advising structure and programming needed?

7   Financial Aid and Scholarship Services

Financial Aid is the most frequented service at brick and mortar campuses, and the same is true for distance delivery programs. According to Clinefelter,

Aslanian, and Magda (2019), 63% of students in distance learning programs are concerned about finances (p. 27). The availability of financial aid and scholarships top prospective learners' criteria for selection and enrollment in a distance delivery program. Over 20% of undergraduate students and 17% of graduate students are concerned about how to pay for college attendance (Clinefelter, Aslanian, & Magda, 2019, p. 23).

Tuition rates factor into prospective students' decisions with 60% of undergraduates and 46% of graduate students sighting affordability as an important factor in deciding where to attend college (Clinefelter, Aslanian, & Magda, 2019, p. 24). While affordability is important, 67% of prospective students are willing to pay a higher tuition rate if the program's schedule and format is ideal for them (Clinefelter, Aslanian, & Magda, 2019, p. 27).

Once a prospective student determines where to attend college they begin exploring how to pay for the cost of attendance. Twenty-six percent of undergraduate students and 20% of graduate students report completing the financial aid application as the most difficult process of enrolling (Asianian, Clinefelter, & Magda, 2019, p. 29). Federal aid is not the only avenue for prospective students to pay for college. One in three distance learners report having their employer pay for college (Asianian, Clinefelter, & Magda, 2019, p. 30). Fifty-eight percent of prospective students believe a scholarship as little as $500.00 would positively impact their decision to attend a college or university (Asianian, Clinefelter, & Magda, 2019, p. 28). Funding scholarships through the budget process generates minimal expense compared to potential tuition revenue. Consequently, considering adding an institutional scholarship as a means of attracting students can pay longer term dividends.

Payment plans can also impact a prospective student's choice of where to attend college. Over 40% of prospective students' report wanting either a monthly or quarterly payment plan (Asianian, Clinefelter, & Magda, 2019, p. 28). Because many distance learners are working while attending school, the offer of paying a little each month or quarter allows them to build college attendance into their personal budget making college seem for affordable.

8   Library

Corbett and Brown (2015) acknowledge distance learning is a global industry (p. 1). Purdue Global's capture of international markets is one example. The national and international appeal of distance education programs allows students from anywhere to gain a college education. Sometimes students' access to libraries is minimal or non-existent. Distance delivery programs must bring the library to students.

Distance delivery requires the library to shift from collections to providing digital information and resources that support students in distance learning environments. Brick and mortar colleges and universities have a long tradition of supporting face-to-face course delivery and on-campus student life activities. To support distance learning, library staff must take on the challenge of shifting to information and resource organization. Professional development for library staff is necessary for broadening their skills for supporting distance learning. Existing library staff can consult their professional organization, the Association of College and Research Libraries (ACRL), for standards for libraries and distance education. In addition to professional development as a strategy for supporting distance learning programs, another strategy is to fill library staff openings with individuals who embrace the information management philosophy or have experience in supporting distance learning programs. Over time, newly hired staff serving as dedicated librarians for distance education will gain a deeper understanding about the correlation of their institutions online course content with resources needed in the library (Hoffman, 2011).

Librarians organizing resources for distance delivery programs can use a common tool, Lib Guides, available in most college and university libraries in the United States. Lib Guides allow for the curation and publication of resources for easy integration into the learning management system. Librarians, working with faculty, design Lib Guides correlated with course outcomes. Many learners enrolling in distance delivery programs while juggling jobs, families, and other commitments find direct support embedded within the LMS essential to assist them with maximizing the time they dedicate to their learning. These learners value the library support they receive when the library is linked into the course and Lib Guides are available to help them begin their research. In addition to developing program specific Lib Guides, librarians wishing to support faculty engage in identifying open educational resources (OER) that correlate with the content of courses.

Discussion:
Returning to the two Universities planning for distance delivery, the student affairs professionals discover different challenges. University A is a research university wanting to maintain the research culture present in their face-to-face programs while developing a similar culture in the distance delivery programs. University B, values ensuring graduates develop skills in information management and evaluation and believe that those skills can be embedded within course assignments. Consider how you would work with the librarians at either University if you were in a leadership role within student affairs.

9   Tutoring and Writing Support

Pratt (2015) reports that students entering distance learning environments after being away from school for several years believe they need support early within their program and courses (p. 17). The nature of the support varies based on program and course. Tutoring and writing supports specific to course outcomes and skills are often available to students who do not even know they exist. Communicating the availability of tutoring and writing centers remains a constant challenge in both distance and traditional learning environments. Embedding communication in all aspects of distance learning programs from orientation to advising conversation and within course shells serves as a reminder to students that these services are available for them at any point when they choose to connect with them.

Embedding tutoring or learning supports within course modules makes learning supports readily available for students who would not otherwise search them out. Such supports can include linking to YouTube demonstrations of essential skills developed by the University or providing virtual appointments with writing coaches to allow for feedback to students on their writing assignments. Within course modules, peer reviews of one another's writing can be effective when enhanced with clear rubrics to guide students in providing meaningful feedback.

Annual learning assessments uncover trouble areas for students and that can become the topic of videos publicized to students upon logging into their course modules. Reinforcing essential skills takes the form of short, just-in-time online workshops. These workshops can be delivered synchronously or asynchronously. Tutoring delivered through virtual meetings provides another form of support for students. Because distance learning can take place across several time zones, virtual, synchronous tutoring meetings become challenging for institutions in one time zone with learners in multiple time zones. Tutoring provided across several shifts may not be possible for an institution. In these situations hiring tutoring services may provide the optimal solution.

10   Career Services

While many distance learners are employed, they still utilize career services. Clinefetter, Aslanian, and Magda (2019, p. 9) report career services are very popular with first generation college students. Over 20% of distance learners use career services for resume creation, self-assessment, job searching, job search guidance, and meeting with a career advisor (Clinefetter, Asianian, & Magda, 2019, p. 39).

Resumes can be submitted on-line to a career advisor who can provide written guidance or advise through remote face-to-face meetings. Mock interviews conducted via video conferencing can be invaluable for learners. Job postings can be available to students through technology solutions such as Handshake. Ten percent of distance learning alumni report plans for continuing with career services in the future (Clinefetter, Asianian, & Magda, 2019, p. 39).

11   Student Life

Students in distance learning programs experience Isolation which hinders persistence (Benke & Miller, 2013, p. 213). Building a sense of community and fostering connectedness in distance learning occurs within courses through interactions between course participants such as virtual introductions, reacting to fellow students' reflections, or group assignments. The co-curricular experience at brick and mortar colleges and universities creates a sense of belonging through continuous face-to-face interactions through. Traditional students, if there is such a category, pursue admission to colleges or universities providing a robust student life. However, distance learning program designers often overlook co-curricular experiences assuming their students reject such traditional experiences. Promoting a sense of community in distance learning environments through co-curricular experiences eliminates isolation, lessening disconnection with other students as a cause for stopping out.

Professional learning environments foster community by providing students access to other students (Benke & Miller, 2013, p. 216). These learning environments include on-line open houses, peer mentoring programs, book discussions, guest speakers and first-year experiences when courses can be sequenced and include moving a group of students through those courses collectively. Clubs and organizations provide ways for students to connect. Technology such as Zoom, Microsoft Teams, Skype and other solutions enable groups of students to meet in real-time around common interests.

Distance learners face similar challenges to traditional college populations and that of society. The emergence of mental health needs among on campus populations and within society signal the need to consider mental health services as necessary for supporting distance learners. Telehealth and on-line screenings make mental health services more accessible for students participating in distance learning programs. Ensuring student success goals depends on supporting students holistically.

The areas of student conduct and Title IX are often evolving and challenging areas of focus for student life professionals within more traditional college and university environments. Yet, distance learning programs lag behind in considering these elements of the student experience. Developing, evaluating, and continuously revising a conduct process including student appeals, student judiciary hearings, and conduct policies applied within distance learning environments remains an area to be addressed for student life professionals working within colleges and universities delivering distance learning programs (Benke & Miller, 2013, p. 208).

Forefront for student affairs professionals is fostering equity and inclusion for all students in traditional campus environments. Equity and inclusion is equally important in distance learning environments. Wheelan (2016, p. 72) reports that students with disabilities are often marginalized within distance learning environments. Instructional designers working with faculty to develop accessible course delivery models is common. However, services must be available to ensure inclusion for all students. Students need access to professionals who can assess whether or not accommodations are necessary for them to succeed. The heterogenous nature of distance learners requires institutions to ensure culturally appropriate curriculum and co-curricular experiences. As mentioned earlier, professional learning groups can enhance student's connectedness to one another. Designing these professional learning groups to appeal to a wide range of diverse cultures and backgrounds further validates learners from all backgrounds.

12   Conclusion

Within the higher education sector calls grow for improved student outcomes and success. Simultaneously, distance learning environments grow providing non-traditional learners avenues to maintain personal and employment responsibilities while gaining advanced knowledge and skills. Throughout the evolution of distance delivery, student affairs professionals must take their skills into distance delivery programs and closely examine their roles and value for serving students who engage in these environments. Relying upon student development theory and committing to equity and inclusion fosters co-curriculum and support services. Enhancing the institutional mission through distance learning is the new frontier for student support services, whether the institution focuses on distance delivery or traditional face-to-face delivery.

Discussion Questions:
- What processes would you use if you were the Vice President of Student Affairs at either University A or University B to determine how to design or redesign student affairs programming and supports for a distance learning program? Consider the following questions.
- What role will your library and the librarians play in your distance education program?
- How will tutoring be delivered?
- How will you consider the needs of the learners?
- What technology needs will the learners have and how will you support them?

References

Benke, M., & Miller, G., (2013). Optimizing student success through student support services. In G. Miller, M. Benke, B. Chaloux, L. C. Ragan, R. Schroeder, W. Smutz, & K. Swan (Eds.), *Leading the e-learning transformation of higher education*. Stylus Publishing, LLC.

Capranos, D., & Dyers, L. (2020). *Online student behaviors and attitudes: A survey of prospective students, current learners, and recent graduates of Wiley education services' partners*. Wiley edu, LLC.

Clinefelter, D. L., Aslanian, C. B., & Magda, A. J. (2019). *Online college students 2019: Comprehensive data on demands and preferences*. Wiley edu, LLC.

Corbett, A., & Brown, A. (2015). The roles that librarians and libraries play. *Online Journal of Distance Learning Administration, XVIII*(2).

Dabbagh, N. (2007). The online learners: Characteristics and pedagogical implications. *Contemporary Issues in Technology and Teacher Education, 7*(3), 217–226.

Magda, A. J., Capranos, D., & Aslanian, C. B. (2020). *Online college students 2020: Comprehensive data on demands and preferences*. Wiley Education Services.

Mehran, F., & Mahdi, M. (2010). The study of relation between students support services and distance students' academic achievement. *Prodedia – Social and Behavioral Sciences, 2*(2), 4451–4456.

Pratt, K. (2015). Supporting distance learners: Making practice more effective. *Journal of Open, Flexible and Distance Learning, 19*(1).

Thompson, M. M. (1998). Distance learners in higher education. In C. C. Gibson (Ed.), *Distance learners in higher education* (pp. 9–24). Atwood Publishing.

Wheelan, P. (2016). Flipping student support services to improve outcomes. *Change: The Magazine of Higher Learning, 48*, 36–41. doi:10.1080/00091383.2016.1247581

CHAPTER 13

Student Success

Administering Distance Education for Student Success

Ormond Simpson

Abstract

At the conclusion of this chapter, you will be able to identify ways to administer:
– a system of input into course design
– a system of student support both academic (teaching) and non-academic
– to enhance student success in your institution.

Keywords

student dropout – student support – cost benefits – distance course design – proactive
support – barriers – predictive methods – motivation

• • •

You learn best when you have someone who cares that you learn.

• •
•

1   Setting the Scene

Welcome to this chapter on student success. I'm Ormond Simpson, most
recently Visiting Professor at the Open Polytechnic of New Zealand. I've written a book *Supporting Students for Success in Online and Distance Education*
(Routledge) on which this chapter is partly based.

I'm imagining that you're an administrator working in a university that
includes distance learning opportunities. You're sitting in your office and the
University President has just called to tell you that you've been promoted to be
the institution's new 'Director of Distance Learning' (Congratulations! What's
your new salary?).

Like any new job it feels quite overwhelming. What can you do? Where can you start? Let's set the scene first.

1.1   *Student Success – Why the Focus?*
Everything in this book is ultimately aimed at turning out successful students. But there are two reasons for focusing specifically on student success in distance learning:
– the much higher dropout rates in distance education,
– the effects that has on both distance institutions and their students.

1.1.1   Retention Rates in Distance Education
There is now general agreement amongst researchers that retention rates in many distance online education institutions are lower – sometimes much lower – than in conventional education (Figure 13.1).

Average conventional education retention rates in the US are almost double those of full time distance education rates (63% vs 33% – a difference of *33% points*). Outside the US an example is the International Programme of the University of London where exactly the same courses are presented in two modes – 'institution based' with face-to-face teaching, and 'distance based' which is all online. The difference between them is around *46% points* in favor of the face-to-face mode. I think of these differences as the *Distance Education Deficit*.

Does moving online increase retention in distance education? The distance institutions in Figure 13.1 are all practically 100% online. But the UKOU was

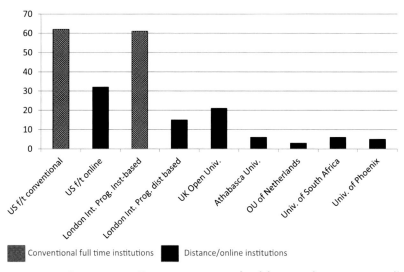

FIGURE 13.1   Some retention % rates in conventional and distance education compared[1]
(Lederman, 2018, and Simpson, 2013)

initially a classic correspondence institution when it first opened in 1971, sending teaching materials by mail and offering face-to-face tutorials. Since then it has moved steadily to an almost entirely 100% online delivery. During the process its graduation rate has declined from 59% in 1982 to around 13% in 2016 (Figure 13.2).

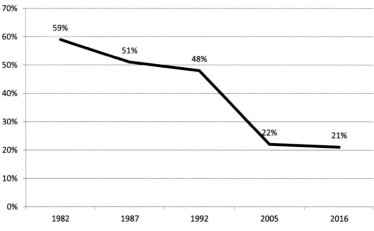

FIGURE 13.2   UKOU graduation rates 1982–2016 (Simpson, 2013)

While the decline could be due to a number of factors, it seems clear at the very least that moving online has not helped the UKOU maintain its original graduation rate.

One factor behind the decision of the UKOU to move online (as for many distance institutions) was an expected reduction in the costs of providing distance education. In fact, a recent OECD report (2020) cautions that online teaching is just as expensive as in-person instruction. This is in part because instructors teaching in distance courses report that smaller class sizes are needed to keep students engaged and retained at the same level as conventional education.

1.2   *Do Low Retention Rates Matter?*

In the move to online learning retention has been somewhat overlooked. But such low rates are damaging for both institutions and the students involved.

1.2.1   Effects of Low Retention on Distance Institutions

Whether distance education institutions are funded directly by governments or indirectly through student loan schemes, high dropout rates will affect their incomes eventually. Drops in income will then lead to cuts in staffing with cuts in services to students in a vicious circle of increasing dropout. The resulting financial problems can then lead to closure. In the US, dozens of higher education institutions close every year, both private and public. For example, 'Education Dive' (2019) reported that

> In 2016 the Obama administration stripped federal recognition of the accreditor responsible for two large chains – ITT and Corinthian Colleges – whose collapses drew attention to issues of misrepresentation and *poor student outcomes* [emphasis added] within the sector.

Of course, by no means all the institutions closing are online. But if retention rates for online institutions are much lower and lead to 'poor student outcomes' then they are very likely to be the first to go.

A few years ago I was invited to the Open University of the Netherlands to talk about student retention in open learning. The OUN was financed directly by the Dutch Government who had threatened to withdraw its funding on account of its high dropout rates. So far it has survived the threat (but I can take no credit for that).

1.2.2 Effects of Low Retention Rates on Students

A student is investing (possibly in the form of their loan) in order to obtain an eventual return on that investment (RoI). The RoI is usually in the form of increased income as a result of graduation (depending on the 'resale value' of their degree – law and economics graduates tend to do best – humanities less well). But there are other benefits – graduates tend to live longer, lead healthier lives and volunteer more (APLU, 2015).

But a student's investment carries a risk – the possibility of dropping out. In theory a student's 'Willingness to Pay' (WtP) would depend on their evaluation of that risk. But of course, institutions are very skilled at recruitment and spend a lot of money on it. Thus, their WtP barely registers in potential students' thinking. However, a distance education institution will ultimately suffer financially when students' WtP declines as a result of its reputation for high dropout.

So, what happens to students who drop out? Clearly dropped out students will suffer financially either through the loss of their upfront fee payments or through increased indebtedness because of their student loan.

The consequences of student indebtedness has been turned into fiction in a recent John Grisham (2017) novel *The Rooster Bar*. Three heavily indebted students drop out and plot to get revenge on the billionaire who not only owns their law school, but the company that loaned them their fees.

But there are other consequences. A longitudinal researcher Professor John Bynner (2001) followed up a UK school leavers cohort over a number of years.[2] Figure 13.3 shows the relative probability of experiencing depression, unemployment and (for women) violence from their partners, for various educational qualification levels – including non-completion.

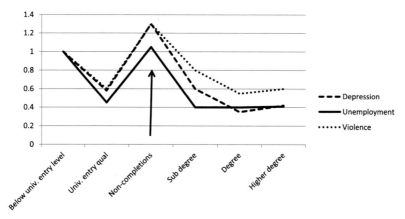

FIGURE 13.3   Probability of experiencing depression, unemployment and partner violence for various educational qualification levels in UK (adapted from Bynner, 2001)

The graph shows that non-completing students have up to one third higher probability of subsequent depression, unemployment and partner violence, than either graduates or (alarmingly) people who never went to university in the first place.[3]

Depression. Kessler (2012) found that major depressive disorder (MDD) in the US predicted low marital quality, low work performance, and low earnings as well as higher risk of early mortality due to a wide range of disorders and suicide. With more than 20 million students in higher education in the US the number dropping out could be around 5 million a year, many of whom may be suffering depression as a result. This can only add to the overall cost of depression in the US, estimated at $210 billion a year (Greenberg, 2015).

Worst case scenario. All this of course is a worst-case scenario. There are many caveats. The depression data is for full-time UK students – US students may be more resilient. We might expect that distance students may be more flexible and able to return to study after dropping out.

Win some, lose some? Despite my over-egging this dropout pudding, I hope I have persuaded you that dropout isn't a case of shoulder shrugging – 'it's always been like that – win some, lose some.' *Dropout is a billion-dollar tapeworm in the guts of the distance education business.*

> *Query 1:* What's your experience of dropping out – of anything? How did it make you, feel?

> *My response:* I have a fair bit of dropping out experience ... My most recent was trivial – I gave up my gym membership. But I still feel guilty and make excuses for myself.

2   Understanding Dropout

> The philosophers have only interpreted the world, in various ways. The point, however, is to change it. (Karl Marx)

Why do distance students drop out more than conventional students? This is a simple question, but very difficult to answer. Dropout is 'multi-factorial' with many possible causes. So there are many theories to try to explain it, such as Vincent Tinto's classic 'Institutional Departures' model (2007). But few existing theories satisfactorily explain the 'distance education deficit'. It is more useful to ask what the main barriers to student success in distance education might be, and how they might be overcome.

2.1   *Barriers to student success in distance education*

> The biggest barrier to success in an institution is the institution itself. (Veronique Johnston)

I suggest that there are four principle barriers:

i.   *Lack of resources.* There will always be arguments about resources in any institution – how much and where should they go – research, recruitment, course production or student support. I'll come back to that.

ii.   *Technology as a barrier to learning.* Whilst online devices enable learn-
      ing, they can also be barriers to learning, not least because reading off a
      screen can be considerably less effective than reading print. For example:

> Regardless of topic, text length or the inclusion of visuals, ... com-
> prehension is better when reading occurs in print ... [for] things like
> pulling details, key facts, numbers, and figures, participants do a lot
> better after reading print. (Trakhman, 2019)

And of course there are the endless distractions of pop-up videos, as well as
viruses, spam, scams, crashes, Wi-Fi outages and so on.

iii. *Institutional attitudes as barriers to learning.* There is an invisible barrier
      to success in the form of ambivalent attitudes in institutions about drop-
      out, which may be more prevalent in distance education where dropout
      may be less immediately obvious. I argue that there are three kinds of
      university teachers:
      – 'Darwinistas' – who believe their role in teaching is to 'weed out the
        unfit' who shouldn't pass
      – 'Fatalistas' – who say that their job is to teach and that it's all up to the
        students
      – 'Retentioneers' who believe their job is to help students be the best
        they can be, even if their students ultimately don't succeed.

It's the latter group who really care about retention (Johnston and Simpson,
2006).

> *Query 2*: How would you rate your own institution on an arbitrary scale of
> 0 to 100 where 0 is not at all Darwinista and 100 is completely Darwinista?
>
> *My response*: I've asked this question of distance education colleagues at
> various places around the world. For example the two most Darwinista
> institutions were the Korean National Open University and the University
> of Papua New Guinea at around 85 on my arbitrary scale. The least was the
> University of South Africa at 6. I've not yet related this to student success,
> but my impression is that the closer the personal relationship between stu-
> dents and staff in an institution, the lower the Darwinista rating.

iv.   Loss of motivation. But because dropout is such a complex phenome-
      non, sometimes a simple formulation can be helpful, such as that due to
      Anderson (2003) who said:

> The best predictor of student retention is motivation … most students drop out because of reduced motivation.

So motivation will be a principal focus of this chapter.

3 Taking Action

> Almost everything works. (John Hattie, Melbourne University, Australia)

So here you are about to start your new role as Director of Distance Learning. You have two main areas of distance learning over which you can have some effect in increasing student success:
– Distance course design
– Student support.

3.1 Designing Distance Courses to Increase Student Success

> When it comes to eLearning, content means everything. If eLearning content is not masterfully designed, all the rest will just go down the drain. (Christopher Pappas)

I'll assume that you won't have very much control over actual course content which will be determined by Faculty. But there will be areas that you can influence that critically affect student success. These might be:
– Course selection – how students are helped to choose the course
– Course workload – how much is in the course
– Course structure – how the course is organized
– Course assessment and feedback strategies – how students are assessed and given feedback
– Course psychological design – how the course motivates students to learn

As Director of Distance Learning your influence on these aspects of your institution's courses will be vital, as no amount of student support will overcome the problems of a retention-hostile course. So, it will be helpful to have access to course retention data.

Course retention data. Hopefully you'll have the ability to identify courses that have unduly high dropout or poor student feedback. One of my previous universities now uses a 'predicted probability of success' (see later) of students starting a course, to estimate what the retention rate should be on that course.

Course writers whose retention rates are considerably lower than predicted are politely asked if they know why.

While this is a sophisticated system, simply collecting the retention data for a course and approaching the writers of high dropout courses or courses with poor student feedback, may give you a chance to influence retention rates.

3.1.1   Course Selection and Retention

One of the most common reasons that students give for dropping out is the general issue of time – either being unable to find enough time to study or getting too far behind.

However, the second biggest reason that students often give for dropping out is that they were enrolled in the wrong course. There does not appear to be a great deal of attention paid to how distance students choose the right course for themselves ('right' in this case meaning that a student registers in a course with the content, level and pace most appropriate for them). I once suggested (Simpson, 2004) that distance institutions should explore the following devices for their efficacy in correct course choice:

– Taster materials – the ability to see samples of course material before enrolling
– Student course reviews – the ability to see previous students' reviews of a course
– Diagnostic materials – quizzes to enable prospective students to measure their readiness to take a particular course
– Course statistics – data about a course such as completion rates.

Diagnostic quizzes. Some years ago I used a binary logistic statistical program that enabled me to attach a 'predicted probability of success' (pps) to new students entering the University where I was working. It was based on the results and related characteristics of previous students and was reasonably accurate in forecasting which new students would eventually drop out (see later).

I went on to devise a diagnostic quiz which would allow a new student to work out their own pps before starting a course. But I was discouraged from piloting this on the grounds that it might unreasonably deter new students from enrolling – a 'recruitment versus retention' dichotomy.

'Recruitment versus retention dichotomy.' As the Director of Distance Learning, you may run into barriers if you introduce some of these concepts. In any institution there can be a 'recruitment versus retention' tension because:

- the wider you recruit the more likely you are to pick up students who will not succeed – the 'false positives' problem
- The more narrowly you recruit the more you exclude the 'false negatives' – student who although not picked up by your program could still have succeeded.

You may also meet questions from your institution's marketing department who will be uneasy at what they see as extra barriers to recruitment.

Query 3: Given no recruitment program is ever entirely accurate, which problem would you rather have – the 'false positives' or' false negatives'?

My thoughts: My background has always been in widening participation and access. So I'd be happier with the false positives. *But only as long as students had a reasonably good idea of their chances of success and how they could increase those chances.* I can also see the arguments for the false negatives approach as minimising the damage done by dropout (q.v.).

3.1.2 Course Workload

It's difficult to find clear evidence linking course workload with student dropout. Yet it would seem very likely that course workload will affect student completion rates, especially given the feedback from students about their time issues.

A number of years ago I taught a course on 'The Technology of Music.' It rapidly became clear that it was very overloaded for its credit rating. I thought it was a victim of 'course exuberance syndrome' – the course team who wrote the course couldn't resist throwing in everything that interested them. The dropout rate was very high and the course eventually had to be rewritten.

'Course exuberance syndrome' can be a serious problem for people writing online courses. It's very easy to add extra material to a course in the form of additional websites to visit, video and audio clips, social networking sites, podcasts, forums, extra reading lists and so on. But unless you're sure that such extras actually help students learn the course material more effectively, they may have the opposite effect and reduce retention – see Keller's 'Relevance' later.

The 'Student Workload Tool.' Recently the UK Open University developed a 'Student Workload Tool' which estimates the student workload for any module. It takes the various components in a module and assesses how long they should take. For example, the Tool suggests the following rage of study speeds according to the level of difficulty of the text:

- 20 words per minute (wpm) for extremely challenging texts – e.g. mathematical equations in text or for complex musical scores
- 35 wpm for challenging and concept-dense texts
- 70 wpm for medium texts
- 120 wpm for easy texts and
- 200 wpm for scanning texts – e.g. reading novels or skim reading other materials.

Other material such as visual images, tables, figures can also be assessed for study speed and an overall projected study proposed.

This program is in its early days and I'm not sure how accurately it measures actual student workload in practice. But as Director you might want to see if such a tool might work for you.

> *Query 4*: How fast do you think you're reading this chapter?
>
> *My thoughts*: I don't know how fast your reading speed is – I can only tell you that my writing speed is much, much slower … There are about 3000 words left from this point in this chapter which according to the Tool should take you about 40 minutes, allowing for quizzes and tables. You might like to time yourself and see if you think the Tool might be anywhere near accurate.

3.1.3   Course Structure

By course structure I mean the way the different elements of a distance course are organised together. As I suggest previously, in an on-line course it may be possible to overload a course with elements.

> My Technology of Music students used to tell me that it wasn't just the quantity of material, but the sheer number of new, different and often unrelated concepts that was the problem. It is easier to learn a large amount of material if it all relates together tightly.

Course structure might also cover the way that students are meant to navigate their way through the course – what they are required to do and when. Crook (2005, as cited in Simpson, 2008) analyzed a course which had remarkably high retention and compared it with similar courses in her university which had much lower retention rates. She came to the conclusion that flexibility is the key to a retention-friendly course – giving students a choice of how they navigate the course, in terms of material, time, and assessment. Perhaps distance students need flexibility to be able to fit their studies into their everyday lives.

3.2.4 Course Assessment and Feedback Strategies

Assessment drives learning: but assessment also drives dropout. (Anon)

There can be two kinds of assessments – summative and formative.

Summative assessment – used for grading. As Director of Distance Learning you are unlikely to have any say over assessment strategies, areas which Faculty tends to hold dear. However, although assessment is an essential part of any distance course, an assessment can also present a hurdle at which a student can fall. But if your student feedback is sufficiently precise you may be able to identify particular assessments in a course which are driving dropout. One of the simplest motivational theories is due to Eccles and Wigfield (2002):

Learning motivation

= (a student's assumed possibility of accomplishing a task) × (the perceived value of the task)
If either factor is zero then motivation is zero

So, assessments need to be carefully designed for appropriate difficulty at every stage of a course.

Formative assessment – informal feedback to students to allow them to check their understanding at any point, such as self-assessed quizzes. Professor John Hattie of New Zealand conducted a 'meta-survey' – that is surveys of surveys. His aim was to try to find out which of the many methods that can be used to improve learning have been most effective, by calculating their statistical 'effect size.' A sample from the top of the list of 195 effects is shown in Figure 13.4.

Hattie's analysis did not focus specifically on distance education, but I think his findings are very pertinent to the field. He found that almost all these methods had some positive effect. But what was important was the effect size. He found that the most effective teaching method is 'Teachers' Collective Efficacy' – essentially how far teachers believe together in their ability to make a difference to their students' learning.

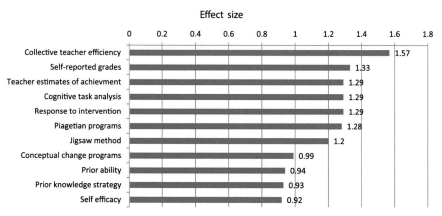

FIGURE 13.4   The top 11 most effective methods to improve learning out of 195 methods, analyzed with their effect size (from Hattie, 2008)

But it's the second of Hattie's effects that is the most important for distance course design. It's *'Self-Reporting'* – meaning that students must be given as many opportunities as possible to check on their progress – i.e. *that a student should know how well they're doing.* And there is a lot of evidence that formative assessment improves retention – for example Yorke (2004).

3.2.5   Course Psychological Design – How a Course Motivates Students
             to Learn
If student dropout is often due to a loss of the motivation to learn, is it possible to write course material that motivates students to complete it?
     There are a number of possible theories of motivational course design, but arguably one of the most useful is Keller's 'ARCS' theory.

3.2.5.1   *Keller's ARCS Theory*
Keller argues that for a course to motivate students to learn it must:
– Get their *A*ttention
– Ensure everything is *R*elevant to their needs
– Enhance their *C*onfidence in the process
– So that they are *S*atisfied with the outcomes.

i.   *Attention.* There are two aspects to students' attention – getting it and keeping it.
   – Getting attention. According to Keller there are a number of ways of getting attention, most importantly through:
       – Occasional incongruity – humour is the best example
       – Displaying empathy – difficult in text but stories and sharing personal thoughts can go some way
       – Authority – displaying expertise

Sometimes distance texts seem to take an opposite line:
– They are serious – humour seems to out of place
– They are written in impersonal terms, ignoring (for instance) that students may be feeling anxious about the material they're trying to learn.

Keeping attention probably needs the same qualities as getting attention, but with adding in 'readability' – matching text to students' reading skills. I once analyzed introductory courses at my own institution using the Flesch Reading Ease Score (FRES), a readability measure based on sentence length and number of syllables per word (see Table 13.1). (In the FRES the readability of a text increases with the score.)

TABLE 13.1   The Flesch reading ease scale – examples

Flesch reading ease score	Readability level	Education level	Example
0–29	Very difficult	College Graduates	Some insurance policies – 10
30–49	Difficult	College	Harvard Law review – 32
50–59	Fairly difficult	Senior High School	Time magazine – 52
60–69	Plain English	13 to 15 year-olds	Reader's Digest – 65
70–79	Fairly easy	12 year-olds	Tabloid newspaper – 71
80–89	Easy	11 year-olds	Some adverts – 82
90–100	Very easy	10 year-olds	Children's comics – 92

I found the initial 'Introduction to Distance Learning' was rated as 'Difficult.' Clearly at some point in their career students will have to be able to read texts rated as difficult. But it may not be wise to face them with such a text right at the beginning of their studies.

As yet there have been few attempts to relate readability to students' learning success. However, it is relatively easy to change the readability of a text without changing its level of academic content, by using shorter sentences, more frequent paragraphs and simpler vocabulary.

Query 5: how would you rate the readability of this chapter as far as you're concerned up to now – Very Difficult/Difficult/Fairly Difficult/Plain English?

My thoughts: The FRES of this text so far is 50.2 – right on the boundary between Fairly Difficult and Difficult. I'm a little disappointed by that; I was hoping to get nearer Plain English.

There are of course other differences which can make a text more readable such as layout (ragged right is often easier to read than justified left and right, even if it does not look as elegant), using columns (which shorten eye movements), text boxes, and frequent headings.

ii.   *Relevance.* See my comment in Confidence below about 'enlivening' elements in writing.

iii.   *Confidence.* Keller says students should have confidence in the text they are working with. For example in a survey of what qualities distance students wanted from their teachers (Gaskell & Simpson, 2000) the two most important by far were that teachers should be experts in the content of the course, but should also be 'approachable' – not intimidating, abrupt or status-conscious (expertise combined with approachability might be the qualities that you want from your doctor).

   Expertise and approachability in a text could be demonstrated through the backgrounds of the authors, and through expressions of personal stories, and acknowledgement of students' potential difficulties. So when writing a course I tend to use 'enlivening' elements – pictures, examples, jokes, cartoons, stories, games and even poems, as well as humor and personal stories to make a point – *as long as everything is relevant.* But I must also try to avoid sounding patronising.

iv.   *Satisfaction.* Keller's 'S' stands for Satisfaction – that a student should be satisfied with their learning experience. This echoes Professor John Hattie's findings on the importance of 'Self-reporting.'

3.2.5.2   *Other Theories*

Other theories of course design for success are available. And there are now motivational apps such as 'Study Bunny' to help students keep their motivation going while reading. But you needn't be an expert in learning design; you just need to know enough to help course writers write the most retention-friendly courses possible.

> Years ago I came across a course in my university that had very high dropout rate. Being young and even more naïve in the ways of academia than I am now, I contacted the writers to draw attention to their dropout rate. "Yes," they said, "We know it's high – it's a difficult course!"
>
> At that time I really had no reply. Now I think I would suggest (gently – hopefully I've at least learnt some tact in the last 40 years or so) that there didn't seem much point in offering a course that failed to teach anything. I might also (even more gently) wonder if it wasn't a little unethical to do so without at least warning the students that their chances of success were very low.
>
> Now I would wonder if the object of offering such a course wasn't more to enhance the prestige of the writers, than for any other reason. But I wouldn't say that out loud …

3.3 *Designing a Student Support Program for Success*

As Director of Distance Learning you are obligated to design your institution's student support program as well as influence its course design. But you will still be limited by several factors – most importantly your financial resources and the skills of your staff.

Resources. Your first task as director may be to copy Oliver Twist and ask for more. You will need to argue your case against opposition from other interests, so it will be very helpful to be able to carry out cost-benefit analyses. Hopefully these can show how your work increases retention, bringing in increased fee income from more students carrying on, which then makes a surplus for the institution.

You may also have to occasionally defend yourself against the inevitable round of cuts which seem to be characteristic of higher education the world over.

> In one of my previous institutions there were often rounds of cuts which seemed, to my biased eye, to focus largely on student support. No-one was doing a cost-benefit analysis to decide where cuts should occur so I had a go myself (Simpson, 2005).
>
> It turns out that it's pretty difficult to 'Follow the Money' in complex institutions, but it's not impossible. Universities often have access to highly talented mathematicians, accountants and statisticians so there's no reason not to try. After all if universities were real businesses they'd know exactly where to put their investment to produce the maximum output.

Staff skills. There are many books on staff development and it's too big a topic for this chapter. But one thing I've learnt from training any distance education staff, whether faculty, instructional designers or administators, is that the methods you use should reflect the methods you hope they will use. Or as Anderson (op. cit.) puts it 'Those who are expected to promote retention should have the same personal support as they are expected to give to students.'

3.3.1   Academic Support – Teaching

> Learning and teaching are not inherently linked. Much learning takes place without teaching, and indeed much teaching takes place without learning. (Jane Bozarth)

To begin, it's helpful to divide student support into two areas: 'academic support' – that is teaching, and 'non-academic support' – everything else.

By academic support I mean all the activity outside the course text that helps student learning, such as:
– Explaining the course – answering questions and clarifying queries
– Assessing and giving formal and informal feedback
– Chasing up student progress

Every institution I've worked at has administered its teaching differently, perhaps using adjunct or part time instructors. But whatever administration system you have, hopefully you will have some input into teaching in conjunction with faculties and instructional designers. You may for instance be able to appoint, monitor and train instructors.

'Category error.' But just one note: the word teaching has to be used carefully. Specifically, the term 'e-learning' is used very loosely, in what philosophers would call a 'category error.' When an organization says that it is doing 'e-learning,' it is really doing 'e-teaching.' E-learning is what the students are doing – we hope. It can have significant implications to confuse hoped-for-ends (learning) with the means to that end (teaching).

3.4   *Non-Academic Support*

> Student self-referral does not work as a mode of promoting retention. Students who need services the most refer themselves the least – Anderson. (op. cit.)

Support can be reactive – students asking for help, or proactive – reaching out to students to help.

3.4.1   Reactive Support – Responding to Students Asking for Help or
          Advice

Your unit will have to be able to be able to respond to the many and varied
queries students can pose:

- 'Can I submit this assignment late?'
- 'If I withdraw now will I get my fees back?'
- 'I'm going into the hospital next week – what can I do?' – and so on.

Queries will arrive by all kinds of media – email, phone, WhatsApp or VLE.
You might be under pressure to provide an out-of-hours service as students will
need quick answers. A student's dropout decision can be made very quickly so
your service will need to be prompt.

To ensure promptness and keep costs down you might be able to use
Artificial Intelligence like the Georgia Institute of Technology (2016) which
developed a program called 'Jill Watson.' It's now claimed she (it) can answer
student' questions with a 97% certainty. Students are said to not mind interacting with AI.

And of course you can provide all kinds of support materials online with
FAQ's to cover almost most eventualities. But although you must provide these
services, they may not have much effect on retention.

> My wife is a dyslexia adviser at our local university where her students defi-
> nitely need help – or, as one says, "I defiantly need help." She often points
> out to them that there is a huge range of learner support materials on the
> university's website. They are very surprised, having never looked. And even
> then she knows they won't use them.

3.4.2   Proactive Support

> Effective retention services take the initiative in outreach and timely
> interventions with those students. (Anderson, op. cit.)

If you decide to setup a contact program of proactive support there are a number of questions:

- what the content will be,
- how it will be organized,
- who it should be aimed at,
- how frequently,
- how much can you afford?

i.   Proactive support – content.
If motivation is the key in retention, what models of learning motivation might be most helpful? There are many to choose from – 'Self-Determination Theory,' 'Achievement Goal Theory,' 'Self-Efficacy Theory,' 'Epistemological Identity Theory' and 'Self-Concordance Model' among others. Some offer useful insights; for instance 'Epistemological Identity Theory' suggests that motivation depends on students feeling that they are doing exactly the right things for themselves – for example that they are on the right course for them.

There are two that are particularly helpful:

a.   *Self Theory* (Dweck, 1999). I'll illustrate Professor Dweck's theory by asking you two questions:

> Q1. You have a certain amount of intelligence and can't do much to change it. Answer True or False
> Q2. Success = X% intelligence + Y% effort. Give values for X and Y

What did you answer? Dweck says that if you said 'True' to 1 and your value of X > Y you may be an *'entity'* theorist.

If you said 'False' to 1 and your value of X < Y you may be an *'incremental'* theorist.

(If your value of X + Y didn't equal 100 do check your math …).

She further says:
'Entity' theorists believe that their intelligence is fixed and cannot be altered through effort. They will study but give up easily when they encounter difficulties or failure.

'Incremental' theorists' believe that intelligence is malleable and can be changed through effort.

Incremental theorists will keep trying despite initial difficulties or failure. They are therefore more likely to succeed overall.

Having tested her theory by teaching it to classes in New York school, Dweck found that there were positive effects on success that were 'far beyond what you might expect from the simplicity of the interventions.'

Dweck's theory implies that you need to persuade your students (and your staff) that they should be 'Incremental' theorists rather than 'Entity' theorists. (I see 'Darwinistas' and 'Fatalistas' being Entity theorists and 'Retentioneers' being Incremental theorists).

b.   *'Self Determination Theory.'* The other theory that might be helpful is Deci
      and Ryan's 'Self Determination Theory' (Ryan et al., 2000). Deci and Ryan
      claim that self-motivations are more important than external motiva-
      tions and that there are three innate needs for success:
      – C = Competence – an increasing competence increases motivation
      – A = Autonomy – having control over your learning
      – R = Relatedness – relationship with a person who cares about your
        learning.

      In distance education:
  – *Competence* – should increase steadily in a course that is well-designed with
    carefully graded feedback (Hattie, 2008).
  – *Autonomy* – an advantage of distance education is that a well-designed
    course can already offer some control over your education, at least in terms
    of distance and scheduling (Crook, 2005, as cited in Simpson, 2008).
  – *Relatedness* – this is where the real weakness of distance education arises.
    The challenge is to make distance education personal.

      So it's vital that your support be 'personalized.'

> In 2016 Ben Wildavsky of the Rockefeller Institute of Government in New
> York, wrote 'The UK Open University at 45: What can we learn from Brit-
> ain's distance education pioneer?' He thought its "biggest accomplishment
> is combining scale with personalization," and that *"for many students ... this
> personal relationship with an instructor is the key"* [emphasis added].
>   Alas, while Professor Wildavsky was right historically, in the last few
> years the UKOU has substantially damaged this personal link through cost
> cutting, adding (I believe) to the consequent decline in its graduation rates
> illustrated earlier.

iii.   Organizing proactive personalized support
       'We must reach the quiet student' (Bogdan, Eaton et al., 1995)
       You'll need to make a number of decisions within your budgetary con-
       straints:
       – *Who will make the contact?* Will it be full time staff or part-time adjunct
         faculty, perhaps combined with a teaching role? The contact will prob-
         ably work best if there is continuity, so that the same person makes
         the contact, whether they are called a student's counsellor, advisor, or
         'learning coach.'

The Open Polytechnic of New Zealand (OPNZ) has a section called 'Outward Bound' which Faculty can ask to make contact with students on their behalf. The section used a variety of part-time staff ranging from OPNZ retirees to young undergraduates from a local university. I heard one of these talking to a student on the phone. He was congratulating them on some achievement and saying "Wow! That's so cool. Totally awesome!"

I asked the Outward Bound manager if some OPNZ students (average age often about 40) felt patronized by this kind of thing. "Absolutely not" she said, "they love the enthusiasm these kids bring to the job."

- *What media will they use – phone, email VLE etc.?* Each will have its own cost and effectiveness with phone most costly but possibly most effective. At the University of London we used plain un-personalized emails and still got a modest but cost-effective retention increase (Inkelaar et al., 2015).
- *How frequently should contact be made?* That will be determined by experience. For example, in their particular situation Case and Elliot (1997) found that 2 to 5 phone calls per semester were the most effective.
- *Who should you contact?* This is more difficult – ideally you want to contact all your students. But your budget may not run to that. So perhaps you could focus on the most vulnerable where you might hope for the best results. But there are ethical issues here ...

Query 6: working in an open entry institution I once came across a student whose 'predicted probability of success' (see below) was only 10%. Should I have told him that and risked him giving up immediately? After all, the 10% figure just meant that he was in a group where only one in ten succeeded – he could be that one. Or should I keep mum and risk the high probability that he would waste his time and money and end up worse than before? Would you tell or not?

My thoughts: I copped out and didn't tell him. He failed.

The *'predicted probability of success model.'* A few years ago a tame statistician developed an algorithm (a binary logistic analysis) for me that enabled us to attach a 'predicted probability of success' (pps) to each of our 30,000 new

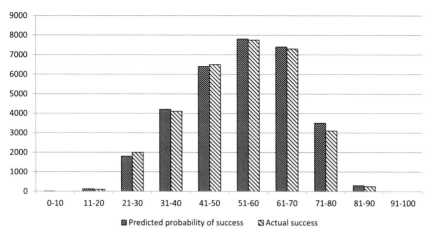

FIGURE 13.5   The number of students in each 'probability of success' band in that year

students each year at the start of their course. This prediction was based on previous students' characteristics such as age, sex, GPA and so on. The predictions turned out to be surprisingly accurate (see Figure 13.5) (Simpson, 2006).[4]

We used this result to make proactive phone contact starting with the students with the lowest predicted probability of success (our most vulnerable students) and working our way up the pps list till the budget ran out. We contacted about 2000 students and found a steady increase of around 5% in retention (Simpson, 2006). Not huge, but it was the result of just one phone call and had a return on investment of around 250%.

3.4.3   Other Sources of Support

Given your budget limitations and the large numbers you are probably dealing with, it will be important to look for other sources of support for your students. Asbee et al. (1998) asked students where they got their most important support. In order of importance it was (see Table 13.2):

TABLE 13.2   Where distance students get their support

Importance to students	Source
Most important	From families and friends
↓	From tutors/instructors
	From other students
Least important	From employers
	From the institution directly

i.   From families, friends, and employers. Despite its importance to students this seems often surprisingly neglected by many institutions. Yet it's important and free. So there should be a way of allowing students (if they wish) to tell families, friends, and employers what they're doing and how families and friends might best support them – usually motivationally. One route is through a dedicated website.

ii.   From instructors. This finding was in an institution that used adjunct faculty instructors and where there was a strong element of personalization.

iii. From other students. There are two ways in which students can help each other:

- Peer support – students on the same course helping each other in pairs or groups. There's a lot of emphasis on peer support in the distance education literature, but not always clear evidence of such support increasing student success. While it can be very motivational, I worry about pairs or groups when one or more students drop out. Will that actually demotivate the others? Nevertheless the use of online forums of one kind or another remains a key tactic in student support, although perhaps more important for humanities than science subjects?
- Mentoring support or 'Supplemental Instruction' – using previous students on a course to help new students on that course. There is evidence that this does increase retention. A project between New Zealand, South Korea and the UK increased retention with a positive return on investment, even given the substantial administrative time needed to set the program up (Boyle et al., 2010).

iv. From employers – perhaps by giving students material about how their employers can support them that they can give to their employers if they wish.

v.   From the institution itself – the fact that this is the least important source of support might tell us something about the importance of proactive support relative to reactive support.

3.4.4   Other Support Ideas

There are other support activities associated with student success that I've not addressed. This is because I believe well-designed courses and support programs will automatically develop them. For example there are activities that are:

i.   *Necessary but not sufficient.* These are activities that you must do, but which may not be sufficient to ensure student success, such as:

- *Online readiness classes.* While you must supply these, as Anderson (op. cit.) says "Don't expect non-credit materials to do what credit materials have to do." Or as I overheard at a US retention conference – "there's more to a party than issuing invitations."

- *Online learning skill materials.* As I argue previously these may not reach the students you need to reach. And as Morgan (1999) notes 'Learning skills training that does not consider motivation ... may result in little skill improvement.'

ii. *Necessary and will follow.* These are things that are necessary, but will follow if the program of proactive support is well developed, such as:
- Student engagement. Students will feel well-engaged with the institution if they receive proactive personalized support.
- Self-regulation. Students will regulate their learning if the courses they are taking are well-structured, the assessment systems are well designed and support is timely and appropriate.

3.4.5   Retrieval, Evaluation and Research

Finally there will be other things that you will be doing if you have the resource and which I haven't the space to cover:
- Retrieval. Getting dropped out students back on course, possibly at the next presentation.
- Evaluation. Developing appropriate criteria and evaluating your own performance.
- Research. Hopefully you will also find the resource to undertake and publish your own research. Publication isn't the prerogative of faculty! That research should include intelligence – keeping watch on what other people are doing.[5] As my old Sergeant Major used to say to me, "Laddie, time spent in reconnaissance is never wasted."

4   Recap

> Trying everything that works, doesn't work. (Johnston)

You can't do everything. And even if you could, how would you know which of the many things you were trying had been the most successful and cost-effective? So what might be your priorities in the two areas that most affect student success – Course Design and Student Support?

4.1   *Course Design*

Try to influence the development of retention-friendly courses in the following areas:
- Course selection – getting students on the right course for them
- Course workload – ensuring that the course workload is appropriate

- Course structure – monitoring how far the different parts of a course work together smoothly
- Course assessment – trying to ensure that the course assessment strategies encourage progress rather than drive dropout
- Course psychological design – encouraging course writers to make their courses motivational.

To help do that you can:
- monitor course retention data and student feedback.

You may also need diplomatic skills in working with faculty and instructional designers who will naturally have their own ideas about writing and design.

4.2   *Student Support*

Design a student support system which is:
- *Proactive* – reaching out to students rather than waiting for them to contact
- *Personalized* – helping students feel that there are people who know them and care about their learning
- *Prompt* – reacting to students' needs as promptly as possible.

Such a support system will enhance student engagement and consequence success.

To help students in large numbers with a small budget you may need to use mentoring or other sources of support.

> *Final query*: Have you found this chapter helpful?
>
> *My thoughts*: Obviously I hope that there's been something in this chapter that you've found interesting. You may well not be a Director of Distance Learning (at least not yet) but student success is the business of everyone in distance education, whatever your role.[6]

Finally: Good luck in your role whatever it may be! And remember the old saying "If everything you do works – you're not trying hard enough."

Notes

1   The other rates illustrated are a selection of those which are available from an international range of sources. They show that the retention rates for some distance institutions are in single figures.

2   I have used UK findings as I've not been able to find similar longitudinal US data. I believe
    that the effects of dropout will be broadly similar, not just in the US but in Europe.

3   Obviously some students dropped out because they became depressed, rather than becom-
    ing depressed because they had dropped out. We don't know the proportion.

4   This kind of analysis can reveal unexpected predictors. Johnston (2002) found that one pre-
    dictor of student success was taking paid work. Dropout was higher among students working
    more than 15 hours a week or not working at all. Dropout was least among students doing
    around 10 hours paid work a week.

5   Apart from AI, one development to watch will be the area of 'Learning Analytics.' As yet, I've
    not seen clear evidence of retention effects of LA.

6   If you'd like to read more or argue with me, you can read my book *Supporting Students for Suc-
    cess in Online and Distance Education* (Routledge), visit my website www.ormondsimpson.com
    or email me ormond.simpson@gmail.com

References

Anderson, E. (2003, July 13–16). *Retention for rookies* [Conference presentation]. National
    Conference on Student Retention.

APLU – Association of Public and Land-Grant Universites. (2015). *How do college grad-
    uates benefit society at large?* https://www.aplu.org/projects-and-initiatives/college-
    costs-tuition-and-financial-aid/publicuvalues/societal-benefits.html

Asbee, S., & Simpson, O. (1998). Partners families and friends. *Open Learning, 13*(3),
    56–59.

Bogdan E. S., & Bean, J. P. (1995). An approach/avoidance behavioral model of college
    student attrition. *Research in Higher Education, 36*(6), 617–645.

Boyle, F., Kwon, J., Ross, C., & Simpson, O. (2010). Student-student mentoring for reten-
    tion and engagement in distance education. *Open Learning, 25*(2), 115–130.

Bynner, J. (2001). *The wider benefits of higher education.* Report No. 01/46. Higher Edu-
    cation Funding Council for England. https://webarchive.nationalarchives.gov.uk/
    20091112203624/http://www.hefce.ac.uk/pubs/hefce/2001/01_46.htm

Case, P., & Elliot, B. (1997). Attrition and Retention in distance learning programs,
    problems strategies, problems and solutions. *Open Praxis, 1,* 30–33.

Dive, E. (2019). *How many nonprofit colleges and universities have closed since 2016?*
    Education Dive. https://www.educationdive.com/news/how-many-collegesand-
    universities-have-closed-since-2016/539379

Dweck, C. S. (1999). *Self-theories: Their role in motivation, personality, and development.*
    Taylor & Francis.

Eccles, J. S., & Wigfield, A. (2002). Motivational beliefs, values, and goals. *Annual Review
    of Psychology, 53,* 109–132. https://doi.org/10.1146/annurev.psych.53.100901.135153

Gaskell, A., & Simpson, O. (2000, March 16–17). *Tutors supporting students.* Research
    and Innovation in Open and Distance Learning: 1st EDEN Research Workshop,
    Prague. https://www.eden-online.org/eden_conference/eden-eventsresearch-
    workshopsprague-html/

Georgia Institute of Technology. (2016). Artificial Intelligence course creates AI teaching assistant [Press release]. http://www.news.gatech.edu/2016/05/09/artificial-intelligence-course-creates-ai-teaching-assistant

Greenberg, P. (2015). The Growing Economic Burden of Depression in the U.S. [Blog post]. https://blogs.scientificamerican.com/mind-guest-blog/the-growing-economic-burden-of-depression-in-the-u-s/

Grisham, J. (2017). *The rooster bar*. Double Day.

Hattie, J. (2008). *Visible learning: A synthesis of over 800 meta-analyses relating to achievement*. Routledge.

Inkelaar, T., & Simpson, O. (2015). Challenging the 'distance education deficit' through 'motivational emails'. *Open Learning, 30*(2), 152–163 https://doi.org/10.1080/02680513.2015.1055718

Johnston, V., & Simpson, O. (2006). Retentioneering higher education in the UK: Attitudinal barriers to addressing student retention in universities. *Widening Participation and Lifelong Learning, 8*(3), 28–36. https://www.ingentaconnect.com/content/openu/jwpll/2006/00000008/00000003/art00004

Keller, J. M. (2010). *Motivational design for learning and performance: ARCS model approach*. Springer.

Kessler, R. (2012). The costs of depression. *Psychiatric Clinics of North America, 35*(1). https://doi.org/10.1016/j.psc.2011.11.005

Lederman, D. (2018, June 20). Online options give adults access, but outcomes lag. *Inside Education*. https://www.insidehighered.com/digital-learning/article/2018/06/20/online-education-gives-adults-access-student-outcomes-lag#.WypGgexaCY8.twitter

Morgan, C., & Tam, M. (1999). Unravelling the complexities of distance education student attrition. *Distance Education, 20*(1), 96–108. https://doi.org/10.1080/0158791990200108

Organisation for Economic Cooperation and Development (OECD). (2020, June, 18). *Resourcing higher education – Challenges, choices and consequences*. https://tinyurl.com/y2p5jugf

Ryan, R., & Deci, E. (2000). Self-determination theory and the facilitation of intrinsic motivation, social development, and well-being. *American Psychologist, 55*(1), 68–78. https://doi.org/10.1037110003-066X.55.1.68

Simpson, O. (2004). Student retention and the course choice process. *Journal of Access Policy and Practice, 2*(1). https://www.researchgate.net/publication/42795979_Student_Retention_and_the_course_choice_process_the_UK_Open_University_experience

Simpson, O. (2005). The costs and benefits of student retention for students, institutions and governments. *Studies in Learning Evaluation Innovation and Development (Australia), 2*(3), 34–43 http://oro.open.ac.uk/6761/

Simpson, O. (2006). Predicting student success. *Open Learning, 21*(2), 125–138
     https://www.researchgate.net/publication/42792547_Predicting_student_success_
     in_open_and_distance_learning

Simpson, O. (2008). Motivating learners in open and distance learning: Do we need a
     new theory of learner support? *Open Learning, 23*(3). https://doi.org/10.1080/
     02680510802419979

Simpson, O. (2013). *Supporting students for success in online and distance education.*
     Routledge.

Tinto, V. (2007). Research and practice of student retention: What next? *Journal of Col-
     lege Student Retention, 8*(1), 1–19.

Trakhman, L. (2019). *Medium matters: The effects of print and digital texts on comprehen-
     sion.* https://impact.chartered.college/article/medium-matters-effects-print-digital-
     texts-comprehension/

Yorke, M., & Longden, B. (2004). *Retention and student success in higher education.*
     McGraw-Hill.

CHAPTER 14

Support Technologies

Tonia A. Dousay and Cassidy S. Hall

Abstract

At the conclusion of this chapter, you will be better prepared to administer the following:
- Select relevant technologies to design, organize, and deliver an engaging distance learning experience depending upon the affordances and constraints at your institution
- Design and assess learning in a distance learning context using the appropriate traditional or authentic tools and strategies
- Curate and produce media for digital engagement and content presentation following ethical and legal guidelines
- Conceptualize ways to personalize learners' distance learning experiences using established practices and emerging trends in technology.

Keywords

selecting technology – assessment technologies – digital ethics – campus technologies – distance learning technologies

1 Introduction

Thinking about or even engaging in a discussion on support technologies for distance learning may sound daunting. However, it need not be if you break the task into three main categories: hardware and equipment; learning design, delivery, and access; and personalizing the learning experience. Beginning with hardware and equipment, you can start to envision baseline needs to design and deliver quality distance learning for a variety of modalities. Attention to the design, delivery, and access aspects helps fine-tune the hardware and equipment decisions, scoping outward to consider the design and delivery and how we access the variety of resources involved in learning today. Digital ethics also informs several decisions related to curating and producing media for distance learning. Lastly, trends in personalizing the learning experience reveal exciting possibilities with artificial intelligence and learning analytics to address motivation and persistence challenges. We conclude this chapter with a caution to remember the parallel administrative decisions in tandem with selecting technologies and a checklist to help you plan and administer these three categories based on your institution's needs.

2   Hardware & Equipment

It may help to frame hardware and equipment needs in terms of three contexts. First, think about the faculty who teach their courses from a desktop or laptop computer. Second, consider specialty rooms explicitly designed with video conferencing or streaming in mind. Third, don't forget to recognize the value of traditional lecture halls and multipurpose classrooms. With these three contexts in mind, you can focus on video and audio demands relevant to learning environment constraints, instructor/learner needs, and other accessories and space configurations.

Every master needs the proper environment in which to practice their craft. For example, you likely wouldn't ask a chef to prepare a three-course meal outdoors without any pots or pans. Similarly, a mechanic can work on a vehicle more efficiently and effectively when provided access to a proper garage with tools. As educators, we also need learning environments equipped with a few necessities. The face-to-face classroom has long retained a basic appearance, but this is changing in the wake of distance learning that encourages flexibility.

Consider the following questions:

1. When you think of a typical classroom at your institution, what furniture is present, and how is it configured? What technologies are commonly or occasionally available?
2. Does your institution have special rooms designed for distance learning, or have you encountered these kinds of layouts?
3. What accessories do you prefer having available when you participate in video conferences?

From specialty to multipurpose classrooms and faculty workstations, the necessary hardware and equipment to sustain quality distance learning experiences bear careful consideration. Regarding budgets, these components often represent a significant expense as maintenance and upkeep are also necessary.

FIGURE 14.1
Physical spaces

Administrators must first tackle the necessary technology for video and audio needs in all three contexts. Standard workstations for faculty and course designers often provide the hardware required for the first context. However, the second context requires careful planning that may inform or otherwise support the third context. Those designing specialty rooms to support distance learning, especially synchronous video, should consider overall floorplans and furniture layout to determine video needs. For example, wide spaces might need panoramic or 360 video cameras, and larger rooms may need multiple stationary cameras or pan-and-tilt cameras, responsive to audio for dynamic displays.

Similarly, quality audio pickup, transmission, and playback require microphones and speakers distributed throughout classrooms. Current microphone array systems take the place of previous methods with distributed mics with user controls. These systems also integrate with dynamic video cameras for the responsive capability noted previously. Without these kinds of integrated technologies, administrators must consider using stand-alone web cameras and microphones or multidirectional microphones with panoramic cameras, such as the Meeting Owl from Owl Labs, to accomplish the same tasks. Although integrated systems cost more, these expenses typically include service and support contracts, whereas custom systems created with independent technologies cost less but require more independent support. The other benefit of an integrated system lies in the ability to connect with control systems increasingly found at teaching stations to ease switching between different inputs or displays.

Accessories require additional attention to enhance the quality of the distance learning delivery environment and likely arise more often concerning the first context (faculty workstations). Accessories refer to the extra equipment that helps with particular aspects of teaching online. Consider how most faculty offices are not well-lit or at least not designed with video conferencing and production in mind. To this end, some faculty may need portable LED lighting in the form of a clip-on desk or ring lamp to illuminate their faces while on camera and reduce shadows. Similarly, although many video conferencing platforms now offer built-in features to obscure surroundings or use virtual backgrounds for privacy, some faculty may need to use portable or fixed green screens. These setups allow a presenter to dynamically present other digital content that can be inserted post-production, facilitating unique learning experiences. Additional accessories may be desirable based upon discipline-specific practices, and faculty should be consulted when making decisions about what to use.

Space configurations affect all three contexts and refer to the orientation and layout of equipment. In the first context, faculty workspace, special considerations may need to be applied to audio to address constraints, such as lack of privacy and constant background noise (offset by noise-canceling headphones, quality microphones, and features in software). The use of accessories can also enhance video, depending upon the relative brightness of the workspace, and engagement. These accessories might include a second monitor of equal or greater size to facilitate ease of access and interaction during video conference meetings that require split attention on chat windows, participant reactions, and content presentations/shared screens.

In the second context, rooms specially designed for distance learning, administrators might refer to the HOTS (Zydney et al., 2019) or e-SyMS (Dousay et al., 2019) models for potential room layouts, including seating arrangement and audio/video placement. For traditional and multipurpose classrooms, the third context, keep in mind the possible need to retrofit these spaces with the audio and video recommendations described previously. Additionally, be prepared to re-examine how seating and tables are arranged in these spaces, potentially necessitating a shift to flexible and portable furniture or recommended seating charts to cluster learners appropriately for distance learning enhanced classes.

3   Learning Design, Delivery, & Access

This section, like some models of learning design, begins with the end in mind, assessing the learner, including identity management (see Chapter eight). From here, the discussion flows into associated media to support the learning content (producing and curating). With design considered, attention shifts to delivery and the technologies for collaboration and engagement. Lastly, the section addresses access to tools and courses by way of learning management systems and campus portals.

3.1   *Assessment*
The nature of distance learning contributes to new forms of interactions and assessment, generated through engagement, and by extension, student expectations for continuous feedback and varied types of assessment (Markova et al., 2017). Further, we need to remember that a fundamental difference exists between testing and assessment. Testing, often in the form of formal or standardized exams and a kind of assessment, involves precise procedures to administer and score; whereas, assessment includes all measures of the various ways in which learners achieve and perform (Dikli, 2003). Additionally, Gibbs and Simpson (2004) remind us that assessment must prioritize supporting

learners instead of measuring outcomes. Thus, this section addresses support technologies and relevant factors for testing (traditional approaches to assessment) and authentic forms of assessment encountered in distance learning contexts. Of note, administrators should ensure that supported platforms and services allow faculty and course designers to use both types of assessments as appropriate to the context and course goals.

Think about the different types of assessments you've experienced as a learner. Perhaps traditional or standardized testing comes to mind, with multiple-choice scantron or computer-based tests. Related, maybe you've experienced some of the more innovative question types with hotspot images, drag and reorder statements, or matching. Perhaps you enjoyed more authentic forms of assessment, such as inquiry projects that allowed you to create and express yourself with evaluation through a rubric.

Consider the following questions:

1. As a learner, what types of assessments do you find most engaging and useful? Traditional or authentic?
2. Have you ever had to take a proctored exam or verify your identity (in person or online)? What was that like, or what do you think it would be like?
3. What concerns do you have about assessment in distance learning?

Even the most experienced educators feel challenged by assessment. The shift into distance learning brings changes in how we communicate, interact, and assess, adding additional challenges. Administrators and faculty must simultaneously attend to the technological logistics as well as quality assessment designs.

FIGURE 14.2
Making the grade

Traditional assessment technologies include exam building platforms or internal capabilities of a learning management system. Identity/integrity management and test proctoring are the two primary issues when considering distance learning assessment technologies. The field of distance learning generally accepts two fundamental approaches to mitigate identity and integrity management. First, clear academic dishonesty policies must be drafted and made available to students (Simonson et al., 2019). Second, quality instructional design practices should incorporate authentic assessment strategies, such as collaborative projects, and e-portfolios and requiring drafts or formative components of final projects, to mitigate identity and integrity challenges (Bobak et al., 2004; Teclehaimanot et al., 2017). However, verifying student identity in distance learning rose to the top of administrators' priority lists with the passage of the Higher Education Opportunity Act (HEOA) in August 2008 (Aceves & Aceves, 2009).

The HEOA policy shift resulted in a need for distance learning administrators to recognize two critical factors for identity management: connecting institutional electronic records of a learner with their real identity and creating a way for the learner to link to and access their digital files (McConahay & West, 2012). The three additional considerations interconnecting with these factors include Family Educational Rights and Privacy Act (FERPA) compliance (ensuring that only approved individuals have access to records and intended recipients receive communication), accreditation concerns (accurately reporting identity management practices as supported by quality evidence), and cybersecurity (maintaining system integrity and protection against identity theft). Unfortunately, McConahay and West (2012) noted a lack of common practices or standards in identity proofing. This shortcoming gave way to TIER (Internet2, 2020), "a community-driven effort to develop a consistent approach to identity and access management (IAM) that simplifies campus processes and advances inter-institutional collaboration and research" (para. 2). Supported by a four-institution community investor council, TIER provides a federated management system to meet the demands of identity and access management. Additionally, the network supports these technologies' evolving needs through ongoing research with partners and the adoption of the system by new partners (see Woodbeck, 2019). Though the technical requirements of assessment begin with identity management, administrations must also tend to the more detailed nuances of traditional assessments, such as test and exam creation, proctoring, digital grading, and authorship assurance.

3.1.1   Traditional Assessments

Test creation, and to some extent delivery, can take one of two approaches. First, some exam creation and delivery tools accompany or integrate with digital textbook packages from publishers (such as Pearson's MyLab and Mastering products). Second, others originate within or integrate with the learning management system, such as native exam/quiz creators or third-party systems (such as Top Hat). Deciding which approach to use depends upon internal policy on course design and delivery, though administrators should generally allow for the most flexibility so that a variety of test question types are available. To aid administrators with the everyday challenges of proctoring, learning management systems (LMS) moved to make it possible for third-party providers to integrate with their platforms. Respondus, Examity, and Proctor U produce proctoring tools commonly integrated with LMSs to make it easier for administrators and faculty to implement proctored tests.

Decisions regarding digital grading for traditional assessments often turn to automated essay scoring (AES), as test and exam builders often include automatic scoring based on the co-constructed answer key. It bears noting that AES, as successfully implemented in a variety of proprietary assessment contexts such as college and graduate school entrance exams, focuses on assessing general writing quality. Products in this market include Intellimetric, eRater, and Project Essay Grade (PEG®), and their specifications all emphasize the use of human-scored writing samples as training evidence to build a model. Thus, the resources and time necessary to generate a reliable and valid model on every essay question possible are not practical, nor should we consider standardizing all essays across disciplines for easy assessments. However, AES technologies may find a home with formative assessment, serving to support written communication development in general as a core educational outcome. In this case, practices include making tools such as Grammarly available to learners and adding the eRater features of Turnitin as assessment evaluation tools to assist faculty in their feedback processes.

Given the wide variety of approaches now available, authorship assurances run tangential to digital grading decisions. The inclusion of third-party tools throughout this discussion highlights the robust market that supports assessment and feedback in general. Just like Turnitin integrates eRater to assess writing quality, it also serves to verify authorship, comparing the submission to millions of other assignments and publicly available documents to evaluate academic integrity. Administrators should carefully consider all technologies available for these purposes, however. Ongoing efforts to maintain students' data privacy and intellectual property protections should be carefully considered when deciding on which tools to adopt. Administrators seeking strategies for authorship assurances should consult Amigud et al.'s (2018) comprehensive overview of approaches to plagiarism detection, traditional proctoring, remote proctoring, behavioral biometrics, instructor validation, computer lockdown, network monitoring, instructional design, and policy.

3.1.2 Authentic Assessments

Authentic assessments in distance learning can take many forms, given the ability to connect within and across platforms and tools. Formative assessment transforms through social interaction when students use whiteboards or collaborative document creation to share their processes and thoughts. These same tools help bring together teams of students as they conduct group projects, documenting their processes, and preparing final reports and presentations. Other applied projects, individual or collaborative, might connect learners with industry-standard software and require them to complete performance-based tasks they might encounter in the workforce. Additionally, the use of discussions in distance learning takes on new dimensions when allowed to flourish with quality designed prompts and/or the use of media-enhanced responses with videos or third-party tools like Flipgrid and VoiceThread. Within some LMSs, course designers and faculty may use electronic portfolio systems to encourage the use of performance-based measures and student artifacts, such as papers, presentations, and other supporting media to demonstrate achievement and growth. Portfolios can be used individually within a single course or comprehensively, across a student's career to express their total development while enrolled. These examples highlight only a few approaches to authentic assessment but also reveal a wide variety of technological capabilities necessary, though these are all capabilities widely available. Administrators should note that some of the tools mentioned here, e.g., Flipgrid, have an internal evaluation or scoring mechanism that might be integrated into the LMS or other grading systems.

Underlying all of these authentic assessment options is a need to ensure objective assessment through quality rubrics. Much has been written about rubrics and approaches to their construction, including how to draft criteria and quality levels (see Brookhart, 2013; Mertler, 2001). This section focuses on technological considerations related to rubrics. Though LMSs inherently include rubric building settings for assessment, administrators may find value in referencing or incorporating third-party resources to help faculty and course designers generate quality rubrics. Systems like RubiStar are favored by some faculty for discipline-specific templates. Other tools like iRubric and Quick Rubric offer fast solutions to conceptualize and build criteria tables with quality measurement statements. The rubrics generated may be imported into some LMS assignments or grade book settings or manually added.

Once rubrics are added to an LMS, some administrators may find value in ways to assess the quality of rubrics used as part of the broader institutional assessment strategy. Work by Arcuria et al. (2019) shows promising evidence of combining baseline quality expectations with LMS-derived features to generate a score on rubrics for such approaches. Ultimately, all decisions regarding assessment tools need to take into account institutional needs to aggregate and report data for various reasons and stakeholders. Thus, strategic administrators will take note of how systems communicate and share data.

3.2   *Media Curation, Production, & Sharing*

Media used in and generated for course content take many forms. From text to static/dynamic images to video, we have a variety of ways to present and consume learning content. We also must attend to the accessibility of these media for our learners. However, we must briefly examine digital ethics before any discussion can look at the technologies related to producing, curating, or even distributing media.

Think about an instructional video that you've watched. If it's been a while, visit YouTube and search for something you find interesting, such as how to tie a fishing fly or how to cook your favorite dish.

Consider the following questions:

1. What do you think it took to create the video? What kinds of cameras or lighting might have been needed?
2. Have you ever produced a video, including editing and publishing to a website? Did you enjoy the process or find it difficult? Why or how?
3. Have you ever used images you've found online in your lessons? What are your assumptions about copyright and educational use?

Before we can explore how to curate and produce media for distance learning, we must first examine the digital ethics underlying the process. A solid foundation in good practices then forms the basis for how to select and/or create other media, ensuring accessibility for all learners.

FIGURE 14.3
Lights, camera,
action!

3.2.1   Digital Ethics & Media

In this case, digital ethics refers to copyright, one of the more complicated and contentious challenges for educators in the digital era. Where educational use of media once felt safe and familiar, the provisions in the Digital Millennium Copyright Act (DMCA) complicated definitions, effectively rendering intent or prior/alternative access moot (Sharp, 2008). Further, provisions of the Technology, Education and Copyright Harmonization (TEACH) Act place requirements on institutions that are no longer dismissible with well-meaning intentions (Crews, 2002). Institutions have responded with the necessary policy changes and gate-keeping mechanisms, such as requiring student or faculty credentials to sign-in and access materials. Still, obtaining full permissions to use some media can be cumbersome and less than ideal.

To address this challenge, institutions increasingly turn to open education resources (OER) as an alternative to traditionally copyrighted materials. OER refers to content that is open in terms of cost and permissions related to copyright (Wiley et al., 2007). The resource (e.g., book, article, image, or video) is free to access and may also be reused, revised, remixed, and/or redistributed. Creative Commons licensing provides simplified guidance for determining which permissions are allowed. Generally speaking, all Creative Commons licenses require attribution. However, other permissions may be granted or controlled, such as allowing derivative works that must be similarly licensed, restricting open use to non-commercial contexts, or restricting all derivative works (OER Commons, 2018).

OER licensing applies when sourcing content from third parties and producing content internally. When sourcing OER, administrators can turn to popular repositories. Now in the dozens, OER repositories can house everything from entire courses to individual images and everything in between. Some repositories may focus on types of content, such as promoting complete courses or textbooks, whereas others may serve to make individual lessons and activities available. Still, others focus on specific content such as images and videos or data sets. All of these categories represent opportunities to capitalize on existing quality content to use in course design. Depending upon the source platform of an OER, it may be possible to take advantage of integrations with campus systems to easily use or remix materials. For example, the open publishing platform PressBooks allows users to remix textbooks, where permissions have been granted, and combine sections and/or chapters of different books into a new text that can be assigned through an LMS. Administrators should check with institutional library services to determine what existing services and tools for OER are currently under testing or adopted.

Speaking of quality, it bears mentioning that repositories increasingly have vetting or reviewing processes in place, and designers should take these into consideration when curating OER. Media selection processes should take into consideration quality control (pre-publication peer reviews and/or field testing), beta versioning (testing in related contexts), editability of source files (for derivative needs), version control (tracking significant revisions), and the publishing process (how the resource was produced for sharing), as these details contribute to determining suitability for your context (Walz & Guimont, 2019). Additionally, selection should attend to available reviews and ratings as well as the Creative Commons license granted, to ensure compliance. These same considerations apply when creating media, regardless of whether or not the intent is to catalog course content. Designers should begin by assigning a license to the media,[1] and completing the guided tool to generate a Creative Commons license based on the intended use. The media should also undergo an internal quality control review before being added to an OER repository, whether internal or as part of a popular repository.

Regardless of whether an institution chooses to use or produce OER, digital ethics must be attended to concerning media used and created for distance learning. Administrators should consult with institutional library services to determine what policies and practices might exist regarding how to curate and integrate digital subscriptions, including texts or other media. Additionally, some institutions may have staff or units dedicated to OER-related initiatives, such as open data or publishing, that should be consulted for strategic decision making.

3.2.2   Media Production

Standard media production needs refer to the technologies that all designers and faculty might need, whereas specialty production needs typically apply to a smaller subset of users. Concerning standard requirements, most workstation computers provided to faculty or course designers likely have all of the capabilities necessary to create presentations, record brief videos, and distribute this content. However, if systems need to be retrofitted with peripherals or other reasons dictate the need, standard media production technologies should allow for medium quality as opposed to production quality, and video and audio recording at a minimum. Medium quality refers to the general availability of a multidirectional microphone (either as part of the computer or external) and standard definition camera (either built-in to the display screen or external). Additionally, don't forget to address the lighting issues described previously in this chapter and storage for draft media and source files for later editing.

Specialty needs might include a high definition camera for videos intended to be archived or re-purposed or greenscreens for dynamic presentations. Similarly, your institution may require rapid eLearning authoring tools, such as Articulate 360 or Lectora, though these tools are more likely to be encountered in industry training. Increasingly, faculty and course designers also find value in screencasting. This particular aspect might be considered a specialty since faculty and designers often design these media as one-off products. The software products of this type have varied over the years, but making one of these tools available along with the hosting of videos and animated gifs should be considered. Some institutions may find success in hosting media embedded within their LMS or on another cloud storage service, especially if they have access to Microsoft Stream or YouTube through enterprise licensing.

Other visual media, such as photos, illustrations, and infographics, serve essential purposes in distance learning and require additional considerations. Whether curating or creating, commonly available software, such as Adobe Creative Cloud, provides easy access to editing and modifying files, regardless of file type. Additionally, browser-based tools like Adobe Spark and Canva allow creators to consider a variety of layout and presentation styles. Similarly, tools such as LucidChart help designers quickly create technical diagrams.

Many of these tools and services continue to offer reduced or free versions for educational purposes or operate on freemium models (see Segal, 2019). Administrators might consider promoting (or creating) internal design style guides and quality message design practices through professional development and templates. These efforts serve to reinforce good learning design and brand management with our increasingly digital creations.

Don't forget to consider student creativity in the media curation and production discussion. Active learning strategies increasingly encourage students to create media in addition to consuming it. Many of the technologies and tools described previously are also necessary for learners to complete their learning activities. Thus, consider adapting some of this advice into student guides and making the same technologies available to learners. For example, students may benefit from access to Adobe Creative Cloud or LucidChart to complete course assignments.

3.2.3 Media Accessibility

We cannot stress enough the importance of ensuring all media produced follow accessibility guidelines. New administrators or administrators unfamiliar with accessibility guidelines and practices for media may find value in a few different resources. The W3C Web Accessibility Initiative's (2019) making audio and video media accessible design and development guide should accompany or integrate with any internal design processes. Additionally, a variety of accessibility checking tools make verifying media easier for designers and faculty. For example, Blackboard Ally integrates with many LMSs and quickly scans all media within a course, generating score reports with suggestions for improving the accessibility of individual files. This tool can self-develop designer and faculty accessibility awareness as they follow the prompts to improve the quality of their images, documents, and videos. Lastly, design processes practicing universal design for learning can mitigate many accessibility issues (CAST, 2018). This discussion highlights the need for a strategic approach to accessibility, making it a priority when discussing what technologies to adopt and how to ensure quality and equal access.

3.3 Collaboration, Exploration, and Engagement

Collaboration, exploration, and engagement all form foundational pillars of active learning. When Veletsianos (2020) described interactivity, engagement, participation, practice, community, and student agency as elements of excellent online courses, he also provided a framework for thinking about the necessary support technologies to accomplish these goals. Native LMS features, video conferencing, and integrated communication used in tandem with cloud-based productivity tools (e.g., G Suite and Office 365) represent the necessary foundation for this framework. Building off of these experiences, serious games, simulations, and mixed realities represent the next level of interactivity and engagement. Lastly, we must also shape the framework with attention to digital wellbeing in these spaces.

Think about favorite learning experiences you've experienced throughout your life and career. You might be envisioning something from high school, or more likely, your undergraduate preparation. Think about other experiences like graduate school or professional development opportunities.

Consider the following questions:

1. What were the personality characteristics of the instructors and facilitators who came to mind?
2. How were the content and other resources presented? Were they made available to you during and/or after the experience?
3. How much did you get to interact with your classmates, and in what ways?

Good learning design incorporates active learning strategies to engage students in the process, capitalizing on social interactivity with all members of a learning community. This statement encompasses all course designs, regardless of modality. However, the strategies we might use in distance learning involve a wide variety of applications and software.

FIGURE 14.4
Distributed active learning

3.4   *Foundational Technologies*

Interactivity in distance learning can take many forms. Text- and video-based, threaded discussions native to many LMSs, or integrated with third-party tools, allow community discussions to blossom when designed expertly with quality prompts. Related to LMS features, some integrations feature additional tools like interactive textbooks or puzzle builders. Video conferences allow for synchronous engagement and now integrate with unified platforms or exist separately from these entities. Administrators should consider all of the potential ways in which video conferencing might be of use to the institution, including educational (one on one meetings, small groups, large groups, formal learning, non-formal learning, webinars, etc.) and business needs. Perhaps underutilized, integrated communication through unified platforms also provides opportunities for engagement.

Examples here include Microsoft Teams, Slack, and Discord. These platforms facilitate small community interactions, perfect as microlearning environments, to exchange ideas and track documentation. Microsoft Teams integrates with Office 365; but organizations using G Suite from Google might consider Slack or Discord, which both offer integrations. Do not forget to discuss local and regional bandwidth constraints when implementing these technologies. Many rural learners still lack adequate broadband access, and existing high-speed networks face an aging infrastructure (Shein, 2019).

Further considerations regarding these technologies include network privacy and security, including tracking users and storing and sharing recordings. Administrators need to consult current security and privacy guidelines, especially as they pertain to encryption when making decisions regarding platforms and system-level settings. As with all technologies, rapid advancements and new releases continuously bring to light new challenges and unintended consequences requiring vigilance and due diligence. Also, keep in mind that the more restrictive system-level settings are, the less flexibility faculty and designers have with using these tools. For example, some video conferencing tools allow for attendee attention tracking. An institutional policy to activate such a feature institution-wide may not consider how it might compromise a learning community or provide an invalid measure considering there are legitimate reasons for the video conference window not being the "active window." Thus, administrators must balance maintaining protocols, respecting learners' privacy, and encouraging creativity with course designs.

3.4.1   Enhanced Technologies

Games and simulations should also receive attention when considering how learners might engage and practice their learning. When evaluating games, be sure to clarify the difference between game-based learning and games for learning. Any of the technologies described in this chapter might be connected to engage learners in a game-based learning approach. However, games for distance learning might involve using massive multiplayer online roleplaying games (MMORPGS) (Childress & Braswell, 2007) or other PC, mobile, or video games (Demirbilek, 2009). Similarly, simulations bring a variety of opportunities for students to engage with and practice content. Subjects from business to science (labs), and everything in between, benefit from the use of simulations, and distance learning contexts make it easy to integrate these activities into the learning experience (Dede et al., 2017; Ferrero & Piuri, 1999; Gibson et al., 2014; Lamont, 2001).

Games may take the form of web-based apps or platform-based software. Simulations may be independent apps, web-based activities, or immersive platforms. Complicating this discussion, note that simulations may be configured within virtual reality environments, as discussed later in this chapter. These varied formats do pose challenges for administrators, particularly concerning account creation/maintenance and student records/data privacy. However, the constraints are not barriers to adoption. Strategies to mitigate these constraints include using platforms or tools that integrate with existing data management systems or using games and simulations that do not store student information.

Among enhanced technologies, extended realities likely pose the most interest and confusion for administrators. The following terms and definitions may help. All of the real and virtual components of the learning environment represent extended reality (XR). To this end, we might consider a learner in a completely LMS-based distance learning program in an XR learning environment. In other words, the virtual discussions and interactions happen through their real environment (their personal devices). XR becomes more complex when we add in additional technologies like wearables, such as trackers, headsets, or immersive goggles.

Shifting to these additional technologies, virtual reality (VR) includes all virtual experiences, such as those filmed in 360 videos and images or computer-generated videos and images. For example, you can use your smartphone to take a 360 photo of a landscape. This photo could then be used in geology or geography class to introduce or convey a particular concept. Be sure to include the potential for VR content when making decisions related to media production.

When we take computer-generated virtual content and overlay it on to the real world, augmented reality (AR) alters our perception of information. Pokémon Go illustrates a well-known example of society and education embracing AR for both learning and fun (Rauschnabel, 2017). Other areas of application include architecture and design. Drawing from the retail industry and apps from companies like Home Depot and IKEA, consider the ability to hold your smartphone, see replicas of artifacts or environmental features, and interact with them to enhance your learning. Continuing this line of thought, mixed reality (MR), represents the highest level of virtual interactivity in which computer-generated objects (AR or VR) impact the physical environment and vice versa. More simply, all mixed reality is augmented reality, but not all augmented reality is mixed reality. In other words, AR is composite and static, whereas mixed realities are interactive.

Administrators considering these enhanced technologies may have concerns regarding specialized hardware required for access. Thankfully, rapid technological advancements contribute to these baseline capabilities in ubiquitous tools readily available on the consumer market. For example, CNET's (n.d.) Virtual Reality 101 guide promotes Google Cardboard, Samsung Gear VR, Oculus Rift, HTC Vive, and Sony PlayStation VR to work with popular smartphones,

PCs, and gaming consoles. Smartphone VR experiences are usually app-spe-
cific. For PCs, virtual reality might take the form of web-based applications
or stand-alone applications, such as Minecraft and AltSpaceVR (accessible
through Steam). Other accessories, such as 360 treadmills or haptics, extend
the virtual learning experience but represent more advanced designs beyond
this text's scope.

Note that all of these collaboration, exploration, and engagement tools do
not supplant distance learning but comprise one aspect of the distance learning
environment in a holistic approach. Further, some disciplines, such as medical
and STEM education, use these foundational and enhanced technologies extensively, and colleagues within these fields have much experience to contribute by
way of mitigating technical and ethical challenges (Craig & Georgieva, 2018a).
For example, administrators must consider how policy and practice intersect
with harassment; student data, privacy, and consent; accessibility; and access
through learning with these technologies (Craig & Georgieva, 2018b).

3.5 *Learning Management Systems*

Up to this point, the discussion has focused mainly on technologies that
require accessing a variety of systems, apps, or other resources. The formal
distance learning environment, though virtual, typically involves a delivery
mechanism that organizes these technologies. In the broader history of distance learning, we might discuss delivery via postal service, radio, or broadcast
television. Learners could complete lessons or entire courses by mailing away
for printed materials and forms or submitting verification of their participation in a radio or television lecture. In the modern technologically-enhanced
era, learning management systems (LMS) serve as the primary mode of distance learning delivery (Sulun, 2018). An LMS serves as the primary gateway by
which all stakeholders plan, develop, deliver, administer, and access distance
learning and related processes (Ellis, 2009).

First used in the 1990s, LMSs rose to popularity for their ability to help
faculty organize course content and automate administration (Coates et al.,
2005). Approaches to course design and delivery within LMSs vary. Some institutions take an open plan, allowing faculty the autonomy to design and develop
courses. Faculty designers may freely choose templates and add/organize content. At the other end of the spectrum, some institutions control all course
design aspects from template to content allowed and organizational structure.
Further, these design environments may restrict editing to an instructional
designer and require instructors to log issues or errors for correction during
scheduled update cycles. Other examples of how to facilitate design and monitor quality control run the gamut between these two extremes.

Good learning design incorporates active learning strategies to engage students in the process, capitalizing on social interactivity with all members of a learning community. This statement encompasses all course designs, regardless of modality. However, the strategies we might use in distance learning involve a wide variety of applications and software.

Consider the following questions:

1. What LMSs are you familiar with? Examples: Angel, Blackboard, Canvas, Desire2Learn, Google Classroom, Moodle, WebCT?
2. How many LMSs have you used before? As a learner? As an instructor or teaching assistant? As a course designer?
3. Has your institution changed LMS platforms during your time there? If so, what challenges and benefits emerged?

LMSs help us organize and safely store big data related to learning in our organizations. This helps with resource allocation, progress/performance monitoring, enhancing accessibility, and personalizing the experience. However, the relatively short history of LMS launches and mergers provides insight into why and how these platforms have evolved in the learning design landscape.

FIGURE 14.5
Organizing learning resources

In some cases, course designers might be instructional designers with undergraduate or graduate degrees in the field. In others, course designers may have other educational or technical experience to guide their work. Similarly, some institutions hire faculty of practice who serve as instructional designers instead of conducting research and teach courses in the subject area of their undergraduate or other degrees. When planning professional development for designers, sessions and topics should address both design quality and technical aspects of the technologies described in this chapter.

LMS providers work to make their platforms accessible by third party vendors for integrations. Think of these integrations in terms of six categories:
- web services (social media and communication)
- collaboration (video conferencing and cloud-based productivity tools)
- authoring assurances (see previous discussion)
- multimedia (images and videos to enhance content)
- course imports (from other LMSs)
- course cartridges (from publishers or other third-party producers).

Administrators need to consider these integrations from both a systems approach, such as making Kaltura available to all faculty and course designers and individual course approach, such as a faculty member embedding a Twitter stream around a class hashtag on a page within a course. Ultimately, these integrations help faculty and course designers fully realize the power of technology in distance learning by easily connecting services learners use commonly to the learning experience.

An institution's LMS should provide an agile platform for efficiently distributing and tracking learning activities. The platform serves to integrate content, users, and data (Lin, 2015), sharing the details of these integrations with other campus systems for student record management and additional reporting. Institutional priorities shift, and technological advances change rapidly, resulting in a need to periodically evaluate if you are still using the platform that meets your organization's needs (Altieri, 2018; Wright, Lopes et al., 2014; Wright, Montgomerie et al., 2014).

3.6   *Campus Portals*

The distance learning administrator likely has little direct oversight over campus portals; however, they should be part of the broader campus engagement. Thus, this brief section focuses on why to consider portals and how other technologies relate to the discussion. Campus, or intranet, portals serve to organize access to campus services and information. These gateways provide quick access to different web-based resources, so that faculty and learners do not have to rely on remembering direct links or recalling the names of these services.

Approaches to portal design, evolving for two decades, stem from attempting to simplify navigating the digital landscape, including an increasingly complex digital ecosystem of applications, websites, and systems (Helwig, 2016). Consider how learners may need to visit one system for course registration and another to complete the course. Now consider that web-based email access requires one link, but web-based access to productivity apps and cloud storage requires another link. Layered between these systems are other technologies such as online advising systems and student financial accounts. The number of different systems and websites accessed during the regular course of business and teaching grows when we turn our attention to staff and faculty. Thus, the particular challenge of campus portals requires stakeholder input from across the campus community, as it is as much a social exercise as it is technical (Bunt & Pennock, 2006).

Ideally, portals move beyond displaying columns of links and visually organize content into easily identifiable categories, though requiring great technical agility to connect often disparate systems (Jafari & Sheehan, 2003). Campus portal design should center on the user experience, focusing on actions and outcomes (Helwig, 2016). One way to prioritize the focus lies in using personas and empathy maps to guide the process (Ferreira et al., 2015; Siegel & Dray, 2019). Empathy map exercises need to identify key personas around users (e.g., faculty, students, staff, friends/community) to capture characteristic thoughts,

Once upon a time, shoppers walked into a retail shopping center, finding a giant illuminated map illustrating the locations of all establishments and an accompanying legend to organize the establishments by theme. In an overwhelming situation, shoppers could reliably use this visually arranged portal to quickly locate the type of product or service they were looking for or at least the types of stores that might sell such a thing. Today, this manifests through online shopping portals. If you log on to Amazon, there's a visual map organizing the types of products and services they offer, and you're likely to want. There's also a side menu to view past orders, connect with support, and access related services. Depending on whether or not you're logged in to the website and what levels of service you use (e.g., Basic user versus Prime subscriber), these menus and options change.

Consider the following questions:

1. When did you first learn how to access your institutional email? Has this changed since your arrival, or have you changed institutions, necessitating a new platform or process?
2. How many different online services does your institution provide to faculty, staff, and students? How do you typically access these?
3. How does your institution differentiate between user roles for accessing different platforms (e.g., faculty, student, staff, administrator)?

Institutions provide many services to their faculty, staff, and students. Figuring out how to navigate these spaces can be overwhelming for new users, whether they are just starting out or transitioning from another organization. Visually organized portals to curate access points help improve satisfaction and reduce user errors.

FIGURE 14.6
Organizing access

actions, and feelings. These maps should be consulted in tandem with the list of services to be organized to help determine how to best group and display the content dynamically based on persona needs and preferences. For example, if an institution subscribes to Kaltura, users may not need direct access as courses embed specific videos for course content, and the library facilitates access through database searches. Thus, determining which services to include on a campus portal depends on how users typically access the portal.

4   Personalizing the Experience

No longer science fiction, artificial intelligence (AI) manifests frequently in transportation, manufacturing, education, communication, sports, media, and healthcare (Techjury.net, 2019). Specialty applications of AI in education include Pennsylvania State University's First Class, a virtual environment where future teachers interact with six AI students, and Georgia Tech's AI teaching assistant, who answers questions in an online forum (Bowen et al., 2017). Other, more familiar ways AI manifests in education already include differentiated instruction (e.g., Carnegie Learning's AI-powered digital learning platform), accessibility (e.g., Microsoft's Presentation Translator for real-time subtitles), and personal assistance (e.g., Amazon Alexa in the classroom) (Dousay & Hall, 2018; Marr, 2018). These examples highlight how AI has the potential to adapt and personalize the learning experience.

Tangential to the increased presence of AI, learning analytics capitalizes on individual learners' behaviors to personalize the experience. "As learners participate in online activities, they leave an increasingly clear trail of analytics

The following description may sound familiar if you're familiar with wearable technologies such as smartwatches and fitness trackers. Consider what it would be like to have access to a device that helps track personal information such as heart rate, steps/distance walked, the intensity of activities, quality of sleep, calories burned, weight, and hydration. This non-invasive device keeps tabs on all of this data simultaneously and stores it for you. By extension, the app that accompanies the device displays your data in easy to read and interpret charts and diagrams. It will even let you set goals for some of these data points.

Consider the following questions:

1. If you don't use (now or in the past) this type of wearable technology, have you ever tried to track any of the types of personal data described? What was that experience like? If you do use these technologies, how do you interact with the data? Do you interact with the charts or set and track goals?
2. Have you ever tried to set goals to support your learning or scholarship, like setting aside one day or certain times of the day during the week to work on certain types of projects? How successful were you?
3. Do you shop on Amazon or other large online vendors? Did you know that machine learning helps drive the recommended items you see? Have you ever interacted with a company, such as insurance or a bank, using the online chat feature? Did you know that these are increasingly chatbots and not humans?

It may sound futuristic or science fiction, but we really are living in the age of artificial intelligence. Big data takes the basic form of timestamps and targets of clicks to engage with course content and drives the rise of learning analytics, revealing how and when learners are active. When combined together, powerful possibilities emerge that let us tailor the learning experience to mitigate challenges with persistence.

FIGURE 14.7
Trends to consider

data that can be mined for insights" (Johnson et al., 2014, p. 12). When combined with learning design, these data inform everything discussed in this chapter, especially how we design learning and assessment (Allen et al., 2017; Holmes et al., 2019). Further, these data guide recruitment/retention strategies, assess learner performance indirectly and provide personalized learner feedback (Meigs, 2016). For example, personalized feedback might take the form of summary statistics about how an individual learner performs on an assessment compared to peers, along with recommendations on how to correct misconceptions based on indicated areas. For a different type of example, consider how data about how (in)frequently students access a particular resource might guide our decision to redesign or exclude that resource. These are simple illustrations of how data influences administrators.

To truly unlock the personalization power of learning analytics, however, we must combine them with AI. Consider the previous example of personalized feedback. With learning analytics, baseline data provided to learners might include just a score, indication of questions missed, and a recommendation of which topics of the course to re-visit (if the designer included this detail in the assessment). When integrated with AI, this feedback transforms with additional system data about the learner. Consider this extended example. Now, when the learner completes an assessment, the system also tells them what they scored (and missed) as well as recommending that they work on assessments during a particular time of day or day of the week based on the learner's past performance. The system can direct the learner to supplementary material or refer them back to material for repeated study. "In theory, the application of AI and personalized learning sounds like an ideal solution to some of the most common educational issues. However, the technology still has a long way for to go before it can fully meet its potential" (Rouhiainen, 2019, para. 5).

With room to mature, AI and learning analytics add significant digital ethics concerns to the discussion. Society at large still struggles with data ownership and how we ethically use data in transparent and equitable ways. From data as currency (see Schaffel, 2018) to the potential for algorithms to exploit and amplify inequalities (see Benjamin, 2019), learning technologists and administrators alike have a challenge. Informed skepticism should guide our decisions as we follow trends and strategically solve problems and seize opportunities with distance learning technologies.

5   Conclusion

Notice how the discussion in this chapter fluidly interchanges "distance learning" and "learning experience." This was intentional. The technologies and practices described herein do not rely on mode or proximity. As distance learning increasingly looks hybrid and flexible, the technologies described herein work across the spectrum and function as layers of engagement and interaction for the learning process. However, administrators would do well to heed one significant piece of seminal advice. "Selecting technology is perhaps the easiest part of developing a distance learning program" (Gellman-Danley & Fetzner, 1988, p. 1). Policy development must accompany this process, and the other chapters of this text help you with integrating the decisions relevant to the issues presented here.

[ ] Hardware and equipment for delivery
   [ ] Contexts to consider
      [ ] Faculty workstation
      [ ] Specialty rooms
      [ ] Traditional & multipurpose classrooms
   [ ] Needs to consider
      [ ] Audio
      [ ] Video
      [ ] Accessories
   [ ] Room configuration
      [ ] Specialty designs for distance learning
      [ ] Retrofitting or reconfiguring
[ ] Learning design, delivery, & accessories
   [ ] Assessment
      [ ] Identity/integrity management
      [ ] Federal policy
      [ ] Traditional assessment tools
      [ ] Authentic assessment tools
   [ ] Media curation, production, & sharing
      [ ] Digital ethics (copyright)
      [ ] Open education resources (OER)
      [ ] Media production
      [ ] Media accessibility
   [ ] Collaboration, exploration, & engagement considerations
      [ ] Foundational technologies
         [ ] Text- and video-based discussions
         [ ] Unified platforms
         [ ] Cloud-based productivity
         [ ] Privacy and security
      [ ] Enhanced technologies
         [ ] Games and simulations
         [ ] Extended and mixed realities
   [ ] Learning management systems
      [ ] General-purpose
      [ ] Third-party integrations
   [ ] Campus portals
[ ] Personalizing learning
   [ ] Artificial Intelligence
   [ ] Learning Analytics
   [ ] Digital ethics

FIGURE 14.8
Planner's checklist of decisions

Note

1   This can be facilitated by visiting https://creativecommons.org/choose/

References

Aceves, P. A., & Aceves, R. I. (2009). Student identity and authentication in distance education: A primer for distance administrators. *Continuing Higher Education Review*, 73, 143–152.

Allen, J., Cavanagh, T., Gunkel, M., & Witmar, J. (2017). *Developments in learning analytics*. ELI 7 Things You Should Know About. https://library.educause.edu/resources/2017/7/7-things-you-should-know-about-developments-in-learning-analytics

Altieri, A. (2018). *The LMS is not dead*. ATD Links. https://www.td.org/newsletters/atd-links/the-lms-is-not-deadyet

Amigud, A., Arnedo-Moreno, J., Daradoumis, T., & Guerrero-Roldan, A. E. (2018). An integrative review of security and integrity strategies in an academic environment: Current understanding and emerging perspectives. *Computers and Security*, 76, 50–70. https://doi.org/10.1016/j.cose.2018.02.021

Arcuria, P., Morgan, W., & Fikes, T. G. (2019). Validating the use of LMS-derived rubric structural features to facilitate automated measurement of rubric quality. *ACM International Conference Proceeding Series*, 270–274. https://doi.org/10.1145/3303772.3303829

Benjamin, R. (2019). *Race after technology: Abolitionist tools for the New Jim Code*. Polity Press.

Bobak, R., Cassarino, C., & Finley, C. (2004). Three issues in distance learning. *Distance Learning*, 1(5), 15–18.

Bowen, K., Riedel, C., & Essa, A. (2017). *Artificial intelligence in teaching and learning*. ELI 7 Things You Should Know About. https://library.educause.edu/resources/2017/4/7-things-you-should-know-about-artificial-intelligence-in-teaching-and-learning

Brookhart, S. M. (2013). *How to create and use rubrics for formative assessment and grading*. Association for Supervision & Curriculum Development.

Bunt, R., & Pennock, L. (2006). Of portals, policies, and poets. *EDUCAUSE Quarterly*, 2, 41–47. http://www.educause.edu/ero/article/portals-policies-and-poets

CAST. (2018). *The UDL guidelines version 2.2*. http://udlguidelines.cast.org/

Childress, M. D., & Braswell, R. (2006). Using massively multiplayer online role-playing games for online learning. *Distance Education*, 27(2), 187–196. https://doi.org/10.1080/01587910600789522

CNET. (n.d.). *Virtual reality 101*. https://www.cnet.com/special-reports/vr101/

Coates, H., James, R., & Baldwin, G. (2005). A critical examination of the effects of learning management systems on university teaching and learning. *Tertiary Education and Management, 11*(1), 19–36. https://doi.org/10.1080/13583883.2005.9967137

Craig, E., & Georgieva, M. (2018a). From VR and AR to our XR future: Transforming higher education. *EDUCAUSE Review.* https://er.educause.edu/blogs/2018/8/from-vr-and-ar-to-our-xr-future-transforming-higher-education

Craig, E., & Georgieva, M. (2018b). VR and AR: The ethical challenges ahead. *EDUCAUSE Review.* https://er.educause.edu/blogs/2018/4/vr-and-ar-the-ethical-challenges-ahead

Crews, K. D. (2002). *New copyright law for distance education: The meaning and importance of the TEACH act.* https://alair.ala.org/handle/11213/9244

Dede, C., Grotzer, T. A., Kamarainen, A., & Metcalf, S. J. (2017). Virtual reality as an immersive medium for authentic simulations. In D. Liu, C. Dede, R. Huang, & J. Richards (Eds.), *Virtual, augmented, and mixed realities in education* (pp. 133–156). Springer Nature. https://doi.org/10.1007/978-981-10-5490-7_8

Demirbilek, M. (2009). The use of electronic games in distance learning as a tool for teaching and learning. In P. L. Rogers, G. A. Berg, J. V. Boettcher, C. Howard, L. Justice, & K. D. Schenk (Eds.), *Encyclopedia of distance learning: Vol. IV* (2nd ed., pp. 2209–2211). IGI Global. https://doi.org/10.4018/978-1-60566-198-8.ch327

Dikli, S. (2003). Assessment at a distance: Traditional vs. alternative assessments. *Turkish Online Journal of Education Technology, 2*(3), 13–19. http://www.tojet.net/articles/v2i3/232.pdf

Dousay, T. A., & Hall, C. S. (2018). "Alexa, tell me about using a virtual assistant in the classroom." *Proceedings of EdMedia: World Conference on Educational Media and Technology,* 1417–1423. https://www.learntechlib.org/primary/p/184359/

Dousay, T. A., Kitchel, A., & Carr-Chellman, A. A. (2019). *Electronic Synchronous Multi-Site (e-SyMS) learning: Design & research recommendations.* Session presented at the Association for Educational Communications & Technology Annual Convention, Las Vegas, NV.

EDUCAUSE. (2014). *7 things you should know about VR headsets.* https://library.educause.edu/resources/2014/12/7-things-you-should-know-about-vr-headsets

Ellis, R. K. (2009). *A field guide to learning management systems.* American Society for Training & Development. http://web.csulb.edu/~arezaei/ETEC551/web/LMS_fieldguide_20091.pdf

Ferreira, B., Silva, W., Oliveira, E., & Conte, T. (2015). Designing personas with empathy map. In *Proceedings 27th international conference on software engineering & knowledge engineering* (*SEKE 2015*) (pp. 501–505). KSI Research Inc. https://doi.org/10.18293/SEKE2015-152

Ferrero, A., & Piuri, V. (1999). A simulation tool for virtual laboratory experiments in a WWW environment. *IEEE Transactions on Instrumentation and Measurement*, *48*(3), 741–746. https://doi.org/10.1109/19.772214

Gellman-Danley, B., & Fetzner, M. (1998). Asking the really tough questions: Policy issues for distance education. *Online Journal of Distance Learning Administration*, *1*(1).

Gibbs, G., & Simpson, C. (2004). Conditions under which assessment supports students' learning. *Learning and Teaching in Higher Education*, *1*, 3–31. http://eprints.glos.ac.uk/id/eprint/3609

Gibson, D. C., Knezek, G., Redmond, P., & Bradley, E. (Eds.). (2014). *Handbook of games and simulations in teacher education*. Association for the Advancement of Computing in Education (AACE). https://www.learntechlib.org/p/147471/

Helwig, J. (2016). Beyond portals: A next generation, action-oriented service delivery platform for rich campus applications. *EDUCAUSE Annual Conference 2016*. https://events.educause.edu/annual-conference/2016/agenda/beyond-portals-a-nextgeneration-actionoriented-service-delivery-platform-for-rich-campus-applications

Holmes, W., Nguyen, Q., Zhang, J., Mavrikis, M., & Rienties, B. (2019). Learning analytics for learning design in online distance learning. *Distance Education*, *40*(3), 309–329. https://doi.org/10.1080/01587919.2019.1637716

Internet2. (2020). *About TIER*. Trust & Identity in Education & Research. https://www.internet2.edu/vision-initiatives/initiatives/trust-identity-education-research/about-tier/

Jafari, A., & Sheehan, M. (Eds.). (2003). *Designing portals: Opportunities and challenges*. IGI Global. https://doi.org/10.4018/978-1-59140-108-7

Johnson, L., Adams Becker, S., Estrada, V., & Freeman, A. (2014). *NMC horizon report: 2014 higher education edition*. https://library.educause.edu/resources/2014/1/2014-horizon-report

Lamont, L. M. (2001). Enhancing student and team learning with interactive marketing simulations. *Marketing Education Review*, *11*(1), 45–55. https://doi.org/10.1080/10528008.2001.11488731

Lin, S. (2015). *The beginner's guide to LMS integrations*. eLearning Industry. https://elearningindustry.com/beginners-guide-lms-integrations

Markova, T., Glazkova, I., & Zaborova, E. (2017). Quality issues of online distance learning. *Procedia – Social and Behavioral Sciences*, *237*, 685–691. https://doi.org/10.1016/j.sbspro.2017.02.043

Marr, B. (2018). How is AI used in education – Real world examples of today and a peek into the future. *Forbes*. https://www.forbes.com/sites/bernardmarr/2018/07/25/how-is-ai-used-in-education-real-world-examples-of-today-and-a-peek-into-the-future/

McConahay, M., & West, A. (2012). Establishing remote student identity: Results of an AACRAO/InCommon Federation survey. *College & University, 87*(3), 59–64.

Meigs, B. (2016). Online learning special issue: Learning analytics. *Online Learning, 20*(2), 1–144. https://onlinelearningconsortium.org/jaln_full_issue/online-learning-special-issue-learning-analytics/

Mertler, C. A. (2001). Designing scoring rubrics for your classroom. *Practical Assessment, Research and Evaluation, 7*(25), 2000–2001.

OER Commons. (2018). *Permissions guide for educators.* https://www.oercommons.org/authoring/5800-permissions-guide-for-educators/view

Rauschnabel, P. A., Rossmann, A., & tom Dieck, M. C. (2017). An adoption framework for mobile augmented reality games: The case of Pokémon Go. *Computers in Human Behavior, 76*, 276–286. https://doi.org/10.1016/j.chb.2017.07.030

Rouhiainen, L. (2019). How AI and data could personalize higher education. *Harvard Business Review.* https://hbr.org/2019/10/how-ai-and-data-could-personalize-higher-education

Schaffel, C. (2018, September 29). No cash needed at this cafe. Students pay the tab with their personal data. *National Public Radio.* https://www.npr.org/sections/thesalt/2018/09/29/643386327/no-cash-needed-at-this-cafe-students-pay-the-tab-with-their-personal-data

Segal, T. (2019). *Freemium.* Investopedia. https://www.investopedia.com/terms/f/freemium.asp

Sharp, J. (2008). Coming soon to pay-per-view: How the digitial millennium copyright act enables digital content owners to circumvent educational fair use. *American Business Law Journal, 40*(1), 1–81. https://doi.org/10.1111/j.1744-1714.2002.tb00910.x

Shein, E. (2019, November). Many rural Americans still lacking broadband access. *TechRepublic.* https://www.techrepublic.com/article/many-rural-americans-still-lacking-broadband-access/

Siegel, D., & Dray, S. (2019). The map is not the territory: Empathy in design. *Interactions, 26*(2), 82–85. https://doi.org/10.1145/3308647

Simonson, M., Zvacek, S. M., & Smaldino, S. E. (2019). *Teaching and learning at a distance: Foundations of distance education* (7th ed.). Information Age Publishing.

Sulun, C. (2018). The evolution and diffusion of learning management systems: The case of Canvas LMS. In A.-P. Correia (Ed.), *Driving educational change: Innovations in action.* PressBooks. https://ohiostate.pressbooks.pub/drivechange/chapter/the-evolution-and-diffusion-of-learning-management-systems-the-case-of-canvas-lms/

Techjury.net. (2019). *How AI is being deployed across industries.* Robotics Business Review. https://www.roboticsbusinessreview.com/ai/infographic-how-ai-is-being-deployed-across-industries/

Teclehaimanot, B., You, J., Franz, D., Xiao, M., & Hochberg, S. A. (2017). Ensuring academic integrity in online courses: A case analysis in three testing environments. In M. R. Simonson & D. J. Seepersaud (Eds.), *40th Annual AECT Proceedings* (Vol. 1, pp. 116–120).

Veletsianos, G. (2020, June). The 7 elements of a good online course. *The Conversation.* https://theconversation.com/the-7-elements-of-a-good-online-course-139736

W3C Web Accessibility Initiative. (2019). *Making audio and video media accessible.* Design and Develop. https://www.w3.org/WAI/media/av/

Walz, A., & Guimont, C. (2019). *Toward best practices for OER quality: A conversation about OER quality and emerging best practice solutions.* Library Publishing Forum. https://vtechworks.lib.vt.edu/handle/10919/90223

Wiley, D. A., Bliss, T. J., & McEwen, M. (2014). Open educational resources: A review of the literature. In J. M. Spector, M. D. Merrill, J. Elen, & M. J. Bishop (Eds.), *Handbook of research on educational communications and technology* (4th ed., pp. 781–789). https://doi.org/10.1007/978-1-4614-3185-5_63

Woodbeck, D. (2019). *InCommon collaboration success program.* https://spaces.at.internet2.edu/display/tiercsp/incommon+collaboration+success+program

Wright, C. R., Lopes, V., Montgomerie, T. C., Reju, S. A., & Schmoller, S. (2014). *Selecting an LMS: Questions to consider.* EDUCAUSE. https://er.educause.edu/~/media/files/articles/2014/4/selecting_lms.pdf?la=en

Wright, C. R., Montgomerie, T. C., Reju, S. A., & Schmoller, S. (2014). Selecting a learning management system: Advice from an academic perspective. *EDUCAUSE Review.* https://er.educause.edu/articles/2014/4/selecting-a-learning-management-system-advice-from-an-academic-perspective

Zydney, J. M., McKimmy, P., Lindberg, R., & Schmidt, M. (2019). Here or there instruction: Lessons learned in implementing innovative approaches to blended synchronous learning. *TechTrends, 63*(2), 123–132. https://doi.org/10.1007/s11528-018-0344-z

CHAPTER 15

Your Distance Learning Community

Anthony A. Piña and Lauren Cifuentes

Abstract

This chapter provides a rational for being a member of a distance learning community; and lists, describes, and provides contact information for the major professional associations for those interested in online/distance learning, teaching, design, and management. Also included is a list of major scholarly and trade journals in online/distance education and scholarly and trade journals in educational technology that frequently feature articles on online/distance education. Ideas for and links to social media sites are also provided. Much of the information in this chapter is compiled from the associations and journals.

Keywords

online education – distance learning – journals – professional associations – social media

1   Introduction

As described in this guide's chapters, becoming a distance learning administrator involves leadership skill, administering employees and programs, as well as applying learning, instructional design, and change theories. Beyond that, quality administration involves networking with other professionals from whom you can learn and with whom you can collaborate. From others in the profession you can gain deep understanding of the norms of the field and your responsibilities as a distance learning administrator. In addition, through professional organizations you can contribute your growing insights to other professionals. Assuming that your personal life is enriched by your professional passions, knowledge and experience, then building a network of fellow professionals who you count as your friends is a valuable professional and personal pursuit. Fellow professionals create and share ideas and problems as well as problem-solutions.

Networking face-to-face at regional, national, and international conferences enhances your professional competence and allows you to be socially involved in your field. In addition, serving in professional associations; subscribing to, editing for, and contributing to publications in professional journals; and consuming and producing contributions on social media, help you build a professional network. Professional associations typically have a presence on social media platforms. For instance, hundreds if not thousands of knowledgeable professionals posted useful strategies for addressing the need to rapidly learn how to teach online on Twitter and Facebook during the Covid-19 crisis. Through social media sites, collaborative teaching and learning are no longer limited to formal classes and workshops but are globally distributed.

Creating your professional learning community requires embracing a "culture of contribution" (Atkins et al., 2007, p. 3) by seeking feedback from others and by sharing and promoting one's own contributions to the field. This can be accomplished by:

- reading others' journal articles and attending talks and workshops at conferences and in webinars;
- writing and publishing articles and presenting at conferences and in webinars;
- serving as an officer in associations of your choosing;
- serving on editorial boards for journals;
- following participants in social media and establishing and regularly contributing to social media accounts of your own.

2   Distance Learning Professional Associations

Conferences, journals, and social media links are posted on their websites.

Association for the Advancement of Computing in Education (AACE)
The Association for the Advancement of Computing in Education (AACE), founded in 1981, is an international, not-for-profit, educational organization with the mission of advancing Information Technology in Education and E-Learning research, development, learning, and its practical application.
P.O. Box 719
Waynesville, NC 28786 USA
www.aace.org

Association for Distance Education and Independent Learning (*ADEIL*)

The Association for Distance Education and Independent Learning is a professional association for anyone engaged in or interested in distance education. The goal of the organization is to provide professional development opportunities as well as opportunities for collegiality and interaction.

21 N. Park St. Room 7101
Madison, WI 53715 USA
www.adeil.org

Association for Educational Communications and Technology (*AECT*)

Established in 1923, AECT is an international professional association for those actively involved in the design of instruction and a systematic approach to learning design. AECT provides national and international leadership in scholarship and best practices in the design, creation, use, and management of technologies for effective teaching and learning in a wide range of settings.

320 W. 8th Street, Suite 101
Bloomington, IN 47404-3745 USA
www.aect.org

EDUCAUSE

Educause is a nonprofit association of information technology leaders and professionals committed to advancing higher education. Members of EDUCAUSE include U.S. and international institutions of higher education, corporations serving the higher education information technology market, and other related associations and organizations.

282 Century Place, Suite 5000
Louisville, CO 80027 USA
www.educause.edu

European Association for Distance Learning (*EADL*)

The mission of EADL is to represent privately-owned and non-governmental European organizations offering high quality and educationally sound distance learning. EADL aims to improve the quality and acceptance of distance learning to ensure the maximum benefit for students. EADL provides its members with a forum for open discussion of all issues related to distance learning and for sharing ideas and good practice.

11 Thorpe Lane, Cawood
Selby, YO8 3SG, United Kingdom
www.eadl.org

Instructional Technology Council (ITC)

An affiliation of the American Association of Community Colleges, ITC members include single institutions and multi-campus districts; regional and statewide systems of community, technical and two-year colleges; for-profit organizations; four-year institutions; and, non-profit organizations that are interested or involved in distance education.

19 Mantua Rd.
Mount Royal, NJ 08061 USA
www.itcnetwork.org

The Inter-American Distance Education Consortium (CREAD)

Founded in 1990, CREAD is a consortium for distance education for North, Central and South America, that provides opportunities for improving educational quality, sharing information and finding greater strength through institutional cooperation. The mission of CREAD is to assist in the improvement of distance education in the Americas and to develop projects related to educational uses of technology.

P.O. Box 4374
Hallandale, FL 33008-4374 USA
www.cread.org

International Council for Open and Distance Education (ICDE)

Founded in 1938 in Canada as the International Council for Correspondence Education, ICDE is a global membership organization in the fields of open learning, distance education, and flexible, lifelong learning.

Pløens gate 2B, 0181
Oslo, Norway
www.icde.org

International Society for Technology in Education (ISTE)

ISTE inspires educators worldwide to use technology to innovate teaching and learning, accelerate good practice and solve tough problems in education by providing community, knowledge and the ISTE Standards, a framework for rethinking education and empowering learners.

2111 Wilson Boulevard, Suite 300
Arlington, VA 22201 USA
www.iste.org

National Council of State Authorization Reciprocity Agreements (NC-SARA)

The State Authorization Reciprocity Agreements, commonly known as SARA, provides a voluntary, regional approach to state oversight of postsecondary distance education. An agreement among member states, districts and territories that establishes comparable national standards for interstate offering of postsecondary distance education courses and programs.

3005 Center Green Drive, Suite 130
Boulder, CO 80301 USA
www.nc-sara.org

Online Learning Consortium

OLC is a collaborative community of higher education leaders and innovators, dedicated to advancing quality digital teaching and learning experiences designed to reach and engage the modern learner – anyone, anywhere, anytime (formerly the Sloan Consortium).

6 Liberty Square #2309
Boston, MA 02109 USA
www.onlinelearningconsortium.org

Open and Distance Learning Association of Australia

ODLAA is a professional association of educators, instructional designers, educational researchers, education consultants, and administrators from across Australia and overseas that is dedicated to advancement of research, practice, and support of education across time and space.

P.O. Box 176, Bathurst
New South Wales, 2795, Australia
www.odlaa.org

Quality Matters (QM)

QM is an international organization that is dedicated to quality assurance in online and innovative digital teaching and learning environments. QM develops quality standards and provides training and certification in the use of its rubrics, tools and practices.

1997 Annapolis Exchange Parkway, Suite 300
Annapolis, MD 21401 USA
www.qualitymatters.org

University Professional and Continuing Education Association (UPCEA)

UPCEA is an institutional association for professional, continuing, and online education. Founded in 1915, Based in Washington, D.C., UPCEA builds greater awareness of the vital link between contemporary learners and public policy issues.

One Dupont Circle, Suite 330
Washington, DC 20036 USA
www.upcea.edu

United States Distance Learning Association (USDLA)

Founded in 1987 USDLA is a professional organization dedicated to support distance learning research, development and praxis across the complete arena of education, training and communications in pre K-12, higher education, continuing education, corporate training, military and government training, home schooling and telehealth.

10 G Street, NE, Suite 600
Washington, DC 20002 USA
www.usdla.org

WICHE Cooperative for Educational Technologies (WCET)

WCET is a national, membership cooperative of institutions and organizations which brings together colleges and universities, higher education organizations and companies to collectively improve the quality and reach of technology-enhanced learning programs. WCET also provides leadership in policy and advocacy of technology-enhanced learning in higher education.

3035 Center Green Drive, Suite 200
Boulder, CO 80301 USA
wcet.wiche.edu

> Identify five organizations from the list above and, using their websites, determine when they typically have their annual conferences and where they will be next year.

3   Online/Distance Learning Journals

The journals listed below have a primary focus on online/distance education.

American Journal of Distance Education

Established in 1987 with the mission of promoting research and disseminating information about distance education in the Americas, AJDE explores topics about all teaching-learning relationships where the actors are geographically separated, and communication takes place through technologies.

www.tandfonline.com/toc/hajd20/current

Distance Education

Distance Education is a peer-reviewed journal of the Open and Distance Learning Association of Australia, Inc. The journal publishes research and scholarly material in the fields of open, distance and flexible education where learners are free from the constraints of the time, pace, and place of study.

www.tandfonline.com/toc/cdie20/current

Distance Learning

Distance Learning is an official publication of the United States Distance Learning Association. It is a professional journal with applicable information for those involved with providing instruction to all kinds of learners, of all ages, using telecommunications technologies of all types. Stories are written by practitioners for practitioners.

www.infoagepub.com/distance-learning.html

The European Journal of Open, Distance and E-Learning

The European Journal of Open, Distance and E-Learning (EURODL) is an electronic, multi-media, open access journal. It publishes the accounts of research and presents scholarly work and solid information about open, distance, online and e-learning in technology-enhanced education and training in its most inclusive definition.

www.eurodl.org

International Journal on E-Learning

IJEL is the official journal of the Association for the Advancement of Computing in Education (AACE). IJEL serves as a forum to facilitate the international exchange of information on the current research, development, and practice of e-learning in corporate, government, healthcare, and higher education.

www.aace.org/pubs/ijel/

International Journal of E-Learning & Distance Education (Journal of Distance Education)

The International Journal of E-Learning & Distance Education (formerly the Journal of Distance Education) is an international open access publication of the Canadian Network for Innovation in Education. Its aims are to promote and encourage scholarly work in e-learning and distance education and provide a forum for the dissemination of international scholarship.

http://www.ijede.ca/index.php/jde

International Journal of Open Educational Resources

The aim of IJOER is to provide a venue for the publication of quality academic research with an emphasis on representing Open Educational Resources in teaching, learning, scholarship and policy.

https://www.ijoer.org/

International Review of Research in Open and Distributed Learning

The International Review of Research in Open and Distributed Learning (IRRODL) is a refereed, open access e-journal that disseminates original research, theory, and best practice in open and distributed learning worldwide. Submissions describe teaching interventions and pedagogical approaches that reference student achievement, performance, or retention.

http://www.irrodl.org/

Internet and Higher Education

The Internet and Higher Education, is an international and interdisciplinary journal devoted to addressing contemporary issues and future developments related to online learning, teaching, and administration on the Internet in post-secondary settings.

www.sciencedirect.com/journal/the-internet-and-higher-education

The Journal of Educators Online

The Journal of Educators Online (JEO) is a biannual publication that highlights research in the broad area of Computer Mediated Learning (CML) which includes distance, online, electronic, virtual, distributed, blended and mobile learning.

www.thejeo.com

Journal of Online Learning Research

The JOLR is an open access peer-reviewed journal devoted to the theoretical, empirical, and pragmatic understanding of technologies and their impact on pedagogy and policy in K-12 online and blended environments. JOLR is official journal of the Association for the Advancement of Computing in Education (AACE).

www.aace.org/pubs/jolr/

Online Journal of Distance Learning Administration

The Online Journal of Distance Learning Administration is a peer-reviewed electronic journal offered free each quarter over the World Wide Web. The journal publishes articles based on original work of practitioners and researchers with specific focus or implications for the management of distance education programs.

www.westga.edu/~distance/ojdla/

Online Learning Journal (Journal of Asynchronous Learning Networks)

Online Learning, formerly the Journal of Asynchronous Learning Networks, is the official journal of the Online Learning Consortium and promotes the development and dissemination of new knowledge at the intersection of pedagogy, emerging technology, policy, and practice in online environments.

onlinelearningconsortium.org/read/olc-online-learning-journal

Open Learning: The Journal of Open, Distance and E-Learning

Open Learning is a leading international journal in the field of open, flexible, and distance learning. The Journal is widely subscribed to and read throughout the world by those in specialist distance education institutions, and also by those using distance, flexible and technology-based forms of learning in conventional education and training contexts.

www.tandfonline.com/toc/copl20/current

Open Praxus

Open Praxis is a peer-reviewed open access scholarly journal focusing on research and innovation in open, distance and flexible education. It is published by the International Council for Open and Distance Education.

www.openpraxis.org

The Quarterly Review of Distance Education

The Quarterly Review of Distance Education is a rigorously refereed journal publishing articles, research briefs, reviews, and editorials dealing with the theories, research, and practices of distance education.

www.infoagepub.com/quarterly-review-of-distance-education.html

Turkish Online Journal of Distance Education

TOJDE is an open-access, peer-reviewed academic distance education journal. TOJDE is intended to provide readers with scholarly and academic perspectives and research in the field of distance education.

www.dergipark.org.tr/en/pub/tojde

4   Educational Technology Journals

The journals listed below focus on various aspects of educational technology, but often feature articles about online/distance education.

Australasian Journal of Educational Technology

The Australasian Journal of Educational Technology (AJET) aims to promote research and scholarship on the integration of technology in tertiary education, promote effective practice, and inform policy.

www.ajet.org.au/index.php/AJET

British Journal of Educational Technology

BJET publishes theoretical perspectives, methodological developments and high-quality empirical research that demonstrate whether and how applications of instructional/educational technology systems, networks, tools, and resources lead to improvements in formal and non-formal education at all levels.

bera-journals.onlinelibrary.wiley.com/journal/14678535

Canadian Journal of Learning and Technology

CJLT is a peer-reviewed journal that welcomes papers on all aspects of educational technology and learning, including learning theory and technology, cognition and technology, instructional design theory and application, online learning, computer applications in education, simulations and gaming, and other aspects of the use of technology in the learning process.

www.cjlt.ca/index.php/cjlt

Educational Media International

Educational Media International (EMI) is a scholarly journal that publishes research, evaluation, and development studies addressing the issues, successes and challenges faced in the design, development, implementation, and evaluation of educational media.

www.tandfonline.com/toc/remi20/current

Educational Technology and Society

Educational Technology & Society (ET&S) is an open-access academic journal that publishes research that bridges the pedagogy and practice in advanced technology for evidence-based and meaningfully educational application.

www.j-ets.net

Educational Technology Research & Development

ETR&D, an official journal of the Association for Educational Communications and Technology, focuses on research and development in educational technology. The Research Section is dedicated to rigorous original quantitative, qualitative, or mixed methods studies. The Development Section publishes research on planning, implementation, evaluation, and management. The Cultural and Regional Perspectives Section welcomes innovative research about how technologies are being used specific to a culture or region.

www.springer.com/journal/11423

EDUCAUSE *Review*

EDUCAUSE Review is the association's open-access digital flagship publication for the higher education IT community. The magazine takes a broad look at current developments and trends in information technology, how they may affect the college/university as an institution, and what these mean for higher education and society.

er.educause.edu

Journal of Computing in Higher Education

JCHE publishes original research, literature reviews, implementation and evaluation studies, and theoretical, conceptual, and policy papers that provide perspectives on instructional technology's role in improving access, affordability, and outcomes of postsecondary education.

www.springer.com/journal/12528

Online Journal of Distance Learning Administration

We repeat here because this journal is of special interest to readers of this chapter. The Online Journal of Distance Learning Administration is a peer-reviewed electronic journal offered free each quarter over the World Wide Web. The journal welcomes manuscripts based on original work of practitioners and researchers with specific focus or implications for the management of distance education programs.

www.westga.edu/~distance/ojdla/

TechTrends: Linking Research and Practice to Improve Learning

TechTrends, an official journal of the Association for Educational Communications and Technology, provides a vehicle that fosters the exchange of important and current information among professional practitioners. Articles published in the journal contribute to the advancement of knowledge and practice in the field.

www.springer.com/journal/11528

Identify the editors of five of the journals above. Check to learn whether or not they have Twitter accounts. If they do, follow them.

CHAPTER 16

Ramping up Distance Learning in a Crisis

Lessons Learned from Covid-19

Robbie Grant, Michelle Lebsock, Daniel Olsson and Timothy Strasser

Abstract

At the conclusion of this chapter, you will be aware of the need to administer:
– a flexible and skilled staff
– scalable and robust software
– quick decision making
– constant and consistent communication
– high quality instructor professional development in online pedagogy and technical skills
– high quality instructor support both technical and pedagogical.

Keywords

canvas – workshops – professional development – training – online learning – transition – distance learning support – Zoom

1   Introduction

At New Mexico State University, our Academic Technology (AT) team watched the progress of COVID-19 wreak havoc on other states in February and early March 2020. Seeing the news and what was occurring at other universities, we knew that our team needed to proactively make preparations to support the university system during a potential pandemic. We began with an analysis of University needs and top priorities in the event that we would need to transition to emergency remote instruction quickly. We also evaluated our departmental needs in order to transition to a work-from-home situation while not just maintaining but increasing our support for faculty and students who would need to adjust quickly to new instructional modalities. We needed (1) to offer all of our workshops online, (2) a means of synchronous communication with our faculty, and (3) a synchronous means of communication within our unit. Luckily, we did not have to start from scratch as we had already begun to shift some in-person workshops to online delivery.

To offer some background at the AT team at New Mexico State University; this unit was created in 1996 as a unit within the Office of Scholarly Technology in Information and Communications Technology. At the time, Scholarly Technology's main task was the implementation, support and training for the WebCT learning management system. AT staff now consists of four employees, which is fewer than what you will find at most peer institutions. The four of us each bring a diverse skill set grounded in a solid foundation in technology administration, higher-education instruction, and creative problem-solving. Our daily unit responsibilities include: managing the academic software and technology tools for instructional delivery; evaluating new software to meet campus needs; providing troubleshooting, answers, and guidance to faculty and students; providing workshops and professional development for instructors; providing instructional solutions for faculty – both in course design and course delivery; providing individual consultation with faculty, departments, and support units; and finding innovative solutions for instructional needs. Today, AT supports the Canvas learning management system (LMS) by Instructure, Canvas Studio video management platform, Zoom video conferencing, Adobe Connect video conferencing, Turnitin originality checker, EvaluationKIT survey tool, Respondus LockDown Browser and Monitor, the Panopto integration with Canvas, and i>Clicker student polling software.

Academic Technology is separate from the University's Information and Communication Technology department (ICT) and is housed under the Provost's office reporting to the Vice Provost for Digital Learning Initiatives. All of the software programs that AT supports integrate with Canvas. Management and support of other technologies are the responsibility of ICT. Our workshops cover the Canvas core tools: Assignments and Rubrics, Quizzes, Home Pages, Modules, MasteryPaths, Student Groups, Gradebook, and Audio/Video in Canvas (now Canvas Studio). We also have workshops that cover the most heavily used LTI tools that are integrated with our Canvas instance, previously mentioned: Adobe Connect, Zoom, Turnitin, and i>Clicker. In addition, we also look for opportunities to develop new workshops to meet faculty needs. Customized support for EvaluationKIT and Panopto in Canvas is provided for individuals or departments.

2 Current Services Offered and Emergent Needs

Historically, AT has offered an intensive one-week "Canvas Bootcamp" workshop cycle of 10 workshops in the span of five days monthly during the summer and at the beginning of each semester to prepare faculty to use technology effectively in their courses. Outside of these strategically-timed Canvas Bootcamp cycles, we found the most success in offering two workshops each Friday, one in the morning and a different workshop in the afternoon, following a set path that repeated each month. With a cap of 15 attendees due to having 15 PCs in our AT computer lab, these workshops were offered face-to-face. In the beginning of the Spring 2020 semester, we began offering a one-week Canvas Bootcamp face-to-face and a one-week Canvas Bootcamp synchronously delivered online using Adobe Connect with the plan to compare the two modalities. We also began to include an online workshop in our standard Friday workshop cycle, offering one face-to-face workshop and one online workshop every Friday, again following a set order.

We had offered online versions of our face-to-face workshops off and on for many years, and had in the last year settled on an online delivery format through Adobe Connect which allowed us to provide robust training and professional development to a wide audience of geographically distant faculty and part-time faculty who were not able to attend face-to-face workshops on campus during our 8 am–5 pm workday. After only a handful of online workshops, we were quickly able to determine that this current online delivery format was successful through tracking attendance and feedback from participant evaluations. In January 2020, our online workshop attendance decidedly outpaced our face-to-face workshop attendance. The immediate success of our online workshop delivery model made us confident that we were meeting the needs of our faculty and that we would be able to scale-up our online workshop delivery to provide high quality, synchronous workshops to all NMSU system faculty. Our objective was to expand our reach to serve more faculty, including part-time faculty. Our timing was good as we were prepared for an emergency transition to remote instruction.

In early March 2020, when the transition to emergency remote instruction occurred, we increased the attendance cap in our online workshops from 15 attendees to 80 attendees. We determined that the best way to support a large number of workshop attendees was to team up to host each online workshop. One team member would deliver the workshop and monitor the chat for questions, and a second team member would provide redundancy in the case of an internet connection failure, provide attendee troubleshooting for the Adobe Connect room, and help to answer questions entered into the chat. With our unit being a relatively small unit with just four staff members, managing online workshops with large numbers of participants was tricky considering all of the other important activities for which this unit was responsible. Typically, faculty participants were eager to learn and were gracious in asking questions and allowing for follow-up feedback to questions and/or guidance that required longer explanation or directions. The internet reliability in the on-campus office was excellent, however when we moved to our home offices, the internet connection stability became less reliable. During a handful of sessions, the main presenter's internet service would either become unstable or turn off completely, leaving the back-up staff member to take over. It was important that the backup presenter was able to immediately take over and continue the training until the main presenter's internet became more reliable. While this only occurred less than five times over six months, it highlighted the importance of having backup on hand to take over if required.

We also knew that we would need to offer our typical beginning-of-the-semester Canvas Bootcamp workshop cycle online immediately mid-semester to help the new online instructors who would have two weeks to move their face-to-face course to an online format. The urgency of this situation also required us to offer workshops more frequently than ever before. We realized we would need to increase our flexibility in order to accommodate faculty schedules so that everyone could access our workshops as needed. Traditionally, AT had not offered recorded versions of our workshops – the reason for this is the software/technology that we support updates so frequently that recordings become outdated quickly. In this urgent situation, however, we knew that we would need to create an on-demand library of recorded workshops to meet faculty needs given the chaos and uncertainty faculty faced while transitioning to working and teaching from home. Our online workshop format provided the flexibility that faculty needed by allowing us to reach them synchronously and reach even more faculty through our on-demand recorded workshop library.

At the start of the crisis, Academic Technology hosted nearly-daily workshops online with faculty attendance nearing the 80-person cap in several of the workshops. These Canvas workshops using Adobe Connect played a significantly important role, especially at the beginning of the move from face-to-face to online. As mentioned already, our workshops, which had traditionally been face-to-face, were already redesigned to be offered online. We cannot overstate how fortunate this decision was. When the university moved to all-courses-online, our staff had already been familiar with online workshops and worked out potential issues before they became bigger issues. This was incredibly important. Once the decision to switch all courses online was made, leading into a special two-week Spring Break, instructors used the two-week window of time to move face-to-face courses online. Our registration and attendance in online workshops spiked dramatically with several workshops, including the Adobe Connect workshop, the Introduction to Canvas workshop, and the Using the Canvas Gradebook workshop, totaling out at approximately 50–75 attendees.

Previous workshops would typically top out at approximately 20 attendees. The increased attendance was not a result of any departmental incentives, but rather because of the increased demand for online teaching training. Since all face-to-face classes were moved online, instructors were faced with the reality that they needed to learn about effective online teaching ASAP.

These online workshops with record attendance played a highly important role in helping faculty. These workshops, which typically lasted 1–2 hours were lengthened by roughly 30–45 minutes in order to adequately answer all of the participant questions, which were typed into a Chat box. Any follow up questions were typically emailed or asked during the next workshop as it was common for faculty participants to attend the same workshop multiple times. The attendance of these online workshops was the highest it had ever been and the reach of these workshops to teach faculty played an important role in helping them.

We knew that the Canvas LMS would be the foundation of our transition to remote instruction. The majority of instructors in the NMSU system used Canvas to support instruction, with different levels of use ranging from minimally as a supplement to a face-to-face course to fully-online course delivery. Since the Canvas LMS is a cloud-based "Software as a Service" (SaaS) system that auto-provisions IT resources to scale-up or down as needed, we were confident that it could handle the additional load as all of our courses transitioned to online-only instruction. At the time of this initial assessment in March, NMSU had just over 3,400 courses published for the Spring 2020 semester in Canvas. At the end of the Spring 2020 semester, the data showed that we offered 3,977 online courses, an increase of nearly 600 published courses. Even before the start of the COVID-19 crisis, NMSU was offering 85% of courses on Canvas in some format (supplemental, blended, hybrid, or fully online). The 3,977 published courses represented 99.4% of all course offerings.

At the very beginning of this crisis, we all agreed that video conferencing was going to be key in supporting faculty and students through the emergency transition to remote learning and also for supporting staff and the missions of non-academic support units. NMSU has been using the individual named host-license version of Adobe Connect for over a decade. Due to instructional needs prior to the Covid-19 crisis, we added an on-premise 500 concurrent-seat term license for integration with Canvas four years ago which had grown from >100 users in the first iteration of the integration to over 15,000 unique identified users. As the demand for synchronous video conferencing continued to increase throughout 2019, we knew that we would need to increase video conferencing capacity and delivery options as well.

Although NMSU already had two licensed versions of Adobe Connect, around 2018–2019 individual instructors and departments began exploring the use of a newer video conferencing software called Zoom. The feedback from faculty users of Zoom was positive and the demand for Zoom started to grow. In a short amount of time, we found that there was significant support across the NMSU system for making Zoom widely available – and the introduction of the new Zoom LTI Pro finally made this option viable. In December of 2019, we serendipitously purchased an enterprise Zoom account with the plan to eventually use Zoom as the main video conferencing software available through Canvas. In our release strategy, we planned a deliberate 6-month implementation timeline including a soft release for the Summer 2020 semester with a full campus rollout in place for the beginning of the Fall 2020 semester. This was following the common wisdom of how to slowly release a new software to an entire campus community to ensure a successful roll-out.

These carefully laid-out plans went out the window quickly. Once it became apparent that NMSU would likely shift to remote teaching and working for the remainder of the Spring 2020 semester, the implementation timeline for Zoom took on its namesake and *zoomed* up. COVID-19 changed this implementation plan from a 6 to 8-month timeline to a 2-week emergency implementation. We identified core needs as a team in our unit-meetings based on our experience supporting online teaching and began the implementation. This new emergency implementation was exhilarating and terrifying – we had just begun the onboarding process with Kathy, our Zoom Education Success Manager and were still in the beginning planning stages of our implementation, including securing a vanity URL and determining the best way to provision user accounts. Our Zoom administrator, Michelle, had scheduled Zoom administrator training with Kathy to begin mid-March, which was no longer an option. We would proceed with the integration without formal training, but with just-in-time support from our Zoom Success Manager and Sales Engineers.

The scope of the Zoom implementation project was larger than any of our previous software integrations in that Zoom would support teaching and learning through Canvas, but would also be available for all staff, faculty, and students across the 5 campuses in the NMSU system. We expected Zoom would support working from home, collaborative research, student outreach and support, faculty outreach and support, community outreach, student clinical hours, and telehealth (through a HIPAA-compliant sub-account). Overnight Zoom became the primary means of meeting synchronously for the entire NMSU system. The emergency implementation was possible and successful due to the Academic Technology team dynamic of providing collegial support, adjusting responsibilities, and working overtime to meet critical deadlines. Thankfully, we had a pre-existing collegial relationship with key ICT Systems personnel who were willing to make Single-Sign-On (SSO) for Zoom an extreme priority. Zoom was available for use outside of Canvas on March 18, 2020 and the integration with Canvas was complete on March 23, 2020.

Zoom quickly became one of the most important software available to NMSU faculty and staff. Many instructors were interested in maintaining some face-to-face continuity online through synchronous Zoom sessions. As we offered support for all learning technologies via Zoom, one of the most common topics was on the use of Zoom itself. First, we communicated to faculty the fact that we were learning Zoom as well. Next, we quickly sought answers to Zoom questions using the resources made available to us from Zoom. At the same time Zoom was actively updating their software to meet the increase in demand internationally across industries, which means that the available features and instructions for use changed frequently.

An important challenge that the AT unit faced was addressing how to offer the same walk-in, one-on-one consultation services and open lab sessions that we had been offering for years. There were several options floated around our virtual offices. The one option that made the most sense was the option to use Zoom as a replacement. The plan was to send out a Zoom meeting link to all of our faculty. The idea was that the Zoom meeting would act like an online Open Lab. It would be staffed Monday through Friday from 8:30 am–11:30 am and 1:30 pm–4:30 pm with all four of the AT staff active and available in the virtual lab. Each staff member would be added to the meeting as an alternative host and would be expected to be in the meeting during the available times unless they were scheduled in another meeting or delivering a workshop. We also received extra support from the Online Course Improvement Program (OCIP) staff and the NMSU Teaching Academy staff to help with the online lab for the first few weeks due to extreme demand at the initial launch of the lab. Using Zoom in this manner allowed us to use Breakout Rooms to provide one-on-one support for multiple faculty at the same time rather than one-at-a-time in the main meeting room. Having our webcams on when faculty first accessed the room allowed us to set up a welcoming environment for stressed and frustrated faculty. We also created a graphic that was titled Online Open Lab that was shared as faculty joined the meeting. Using Zoom in this way not only allowed us to provide on-demand support to faculty, but it also allowed us to model synchronous video conferencing best practices and actively demonstrate the available features. We took advantage of the "waiting room" in Zoom to allow for controlled entry into the meeting. The Zoom "waiting room" also helped prevent unauthorized access to our meeting room by what is being referred to as "Zoombombing." "Zoombombing," a relatively new term, is when uninvited and unwelcome participants access the Zoom session and generally try to be as disruptive as possible; typically the "Zoombomber" uses their microphone, camera, and keyboard to share vulgar and offensive speech and images for shock value and general disruption.

There were points during the first few weeks of this "new normal" that we had approximately eight faculty at a time in the open lab, each in a breakout room with a support person. Originally, we had planned to phase out the "always-available" open lab model in favor of a scheduled, one-on-one consultation model. After a number of internal conversations and the favorable feedback from faculty and administration on the ease of access, we decided to keep the always-available open lab model for the foreseeable future. This model has worked well and the feedback from faculty has been overwhelmingly positive. Faculty knowing that they can simply click a link and get to a support person provided an ease-of-access that faculty found to be just what they needed. The emails of appreciation and public NMSU list-serv notes expressing appreciation for the AT unit communicated to us that the support we were providing was meeting the needs of faculty.

In using Zoom, a key concern for many faculty members was the security of their online assessment. Many of these faculty had very specific practices for how to handle this in a face-to-face setting and were caught completely off-guard and had no idea of how to proceed when the transition to fully online learning occurred. At this time, NMSU had two types of services and software in place to deal with this. The first was ProctorU and the second was Respondus Lockdown Browser (RLDB)/Respondus Monitor (RM). At NMSU, use of the online proctor, ProctorU, needs to be scheduled ahead of time and the service provides a live proctor. This service also requires students to pay a fee in order to take their exams. Alternatively, RLDB/RM was an on-demand service that instructors could enable for any Canvas quiz which used an algorithm to then "monitor" the students during the take. The software would then flag any suspicious activity for review by the instructor and rate by level of severity. This solution however was not implemented without significant difficulty.

One of the greatest difficulties for faculty when using online proctoring services was the fact that their students had originally signed up for a face-to-face course and were not technologically equipped to use the RLDB/RM suite. The faculty also had very little understanding of the technology involved. At the time, only PCs, Macs, and iPads (if enabled) were compatible with this technology. One of the most common issues encountered was either the lack of a suitable webcam or a computer that was incapable of installing the proctoring software. For instance, we encountered many students who used Google

Chromebooks excursively due to the low cost of these devices (Chromebook support was later added by Respondus in beta). Unfortunately, this left them in a situation where their devices would not allow them to participate.

Due to these issues, many workarounds were implemented. Fortunately, our AT unit was able to provide support to both students and faculty to navigate these difficulties. One other option that gained some traction among faculty; a very creative option, included the use of Zoom mobile application as a work-around solution for proctoring. When a student did not have a webcam but they had a smartphone or tablet, they would install the Zoom app to act as a webcam. Faculty found that many students did have a smartphone or tablet which made this a successful strategy for live proctoring to maintain exam security while still maintaining accessibility to students. Several faculty members used this option.

Overall, use of the proctoring solutions RLDB/RM and ProctorU saw a significant uptake in faculty use in April and May. With all assessments moved to online, the urgency and demand for protecting assessment integrity grew sharply. Support sessions with faculty regarding RLDB/RM quickly increased. However, AT staff was able to manage the significant amount of "how-to" questions and be creative to come up with workarounds, as noted in the previous paragraph.

Course evaluations were another area that Academic Technology oversaw through the transition to fully online courses. To provide some historical perspective, when the course evaluation system was originally deployed, the department representatives (most commonly the administrative assistants) were trained in the use of this software. This, however, became very problematic for many reasons. The department representatives would only use this software several times a year which caused them to forget many of the steps and become uncomfortable with its use. This caused Academic Technology to have to deal with drastically increased support issues during peak evaluation periods. The second main issue was that departments used the software inconsistently, creating different user experiences for students evaluating multiple courses. Lastly, some departments opted to not use this tool at all and would conduct their evaluations using paper only.

In 2018, seeing the issues at hand with the course evaluation process, Academic Technology hired an additional staff member to administer and provide department consulting for EvaluationKit which changed the course evaluation process. For departments that were comfortable with the process, they could continue to build their evals as before. For everyone else, a new request form was created from our website that departments could fill out with all of the relevant details. This allowed departments to focus solely on the quality and content of their evaluations while allowing the subject matter experts to handle all of the technical complexities. This caused a drastic increase in use of the software. The new process was fortunately initiated prior to COVID-19 which allowed for a smooth transition when those departments that relied on paper were forced to transition to online delivery. Whether your institution uses standardized or non-standardized evaluations, a solid plan must be in place to administer your evaluations in an online format while remaining scalable to handle unexpected events such as a global pandemic.

3 Include Technology/Technologists in the Crisis Plan before a Crisis Hits

One of the software that we saw instructors use dramatically more of once the pandemic hit was the originality checker, Turnitin. This software had already been used a good deal by faculty who wanted to check papers for plagiarism or matches, but mainly faculty used it as a teaching tool to effectively teach students proper citation and APA/MLA style citing and referencing. Once the move to online happened, use of Turnitin increased in March, April, and May of 2020 with instructors' desire to maintain academic integrity and accountability with their students. The spike in use coincided with a strong uptake in the training workshop attendance for "Using Turnitin in Canvas."

The general sense of the effectiveness of Turnitin in encouraging original work and teaching proper referencing and citation has been overwhelmingly positive. With both instructors *and* students having access to review the Turnitin Originality report, the transparency proved highly beneficial for both roles. For those adopting Turnitin at NMSU, our office recommended that Turnitin be used primarily as a teaching tool rather than primarily as a means for catching plagiarism. We chose the positive message that adoption of the software provides. Our guidance was acknowledged through the use of "draft" assignments. Instructors were encouraged to use draft assignments, which are assignments created in Canvas, specifically communicating the assignment be utilized as a practice submission to be submitted through the Turnitin system. The assignment could be worth some amount of points, worth 0 points, or applied as extra credit. In this type of assignment, students submit the draft assignment with the expectation it will be purely practice and a way to review and analyze the Turnitin Originality report. A separate assignment, the actual high value assignment, would then be used as the "final" submission for the student. The feedback from this guidance of using draft assignments was overwhelmingly positive. The opportunity for students to practice and review the Originality report of their writing gave students valuable insight into what improvements could be made; specifically, in relation to in-text citations and including the appropriate attributions.

As the move to online teaching from face-to-face teaching required time and energy be focused on the transition, providing the use of Turnitin removed the task for instructors of trying to identify plagiarism via the use of search tools such as Google.

4 Faculty Testimonials

Two success stories in working with faculty lie in our work with instructors who are wildly different. Photojournalism instructor Professor A and Geography Professor B.

Professor A is a photojournalism faculty member who had not previously viewed the idea of online teaching favorably. In his own words, he described himself as "rough around the edges" and the "least technologically-familiar person you could find to teach online." In our initial conversations in open lab his stress, anxiety, and frustration were obvious. Professor A might be described as somewhat grouchy when it comes to learning things not in his realm; i.e. online teaching. As soon as he learned of the availability of the Zoom virtual open lab, Professor A frequently visited to seek advice. He clearly was no fan of online teaching and expressed doubt about the effectiveness of this modality; especially, he proclaimed, for teaching his field of expertise, photography. With that said, each time Professor A visited the Zoom virtual open lab, he would learn a little bit more: a different teaching tool in Canvas; a different approach to teaching... Each day, Professor A's dedication and hard work resulted in increased understanding of what was required to effectively move his face-to-face photography course online. As one can expect, there were some challenges and bumps along the way, and Professor A expressed frustration. With at least one of us in AT available to act as a sounding board for him and work with him in a deliberate manner every time, Professor A was able to make important strides in understanding how to use Canvas and Zoom, and develop effective online teaching strategies. Perhaps most important in helping Professor A was being available for him before, after, and sometimes *during* his online class in which he was using Zoom. Support with Zoom was undoubtedly the most important area for Professor A to be successful in moving his course online.

After a couple weeks and frequent, nearly-daily visits to our Zoom virtual open lab, Professor A's stance on teaching photography online did a 180 degree change. He expressed how his motivation related to teaching increased and he stated how he believed in the effectiveness of online teaching. In his own words online teaching is, "maybe more effective in some areas than face-to-face."

In helping Professor A, a major difference-maker was the ability for him to receive support while in his own home and the ease of access to support through our Zoom virtual open lab. The access of faculty to the Zoom virtual open lab during this time period, which totaled six hours a day; 3 in the morning and 3 in the afternoon, was critical for Professor A along with many other faculty members. If he began struggling and needed guidance, he was able to, with a few clicks, join the Zoom virtual open lab and talk to somebody who would listen and give guidance. This was the most important difference-maker for Professor A. Furthermore, with Zoom's ability for users to share their screens, Professor A was able to quickly share his screen which allowed us to walk him through step-by-step or click-by-click to show him how to build content, solve any number of issues and just provide consultation for online teaching ideas. As a learning tool, the share-screen ability was highly effective and efficient.

Professor A was gracious enough to provide the following written testimonial about his experience during this crisis:

> On March 10, 2020, talking with a colleague about the growing Corona crisis, I heard the word "Zoom (software)" for the first time. I tossed it off. "What does it have to do with me?," I asked myself.
>
> On March 12, 2020, we, at NMSU were notified to take what we could carry and leave the building. The Corona Crisis had arrived – full bore – and we were being sent home indefinitely. As I walked to my car I pondered, "How in the world could I possibly teach online?" I never had before nor had I ever wanted to.
>
> My whole idea of teaching goes well beyond just the subject matter. Interaction with students is the key to teaching for me, exchanging ideas in casual conversation not during class, but, subtly discerning a student's needs, trying to expose them to new ideas about, in my case, photojournalism, and about life.
>
> How could you do that via a laptop?
>
> During that coming weekend, I pretty much decided that the semester was actually over. How could an entire faculty, not that geeky in the first place, convert classes to online? In my Department, Journalism, a majority of our courses involve technology and hands-on teaching about cameras, audio recording, video capture, multimedia presentation, and one-on-one interviewing.
>
> How do you do that on a computer? I thought it might be impossible.

So, I grudgingly conceded that over the next two months, I was just going to give my students a couple of assignments, grade them, maybe do it all via email and just let it go.

The Crisis had won.

Then the "cavalry" came to the rescue!

The "cavalry" was NMSU's Academic Technology service.

Immediately after our dismissal from the campus, I kept seeing – couldn't avoid them – emails from something called Academic Technology offering help to do the conversion, with a hot link to them. These came regularly and often. Whoever they were, I thought, they are, at the least, persistent!

By the next Monday, March 16, I hit that hotlink and my teaching would change forever.

This service was well organized, incredibly sensitive to the urgency and anxiety we teachers felt, patient, always cheerful, always generous and most of all, very skillful in helping me to go from zero knowledge about online teaching to becoming thoroughly familiar with the resources available.

The Academic Technology team explained the various modes that could be used, were careful and aware that after twenty-two years of teaching in a classroom, online teaching could be overwhelming.

They listened carefully to my special needs, primarily that what I teach – photojournalism – requires learning technical hands-on skills, and helped me tailor an approach to doing it.

Instead of the dread of having to abandon my tried and true way of teaching, they turned the experience into a great adventure, something that became fun, something that I felt would help me, when school resumed after our break, transfer enthusiasm for the subject matter to our students (who were, naturally, a little "down" from the disruption).

Tim Strasser, Dan Olsson, Robbie Grant and Michelle Lebsock became daily teachers. Well, actually hourly! For two weeks we worked together – many times a day – and it has been one of the finest experiences I have had in academia.

Within two weeks they had prepared me to resume my teaching full speed.

I went from dreading doing this to looking forward to it and I believe (based on their comments) that the students also enjoyed the classes.

One student, after one of our classes (ZOOM), approached me and said, "Thank you so much for holding classes." She told me that many of her classes were just online, faceless, just "paperwork (her word)," not interesting. But ours was just like "going to school."

We were really having classes! I was thrilled.

I have come to think of this new methodology not as a transition from "face-to-face teaching" to "online teaching," but rather, a transition to "Electronic Face-To-Face" teaching.

We had real classes! We held them at their regular times. I rewrote my Syllabus and my assignments to encompass the reality of the sequestration we all were experiencing but I did not change the content of the course whatsoever, nor was I able to continue the aforementioned special aspects of teaching, the "beyond the classroom" interaction, so essential to helping students to mature and prosper.

Our Zoom classes were robust, interactive, full of new and innovative audio-visual presentations (we even created a Photo Gallery to replace the physical one we had back on campus) that would not have been possible had we stayed in the classroom.

Am I suggesting that the classes were better as Electronic Face-To-Face?

Maybe.

Hard to say.

I do know this: the Academic Technology team at NMSU was and is superlative. I owe them great gratitude and I believe our university avoided a complete disaster because of their persistent, cheerful, patient and effective leadership.

The AT Team not only helped us continue a high level of pedagogy, but it very well may have pointed us in the direction of the future of education.

That's not bad for a four-person team!

Professor B, a Geography professor and former Faculty-Senate Chair, could not be more different than Professor A. Professor B is up-to-speed with technology and is willing to try out different software and different tools. He has taught online before and has often used Canvas as a supplement to his face-to-face courses.

At the beginning of this crisis or even when the idea of moving courses online was in the faculty discussion realm, Professor B sought out support at least a few times a week through our Zoom Open Labs. He approached the move from face-to-face to online with some concern. One of Professor B's complicated tasks was to replicate face-to-face group work in a synchronous Zoom class session. In many Zoom sessions, most of which were roughly 30 minutes, sometimes more, we were able to help him step-by-step, with Michelle even going to his Zoom class session to assist. The efforts of the Academic Technology staff and of Professor B were successful and he was a happy faculty member and has since thanked us personally and publicly through the NMSU email listserve called "Hotline," even providing the following write-up of his experience:

> When NMSU went 100% online in response to the COVID-19 epidemic, I was faced with taking 3 classes online in 2 weeks with limited training, and I saw 2 options – do all I could to preserve the F2F nature of the class and the strong connection I have with my students, or move to a 100% asynchronous model with very limited interaction. After consulting with Christina Schaub in IIQ [The Office of Instructional Innovation and Quality], and the entire AT team, I decided to use all the tools at hand to stay in a synchronous model. Over the 2 weeks we had to get things ready to move 100% online, I worked with IIQ and AT staff to learn the basics of Zoom, Zoom breakout rooms, Canvas Collaborations, Google Docs, and a robust way to stay connected to my students. As classes started again on 30 March, we met at the regular class time on Zoom, I took all group activities I deploy in Team Based Learning Model into breakout rooms, I ported all quizzes and exams online with the Canvas Quiz tool, and I made sure I was available for students as needed. Two key things came from this exercise – it was a major lift for me and students to make the leap, and it worked! I lost 3 students out of 60 due to personal issues, and everyone that stayed in the game had a satisfactory outcome. My classes concluded on a very satisfying and successful note, an outcome that was far less than certain when I started the exercise. Special thanks to the IIQ and AT staff for being there for me EVERY DAY I needed help, and to my students who rose to the challenge with courage and hard work.

Professor B and Professor A represent a sample of the experiences we had with faculty during the crisis. Faculty sought out our guidance in large numbers. In using the philosophy of supporting faculty by being patient, being a good listener, and walking faculty through the guidance in a step-by-step, easy-to-understand manner, we were able to find success. It is important to note that credit for this success of supporting faculty is not tied solely to Academic Technology. Seeing as there were 4 Academic Technology staff members, a small number to handle the numerous faculty visits in Zoom, staff from our sister unit "OCIP" and another related unit "Teaching Academy" volunteered either mornings or afternoon on various days to help. A Google sheet was created in which OCIP and Teaching Academy staff could add their names to the days and times they were available to help. This support gave us 1–2 extra support staff on the majority of days during this crisis and provided substantial help all the way through the end of the Spring 2020 semester.

5 Lessons Learned

The lessons learned in this endeavor have been many. Having the responsibility of supporting hundreds of faculty with a diverse online teaching skill set, ranging from experienced with online instruction to no experience at all, has been an enormous challenge. The range of the type of support needed forced the AT unit to be flexible in determining what types of support were needed. Some instructors needed technical support with Canvas or with one of the learning software offered by NMSU. Other instructors needed guidance on how to promote interaction among students. Others needed somebody to be empathetic to the challenges they were facing. Sometimes instructors needed all three.

The lessons learned also highlight the importance of making decisions quickly. In such a short window of time to prepare and to strategize, the AT unit was forced to react quickly. As former UCLA and Hall of Fame basketball coach John Wooden says, "Be quick, but don't hurry," a quote that is highly applicable to our situation. We had to think quickly and clearly about how the process of supporting online faculty would look and how we could be highly effective. In the process, when we noticed areas that needed to change or be improved, we acted quickly being that time to think was not in our favor.

In preparing to assist faculty, it was important to keep top of mind that many of the new online instructors prefer face-to-face teaching and/or even have a negative perception of online teaching. We had to be as welcoming and friendly as possible. It was important to be aware of the stress that faculty were facing, especially for those with limited or no online teaching experience. Being aware of the difficulty of quickly converting face-to-face courses to online was critically important in offering guidance and easy-to-understand language rather than the technical terms we are used to using. It was important for us to recognize that faculty were likely to be stressed and anxious due to the abruptness of moving their teaching methods online. This was an experience no faculty member had dealt with before. Expressing empathy when it was appropriate was critical in diffusing stress/tension.

When it came to online teaching and building content, we had to find a solution that would work quickly and, again, explain it in easy-to-understand language. Moreover, we had to communicate to each instructor that they were welcome and encourage them to re-visit our Zoom virtual open lab as much as they needed. It was important that faculty did not feel inadequate or incapable of teaching online because they didn't know the ins and outs of Canvas. Rather, it was important that faculty make progress in learning how to use Canvas and how to teach online. We not only provided technical guidance; we provided online teaching best practices and engaged in discussions about effective ways to present a quality online teaching and learning experience for instructors and students. All of these strategies combined played a big part in successfully supporting faculty in the rapid switch to teaching online.

As mentioned previously, we used Zoom to hold the open lab sessions to provide answers and guidance. Faculty responded very favorably to the use of Zoom to host online open lab sessions; they found it to be an easy and highly accessible method of finding support. The use of Zoom to offer support greatly expanded access and was overall a huge success. The amount of positive feedback from faculty far exceeded any previous amount of positive feedback from semesters past.

It is important to note that offering virtual open labs to expand faculty access to support was no simple task. The AT unit aggressively marketed the Zoom Open Labs through the NMSU list-serve called "Hotline," through the Canvas Global Announcements tool and through the NMSU direct-to-faculty email list-serve. Eventually we also added a direct link to our Open Lab for faculty under the Canvas Help Menu. Our virtual lab model was also adopted by other departments to better serve students. These marketing and communication strategies undoubtedly helped to inform faculty about how to access synchronous support.

6   Conclusion

As you have seen from this section, a continuous assessment of current services provided is always a best practice. This continuous assessment and flexibility when working with a large faculty population is critical. The following lists the key best practices we have identified:

Innovate and model best practices.
– Use the software tools available at your institution to model best practices (use of synchronous video conferencing).
– Use all methods available to spread the information to faculty about access to support and guidance. For us, these methods included:
  – NMSU email list-servs
  – Canvas Announcements
  – NMSU Hotline list-serv

- Direct communication with department chairs to deliver information to faculty
- Proactively identify non-academic departments that need access to software tools, such as Zoom, to continue to offer services (tutoring, advising, outreach, medical, etc.).
- Customer service focus-
  - Provide support and step-by-step guidance in easy-to-understand language to avoid overwhelming instructors who are not experts in technology.
- In times of crisis act as a sounding board for faculty concerns.
- Key point for executive administration: support innovation and experimentation with new solutions.
- Support faculty in creative ways to address new problems.
- Remind and encourage faculty to stay flexible and keep things manageable; this is a crisis, not a planned move.

In our AT unit, we had actively prepared our campus for a pandemic by building capacity before the pandemic occurred through some combination of foresight and, to be honest, luck. We had a robust professional development program in place and were able to quickly scale up delivery of what we had. During this time period of COVID-19 and going through an emergency mass move to online course offerings, AT relied heavily on the use of Zoom. Ramping up the Zoom integration from 6–8 months to 2 weeks took an amazing amount of time, dedication and focus and the credit for this certainly goes to Michelle Lebsock. As a team we worked to find answers and provide solutions as quickly as possible given the rapid software updates and myriad use cases. Initially our answers about Zoom included "I don't know, but I'll find out as quickly as possible." This experience was the epitome of trial-by-fire. Frequent communication with our assigned Zoom Education Success Manager was also very important.

During this crisis, the Academic Technology staff were able to successfully support NMSU faculty due to remaining flexible, expanding support access to faculty via Zoom, a general sense of responding quickly to faculty inquiries, welcoming faculty, being good listeners, and providing directions and guidance through bite-sized, non-technologically-complex terms. It was especially important to recognize the intensity of the faculty members' senses of urgency and anxiety and it was important to make a conscious effort in being a sounding board; listening, and, of critical importance, being kind and welcoming.

Moving forward and past the Covid-19 crisis, there are several lessons that can be taken from these experiences. In working with colleges and academic departments at our university we will emphasize the importance of flexibility and for faculty who are not experts in online teaching or lack experience, we will encourage them to seek help while keeping things manageable. It is also important to work with the Faculty-Senate, the university faculty governing body, to push and encourage academic departments to greatly increase the value of online teaching experience when hiring faculty and adjunct faculty.

Maybe most importantly, it is invaluable to continue to grow and develop the faculty culture to value being flexible in modes of teaching. Peer-to-peer support within academic departments has proven to be critically important and played an important part in NMSU getting through the Crisis. Last, but not least, it is an important and needed step to expand and grow the online education support department, including adding instructional consultants to help with all things online teaching. At NMSU, it's fair to say the AT unit is under-staffed. With more staff, the benefit potential is tremendous and the continued expansion into the online education world would benefit greatly, which ultimately will be a benefit to NMSU overall.

- Taking advice from this chapter, what practices would ideally be insti-tutionalized before your campus has to close due to a disaster such as a pandemic, weather crisis, or power outage?
- How can you "be quick, but not hurry" as a distance learning adminis-trator?
- What attitudes did this team exhibit while maintaining a service leader-ship perspective?

CHAPTER 17

Conclusions

Lauren Cifuentes

Abstract

This book provides a solid foundation for knowing how to take on the complex task of leading online initiatives in a college or school district. This chapter summarizes recommendations made by authors. Six overarching tasks that distance learning administrators should attend to are described: leadership, building and sustaining systems and infrastructure, learning technologies, providing faculty members professional development in online course design and development, the application of theory, and research and evaluation.

Keywords

Covid-19 – distance learning leadership – online learning leadership – online learning administration – distance learning administration – competencies of online administration – competencies of distance learning leadership

1 Intention

I composed and compiled this book because I had read the thoughtful writings of many of the authors of chapters here in preparation for my leadership position in distance learning at Texas A&M University–Corpus Christi. These authors, among others, did indeed prepare me well to facilitate distance learning and make a smooth transition from serving as a teaching-and-research faculty member to a leadership position. At the time of my hiring into that position I had been a faculty member at a research-1 university for twenty-three years, teaching online and conducting research on the impacts of, and possibilities for, distance learning. It is my hope that this book will provide others with a solid foundation for knowing how to take on the complex task of leading online initiatives in a college or school district.

Over the past decade, much has changed in the field of distance learning, and research findings have provided insight into effective leadership for quality online learning. Distance learning is now fully in the mainstream of college and preK-12 education. In addition, schools at all levels have broadly and rapidly adopted learning technologies and the principles of learning design. New technologies and applications of those technologies in education continuously emerge to help us address the needs of distance learners. Course design, degree-program and certificate-program design, evaluation, professional development, and policies have also evolved, as discussed in these chapters.

Covid-19 broke out while I was writing and compiling writings for this book, and the urgency of the book's lessons became universally clear. Experiencing rapid adoption of online learning has led many higher education presidents, provosts, and faculty members to accept that online courses and programs can match and even exceed the quality of face-to-face courses and programs, depending upon how well they are designed and delivered. Many such leaders only months ago believed that distance learning could not possibly match the quality of face-to-face learning. Through the experience of the rapid transition to online delivery of instruction, some educators have a more positive perspective regarding online education while others have formed a more negative view. However, no one can deny that emergency response to Covid-19 accelerated online education's place in the mainstream. It has become clear to many educational administrators that higher education, and perhaps even preK-12, will never go back to exclusively offering face-to-face instruction.

One positive outcome of emergency response adoption of online learning is that educators around the world are learning first-hand that online platforms afford community formation, interactivity, and personalization in ways that cannot be met in face-to-face classrooms where one expert conveys their knowledge through lectures while learners study in isolation from each other. In contrast, online learning environments provide for collaborative knowledge construction among diverse learners who benefit from both expert knowledge and peers as they build understanding. Creating such environments requires knowledge of learning technologies, instructional design, and learning design. As most instructors today learn how to modify their courses for online delivery, many are also receiving professional development in how to build social-constructivist and sociocultural learning environments. They learn how to use online tools to encourage dialogue, discourse, and collaborative problem-solving so that students with diverse expertise and knowledge can work and learn together with the guidance of their instructor.

2   Recommendations

In addition to the topics of chapters in this book, at least six themes or emphases emerge across several of the chapters. Distance learning administrators must attend to:
– leadership,
– building and sustaining systems and infrastructure,
– learning technologies,
– providing faculty members professional development in online course design and development,
– the application of theory, and
– research and evaluation.

Depending on a reader's professional aspirations or current position, themes may jump out at them from the readings that are different from those I identify here. In each chapter, authors provide recommendations for how to lead effectively according to their chapter topic. Below I summarize some of their recommendations according to the predominant themes.

3   Leadership

To lead most effectively, you should pursue expertise by staying abreast of the field as a member of the broad distance learning community. Network with other DL professionals and invite faculty members in your institution and your staff to join that network. Continuously build your knowledge of pedagogy; theory; emerging technologies; accreditation standards; best practices for meeting students' needs; and institutional and public policy, rules, and regulations as well as laws and ethical principles related to DL. In addition, stay informed regarding hiring, appropriate allocation of resources, and budgeting practices. One way to stay on top of what is new is to closely monitor validated DL social media sites, organizations, and publications.

Explore in order to understand the culture, resources, standards, organizational structures, and operational management of your institution and work within guidelines. You may wish to promote change, in which case you will need to work hard to enfranchise others in the mission of your office. Forming professional relationships with leaders in all departments as well as faculty and student leadership across campus is important for impacting the environment of your campus and lifting barriers to change.

Much of good leadership belongs in the affective domain. You must see yourself as a servant leader and be responsive to stakeholders. One of the first things you must do is to form a committee with representatives from across campus to keep you informed and to strategically inform stakeholders. The best leaders are those who strive for excellence with knowledge, vision, humility, empathy, interpersonal skills, integrity, and accountability.

4   Building and Sustaining Systems and Infrastructure

The Online Learning Consortium's five pillars map the leadership responsibilities for DL:
– access,
– cost-effectiveness and institutional commitment,
– learning effectiveness,
– faculty satisfaction, and
– student satisfaction.

To assure that these pillars are strong as well as ensure the quality of distance learning, most departments in an institution must be involved.

All distance learning students have to be able to easily access their courses and program materials. DL leaders must systematically and systemically address accessibility for online learning in order to comply with ethical principles, best practices, and laws. You will need to strategically monitor campus needs and resources, build infrastructure in response to need, identify software solutions, address personnel issues, provide professional development in accessibility for online learning, and review online materials to assure that they are compliant with government regulations and are serving all students who pursue a degree at your institution.

DL leadership must work with leaders of departments to share the vision and mission for that campus. You must have a solid commitment to building the required infrastructure, because that effort requires an investment in human and technical resources. View your institution as a system of interrelated components that must be aligned to sustain change and facilitate online learning. For instance, success in DL depends on the Chief Information Officer's ability to build the technology support structure that addresses needs of students, administrators, faculty members, and staff members. You need to help the CIO know what is needed for DL to succeed. You will identify not just technical support needs, but also pedagogical, financial, and human resource needs.

Barriers to success reside in each department; the success of distance learning programs depends on recruitment, marketing, the library, registration, institutional research, advising, financial aid offices, etc. Your job is to build or sustain an infrastructure of interconnected departments that provide for institutional, student, administrator, faculty, and staff readiness to play a part in successful DL.

Learning analytics from your LMS, campus surveys, interviews, and focus groups can provide you with knowledge of learning effectiveness so that you can respond to both student and faculty needs. Your findings will help you present high-level reports, guide policy, and ensure compliance with regulations.

You need to know characteristics of your institution's students, and develop and deliver orientations that ready them for online learning. Students require introductions to institutional culture, expected study and technical skills, and self-regulation skills. Work with student services and support, as well as the technology help desk, to assure that services that are available to on-campus students are also available to distant students. Most importantly, you must assure that trained advisors and tutors are available to each student. Ensuring that the institution provides academic, administrative, and technical services to students is paramount.

5   Learning Technologies

Learning technologies are, of course, essential and fundamental to successful administration of online learning. Selecting technologies that put your campus on the cutting edge, within the bounds of what your campus can afford, is often the task of the leader of distance learning, in collaboration with the Chief Information Officer. That role involves managing working groups that help select technologies for designing, organizing, and delivering engaging learning experiences. Once a technology such as an LMS, test proctoring software, desktop videoconferencing system, or plagiarism detection software is adopted, you must publicize the software and provide professional development to promote adoption by faculty and, when applicable, by students. A wise leader audits levels of adoption using qualitative and quantitative methods and learning analytics in order to justify extending or rejecting a contract. The goal is for digital engagement across campus, not just for online courses.

Obviously, technology tools facilitate delivery of content and interaction among learners and instructors. Beyond what campus technologies offer to teachers, distance learning administrators have to lead the campus in preparing students for critical digital literacy and citizenship across the curriculum.

Instructors must receive professional development in how to use online tools to help students explore and represent their identities as scientists, historians, writers, or engineers, etc. They can also explore issues of race and gender as it relates to their educational aspirations. As part of curriculum, students must learn how to determine and challenge online and other media sources' validity. Most important, students need to learn how to use technologies to support life-long learning.

An important task is to design, develop, and maintain a website that reports and sustains distance learning activity on your campus if one is not already in place. Descriptions of programs must be posted for recruitment, marketing, and informing current students. The site needs to also describe office personnel, vision, mission, approach, and special DL events. Descriptions and links to services for faculty, students, and alumni need to be readily accessible from the site.

6   Professional Development in Online Course Design and Development

The lecture-capture approach to online course delivery is all too common, and has served as a rapid response to Covid-19 that may endure beyond the pandemic in spite of being an approach that rarely provides high-quality learning experiences for learners. Delivering professional development that conveys the value of applying connectivism, social constructivism, and sociocultural learning theory is a critical aspect of a DL leader's efforts. Leaders who deeply understand the power of online learning and can convey that message will be necessary for faculty members and upper administration to fully accept online education beyond the emergency response period.

Attending to the entire instructional system will help you to achieve success and buy-in from stakeholders. Ideally, students and instructors form wisdom communities so that they bond beyond collaboration in course-work. Adopting consistent interfaces across online programs and activities will ease access, increase both student and instructor satisfaction, and increase students' perceptions that they have learned.

Providing faculty professional development is one of your most important tasks. Topics discussed include but are not limited to:
- designing for accessibility,
- compliance with copyright law,
- systematic approaches to course design, development, implementation, and evaluation,

– creating a consistent course interface,
– course-mapping,
– design of student-centered courses to include interaction, collaboration, presence, personalization, engagement, and community (the Community of Inquiry model),
– ways to motivate students and help them students self-regulate,
– use of open educational resources, and
– flipping and blending courses.

7   Applying Theory

Supporting teaching and learning is at the center of all the distance learning administrator does. Every author of chapters in this book has a sound foundation in learning theory, and keeps up with the literature on teaching and learning practice. Theory informs our practice, and research on practice grounds our theories. Therefore, you must familiarize yourself with, and help instructors apply, principles from learning theories. These include the community of inquiry, social constructivism, sociocultural learning theory, and connectivism. Lead your campus in design and development of wisdom communities to support cultural inclusion of diverse learners. That effort will facilitate creation of a social environment for transformational online learning.

8   Research and Evaluation

Your ability to address issues will be enhanced through study of others' published research findings, as well as your application of qualitative and quantitative research methods and learning analytics to better understand your complex learning context. You can dispel the widely held belief that online learning is inferior to face-to-face instruction by sharing research findings that provide evidence to the contrary. When faculty members learn that well designed online coursework is actually effective and that students like it, they are more willing to adopt it. In addition, exploring research on effective applications in DL will help you share approaches that best support students and faculty members.

In order to meet desired goals, you will apply research methods to identify needs in the infrastructure as well as in faculty and student services. You will need to evaluate and report on the various campus inputs to online programs and courses on your campus. Case analyses can provide insight in order to advance theory and knowledge of what works at your institution, as well as in online education in general. For instance, studies need to be conducted in various types of educational environments to better understand what institutional factors lead to faculty satisfaction. Also, in our diverse society, the interaction of learner characteristics and the impacts of specific types of learning tasks need to be more deeply understood so that we can better differentiate and personalize learning experiences. Use of social media for learning should be better understood in order to support both teachers and students with their digital literacy. And, administrators and practitioners need to explore applications of advanced technologies.

9   Final Remarks

In conclusion, the goal of all content in this book is to help administrators build a campus infrastructure that will support each student's learning and success. Educational institutions and practices are transforming due to the disruptive nature of online learning. What we know about how people learn in general, and specifically online, constantly evolves and we respond to that new knowledge.

An important topic not covered here is the variety of innovative business models involving distance learning and digital initiatives. These are rapidly emerging and vary tremendously. Ideally, the Chief Financial Officer works strategically with the distance learning administrator.

Many distance learning administrators act as change agents for overcoming systemic differences in students' life chances. They recognize the potential of distance learning pedagogies and technologies to revolutionize and democratize educational systems so that they provide for collaborative, individualized, personalized, student-centered learning. Such leadership and expansion of distance learning opportunities advance the goal of equity in education. I believe and have hope that well designed and managed distance learning can serve as a solution to threats to social justice by making educational opportunity available to all who have access to the Internet. A good start to being part of the solution is to follow the recommendations of the distance-learning pioneers who authored this book.

> What would your first, perhaps five, priorities be as a newly hired DL administrator? Discuss with others what they each chose and why you each identified what you chose? Through discussion, might you change your priorities?

Recommended Support Materials

Journals
Online Journal of Distance Learning Administration – Essential Reading

Sites and Reports Where Leaders Can Find Important Information
Babson Survey Research Group. Report on online learning growth & trends.
  https://www.onlinelearningsurvey.com/highered.html
CHLOE. Survey of chief online officers. https://www.qualitymatters.org/qa-resources/
  resource-center/article-resource/60
EDUCAUSE ECAR. Student use of technology. https://www.educause.edu/ecar
Interregional Guidelines for the Evaluation of Distance Education.
  https://www.wscuc.org/content/interregional-guidelines-evaluation-distance-
  education
National Council for State Authorization Reciprocity Agreements (NC-SARA).
  https://nc-sara.org/
OLC quality scorecards.https://onlinelearningconsortium.org/consult/olc-quality-
  scorecard-suite/
OLC Research Center for Digital Learning & Leadership.
  https://onlinelearningconsortium.org/read/leadership/
Piña, A. A., & Harris, P. (2017). *Utilizing the AECT instructional design standards for
  distance learning.* https://www.westga.edu/~distance/ojdla/summer222/pina_
  harris222.html#:~:text=The%20AECT%20Instructional%20Design%20
  Standards%20for%20Distance%20Learning,into%20courses%20designed%20
  for%20learners%20at%20a%20distance.
WCET. Policy, regulations and e-learning consortia. https://wcet.wiche.edu/
Wiley Market Reports. Survey of online college students.
  https://www.learninghouse.com/knowledge-center/research-reports/

Support Literature
King, E., & Alperstein, N. (2017). *Best practices in planning strategically for online edu-
  cational programs.* Routledge.
Means, B., Bakia, M., & Murphy, R. (2014). *Learning online: What research tells us about
  whether, when, and how.* Routledge.
Miller, G., Benke, M., Chaloux, B., Ragan, L. C., Schroeder, R., Smutz, W., & Swan, K. (2014).
  Leading the e-learning transformation of higher education. Stylus Publishing.
Miller, G. E., & Ives, K. S. (2020). *Leading the e-learning transformation of higher educa-
  tion* (2nd ed.). Stylus Publishing.
Mizell, A. A., & Piña, A. (Eds.). (2014). *Real life distance education: Case studies in prac-
  tice.* Information Age Publishing.

Moller, L., & Huett, J. B. (2012). *The next generation of distance education: Unconstrained learning.* AECT, Springer.

Piña, A. A., & Huett, J. B. (Eds.). (2016). *Beyond the online course: Leadership perspectives on e-learning.* Information Age Publishing.

Piña, A. A., Lowell, V. L., & Harris, B. R. (Eds.). (2018). *Leading and managing e-learning: What the e-learning leader needs to know.* Springer.

Piña, A. A., & Miller, C. T. (Eds.). (2019). *Lessons in leadership in the field of educational technology.* AECT, Springer.

Shelton, K., & Saltsman, G. (2005). *An administrator's guide to online education.* Information Age Publishing.

Index